Advance praise for *Capitalist Value Chains*

The twenty-first century world economy is organized around what corporate CEOs, Wall Street investors and now nearly everyone else are accustomed to call *global value chains*. But what exactly are these value chains that so continuously circulate around the globe? The authors of this book reveal that these are in reality *capitalist value chains*. They then take you on a fascinating journey into the hidden abodes of global capitalist value chain production, exchange, and distribution, and the effects on the relations of labour and capital, Global North and Global South, and humanity and the environment. If you want to know about the political economy of global power in our time, there are hundreds of works you will want to study. *But first read this book.*

John Bellamy Foster, ***Professor of Sociology, University of Oregon, and author,***
The Theory of Monopoly Capitalism

Capitalist Value Chains takes a familiar concept, Global Value Chains, and approaches the empirical evidence with a newly constructed theoretical lens. Unlike most of the literature, it places capital, class struggle, collective action, and geopolitics at the centre of the understanding of the expansion of capitalist production and trade. Anyone who wants a new theory of capitalism and enjoys the company of articulate, provocative, off-beat intelligences should read the book. And maybe pick a fight with it.

Robert H Wade, ***Professor of Global Political Economy,***
London School of Economics

The results are in. The gains from globalization have been captured at the top. In clear and concise prose, Selwyn and Bernhold explain how, and why it could not have been otherwise. Drawing on essential tools of class-relational analysis, Capitalist Value Chains is required reading for anyone who wants to understand the contemporary architecture of uneven development and the accelerated destruction of nature.

Marion Werner, ***Professor, Department of Geography, University at Buffalo,***
State University of New York

Capitalist Value Chains pushes readers to think critically about participation in global value chains as a 'development' tool—reminding us that the exploitation of labour and nature are deeply embedded at the core of capitalism. It shows how capitalism makes it impossible to generalize economic, social, or environmental upgrading and concludes that 'immiserating growth regimes' can only be counteracted by a class-relational conception of labour and by collective action.

Stefano Ponte, ***Professor of International Political Economy, Copenhagen Business School***

Capitalist Value Chains

Capitalist Value Chains

Labour Exploitation, Nature Destruction, Geopolitics

Benjamin Selwyn
and
Christin Bernhold

OXFORD
UNIVERSITY PRESS

OXFORD
UNIVERSITY PRESS

Great Clarendon Street, Oxford, OX2 6DP,
United Kingdom

Oxford University Press is a department of the University of Oxford.
It furthers the University's objective of excellence in research, scholarship,
and education by publishing worldwide. Oxford is a registered trade mark of
Oxford University Press in the UK and in certain other countries.

Published in the United States of America by Oxford University Press
198 Madison Avenue, New York, NY 10016, United States of America

British Library Cataloguing in Publication Data
Data available

Library of Congress Control Number: 2025938054

ISBN 9780198887836

DOI: 10.1093/9780191994906.001.0001

The manufacturer's authorised representative in the EU for product safety is
Oxford University Press España S.A. of Parque Empresarial San Fernando de Henares,
Avenida de Castilla, 2 – 28830 Madrid (www.oup.es/en or product.safety@oup.com).
OUP España S.A. also acts as importer into Spain of products made by the manufacturer.

Preface

This book contributes to debates in international political economy (IPE) and development studies about globalized production. Much of the literature in these academic fields frame such discussion around concepts such as Global Value Chains (GVCs), Global Production Networks (GPNs) or global supply chains. They address costs and benefits of participation in these chains and networks from a firm-centric perspective and they tend to ignore global capitalism's class relational character in general, and exploitative relations of production in particular. By contrast we develop a class-relational IPE approach to analysing these chains. This is a work of applied political economy, where we draw upon and contribute to a range of conceptual categories from the Marxist tradition.

We contribute to this tradition with the novel conceptual category of *Capitalist Value Chains (CVCs)* to explain these chains as historically specific configurations of capitalist class relations that have been re-structured and bolstered through geopolitics. We also show how CVCs generate *immiserating exploitation* and *immiserating growth regimes*, as they work through the (re)production of large, relatively impoverished, labour forces.

We root our analysis in the Marxist tradition's notion of class as a conflictual, exploitative relation of surplus value production (by labour) and appropriation (by capital). This informs our notion of class differentiation, of international class relations, and of workers' ability to improve their wages, conditions, and livelihoods through their own struggles. It informs our understanding of the capitalist state and the imperialist chain that constitutes the inter-state system. We draw upon ecological Marxism's notion of the metabolic rift to elucidate the relationship between CVCs and the natural environment.

While the writing of this book was quintessentially a joint effort, Selwyn and Bernhold took responsibility for lead-writing (many drafts of) a chapter, after which the other co-author contributed their ideas to the next iteration. Moreover, our colleague Dara Leyden generously provided reviews and discussions of all chapters, and although he opts to appear as a contributing author, this book would not be the same without him. Selwyn led Chapters 1, 2, 5, 6, 7, and 11, Bernhold led Chapters 8 (which is adapted from a piece she co-authored with Tomás Palmisano) and Chapter 10. Chapter 3 was drafted by both authors in equal parts. Dara Leyden contributed substantially to Chapters 4 and 9.

While writing this book many colleagues have helped us—Adrian Smith, Benno Teschke, Julian Germann, Tom Selwyn, Dylan Sullivan, Steven Altman, Jenny Chan, Mark Selden, Christian Stache, John Lütten, Emilia Ormaechea, Marwaa Zazai, Klara Kolhoff, Katharina Vöhler, Jonathan Peters, and Sören Horn. Selwyn benefitted from a sabbatical in autumn 2022 in the department of Economics and Management, University of Pisa.

We would also like to extend our heartfelt gratitude to Mjriam and Valentina Selwyn, as well as Romeo (Selwyn's canine companion), Innamana Pettyll, and, again, Christian Stache, whose support and presence have been truly irreplaceable throughout this journey.

At OUP Adam Swallow, Karen Bunn, Mhairi Bennett, and Karthiga Ramu supported this project patiently, attentively and good-naturedly.

Parts of the chapters in this book draw upon and develop arguments previously published. Parts of Chapters 3 and 8 were previously published in Bernhold (2022), parts of Chapter 4 were previously published in *Competition and Change* (Vol. 26, issue 2) and *Monthly Review* (Vol. 73, no. 6), parts of Chapter 6 were previously published in *Monthly Review* (Vol. 74, no. 10), parts of Chapter 7 were previously published in *Competition and Change* (Vol. 23, issue 1), parts of Chapter 8 were previously published *in Journal of Agrarian Change* (Vol. 22, issue 2) and parts of Chapter 9 were previously published in Leyden (2024).

Contents

List of Figures

List of Tables

1
Introduction

In contemporary capitalism, substantial portions of commodities—from basic consumer goods, food, and services to high-tech and heavy capital equipment—are produced in stages across many countries and integrated through value chains. This book is about what we call *Capitalist Value Chains* (CVCs). These are coordinated and managed forms of production and trade, rather than the arms-length markets of many economics' textbooks. This book explores how CVCs are based upon and have restructured class relations within and across countries. Driven by capital and supported by (geo)political state strategies, CVCs have become a key organizational form of today's capitalism. In policy and academic literature, these chains are often referred to as Global Value Chains (GVCs), Global Supply Chains (GSCs), or Global Production Networks (GPNs). We call them CVCs to bring and keep at the fore their capitalist class-relational character.

The mainstream GVC concept denotes the 'full range of activities which are required to bring a product or service from [its] conception' through its design, the sourcing of raw materials and intermediate inputs, marketing, delivery to final consumers, and final disposal after use (Kaplinsky and Morris 2001, 4). According to the OECD, today 'about 70% of international trade involves global value chains (GVCs), whereby services, raw materials, parts, and components cross borders often numerous times before being incorporated into a final product and shipped to consumers all over the world' (OECD 2021, 4). In CVCs, production is geographically fragmented but functionally integrated. For example, the components and inputs into Apple's iPhones—one of the iconic products of CVCs—are made by millions of workers in over 50 countries (Apple 2024). While the globalization of production and trade has always been characteristic of capitalism, today's CVCs represent historically specific ways of organizing relationships between capitalist firms and workers, and among firms, across national borders.

CVCs are often controlled by powerful corporations, commonly referred to as '*lead firms*' in the mainstream literature, which appropriate large parts of the value produced by workers in CVCs. Through a vast concentration

Capitalist Value Chains. Benjamin Selwyn and Christin Bernhold, Oxford University Press.
 DOI: 10.1093/9780191994906.003.0001

of capital and the capacity to '*govern*' a chain, lead firms influence and command what is produced, where, how, and under what conditions. They typically set the prices paid to suppliers and even determine the wages and conditions of workers in supplier firms.

1.1 The CVC Effect

Much critical scholarship highlights the socially and economically deleterious impacts of CVCs from various perspectives (e.g., Baglioni et al. 2020; Selwyn 2007, 2012b; Bair and Werner 2011a; Newsome et al. 2015; Suwandi 2019; Prentice 2021; Zaman and Jenkins 2024). The mainstream GVC literature also describes some of these impacts, albeit without analysing them in the broader context of capitalist class relations.

For example, while in the 1980s cocoa farmers received 18 per cent of the value of a chocolate bar—by the late 2010s they got just 6 per cent (Oxfam 2017, 17). In 2010, Apple's profit for the iPhone constituted over 50 per cent of its final sale price, while Chinese workers' share was less than 2 per cent (Dedrick et al. 2010). An OECD working paper notes that stronger GVC integration 'can put downward pressure on wage growth through the use of foreign workers embodied in inputs who thus become more direct competitors to domestic workers' (Andrews et al. 2018, 21). In their analysis of nine million workers from 24 European countries Dagmar Nikulin et al. (2022, 701) find that 'wages prove to be negatively related to involvement in GVCs'. Examples of such dynamics are to be found across CVCs—in agriculture (Oxfam 2019), textiles and garment production (Clean Clothes Campaign 2020a), and in sectors which are often presented as high-tech bastions of middle-class employment, such as services (Howson et al. 2022). More generally, in a recent study of 93 countries, Roberts and Tran (2022) calculate the relationship between GVC integration and national income inequality, finding that 'GVC integration increases inequality in the global North and South' (2022, 678).[1]

In CVCs, a large part of the labour force is comprised of workers who are paid poverty wages, and who must work excessive overtime to survive (see Chapter 7 for examples). Exploitative relations of production are the norm under capitalism. However, CVCs are used by firms to reshape these

[1] For countries in the so-called Global South they measure GVC integration by (a) manufacturing exports to OECD countries as a percentage of GDP and (b) inward FDI as a percentage of GDP. For countries in the Global North GVC integration is measures by (a) manufacturing imports from non-OECD countries as a percentage of GDP and (b) outward FDI as a percentage of GDP (Roberts and Tran 2022, 696).

exploitative class relations, outsourcing and offshoring production to locations where they can pay extremely low wages. These dynamics are driven by capital and supported by state strategies, facilitating the relocation of production to places with weak labour organizing, and the suppression and fragmentation of workforces. CVCs have enabled the heightened exploitation of workers in peripheral countries where suppliers are mostly located—while also increasing capital's power to depress wages and to increase labour 'flexibility' in leading capitalist countries where lead firms are predominantly headquartered.

The size and power of contemporary lead firms are noteworthy. Many of them are larger than some national economies, when considering their revenues. For example, Walmart, Amazon, and Apple had larger revenues in 2023 than the entire GDPs of Argentina, Austria, and South Africa, respectively (see Table 1.1). Indeed, the combined revenues of the largest 2000 companies in the world, equal to 52 trillion US dollars (USD), were equivalent to approximately half of global GDP in 2023 (Fortune 2024; World Bank 2024).

Table 1.1 Companies bigger than national economies in 2023 (USD)[a]

Company and revenue (2023)	Country and GDP (2023)	Company world ranking by GDP if it were a country
Walmart, US ($657 bn)	Argentina ($641 bn)	22nd
Amazon, US ($591 bn)	Austria ($516 bn)	25th
Apple, US ($382 bn)	South Africa ($378 bn)	39nd
UnitedHealth Group, US ($380 bn)	Colombia ($364 bn)	40th
Berkshire Hathaway, US ($369 bn)	Nigeria (363 bn)	41st
CVS Health, US ($361 bn)	Romania ($351 bn)	42nd
Volkswagen, Germany ($349 bn)	Pakistan ($338 bn)	43rd
Alphabet, US ($318 bn)	Finland ($300 bn)	46th
Toyota, Japan ($312 bn)	Portugal ($287 bn)	46th
McKesson, US ($309 bn)	Peru ($268 bn)	46th

[a] Although national GDP and consolidated corporate revenue are conceptually different—GDP reflecting value added, and revenue reflecting gross income—they are often used as rough proxies to compare the relative economic scale of states and large corporations.

Source: Largest global private corporations (Fortune 2024) versus largest economies (World Bank data 2024, series code NY.GDP.MKTP.CD).

These and other mega firms are well-insulated from democratic accountability—from within and without the firm. Given their lack of internal democracy, if they were countries they would be described as authoritarian dictatorships (Savage 2023). For example, Walmart has 2.3 million employees that do not get to vote for its leadership or policies. Rather, the world's biggest retailer aggressively suppresses workers' attempts to establish any degree of internal democracy (Greenhouse 2015).

The adverse effects of CVCs are not limited to social aspects. CVC hyper-specialization—the fragmentation of tasks across borders—entails an increase in production, transportation, and energy use. This directly accelerates climate breakdown, and the mass environmental ruin caused by capitalism. For example, the shipping industry is central to the functioning of CVCs, and it has contributed to the rise of CO2 emissions (see Chapter 10). Furthermore, as we shall see in Chapters 5 and 6, CVC integration and interlinked dynamics of *uneven capitalist development* are reinforcing geopolitical rivalries, exemplified by the United States' attempts to curtail China's development of high technology. For the purposes of our analysis, we understand uneven development as processes of unequal geographic distribution of capitalist production, exchange, and reproduction within and across countries (see Hadjimichalis 1987, 38). One effect of these uneven geographies of capitalist exploitation is the socio-geographic concentration of wealth, mirrored by the expansion of new forms of poverty and inequality. CVCs—as expressions and mechanisms of international class relations—are causal generators of these political-economic dynamics.

1.2 What the GVC Mainstream Claims

We understand and label the GVC mainstream as scholars and policymakers who promote GVCs as advantageous for social and economic development—despite mounting evidence that shows the opposite. This mainstream is made up of key international institutions, state and NGO actors, and crucially, a vast array of academics (e.g., Sturgeon 2009; Cattaneo et al. 2010; Gereffi and Fernandez-Stark 2016; Taglioni and Winkler 2016; World Bank 2020). They argue that 'upgrading'—where supplier firms, or would-be suppliers, enter GVCs and enhance their competitiveness within them—is a key strategy and the primary mechanism for achieving development (see Gereffi 2018). These advocates of *GVCs for development* are not a homogenous group, and most acknowledge that upgrading is not a straightforward process. However, they do share a common faith that if tailored correctly, GVCs can contribute to raising productivity, boosting economic growth, ameliorating poverty, and even mitigating the worst effects of climate breakdown.

The World Bank's (2020, 3) World Development Report 2020 ('WDR2020'), *Trading for Development in the Age of Global Value Chains,* headline claim is that 'Global Value Chains boost incomes, create better jobs, and reduce poverty'. The Bank has done more, arguably, than any other international organization to promote the ideology of *GVCs for development.* Despite such hyperbolic claims, the WDR2020 itself provides evidence documenting how CVCs have (i) contributed to wage depression, (ii) enabled lead firms to increase their markups while supplier firm markups have fallen, (iii) contributed to reallocating value from labour to capital within national economies, and (iv) accelerated the destruction of the world's natural environment (and see Chapter 4). However, in an act of cognitive dissonance it nevertheless advocates the continuous expansion of GVCs. It is not only the WDR2020 that fails to square the circle. Other mainstream GVC analyses also recognize the power of lead firms and how they use it to enhance their capture of value within GVCs. Yet, like Gary Gereffi (2001, 1622), undoubtedly the most influential thinker within the GVC mainstream, they argue that development 'requires linking up with the most significant lead firm in the industry'.

One of the reasons that the World Bank gets away with endorsing GVCs as beneficial for development is that its notion of poverty is inhumanly low. The Bank has several consumption-based international poverty lines—$2.15 per day (for what it labels as low-income countries), $3.65 (lower-middle-income-countries), and $6.85 (upper-middle-income countries). None of these poverty lines tell us if a worker could survive adequately at this consumption level in these countries, nor how much and under what conditions they must labour to earn enough to reach these consumption levels. These poverty lines are based upon the attainment of 2100 calories a day, without specification of their nutritional value. They do not include the cost of adequate nutrition or health, or the attainment of basic education (Pogge and Reddy 2006; Selwyn 2017; Sumner et al. 2020; see Chapter 7). There are other ways of measuring poverty that do account for what people need to consume to live a decent life—for example, a living wage poverty line, or the calculation of costs of an essential subsistence basket (and see Chapters 5 and 7). Such measures would show that many people classified by the World Bank as 'not poor' or as 'middle class' (as in Ravallion 2010), do, in fact, experience severe social and economic deprivation.

Our book shows how and why CVCs are generating highly exploitative jobs and new forms of poverty, stunting real human development, and destroying the world's environment. We argue that CVCs are historically specific configurations of capitalist class relations that contribute to heightened exploitation of labour and appropriation of nature by capital.

There is a historical irony in the role that the GVC mainstream plays in promoting global capitalism. As we shall see in Chapter 3 of this book, GVC analysis has its roots in the World Systems approach, which explicitly denies the possibilities of *general* upward mobility (or 'upgrading' for all), arguing that global capitalism implies systemic uneven development (Wallerstein 1988a). Gary Gereffi's (1978) earlier work also illuminated some of the deep-seated problems with capitalist development. However, he has played the most significant role in transforming the value chain concept from one that was critical of capitalism into one of its biggest cheerleaders.

Developmentalist Fantasies

As mentioned above, not all GVC analysis is the same. As we shall see throughout this book, a large body of work recognizes the diverse problems with CVC development although they stop short of calling for the dismantling of their underlying capitalist relations and structures (see Chapters 9 and 10 for discussions on social and environmental upgrading). For example, The United Nations Conference on Trade and Development (UNCTAD) 2017 Report provides a strong critique of the developmental impacts of GVCs. It characterizes their increasing concentration of power as representing the creation of 'a new form of global rentier capitalism to the detriment of balanced and inclusive growth for the many', where 'the winner takes most' (UNCTAD 2017, 119, 125). Its 2018 Trade and Development Report notes how the top 200 corporations are increasing their power within (and over many elements of) the world economy (UNCTAD 2018). However, it sees a solution in a 'Global New Deal'—large-scale public investments to boost growth, combined with progressive policies such as living wages (UNCTAD 2019).

In a similar vein, the UN Industrial Development Organisation argues that governments should not prioritize GVC integration as a development strategy in and of itself, but should 'factor in broader public policy objectives, such as the number and quality of jobs created, spill-over effects into other sectors, the noneconomic and environmental impact of industrial activities, and more generally, contributions to economic diversification and resilience' (UNIDO 2015, 13).

While these studies reject the celebratory hyperbole of *GVCs for development*, they do not identify the root cause of the problem. For example, they portray 'global rentier capitalism', rather than capitalism's core social relations as the driver of lead firm power, global poverty, and inequality. They advocate a benign vision of capitalism—where states can govern markets, rather than simply support them, thereby achieving progressive developmental outcomes. Organizations such as UNIDO and UNCTAD propose many policies that assume that CVCs can be tweaked to cure social and environmental exploitation—from living wages to environmental protection. However, as they do not analyse the core drivers of capitalist exploitation and expansion, they are unable to provide a satisfactory explanation for the deleterious developmental dynamics generated by CVCs and how they can be overcome.

1.3 Rationale for this Book

The evidence of CVC's deleterious socio-economic impact needs to be explained in a theoretically coherent fashion. What we find, however, when we read the GVC mainstream is a consistent inability to explain, rather than simply to observe, such evidence. There is, in fact, a jarring disjuncture between claims about the benefits of GVCs and their empirical reality. The reason for this is that most of the GVC mainstream ignores the role of capitalist relations of exploitation, class struggle, and geopolitics, and how CVCs are part of and contribute to the expansion of capitalist production and trade.

We understand capitalism from a class-relational theoretical perspective. Capitalist production is comprised of a unique dialectical relation: (A) Capital pursues profit through the exploitation of labour. (B) Capital exists as many individual capitalists related to each other through the market. As a result of A and B, capital accumulation is competitive, creating a historically unparalleled dynamism. Unlike previous modes of production—including feudalism and slavery—where exploitation occurred through obvious relations of force, under capitalism it is veiled behind the wage contract. Once workers' sell their labour power to capitalists, the latter can put it to work as part of their ceaseless drive to accumulate capital, to generate more value than they paid for the labour power in the first place.

As we discuss in more detail in Chapter 2, in general, the term class represents 'the *collective* social expression of the fact of exploitation' (Ste.

Croix 1981, 43, emphasis added; see Lütten 2021). Exploitation refers to the appropriation by one social class of the product of the labour of another social class. Based on the capitalist ownership of the means of production, exploitation predominantly takes the form of capital's appropriation of surplus value from labour. Wage workers are *relatively* free to change employer, but they must sell their labour power to acquire the wages to buy means of subsistence. Even if they receive the value of their labour power in wages, they produce over and above that a surplus value, which does not remain in their own hands. In this way, the central mechanism of value creation and extraction under capitalism is socio-economic exploitation of labour by capital. This conception of capitalist class relations defines the positioning of actors towards each other through the social relations of production, and thus the distribution of the produced social wealth.

Our core argument is that CVCs represent historically specific configurations of *international class relations*. Through these relations, firms can directly exploit workers offshore, when they make foreign direct investments. Furthermore, lead firms can exert high degrees of control over globally integrated production processes and appropriate a part of the surplus value produced by workers in nominally independent supplier firms. The analysis of international class dynamics is therefore necessary to scrutinize how CVCs emerged out of, and contribute to, the reproduction and deepening of international socio-spatial inequalities.

But labour exploitation is not the only source of wealth under capitalism—so is nature, the devastation of which also has its roots in endless capital accumulation. Through CVCs, capital's appropriation and despoilation of nature has reached new heights. The UN secretary general Antonio Guterres (2022) warns that the world is on a 'highway to climate hell with our foot on the accelerator' (cited in Harvey and Garrington 2022, n.p.). We argue that capitalism is the engine and CVCs are the accelerator.

As mentioned above, mainstream GVC analysis endorses development based upon capital accumulation and ignores the centrality of class relations to its object of study. Consequently, it is firm-centric and thus elitist (Selwyn 2012a). It pronounces firm managers/owners as primary developmental actors and identifies firms' main rationale—of profit-maximization—as the core driver of development. States are, as in the post-Washington consensus, understood as supporting actors to capitalist progress (see Stiglitz 2005). However, such firm-centrism effectively conceals the socio-economic basis of CVCs.

We would not be surprised if mainstream GVC advocates reject our understanding of capitalism, class, exploitation, and ultimately of surplus value. The problem for them, however, is that despite expanding the GVC research agenda for around a quarter of a century, they have not provided their own theory of capitalism. Furthermore, while the GVC approach identifies 'value-added' as a core notion—for its own analysis, and as a competitive strategy for GVC firms—*it does not define value or specify its source.* Rather, it starts half-way through the analysis by investigating dynamics of 'value added' or 'value capture'.

Against such approaches we establish conceptual categories to contribute to a critical CVC approach. The mainstream GVC inability to conceptualize and theorize capitalism undermines its ability to grasp CVC's developmentally deleterious impact. Quite simply, the GVC mainstream's theoretical toolbox is not equipped to explain labour exploitation and impoverishment, capital concentration, the destruction of the natural world, and geopolitics. Our approach, by contrast, shows how capitalist class relations underpin and are impacted by CVCs, and how the latter shape the destructive relation of capitalist society to nature, as well as geopolitical relations.

These are the reasons why our book introduces the term Capitalist Value Chains (CVCs)—to place front and centre of our analysis the capitalist character of value chains. It *defines CVCs as historically specific configurations of international capitalist class relations.* We show that this entails an overall—though geographically differentiated—intensification of exploitation and appropriation of labour and nature by capital.

To clarify, while this book discusses CVCs, it does not claim that value chains are the only game in town. Hence, we eschew seemingly totalizing terms such as 'the age of global value chains (World Bank 2020) 'supply chain capitalism' (Tsing 2009) or 'the GVC world' (Mayer et al. 2017). We are not proposing a comprehensive analysis of historical capitalism and its socio-spatial dynamics of uneven development, which would include many facets—from smaller scale production networks, to the global geographies of uneven production and exchange, the financial system, to the regulation of global trade, to military industrial complexes. However, we do argue that understanding uneven development requires analysing the geographically uneven processes of class-based exploitation and capital concentration in and through CVCs.

International Class Relations

In Chapter 5, we use the US as an example to illustrate how geopolitically charged offshoring not only enabled the exploitation of workers in various countries by US firms. It also reinforced the dismantling of hard-won labour protections in the United States itself. The conditions that attracted US capital to offshore production sites in East Asia were in turn the result of prior class struggles from above, leading to the establishment of repressive labour regimes (Cumings 1984; Deyo 1987; Li 2015). At the same time, the reshaping of class relations in countries like the United States and China respectively were mutually connected. Hence our deployment of the notion of international class relations. Capital investments transcend national borders. However, spaces of capitalist production are characterized by geographically specific socio-economic and political class formation. Through CVCs, lead firm capitals can influence these dynamics in different countries, play these spaces off against each other, and increase their profits.

In this vein, the foreign investments by US and East Asian firms into China from the 1980s onwards are not just cases of capital flows—but also of class formation. China has bequeathed to global capitalism the largest industrial working class the world has ever seen. In the broader East Asian region new capitalists have emerged through accessing and exploiting China's labour force. And at the pinnacle Silicon Valley's capitalist class fraction quite effectively bestrides the globe. Chapter 5 analyses how key states—the United States and China—established the political frameworks for the hierarchical collaboration of leading capitalist class fractions to establish CVCs.

While CVCs are based upon and have contributed to heightened labour exploitation through international class relations, this does not mean that workers are powerless to mobilize for better wages and conditions. The global dispersal of production generates 'choke points' within value chains, where sometimes small disruptions in one link reverberate throughout the chain generating major disruptions and potential losses to capital (Selwyn 2008; Robinson and Rainbird 2013). In late 2024, a three-day strike by 45,000 dock workers across 36 ports on the US East coast disrupted US supply chains. The cost to the US economy was an estimated $US 5 billion a day. The dockworkers collective action won them a tentative agreement for a wage hike of around 62 per cent (Saintano 2024, n.p.). Chapter 9 provides an in-depth analysis of discussions about workers' struggles in CVCs.

Methodological Internationalism

One of the strengths of the GVC approach is its transcendence of methodological nationalism—the analytical prioritizing of the nation state. By taking GVCs as its unit of analysis it enables in-depth investigation of a single chain of commodity production. It illuminates, with a great degree of empirical detail, how processes in one part of the world (e.g., corporate profit-maximizing strategies) impact upon processes in other parts of the world (e.g., developmental dynamics associated with supplier firm upgrading).

However, the mainstream GVC approaches' transcendence of methodological nationalism has come at an intellectual cost. Today, most GVC studies are of single cases/branches of commodity production. The methodological nationalism that chain approaches successfully transcended have been replaced, largely, with a *methodological singularism*—the empirical focus upon, and theoretical extrapolation from, the vantage point of a single value chain. Mainstream GVCs' methodological singularism is rooted, in turn, in an ignorance (quite literally, ignoring) of the *systemic* features of capitalist political economy. It thus generates a *fallacy of composition*—the error of assuming that what is true for one is true for all.

Mainstream GVC approaches assume and build their notion of upgrading-based development upon the argument that *some* successful cases of upgrading and development show that such processes can be generalized. While there are numerous cases of successful upgrading, they tell us only part of the story about CVCs. Among other issues, supplier firm upgrading is, by definition, relative. While some suppliers can and do move into higher value activities, they do so at the expense of other suppliers. Competitively generated gains for one actor are paid for by other actors' competitively generated losses. Competition under capitalism rewards firms that can increase competitiveness whilst punishing those that cannot.

It is true that capitalism is an immensely dynamic system—generating historically unprecedented economic growth and technological innovation. However, as Anwar Shaikh (2016) explains, these dynamics operate through and reproduce uneven development between social classes and geographic regions. CVCs emerged out of and have reshaped, rather than reduced or ameliorated, capitalist dynamics of uneven development. Without a systemic perspective of capitalism, and of CVCs as a particular form of capitalist production and trade, it is impossible to explain adequately why this is so. Instead, mainstream GVC approaches tend to argue that such socio-geographic dynamics of uneven development reflect insufficient GVC integration or insufficient upgrading and urge more of it. But such policies will only generate new rounds of uneven development.

Another problem generated by the mainstream's methodological singularism is its portrayal of the relationship between GVCs and the natural environment. The notion of upgrading is rooted in a largely unspoken assumption of endless capitalist growth, which generates ever-new competitive opportunities for supplier firms. By failing to recognize the systemic environmental harms generated by capitalist production, it is possible for the GVC mainstream to portray what it calls environmental upgrading as potentially reversing or at least alleviating such harms. For example, the World Bank argues that lead firms in GVCs 'are increasingly transferring environmentally friendly technologies to their suppliers and pushing for higher standards' (World Bank 2020, 119).

Such assertions are based on the argument that novel technologies can be deployed to facilitate competitive upgrading. The GVC mainstream contends that they have the additional benefit of enhancing resource efficiency, are disseminated through GVCs by lead firms more quickly than in non-GVC relations, and can reduce environmental harm generated by international trade and production. While such scenarios may be possible for individual firms and even for individual value chains, they are impossible for all CVCs.

While this book embraces the transcendence of methodological nationalism, it rejects the mainstream's methodological singularism. Rather, we view CVCs from a methodological internationalist perspective. This vantage point holds that class relations—and the CVCs that operate through and contribute to reproducing them—are rooted in national political economies, but simultaneously transcend national borders.

Our methodological internationalism is derived from our class-relational conception of capitalism, of the capitalist state, the international system of states, and how CVCs emerged out of, and now effectively articulate, international class relations. It generates a framework that better explains how CVCs facilitate the reorganization of capitalism's intrinsically uneven and exploitative relations of production and trade, and the developmentally deleterious dynamics underpinning and emanating from this reorganization.

To summarize the rationale of this book: We argue, contrary to the academic, political, and policy mainstream, that CVCs are a developmentally deleterious force that have enabled multinational corporations to boost profitability. CVCs were built upon, and contribute to, geographically differentiated but overall heightened rates of labour exploitation, reinforced capital concentration, uneven development, geopolitical rivalries, and environmental destruction. We argue that a class-relational analysis of international production is necessary to comprehend who produces and who appropriates the surpluses in CVCs, under which conditions, why competitive exploitation propels technological innovations and capital concentration, the effects of CVCs upon nature, and the role that collective worker's struggles (can) play in the class dynamics of CVCs. As we show, mainstream GVC analysis—by ignoring the capitalist class-relational character of value chains—effectively veils this reality.

1.4 Emergence of CVCs

Marx and Engels described capitalism's incredibly expansionary dynamics:

> The need of a constantly expanding market for its products chases the bourgeoisie over the entire surface of the globe. It must nestle everywhere, settle everywhere, establish connexions everywhere.... In place of the old wants, satisfied by the production of the country, we find new wants, requiring for their satisfaction the products of distant lands and climes. In place of the old local and national seclusion and self-sufficiency, we have intercourse in every direction, universal inter-dependence of nations.
>
> **(Marx and Engels 1848, 487f.)**

That capital's inner dynamism pushes it to nestle, settle, and establish connexions everywhere does not, however, tell us how it does so. In this book we show how CVCs became a key organizational form of contemporary capitalism. We also highlight how changing geopolitical dynamics—the dissolution of the former USSR and the rapid global integration of much of the former Eastern bloc, including China—were, and continue to be, key elements in (re)producing CVCs.

In the two decades prior to the 1970s crisis, capitalism experienced its 'golden age' of high profitability when the world average return on investment stood at around 15 per cent (Wein 2010, cited in Choonara 2018, 110). In this context, material concessions were made to an important part of the world's working class—reflecting the relative health of capitalist accumulation, the relative strength of working-class movements, and a geopolitical constellation where Western capitalist countries sought to appear as more socially progressive than what they conceived of as their socialist rivals. These dynamics underpinned a Keynesian class-compromise in many core countries (achieved, for example, via productivity-wage links instituted through agreements between states, trade unions, and employers). Many economists proclaimed a new era of post-crisis or non-crisis capitalism (see Harman 1984).

But capitalist crisis returned in the 1970s. In response, increasing numbers of leading capitalist firms and states began reshaping economies—domestic and global—to restructure capitalist class power (Harvey 2005b; Connell and Dados 2014). Key shifts included suppressing the democratic voice of workers, implementing capital-friendly structural adjustment programmes in one society after another, instituting global norms to enhance capital mobility, decoupling productivity from wages, opening up new geographic zones for sourcing and production based on very cheap labour power, and ramping up the appropriation of nature across the globe. These shifts underpinned the growing importance of CVCs—geographically dispersed, functionally integrated systems of capitalist production.

The growing importance of CVCs reached its zenith in the decades following the dissolution of the Soviet Union in 1991 and the increasing integration of China into global circuits of capital—first as an effective assembly platform and later as a producer of increasingly high-tech goods and services (see Chapter 5 for an in-depth account). Throughout this period, neoliberal ideologues claimed that globalization would accelerate development in poorer countries and reboot growth in richer countries (Bhagwati 2004). But the evidence is less accommodating (Davidson 2018). As mentioned above, what did happen was that wealth was increasingly concentrated in the hands of a very few, giant, lead firms. Some lead firms, especially from the United States, expanded rapidly by outsourcing and offshoring production, and establishing new forms of inter-firm control-relations through chain 'governance'. These relations facilitated their capture of the lion's share of surplus value generated through labour-exploitation in CVCs.

CVCs have been constructed upon the incorporation of a growing global working class. The term labouring or working class refers here to those who 'depend—directly and indirectly—on the sale of their labour power for their own daily reproduction' (Panitch and Leys 2001, ix). We deploy the term labouring class here in this sense, denoting those who do not possess any means of production (and thus subsistence), and are therefore de facto wage dependent. This includes productive workers who sell their labour power for a wage within the productive sphere and those who enable them (often in the home or community) to do so by undertaking unpaid labour in the social reproductive sphere (Elson 2010).

The proliferation of CVCs occurred in tandem with, and based upon, the numerical expansion and political weakening of the world's labouring class. Following the dissolution of the Eastern bloc and the global roll-out of neoliberalism, Russian, Eastern European, Chinese, and Indian workers were made exploitable not only for local capitalists, but also for lead firms from Western countries—increasing 'the size of the global labour pool from approximately 1.46 billion workers to 2.93 billion workers' by 2000 (Freeman 2006, 1). By 2017, the global pool of labour power had expanded by another 500 million workers (Kühn 2019, 5). As Freeman (2006, 3) notes, '[t]he impact of these dynamics of labour integration were to reduce greatly the capital to labour ratio ... [shifting] ... the global balance of power to capital'.

But newly proletarianized workers are only one part of the story. Equally important are attacks by capital upon existing workers' organizations to increase the exploitability of the latter in peripheral countries, as in General Pinochet's 1973 civic-military coup in Chile. Even without military interventions, workers' collective positions vis-à-vis the state and capital were substantially weakened by 'liberalization'. Such dynamics included industrial reorganization under structural adjustment programmes, agricultural 'modernization', land grabs, and migration among other processes. Agrarian modernization has, since the late 1970s, pushed about one billion people from their homes to find work and livelihoods elsewhere (Delgado Wise and Veltmeyer 2016). Workers in countries that implemented International Monetary Fund (IMF) restructuring agreements were 60 per cent less likely to be in a trade union after the programme (Martin and Brady 2007, 574).

Through CVCs, parts of the industrial production controlled by capitalist firms from the United States and Europe shifted towards countries that offered cheap labour power, pro-capital political regulation, and weak or inexistent unions. The number of labourers working in export-orientated industries quadrupled between 1980 and 2003 (IMF 2007, 162). As Kizu et al. note in an ILO research paper,

> 453 million people were employed in GSCs [global supply chains] in 2013, compared with 296 million in 1995, in the 40 countries for which estimates are available.... Emerging economies drive most of the overall increase in GSC-related jobs, and contributed to an estimated 116 million more jobs as of 1995.
>
> **(Kizu et al. 2016, 9)**

They observe that integration into global chains generates 'a positive impact on productivity, but not on wages, implying a drop in the wage share' (Kizu et al. 2016, 23). The labour power of growing numbers of workers employed within CVCs is kept and made cheap through a range of divisive strategies deployed by capital and supporting states. Elena Baglioni (2022) uses the notion of labour regimes to analyse such context-specific relations and institutions that shape and constrain work, exploitation, and struggle (see Chapter 9 on social upgrading). Within and through such labour regimes, capital also shapes gendered and racialized exploitation (see Stevano 2023).

Techno-Dynamism and Geopolitics

Dynamics of global capital concentration through CVCs—the emergence and expansion of enormous lead firms—have been turbo-charged by innovations in digital technologies. These facilitate the global dispersal and functional integration of production by enabling real-time communication between buyers and suppliers, precise shipping and warehousing, and increasing rates of supplier firm surveillance. Digital technologies raise the efficiency of production by monitoring it with the intention of reducing duplication of tasks, reducing lead times, and accelerating stock-replenishment. They are also used to surveil labour and to intensify the labour process. Information has become, increasingly, a vehicle for wealth capture, as firms extracting big data organize markets in new ways. Consequently, alongside monopolization tendencies in tangible commodities, CVCs have accelerated the emergence of intellectual monopoly capital (Pagano 2014).

China's rise has been often characterized—by its supporters and opponents alike—as a threat to this US-centred dynamic. However, China facilitated the outsourcing and profit-maximizing strategies of sections of US capital by becoming the 'workshop of the world'. More recently, China has begun to challenge Western capitalist lead firms on several fronts—in particular in technologically advanced chain links (Rosenberg and Boyle 2019; Germann 2023).

Since the Covid-19 pandemic there has been much discourse about processes of 're-shoring', 'friend-shoring', or 'nearshoring' (e.g., Vivoda 2023). Some of this commentary and literature follows in the wake of the 2008 world economic crisis and the emergence of increasingly loud and popular calls to bring production back home, as in Donald Trump's Make America Great Again campaign. Claims that such processes potentially represent the beginning of the end of CVCs are based on scant evidence.

It is the case that the United States—under the presidencies of Obama, Trump, and Biden—attempted to contain China's rise. On the one hand, the United States and its firms want to continue investing in China, trading with it, and importing its very cheap wage goods. On the other hand, the United States is simultaneously attempting to limit China's economic, political, and potentially military power, in high-tech sectors such as computer chips (Miller 2022). The same is true of EU states and firms.

US policies to contain China have succeeded in re-routing some production and trade between China and the United States—to countries such as Vietnam and Mexico. At the time of writing, CVCs between the USA and China remain intact, and the main trend is continued globalization (Alfaro and Chor 2023). In 2022, two-way (intra-industry) trade between the USA and China reached an all-time high of $690 billion (Palmer 2023). Donald Trump's victory in the 2024 presidential election, and his promises to impose tariffs of more than 60 per cent on Chinese imports, may influence these trends. It may be that the shape of globalized production and trade changes radically in the future. For the moment, however, CVCs represent its prime organizational form.

1.5 Organization of This Book

Following this introduction, Chapter 2 outlines our class-relational theoretical framework, which informs our subsequent analysis of the International Political Economy and uneven developmental dynamics of CVCs.

Chapter 3 outlines the origins, evolution and mainstreaming of the GVC framework and the closely related Global Production Network framework. It details how capitalist class relations have been overwhelmingly sidelined from these perspectives, albeit increasingly at the expense of their explanatory power. Chapter 4 provides a detailed deconstruction of World Bank's WDR2020 report. While the World Bank's report claims that GVCs are developmentally positive, it provides evidence to the contrary—showing how they concentrate wealth, repress wages, create many bad jobs (low-wage, low-skill, low-security, and with poor working conditions), and reproduce new forms of in-work poverty. Chapter 5 provides a historical overview of the role of geopolitics in the making of CVCs. Chapter 6 shows how post-Covid 19 notions of supply chain 'resilience' are intimately bound-up with US attempts to contain, geopolitically, China's rise. Chapter 7 outlines theoretically and applies empirically the concept of immiserating growth regimes to illustrate how CVCs generate impoverished labour forces the world over. Chapter 8 shows how upgrading in CVCs occur though processes of class differentiation. Chapter 9 addresses the question of amelioration of workers' pay and conditions in CVCs (often referred to as 'social upgrading' in the mainstream literature)—and argues that positive developmental ameliorations are most likely achieved by workers' collective actions. Chapter 10 outlines the environmental toll of capitalist production in general, and CVCs in particular. Finally, Chapter 11 concludes and argues that a better (empirically and historically informed) understanding of capitalist value chains is vital for challenging the spurious developmental claims of the *GVCs for Development.*

A Note on Terminology

We use the term Global Value Chain (GVC) when we speak about how the mainstream identifies its object of study. We use the term Capitalist Value Chain (CVC) as our analytical description of these international class-based structures of capital accumulation. We introduce and define the concept of the imperialist chain in the following chapter. While we use the terms higher up and lower down the imperialist chain, sometimes we use terms like 'peripheral' or 'leading' states and firms in the same spirit, for ease of readability. At other times we use terms deployed by institutions and writers—such as when we discuss the World Bank's conceptualization of developed and developing countries—without subscribing to the modernization-theory underpinnings of these terms.

2
Capitalism, Class, and CVCs

> In all forms of society there is one specific kind of production which predominates over the rest, whose relations thus assign rank and influence to the others. It is a general illumination which bathes all the other colours and modifies their particularity. It is a particular ether which determines the specific gravity of every being which has materialized within it.
>
> **(Marx 1993, 106f.)**

2.1 Introduction

We define Capitalist Value Chains (CVCs) as historically specific sociospatial configurations of capitalist production, based upon and reproduced through international class relations. Our understanding of capitalist development entails the analysis of inter-class (capital–labour) and intra-class (between different units of capital) dynamics. It is key to comprehending how wealth (of the few) and poverty (of the many) are, through exploitation, two sides of the same coin of CVCs. Through CVCs, units of capital in one part of the world can effectively command the production and appropriation of surplus value in other parts of the world. Additionally, highly monopolized lead firm capitals can make extra profits by capturing parts of the surplus value produced under the direct control of supplier firm capitals.

After the 1970s crisis of profitability, CVCs have increasingly enabled lead firms, initially mainly from the United States and European countries, to profit from these forms of geographical expansion. In and through CVCs, fractions of capital and states have used, and also generated, uneven sociogeographies of capitalism (see Chapter 5 on the making of CVCs). However, the underlying class dynamics—the dialectics of exploitation of labour by capital and competition among capitals—tend to be ignored empirically and conceptually within mainstream Global Value Chain (GVC) approaches. As noted in Chapter 1, this book argues that we need to understand (a) the core

Capitalist Value Chains. Benjamin Selwyn and Christin Bernhold, Oxford University Press.
 DOI: 10.1093/9780191994906.003.0002

dynamics of capitalist production, (b) how CVCs emerge from and are based upon them, and (c) how CVCs impact back upon and intensify capitalism's core class-relational dynamics. Marx's quote above—that in all forms of society 'there is one specific kind of production which predominates over the rest' directs us to analyse the formation, functioning, and developmental processes associated with CVCs from a class-relational perspective. This does not mean that geopolitics, among other hierarchical relations, are unimportant for CVC development. Rather, it is necessary to analyse how the latter are shaped by capitalist social relations of production.

Our focus lies not merely on the distribution of value among firms, but upon surplus value *production and distribution*. This differentiates our analysis from mainstream GVC approaches. The latter speak of 'value-added' and 'value capture', which can yield important insights about inter-firm relations (Kaplinsky 2005, and see Chapter 3). But they ignore how value originates in a historically specific exploitative social relation between capital and labour. By ignoring the question of the social source of value, such approaches can then self-justify sidelining the importance, and historical specificity of, the capital–labour relation. But this is an intellectually ruinous move, as this relation is the fount of value production upon which CVCs rise. The undefined and vague notion of 'value-added' at the heart of mainstream GVC frameworks represent less a theory of value than the ideological veiling of labour exploitation as the foundation of CVCs (and see Chapters 3 or 4).

Cattaneo, Gereffi, and Staritz (2010, 7) suggest that 'GVCs have become the world economy's backbone and central nervous system.' But this is only part of the story. Labour exploitation and competitive capital accumulation are the DNA of capitalism in general and CVCs in particular. A rigorous conception of class relations is not only necessary to comprehend who produces and who appropriates profits in CVCs. It also explains why competitive capital accumulation through labour exploitation (and resistance to it) propel firms to adopt technological innovations, why capital concentration (and consequently monopolization and the predominance of lead firms) is so characteristic of CVCs, why and how workers in many CVC sectors experience poverty wages, and how CVCs depend upon the growing appropriation (and despoilation) of nature. In sum, even if the reader is not interested in understanding the impacts of CVCs upon labour, they do need to incorporate class-relational dynamics into their conception of CVCs to meaningfully comprehend these just-noted processes.

Our emphasis upon CVCs does not presuppose that they are the only way to comprehend international capitalist dynamics of exploitation and uneven development. We are not proposing a new theory of the global political economy and capitalist development in all its facets that includes discussions on the role of unequal production and exchange, national and international rates of profits, currency seigniorage, geopolitics, and militarily secured appropriation of raw materials, among other factors. Furthermore, states have their own specific histories of class formation and articulations with the world economy.

This chapter outlines the conceptual categories—derived from Marx and later Marxists—that will be deployed and discussed in more depth subsequently throughout this book. In the remainder of this chapter, Section 2.2 outlines our understanding of class relations and why class conflict is intrinsic to capitalism. Section 2.3 discusses the class-relational basis of competition and monopoly under capitalism. Section 2.4 argues that CVCs are based upon and reproduced through international class relations. Section 2.5 delves into the relationship between capitalist production, labour regimes, and the social reproduction of labour. Section 2.6 summarizes the sources of workers' power under CVCs. Section 2.7 outlines our comprehension of the capitalist state and uses the notion of the imperialist chain to frame our understanding of the interstate system and geopolitics. Section 2.8 delineates the ecological foundations of CVCs.

2.2 Capitalism, Class, and Class Conflict

As argued above, CVCs have been constructed and work through international class and geopolitical relations. Comprehending these dynamics requires acknowledging the fount upon which CVCs rise—the surplus value produced by labour and appropriated by capital.

Although the term 'class struggle' is associated, often pejoratively, with workers' attempts to ameliorate their conditions, the reverse—struggles from above by capital to reproduce and heighten its exploitation of labour—is the more common reality. As billionaire Warren Buffet quipped, '[t]here's class warfare, all right, but it's my class, the rich class, that's making war, and we're winning' (Stein 2006, n.p.). CVCs facilitate capital's continuous struggle to heighten this class warfare in its favour.

The category of class identifies a social relation of exploitation and domination, and thus 'real mechanisms that have causal force in the lives of people regardless of whether the actors themselves recognize that causal force' (Wright 2015, n.p.). As we briefly mentioned in the introduction to this book, Geoffrey de Ste. Croix (1981, 43) conceives of class as 'the collective social expression of the fact of exploitation'. Accordingly, a class is:

> a group of persons in a community identified by their position in the whole system of social production, defined above all by their relationship (primarily in terms of the degree of ownership or control) to the conditions of production (that is to say, the means and labour of production) and to other classes.... (ibid.)

All class societies are based upon the appropriation of surplus labour—the labour performed above and beyond that necessary to support the livelihood of the direct producers—by superordinate from subordinate classes. Marx formulated the concept of the *capitalist mode of production* to show how this surplus labour takes the social form of surplus value.

While there have been many different forms of class society, capitalist class relations are historically unique. Here, based on the private ownership of the means of production, workers are 'free' in the double sense—politically 'free' to sell their labour power to different capitalists, but also 'free' from ownership of the means of production. Consequently, they *must* sell their labour power on the market to acquire means of subsistence. Once workers have sold their labour power to capital their freedom is diminished. In the workplace capital's extraction of surplus value is achieved through combinations of consent and coercion (including lesser and greater amounts of force exerted by employers). Capital's ability to coerce labour to work harder, longer, and for lower wages, is rooted in labour's lack of control over the means of production. Hence, the freedom generated by capitalism as espoused by liberal economists such as Hayek (1980) and Friedman (1985) is the freedom for capital to dominate and exploit labour.

Workers' sale of their labour power on the market, their generation of surplus value for capital in the sphere of production, and hence socioeconomic exploitation, are part and parcel of capitalism's *differentia specifica* compared to other modes of production.[1]

The 'inner secret' of surplus value and capitalist profit is the value produced by workers over and above the value of their labour power (determined by the socially necessary labour-time necessary to reproduce the worker) that they receive in wages. '[T]he value of labour-power, and the value that labour-power valorizes in the labour process, are two entirely different magnitudes'

[1] While the capitalist mode of production is the key driver of political-economic development, it exists within a broader context of evolving capitalist societies, or *historical capitalism*. Within the latter, relations of domination that are partly pre-existing are shaped by the capitalist relations of production in historically and geographically specific ways, while they also impact back upon class relations. Later in this book we explore examples of how gendered and racialized politics and cultures and forms of forced labour are deployed by capitalists to augment the exploitation of labour (see, e.g., Giménez 2019).

(Marx 1990, 300). From the perspective of capital, the ratio of surplus over socially necessary labour is represented by the rate of surplus value. For labour, however, it is represented by the rate of exploitation. Consequently, a specific form of class struggle—over the rate of surplus value (from capital's perspective) or rate of exploitation (from workers' perspective)—is intrinsic and ongoing, rather than incidental, to capitalist class relations. The social process by which surplus value is extracted in capitalist societies gives formal meaning to this form of exploitation, and inter alia to the notion of capital and labour as social classes with opposing interests.

Capital's attempts to extract as much surplus value as possible from labour is reinforced by the drive for profit under conditions of *endless competitive capital accumulation.* This set of relations—between capital and labour and between units of capital—generates a social dynamic unknown to prior history:

> Fanatically bent on making value expand itself [capital] ruthlessly forces the human race to produce for production's sake; [it] thus forces the development of the productive powers of society.... Accumulation for accumulation's sake, production for production's sake.
>
> **(Marx 1990, 739)**

However, capitalism generates a seemingly paradoxical, and conflictual developmental dynamism. While it expands and generates vast quantities of wealth at an historically unprecedented rate, its basis in labour exploitation means that most of this social wealth is off-limits to capitalism's labour force. This is because, first, the surplus value produced by workers does not remain in their own hands and is not subject to their democratic control. Second, accumulation is based upon capital's endless accrual and competitive re-investment of wealth *through* the reproduction of a property-less wage-labour force:

> On the one hand, the production process incessantly converts material wealth into capital, into the capitalist's means of enjoyment and his means of valorization. On the other hand, the worker always leaves the process in the same state as he entered it—a personal source of wealth [for the capitalist], but deprived of any means of making that wealth a reality for himself... *in short, the capitalist produces the worker as a wage-labourer.* This incessant reproduction, this perpetuation of the worker, is the absolutely necessary condition for capitalist production.
>
> **(Marx 1990, 716, emphasis added)**

The crudest methods deployed by capital to increase the ratio of surplus over necessary labour is the 'prolongation of the working-day'—thus increasing *absolute surplus value* (Marx 1990, ch. 16). The *immiseration* of labour—pushing down wages—is another way for capital to appropriate more surplus value. In Chapter 7 we show how such methods—in Chinese electronics, Cambodian and UK garments, and East and Central European footwear production, are deployed by CVC firms. Historically and logically, however, there are limits to such strategies—including the natural length of a day, workers' physical exhaustion, and their resistance, as well as hard-won social norms that disallow or limit such practices. However, capitalists have an additional means to raise the rate of labour exploitation that does not involve the above strategies and is compatible with the maintenance of a standard set of working hours and stable or even rising levels of workers' wages and/or consumption.

This is *relative surplus value* extraction (Marx 1990, 432), realized by enhancing the productivity of labour, for instance through technological development—where the same number of working hours yields greater output (and see next section). From the spinning jenny in the eighteenth and nineteenth centuries, the assembly line in the nineteenth and twentieth centuries, digital technologies and Artificial Intelligence in the late twentieth and early twenty-first centuries—advances in technologies raise labour productivity. Higher productivity reduces the socially necessary labour time to produce wage goods, making the latter cheaper. This in turn reduces the costs of reproducing labour power. However, whether wage goods are cheap is also a question of politics and uneven geographies of production and exchange. For example, the repeal of the corn laws (mid nineteenth century UK) and the Marshall plan (mid twentieth century Western Europe) when cheap grains were imported, as well as contemporary imports of cheap consumer goods and food (see Chapter 5) have underpinned capitalist growth through reducing wage costs.

Higher productivity and the cheaper reproduction of labour power generates a situation where labourers work less (necessary labour time) for their own reproduction and bequeath more time to the production of surplus value that does not remain in their hands. Thus, the possibilities of relative surplus value extraction generate the potential for some, *albeit always limited*, material concessions to workers. That capital seeks to increase surplus over necessary labour time through increases in productivity is a key driver of capitalism's technological dynamism.

CVCs are an organizational structure of accumulation that enables capital to heighten exploitation by *combining these forms of absolute and relative surplus extraction in new ways through international class relations.* In CVCs, lead firm capital predominantly located in leading capitalist countries strongly influences what is produced, where it is produced, and under which conditions. In these ways lead firms can capture parts of the surplus value initially appropriated by supplier firms (see next section). Several process of production (e.g., of parts and components) are carried out under the direct control of supplier capital or lead firm subsidiaries in CVCs, in various countries, with different conditions of production, class relations, and resulting political regulations. Some of these firms control high-tech production while paying low wages, others heighten exploitation by extending the working days, and still others combine these methods.

When workers are paid below a living wage, we call this *immiserating exploitation* (see Chapter 7 on Immiserating Growth-Regimes for a discussion of the living wage). Our notion of the living wage is derived from the Asian floor wage (itself rooted in the UN's Declaration of Human Rights), which stipulates a standard working week of 48 hours maximum, enables a worker to buy food for themselves and their family, pay for rent, healthcare, clothing, transportation, education, and to have a small amount of savings.

Dynamics of immiserating exploitation are rooted in capitalist class relations, where firms seek to enhance their profits through increased labour exploitation. Immiserating exploitation is most prevalent in peripheral countries where CVC suppliers are concentrated. However, it is not confined to CVC production in these countries. While it is characteristic for capitalist production, for example in Vietnam, Bangladesh, Cambodia, or in Mexico, it also represents a contemporary strategy of accumulation in leading capitalist countries, for example across Europe (see Chapter 7) and the USA (for example in the food sector, see Allegretto et al. 2013). CVCs have heightened exploitative pressures—though unevenly—in all countries participating in them. Before we address this in Section 2.4, the next section discusses our class-relational notion of monopolization and competition—which is key for understanding lead firm power.

2.3 Competition and Monopoly in CVCs

Writing for the World Bank, Cattaneo et al. (2013, 6) argue that GVCs enhance competitiveness:

> [P]articipation in GVCs allows (as well as is the result of) greater competitiveness, better inclusion in trade and investment flows, as well as socio-economic

upgrading, with more and better remunerated jobs, a more sustainable use of resources, and better governance and political stability at large.

The GVC mainstream explains the developmental benefits of GVCs by deploying classical notions of competition—rooted in Adam Smith's notion of specialization and the productivity-enhancing division of labour (see also Chapters 3 and 4). But such a notion represents more a justification for lead firm power than a substantiated analysis of competition in CVCs.

Capital accumulation entails the *expansion* of production by firms through hiring more workers and buying more machinery and raw materials. It also entails *specialization* through investments in new hard and soft technologies—new equipment and new ways of deploying it (management systems)—designed to increase productive efficiency and to raise surplus value generation and extraction (Choonara 2009). Capital's attempt to increase the rate of surplus over necessary labour through continual technological investments raises the minimum amounts of capital required for competitive production in any given sector. Such processes are relative, where some firms undertake them more effectively than others, which is part and parcel of capitalism's tendency towards capital concentration and centralization.

Marx referred to the capitalist class as a band of hostile brothers: hostile because they compete amongst themselves to maximize individual control over surplus value, and brothers because they are united in the exploitation of labour. As we discuss below, while individual capitalists are the first appropriators of surplus value from labour, they are not necessarily the last. In this context, while *individual* capitalists attempt to wrest as much surplus value from each other (a fact tacitly accepted by mainstream GVC analysis in its notion of value capture, see Chapter 3), it is in the capitalist class's *collective interest* that it raises the rate of exploitation of as many workers as possible—to increase the total mass of surplus value.

Monopolies, which we conceive of broadly as firms consistently capturing above average profits, emerge out of capitalism's inner tendencies towards concentration (increasing size and thus control over means of production and labour) and centralization (integration of already-formed capitals into larger firms, e.g., through acquisitions). Capitalist competition rewards the few and punishes the many, the latter often facing expulsion from the market unless they can secure other ways to maintain their profitability. Writing in the mid-nineteenth century Marx already grasped the class-relational implications of these dynamics whereby 'there is an increase in the minimum amount of individual capital necessary to carry on a business under its normal conditions'. Further, 'Capital grows in one place to a huge mass in a single hand, because it has in another place been lost by many.' Marx also grasped, in ways that are cannily relevant to the presence of lead firms in overwhelmingly rich economies, how capital concentration and centralization generated pressures contributing to '[a] new and international division of labour ... suited to the requirements of the chief centres of modern industry' (Marx 1990, 579f.).

Capitalism is immensely dynamic, and it would be mistaken to interpret Marx's analysis as suggesting a movement towards a situation where a few *permanently* monopolized firms control the economy. Rather, his analysis highlights the continual dialectic between competition and monopoly. As Elmar Altvater (1975) notes, capitalism produces a tendency towards big, powerful corporations. At the same time,

> Monopolies are only those individual capitals that can achieve a profit over longer periods that is not subject to the equalizing movements to the average profit rate of society as a whole. However, since these monopolistic, above-average profits are limited in quantity and time, monopolistic positions are constantly being eliminated.
>
> **(Altvater 1975, 131, own translation)**

Monopolization is an ever-present *tendency* of capitalism, and big, powerful corporations shape the uneven geographies of capitalist production and trade. But monopolies are transient and are not necessarily always the same firms, localized in the same countries. The dynamics of capitalist competitive accumulation, which is always geographically uneven, generates new monopolies. As we shall see in Chapter 5, today this is particularly relevant with respect to the rise of Chinese lead firms and associated geopolitical rivalries. Hence, even where monopoly positions appear to represent a permanent feature of the economy, '[c]ompetition as the effect of individual capitals on one another cannot be eliminated' (ibid., 158). Consequently, Altvater explains how monopoly can be understood theoretically '*as a specific moment of competition*', while competition can be understood as a specific moment of monopoly. Further:

> The individual capitals and their 'heads', the company managers, regularly strive for monopoly positions or try to destroy the monopoly positions of other, competing individual capitals. Since competition does not cease to operate

> when individual capitals exist as monopolies, the individual capitalist striving for monopoly positions (because they bring with them above-average profit), is always contradicted by the equalizing movements of [all] individual capitals—in which they constitute themselves as part of the total capital. (ibid., 159, own translation)

For these reasons Marx writes that:

> In practical life we find not only competition, monopoly and the antagonism between them, but also the synthesis of the two.... Monopoly produces competition, competition produces monopoly. Monopolists are made from competition; competitors become monopolists.
>
> (Marx 1847, n.p.)

Various forms of monopoly exist under capitalism. These include technological advantage (as in contemporary micro-chip production), the superior access to natural resources compared to rivals (such as more fertile land, as in Ricardo's famous example, or fossil capital (Malm 2016)), and 'artificial' monopolies constructed by states—such as through trade restrictions, or through patents and copyrights (as established under the WTO). Altvater (1975, 181) also identifies a form of monopoly that is particularly prominent in CVCs. 'Manipulated monopolies' exist where firms can purposefully structure the markets within which they are dominant to augment their dominance. For instance, the global retail 'revolution' of the late twentieth century saw a few mega supermarkets increasingly dominate markets, excluding rivals and smaller producers, in part through setting product quality standards (see Reardon and Hopkins 2006; Selwyn 2013a). Several of these forms of market power have been identified by Raphael Kaplinsky (2005) as forms of economic rent. While he explains how powerful firms *capture* value through rents, the conception of monopoly outlined here, rooted in capitalism's core social relations, specifies how that value is *created* in the first place: monopoly rent is a part of the surplus value produced by workers. Moreover, it analytically specifies how monopoly arises out of capitalist class's continual attempts to increase the rate of labour exploitation. In this vein, lead firm power is always based on previous rounds of accumulation.

CVC-lead firms use their market power—itself rooted in either the direct extraction of surplus value, or the ability to wrest it from other firms—to determine the flow of goods, the conditions under which they are produced, and the prices for which they are bought and sold. The ability to achieve monopoly positions—the relatively long-term ability to gain above average profits—facilitates the appropriation of portions of the surplus value produced under the direct control of other (subordinate) capitalists. This transfer in turn enables lead firms to invest in furthering their monopoly positions.

Shifts in the uneven geographies of monopoly and competition are not random in the sense that any and all firms can challenge monopolistic positions. In historically and geographically particular contexts, for example, US corporations challenged former British monopolies while today, some Chinese firms are becoming competitive with US high-tech corporations (and see below and Chapters 5 and 6).

2.4 CVCs and International Class Relations

As mentioned above, CVCs represent international configurations of class relations that generate systemic downward pressure upon workers' wages across the world. We thus remain skeptical of exchange-based perspectives on 'Global North' countries exploiting 'the Global South.' It is more accurate, we suggest, to say that capitalist classes in both countries, connected through CVCs, seek to heighten labour exploitation. However, leading capitalists and states (see our notion of the imperialist chain below) have outcompeted weaker capitalists and peripheral states in controlling the development of core technologies and enhancing strategies to appropriate profits. Thus, as mentioned before, the capacities to profit from capitalist production, exchange, and reproduction are distributed highly unevenly. Furthermore, powerful capitalist firms, predominantly located in leading capitalist countries, can either *directly* control production in other countries, and/or appropriate a portion of surplus value produced by workers in supplier firms.

The 'international' in our definition signals a rejection of notions of *methodological nationalism* and *methodological globalism*. Methodological nationalism refers to the theoretical 'equation between the idea of society as social theory's key conceptual reference and the historical processes of modern nation-state formation' (Chernilo 2011, 99). Methodological globalism, by contrast, refers to 'the tendency to consider that the main explanatory factors of most social phenomena lie at the global scale' (Pleyers 2024, 184).

To say that class relations are international is to adopt a *methodological internationalist* perspective, which holds that class relations are neither formed as a uniform global structure (methodological globalism), nor that they are entirely constituted within national spheres (methodological nationalism). First, class relations are formed and organized at the national scale, for example, in China and the USA—while at the same time they are dialectically shaped internationally. Second, capital, to a greater extent than labour, can move across borders. It can utilize geographical differences in class relations (including wages) to increase profits. Capital from some, especially leading countries thus plays an important part in socio-economic class relations and political class formation in other countries where it operates. We discuss examples of this in Chapters 5 and 9, including how offshoring and outsourcing strategies of US capital in the 1970s strengthened class struggle from above in the United States against previously won wages and labour protections. The class relations in East Asian or Latin American countries that made investments profitable for US capitals were, in turn, the result of prior class struggles from above resulting in repressive labour regimes—historically shaped by both local capitals and the involvement of economic and political actors from key imperialist countries (e.g., Glassman 2011). In this way, the reshaping of class relations in the United States, and the reshaping of class relations in East Asian and Latin American countries were mutually connected and internationally articulated.

In sum, the formation, functioning, and reproduction of CVCs is not a simple outcome of a supposedly abstract logic of capitalism, but of historically contingent, internationally related, capitalist development and class struggles. Under capitalism, exploitation and the conditions facilitating it are geographically uneven and socially differentiated. These conditions and social dynamics have been deployed and transformed by lead firms as part of their accumulation strategies. As capital from the United States and other leading countries sought out cheap labour power across the globe, it simultaneously and consequently weakened domestic workers' bargaining power. In this way, CVCs have contributed to rebooting global capitalism. They have impacted upon the wider capitalist system in another way: By accelerating the mass production of cheap wage goods, they contribute to cheapening the cost of reproducing labour power in general. This has in turn further facilitated wage repression across many countries (a fact partially recognized by the World Bank itself, see Chapter 4).

Until now we have discussed international class relations in terms of capital exploiting labour. As noted at the start of this chapter, however, theorizing and investigating intra-class relations is a key element of CVC analysis. For the purposes of our analysis of CVCs, the distribution of surplus value among capitals is pivotal. Here, we build on Marx's observation that while a single capitalist is the first appropriator of surplus value generated in their workplaces, they may not be the last:

> The capitalist who produces surplus-value—i.e., who extracts unpaid labour directly from the labourers, and fixes it in commodities, is, indeed, the first appropriator, but by no means the ultimate owner, of this surplus-value. He has to share it with capitalists . . . who fulfil other functions in the complex of social production. Surplus-value . . . splits up into various parts . . . and take on various mutually independent forms, such as profit, interest, gains made through trade, ground rent, etc. . . .
>
> **(Marx 1990, 709)**

While Marx's discussion of the splitting up into various parts of surplus value alludes to the fractions and functions of industrial, commercial, and finance capital, it does not explicitly theorize these dynamics in geographical and international terms. The latter, however, is an essential element of CVCs. Writing during the gestation period of CVCs Costis Hadjimichalis (1984, 338) observed as one element of uneven development the phenomenon of the geographic transfer of value (GTV), which he defined as

> the tendency or process through which the value produced for exchange by workers at one locality: (a) is realized by the capitalists who have employed these workers, but profits have been reinvested elsewhere and/or (b) is at least partially realized by the capitalists who have employed these workers and is added as excess profits to other capitalists in other localities.

Hadjimichalis argues that examples of indirect GTV include sectoral transfers of surplus value, associated with the equalization of the rate of profit across space (Hadjimichalis 1987, 53f.), and mechanisms of unequal exchange (a much debated concept, the further discussion of which would go beyond the scope of this book (see, e.g., Busch 1973; Suwandi 2019)). Practices of direct GTV include profit repatriation (Parnreiter et al. 2024) and highly monopolized lead firms' ability to determine, to a large degree, production costs in one location and sale prices within another location. Such geographically spatialized and functionally integrated systems of labour exploitation and capital accumulation are operationalized through 'concrete space materialised in socio spatial relations which are particular to a place' (Hadjimichalis 1984, 339). Key determinants are 'local class structure, the local labour market, and local general conditions of social production' (ibid.) which are presided over by local states. While Hadjimichealis did not specify how class relations of exploitation were articulated internationally in CVCs, two of the core concepts associated with the mainstream GVC approach—lead firms with significant market power and chain governance—provide us with a necessary component of the story of direct GTV. As mentioned before, lead firms' chain governance strategies are rooted in diverse forms of monopoly power.

In fact, mainstream GVC theorists go to considerable lengths to establish typologies of various forms of chain governance (Gereffi et al. 2005). However, they do so without interrogating the original source of (lead) firm's power, rooted in the capital–labour relation, and competition among capitalists. As the previous section on monopoly and competition argues, the power to govern a chain needs to be explained by the historically attained class power of leading capitalists to outcompete other capitals in controlling the development of the productive forces, profiting from the exploitation of workers, and enhancing strategies to appropriate profits.

While monopoly emerges out of competition, it subsequently enables lead firms to purposefully manage increasingly asymmetric and hierarchical forms of competition amongst and between their suppliers. David Quentin and Liam Campling (2018, 41) note how

> Lead firms tend to exist in nodes that function as choke points in the chain. The ability to set out barriers to entry and thereby reproduce quasi-monopolistic or quasi-monopsonistic practices in a node is a fundamental piece in the puzzle of 'business success'.

Lead firms' value capture strategies include heightened control over, and increasing the intensity of competition amongst, their suppliers. Competition amongst suppliers is orientated to gaining/maintaining supplier status, rather than competing directly with lead firms. Practices of control include requiring suppliers to open their books, which further augment lead firms' power by, for example, determining from whom suppliers source inputs and at what prices (Miller 2013).

2.5 Labour Regimes and Capitalist Social Reproduction of Labour

The reproduction of capitalist exploitation under historical capitalism requires relations of domination. However, like exploitation, the latter, too, are largely invisible to, or deliberately ignored by, mainstream GVC analysis.

This is in part because these approaches adopt a relatively technical and a-social concept of production (and see Chapter 3). By contrast, Harry Braverman noted how 'what the worker sells and the capitalist buys, is not an agreed amount of labour, but the power to labour over an agreed period of time'. Consequently, 'it thus becomes essential for the capitalist that control over the labour process pass from the hands of the workers into his own' (Braverman 1998, 37, 79; see Smith 2006; Knights and Willmott 2016). Capital deploys a range of forms of domination in and beyond the production process—through selecting, designing, and developing machinery, organizing work schedules and task-targets—to maximize the production of surplus value (Brighton Labour Process Group 1977, 13).

That capital employs labour on an exploitative basis in the workplace requires the existence and social reproduction of a sufficiently disciplined, hard-working labour force, employable at sufficiently low rates of pay, as to enable sustained profits to capital. Workers' maximum work effort is secured within labour regimes, depending on geographically concrete situations, through consent or coercion (Burawoy 1982). The labour regime concept denotes:

> the set of social relations ... that shape and construct exploitation at multiple scales and through different spheres across the 'global economy'. Labour regimes are the ... infrastructures that mobilise workers for factories, farms, and offices, and that extend and intensify work.
>
> (Baglioni et al. 2022b, 82; see Taylor and Rioux 2017)

We show in Chapter 7 how combinations of domestic and international capital in concert with states often collaborate to reproduce a poor labouring class. The latter are subject to immiserating exploitation (where base wages are not living wages) as part of capital's accumulation drive. For example, Dae-Oup Chang (2022) shows how as part of its strategy of CVC integration the Cambodian state established and maintained, often through harsh repression, a highly exploitable and largely poor labour force to attract investments by international garment companies. Further, as we discuss in more detail in Chapter 9 (on social upgrading), labour regimes have been gendered and racialized in geographically specific forms under historical capitalism. Martha Giménez (2019) shows how capitalist class relations shape existing forms of gendered and racialized oppression each in specific ways, modifying their particularity, as in Marx's quote introducing this chapter. Capital also deploys these oppressive strategies to increase exploitation and maximize profits. Social and political landscapes of oppression are thus moulded by the capitalist mode of production—and CVCs are no exception.

Jennifer Bair (2010, 224) for example notes how a powerful strategy by capital is its leveraging of racist and gendered relations as markers of social difference within CVCs to heighten exploitation.

A book about capitalist societies would delve deeply—empirically and theoretically—into the historical processes by which class relations re-shape racist and gendered relations, and how the reproduction of labour is organized across states and localities. Within the frame of this book, it suffices to note that capitalist social reproduction (Giménez 2021), including the concrete historical making of workforces, takes place in various spheres. Hannah Schling (2022) notes, for example, how 'dormitory' or 'hostel' arrangements represent increasingly important strategies by capital in CVCs to secure near-continuous supplies of disciplined workers. Under such arrangements, workers are housed, or more accurately 'stationed', near their workplaces and are subject to heightened control by their employers. Pattenden (2018) also highlights how the socio-geographic circulation of migrant labour—often from rural households to urban factories—is a way for firms and states to regulate the 'release' and 'reabsorption' of labour in ways advantageous to capital (see Chapters 5, 7, and 9).

The establishment of labour regimes (nationally and locally) is determined to a significant extent by states (see Section 2.7). For example, Birke and Bluhm (2019) discuss how the regulation of migration facilitates the intensive exploitation of migrant workers in the German meat industry. In Chapter 5 we discuss, first, how the *hukou* system in China facilitates the availability of vulnerable workers in the right place at the right time (as workers leave the countryside and return there when they are not needed by firms in urban centres). Second, the dormitory system is a mainstay of labour control in key sectors such as electronics (Pun and Smith 2007). In the Czech Republic, Foxconn deploys a dormitory regime to ensure a continuous supply of disciplined workers (Andrijasevic and Sacchetto 2014; Schling 2022).

The power relations required to reproduce the capitalist production process flow directly from the private ownership of the means of production. While workers generate new surplus value objectified in commodities, the commodities they produce are not theirs. Capitalist production is systematically not designed for democratic decision-making over production: The capitalist workshop is, rather, despotic (Marx 1990).

For capitalists the market represents a sphere of opportunity (through which to buy surplus value-generating labour power) and a sphere of either competing successfully against other firms or going bust. While the price mechanism provides (imperfect) information to firms about where to invest, capitalist markets are anarchic in the sense that there is no system-wide planning. Firms' attempts to raise their competitiveness increases the pressure upon other firms to follow suit. The anarchy of markets exacerbates capital's requirement to control production to maximize surplus value extraction—to generate larger profits and to enhance competitiveness. Despotism in the workplace, capital's *attempt* to control as fully as possible the labour process (Burawoy 1984, 251), is dialectically related to both the quest for profits and the anarchy of markets.

The GVC conception of chain governance shows, however, how lead firms attempt to transcend or at least reduce some of the anarchic aspects of the world market through planned inter-firm coordination. They do this, for example, through the explicit coordination of production, distribution, and exchange of raw materials, intermediate components, and finished goods. Mainstream GVC analysis explains chain governance from a transaction cost perspective that emphasizes lead firms' role in *coordinating* the complexities of international production, distribution, and exchange (and see Chapter 3). This mode of explanation, however, excludes the class-relational content of chain governance—the process of creating, employing, and managing geographically dispersed, functionally integrated workforces.

2.6 Workers' Power in CVCs

Despite capital's predominance over labour, workers possess several sources of power to confront increases in exploitation (Adler and Webster 1995; Wright 2000; Silver 2003, see Chapter 9). In CVCs these have been conceptualized as deriving from 'choke points' arising from the complexity of international production, which can generate 'bullwhip effects'. Choke points refer to 'critical nodes' in the CVCs, which can disrupt just-in-time production (Alimahomed-Wilson and Ness 2018, 2). Bullwhip effects refer to the impacts of workers disrupting production, especially at strategic choke points, where a small disruption in one part of the chain is magnified elsewhere in the chain (Selwyn 2008; Fox-Hodess 2022).

Recognition of workers' collective power resources, which are further introduced in Chapter 9, represents a conceptual counterbalance to capital-centric notions of development where, as in mainstream GVC analysis, the amelioration of workers' conditions is understood largely as dependent upon economic upgrading—greater firm-level competitiveness. Rather, it becomes visible how improvements could be achieved for workers through their collective action in its varied forms and settings.

However, there is a danger that such analysis falls into the trap of methodological singularism, by focussing on workers' power in single chains or sectors. While workers in some chains may have more or less disruptive/organizational/bargaining power than those in others, they still exist as exploited workers in relation to capital. As Marx notes:

> In reality, the worker belongs to capital before he has sold himself to the capitalist. His economic bondage is at once mediated through, and concealed by, the periodic renewal of the act by which he sells himself, his change of masters, and the oscillations in the market-price of his labour.
>
> **(Marx 1990, 723f.)**

This brings us back to the above argument that the power of capital over labour is enhanced further internationally through CVCs. In fact, CVCs have facilitated a strategy by dominant sections of capital to reproduce its collective power over labour by interrelated processes of expanding the global labour force and increasing the rate of labour exploitation. Capital's structural power to weaken the possibilities of workers' collective action takes various forms, including establishing or sourcing from production facilities in new employment zones where labour is relatively unorganised, pressurizing states to enact repressive labour regimes, threats of relocation if workers organize for improved wages and conditions, legal and illegal profit repatriation, establishing zones of cheap wage good production to devalue labour power, the racialization and gendering of labour, and various other strategies designed to reproduce labour's subordination to capital.

These observations do not negate the political economic importance of identifying diverse power resources at labour's potential disposition. They do, however, caution against overly optimistic readings of workers power in particular sectors and places, which all exist within an exploitative, dominating system of capital accumulation.

2.7 States and Geopolitics in CVCs

States have been conceptualized within the mainstream GVC literature as facilitators for supplier firms to enter GVCs, as regulators of business-to-business relations, as direct producers, and as buyers (Horner 2017). States have also been regarded as parts of public–private–civil society partnerships that can achieve upgrading through synergistic governance (Lee and Gereffi

2015). These observations go beyond a basic notion of the state as representing part of the 'institutional environment' of predominantly market-based firm-to-firm relations through CVCs. However, they do not consider the more profound relationship between states and the capitalist relations of production that, as we argue here, underpins the variety of roles states play in regulating and promoting CVCs.

States, as the political form of capitalism, are *relatively* independent of the social relations of production. Capital is not identical with the state's ruling elite. There is, as Marx says, a 'particularization of the state' (Marx 1844a, 78). However, this particularization does not imply that the state is independent from the capitalist economy.

Capitalist states defend and promote capital's property right to extract surplus value from labour and to deploy it for its own purposes. They monopolize the use of force to the advantage of capital, and maintain wage-labour forces—sometimes through force—willing and able to sell their labour power to capital relatively cheaply (Gerstenberger 2022). That state bureaucracies enjoy a relative autonomy from capital (Poulantzas 1969) implies that they may discriminate against sections of capital (through, for example, preferential subsidies, targeted tariffs and even the nationalization of capitalist property here and there). But as material condensations of the relation of *forces* between social *classes (capital and labour)* and *class* fractions (of capital) they are effectively class states of capital—committed to reproducing the capital–labour relation, and to develop shared policies that can integrate the interests of different factions of the ruling class.

However, states under pressure states can be responsive to demands from organized labour and social movements. Their management of the capital–labour relation is an ongoing, dialectical process, and consequently the production and reproduction of state institutions is 'incomplete, provisional, and unstable, and ... coevolve[s] with a range of other complex emergent phenomenon' (Jessop 2001, 1228; see Smith 2015). Hence, from founding welfare states, to granting workers' rights that infringe upon *some* capitalist property, capitalist states can—depending on the political-economic situation and the balance of class power—incorporate some of labour's demands without losing their capitalist character (Esping-Andersen 1990; Wolford 2010; Sitrin 2012). These observations are illuminated by Kanchana Ruwanpura's (2016) work on Sri Lanka's export garment sector. She notes how 'The colonial and post-colonial capital–labour struggles were catalytic in shaping Sri Lanka's development trajectory, legal framework and institutional structure—which continue to reverberate positively' (Ruwanpura 2016, 426f.).

As we discuss in Chapter 9, such struggles are key to improving workers' conditions in CVCs. That said however, first, capitalist states remain effectively class states of capital. Second, just as class struggles from below can yield developmental gains to and for workers, so too can class struggle from above take them away and establish the ground for increasingly exploitative employment relations that benefit capital. The story of CVCs is, overwhelmingly, the latter.

Capitalist states exist in the plural (Barker 1978), in hierarchies of what Leon Trotsky, following Lenin, conceived as imperialist chains (see Callinicos 2009; Trotsky 2020). In leading imperialist states with relatively high economic, political, and military strength, capitalist class formation entails (among other aspects that the exceed the scope of this book) a geographical convergence of monopolized capitals and their profits. These control (the production of) key means of production—including key technologies and natural resources— have the potential to partially control (financial) markets and to preside over and influence the geographical transfer of profits, enjoy favourable conditions in the competition for 'mobile capital' (Arrighi 1994), and the ability to outperform competitors in these fields. It is out of such relations that CVC-led firms have emerged and reproduce their power internationally on an expanding scale.

In accordance with our previous discussion (see Section 2.4), different states in the imperialist chain can be understood as institutional materializations of international class relations. In that sense, the imperialist chain 'is the terrain on which a variety of national strategies, often contradictory and incontestably unequal in power, are constituted' (Milios and Sotiropoulos 2009, 189). Leading states deploy their economic, political, and military power to incorporate other states into their spheres of influence through geopolitical relations. The United States presides over the contemporary imperialist chain, and it has done the most to establish the rules of the game within which CVCs emerged and expanded.

The crucial role of the United States in making post 1945 global capitalism is described by Leo Panitch and Sam Gindin (Panitch and Gindin 2005). They also show how, following the crisis decade of the 1970s, the US state played the decisive role in establishing neoliberal globalization (see Chapter 5). The US Military Industrial Complex—its hidden 'developmental state' (Block 2008)—established the key technologies that facilitated the operation of CVCs. But it did much more than that. Following the dissolution of the Eastern bloc in 1991, the United States sought to establish a hegemonic American form of global capitalism—rooted in its economic, political, military, and cultural primacy, as well as its capacity to make material concessions and act in favour not only of its own interests, but also those of its allies. In this way, it established itself as first amongst equals (see Abu-Manneh 2003). Its actions are captured succinctly by Robert Wade, who notes how the US state established a global system of

> [f]irst, free capital mobility. Second, free trade (excepting imports that threaten domestic industries important for your re-selection). Third, international investment free from any discriminatory favoring of national companies through protection, public procurement, public ownership or other devices, with special emphasis on the freedom of your companies to get the custom of national elites for the management of their financial assets, their private education, health care, pensions, and the like. Fourth, your currency as the main reserve currency. Fifth, no constraint on your ability to create your currency at will (such as a dollar-gold link), so that you can finance unlimited trade deficits with the rest of the world. Sixth, international lending at variable interest rates denominated in your currency, which means that borrowing countries in crisis have to repay you more when their capacity to repay is less.
>
> (Wade 2002, n.p.)

CVCs arose and have become one of the core structures of contemporary global capitalism within this US-centred system. Panitch and Gindin's portrayal of the US geopolitical strategy represents a useful corrective to much of the mainstream GVC literature which ignores or takes as given US primacy, to the extent that it merits little attention. However, it does not contain sufficient conceptual space to comprehend the uneven dynamics of capitalist development and geopolitical resistance to US hegemony.

Leon Trotsky and Alexander Gerschenkron recognized how economically less powerful states could, under historically particular circumstances, draw upon advanced technologies to affect rapid catch-up development (Gerschenkron 1962; Trotsky 2009; Selwyn 2011). Contemporary China represents a contemporary case of catch-up development. Its immense size, vast, highly disciplined, and low-paid working class, and its relative political independence from leading imperialist states are some of the conditions that have provided it with the resources to pursue an historically specific form of socio-economic transformation. In this context the Chinese state has effectively integrated and coordinated the accumulation strategies of capitalists from across the globe. Its unique development experience does not offer ready-made 'lessons' to other states—but reflects the particularities of catch-up development within the contemporary imperialist chain.

CVCs have reshaped the global geography of capital accumulation, the international class relations through which it occurs and, consequently, the power relations between states within the chain. Whilst the United States occupies the prime position in the imperialist chain, its strategic planners are increasingly concerned about how, over the next two to three decades, China may emerge as a serious economic, political, and military competitor (see Chapters 5 and 6). These fears have given rise to 'pre-emptive' attempts by the US state to forestall China's rise. Such actions fit a broader tendency under historical capitalism—of economic competition assuming increasingly militaristic dimensions. As Harry Magdoff (1992, 45) once wrote:

> Centrifugal and centripetal forces have always coexisted at the very core of the capitalist process.... Periods of peace and harmony have alternated with periods of discord and violence. Generally, the mechanism of this alternation involves both economic and military forms of struggle, with the strongest power emerging victorious and enforcing acquiescence on the losers. But uneven development soon takes over, and a period of renewed struggle for hegemony emerges.

In sum then, capitalist states play a central role in reproducing the possibilities, and actualities, of capitalist exploitative practices, as well as in facilitating economic transformations ('development') in a geopolitical context. This is simply to prefigure our arguments in Chapter 5 that capitalist states are key actors in the continued development (evolution and expansion) of capitalism.

2.8 CVCs and the Destruction of the Natural World

Most mainstream GVC literature ignores the relationship between capitalism and nature. It ignores how nature is, in political-economic terms, appropriated as a 'free gift' by capital in general, and within CVC-based production in particular. The unwillingness to theorize the societal nature relations underpinning CVCs weakens the mainstream's comprehension of the role CVCs play in accelerating environment destruction. Even worse, many mainstream thinkers and institutions argue that GVCs can contribute to mitigating climate breakdown and environmental destruction. This section provides a brief introduction to our conception of how capitalism destroys the natural world which is taken up in detail in Chapter 10.

While all societies draw upon non-human nature, the notion of the metabolic rift specifies how capitalism does so to an unprecedented, qualitatively different, and ruinous degree (Foster et al. 2010). The notion of metabolism refers to the bio-physical processes that occur within a living organism for it to maintain its life. The notion of rift denotes damage. The concept of the metabolic rift signifies the relationship between capitalism's relatively short-term natural extractivist economic cycles, and the much longer-term cycles of natural creation and restoration (Foster 1999). It highlights capitalism's unplanned, anarchic, and ultimately destructive drawing upon nature.

Marx derived the notion of metabolic rift from the German chemist Justus von Liebig. The latter observed how the use of chemical fertilizer—to maintain food production in the context of declining soil fertility caused by excessive production—was exhausting the earth's nutrient cycles. Liebig called this the 'robbery system'. Marx broadened the notion of the metabolic rift from industrial agriculture to capitalism's entire socio-ecological metabolism (Foster 1999).

Marx also specified how '[l]abour is *not the source* of all wealth. *Nature* is just as much the source of use values (and it is surely of such that material wealth consists!) as labour' (Marx 1875). The subordination of nature to the dynamics of capital accumulation was facilitated through the separation of direct producers from the land and the transformation of the latter into capital. Marx used the term primitive accumulation to specify the process whereby this class distinction between possessors and non-possessors of means of production emerged. In Britain this separation took place through the enclosure movement. In the wake of colonial expansion, it occurred through the 'extirpation, enslavement, and entombment in mines of the indigenous population' (Marx 1990, 915). Such extirpation enabled the subsequent dual process of commodification—of labour power and of land (nature).

While the process of primitive accumulation continues in global capitalism, Chapter 10 shows how and why (a) capitalist production systematically abstracts from the functioning of ecosystems, the wellbeing of animals, and the reproductive capacity of non-human nature in general, and, (b) the resulting transformation and destruction of nature occur on an expanding scale. Capital accumulation is rooted in the conjoined processes of the exploitation of workers on an ever-extended scale, which in turn requires an increased appropriation of nature—for use as inputs to production, technological advances, logistics, and disposal/waste. As Marx notes, 'the progressive development of the social productivity of labour' is

> demonstrated precisely by the fact that the same number of labourers, in the same time, i.e., with less labour, *convert an ever-increasing quantity of raw and auxiliary materials into products*, thanks to the growing application of machinery and fixed capital in general.
>
> **(Marx 1991, 318, emphasis added)**

Under capitalism, technological innovation is primarily for profit, not to safeguard the environment. Furthermore, it increases what Marx labelled the 'technical composition of capital'—the ratio of means of production to the amount of labour power employed on them (greater capital intensity). The consequences for the environment of capitalist production and a rising technical composition of capital are the continual and increased use (and destruction) of nature.

Capitalism's incessant drive to accumulate through labour exploitation and natural extraction generates a situation where it 'only develops the techniques and the degree of combination of the social process of production by simultaneously undermining the original sources of all wealth—the soil [and nature more generally] and the worker' (Marx 1990, 638). One consequence of capital's growing appropriation of nature is that 'the view of nature attained under the dominion of private property and money is a real contempt for and practical debasement of nature' (Marx 1844b, n.p.). But, in words that could have been written about contemporary environmental collapse, Engels warned: 'Let us not ... flatter ourselves overmuch on account of our human conquest over nature. For each such conquest nature takes its revenge on us' (Engels 1883, n.p.). In Chapter 10 we theorize in greater detail the relationship between capitalism, CVCs, and nature, and provide an empirical analysis to show how CVCs are rooted in heightened appropriation (and destruction) of natural resources.

2.9 Conclusions

This chapter has provided an outline of our conception of the capitalist relations of production and how they underpin, and are reproduced on an expanded scale through, CVCs. Unlike mainstream GVC approaches, we place the exploitation of labour by capital, endless competitive capital accumulation, and capital's increasing appropriation of nature at the centre of our analysis. The relations between capital and labour and between firms generate continuous forces of uneven capitalist growth, mediated by states. CVCs' impact upon nature is ruinous. It is also ruinous for the majority of the world's workers. Little wonder then that the mainstream 'GVCs for development' agenda ignores these essential capitalist dynamics. However, as we show in the next chapter, while this ignorance (quite literally, leaving out of the picture) has facilitated the mainstreaming of the GVC approach, it has progressively undermined its ability to explain the forces of poverty, inequality, and environmental destruction arising from CVCs.

3
The Mainstreaming of GVC Theory

> Theory is always for someone and for some purpose.
>
> **(Cox 1981, 128)**

3.1 Introduction

As a concept for identifying empirically the global dispersal and functional integration of production, the Global Value Chain (GVC) approach is eminently useful. As a framework for analysing exploitation and the uneven developmental dynamics arising out of this organizational structure, it is wanting.

This chapter discusses the origins and mainstreaming of the GVC concept and how it has evolved from a radical critique of the capitalist world system to a conceptual tool for promoting capitalist development through upgrading. GVC mainstreaming has two interlinked elements—the marginalization of critical theoretical elements from its earlier iterations, and the widespread adoption of the notion by international organizations and academia. As Robert Cox's quote above recalls, theory serves a political purpose.

The weaknesses of the mainstream GVC approach are considerable. Its core notion—of the developmental possibilities open to supplier firms through upgrading—is beset by a fallacy of composition: the logically untenable assumption that if one firm can upgrade then so can all firms. Leading advocates of the GVC approach have recognized that '[s]ustainable income growth requires the capacity to protect oneself from competition' (Kaplinsky and Morris 2001, 79). Displacing competition onto others implies successful upgrading at the expense of other firms. This means that upgrading cannot be deployed, in theory or in practice, as a general development strategy. It could be used to explain the reproduction of uneven development, where some firms and regions rise and some fall, but this is not the objective of the GVC mainstream.

Mainstream GVC analysis' internally contradictory notion of upgrading is closely related to its second core weakness—its inability to properly explain

Capitalist Value Chains. Benjamin Selwyn and Christin Bernhold, Oxford University Press.
 DOI: 10.1093/9780191994906.003.0003

the existence of lead firms and their power over suppliers. Such power is often assumed rather than explained.

The reason for mainstream GVC's weaknesses is that it does not possess a coherent analysis of capitalism and its class-relational foundations. Such an analysis would place front and centre the ability of capital to extract surplus value from labour, the ability of more powerful firms to capture surplus value from weaker firms, how these age-old capitalist dynamics are reproduced anew through CVCs, and the developmental effects thereof. Instead, it avoids recognizing the capitalist nature of CVCs by restricting itself to a narrow analysis of buyer–supplier interactions in individual economic sectors.

Following this introduction, Section 3.2 reflects upon the origins and evolution of GVC analysis, showing how while class relations were never adequately theorized from the start, they were at least recognized. However, with each successive iteration, the GVC approach has increasingly sidelined notions of power and class relations. Section 3.3 discusses the two core concepts associated with GVC analysis—of supplier firm upgrading and lead firm governance—and shows how their obscuring of questions of class-based exploitation and power limits their ability to explain the intrinsically uneven developmental impacts generated by GVCs. Section 3.4 discusses the most popular iteration of the Global Production Network (GPN) approach ('GPN 2.0') and argues that it attempts, but ultimately fails, to overcome the limits to mainstream GVC analysis' firm-centrism, because of its lack of a rigorous political economy starting point.

3.2 GVC Analysis: Origins, Evolution, and Mainstreaming

Over four decades, the GVC approach has gone from an academic sub-discipline of critical political economy to one of the primary modes 'of analysis and of intervention amongst development institutions' (Werner et al. 2014, 1219). One of the reasons for the approach attaining its mainstream status is its utility in highlighting and seeming to explain the historically novel sets of inter-firm relations that characterize CVCs. The other is the gradual sidelining of capitalism and class from the framework and, inter-alia, the formulation of firm-centric notions of intra-firm power (see Table 3.1). The World Bank's World Development Report 2020 (see below and Chapter 4) represents the culmination of this long-term process whereby the empirical existence and conceptual importance of exploitation and unequal power relations virtually disappear.

Table 3.1 GVC frameworks

Framework	Concept of power	Developmental implications	Key texts
Commodity Chain (1970s/1980s)	Monopoly power, unequal exchange, surplus drain	Reproduction of core-periphery unequal relations	Hopkins and Wallerstein (1977, 1986), Arrighi and Drangel (1986)
Global Commodity Chain (1990s)	Lead firm governance in buyer and producer-driven chains	Supplier firms subject to concentrated lead firm power (e.g., over product standards, price, etc.)	Gereffi and Korzeniewicz (1994)
Value Chain (2000s)	Lead firms capture rents by constructing and protecting scarce assets	Rising entry barriers suppress supplier firm upgrading	Kaplinsky and Morris (2001)
Global Value Chain (2000s)	GVC structure determined by minimization of 'transaction costs'	Continuum of relations from market to 'captive', whereby suppliers are highly dependent upon lead firms	Gereffi and Kaplinksy (2001), Gereffi, Humphrey, and Sturgeon (2005)
Comparative advantage GVCs	Relational GVCs	Mutual gains for supplier and lead firms through complementary specialization	WDR 2020 (World Bank 2020)

Source: Reproduced from Selwyn and Leyden (2022, 178), Table 1.

Given this trajectory of GVC mainstreaming, it would be tempting to argue for reverting to first principles, in the shape of its original iteration as the Commodity Chain framework within the World Systems approach. Unlike later variants, this iteration does theorize capitalist exploitation. However, as we shall see, it is conceptually weak in identifying the relations between evolving class relations and uneven capitalist development. For these reasons, even the best iteration of the GVC approach does not suffice in identifying the core dynamics of contemporary CVCs.

Before setting out on this discussion, it is worth pointing out that there exists a variety of critical GVC approaches. These include current debates that revisit and discuss world-systems analysis (Bair 2014; Parnreiter and Bernhold 2020), the disarticulations approach by Jenn Bair and Marion Werner (Bair and Werner 2011a, 2011b), the articulations of global capitalism approach by Pickles and Smith (2016), and the global destruction networks approach by Herod et al. (2014).

The disarticulations approach investigates the role of social relations in the pre-history of chain formation, and ongoing chain reproduction, and how these relations are causal effects and outcomes of chain inclusion/exclusion (for a critical discussion see Bernhold 2022). Pickles and Smith (2016) investigate how different fractions of capital articulate with different social forces to generate diverse and uneven geographies of development. Herod et al. (2014) investigate how chains simultaneously 'end' and start again through workers transforming previously used parts for inclusion into new commodities (see Selwyn et al. 2023 for a discussion). While these are useful contributions to critical chain analysis our approach, by contrast, places the capital–labour relation at its conceptual core, and it is from this perspective that we comprehend the evolution and mainstreaming of the value chain literature.

The World Systems Apprroach and Commodity Chains Analysis

The first variant of the GVC approach—the Commodity Chain (CC) concept—originated within the World Systems Approach (WSA) (Hopkins and Wallerstein 1977, 1986; Arrighi and Drangel 1986). WSA is primarily concerned with the *long-term reproduction of global inequality* (Wallerstein 1974a, 2011a; Chase-Dunn and Rubinson 1977). According to the approach, world capitalism—defined as *production for profit for the world market*—is constituted by, and continually reproduces, core, semi-peripheral and peripheral zones. The former is characterized by high value-appropriating economic activities, the latter by low value-added activities, and the intermediate zone by a mix of both sets of activities (Arrighi and Drangel 1986). Core–periphery relations 'designate the unequal distribution of rewards among the various activities that constitute the single overarching division of labour and bounding the world economy. All these activities are assumed to be integrated into commodity chains' (Arrighi and Drangel 1986, 16).

While shifts of periphery-like towards core-like activities are regarded as possible, such moves do not imply the feasibility of equal development within and across the capitalist world system. Rather, the world system is characterized by the continual unequal distribution of rewards and the corresponding perpetuation of uneven development. According to the WSA perspective, therefore, the prospect of general upward mobility is a 'developmentalist illusion' (Arrighi 1990; see Brewer 2011).

The WSA iteration of commodity chain analysis was as far as it is possible to get from the mainstream developmentalism characteristic of contemporary GVC analysis. For a start, it was rooted in critical political economy and, as mentioned above, drew upon the notion of a world economy permanently stratified between core and periphery, where 'core activities are those that command a large share of the total surplus produced within a commodity chain and peripheral activities are those that command little or no such surplus' (Arrighi and Drangel 1986, 11f.). Hopkins and Wallerstein (1982, 125) therefore speak of 'cores-in-relation-to-peripheries and peripheries-in-relation-to-cores'. This explains the above-mentioned notion that generalized development (all peripheral regions becoming core regions) was considered impossible. The WSA iteration drew upon Schumpeter's conjoined notion of cycles of economic growth and monopolization, where a small minority of monopolistic firms grabbed the lion's share of value produced in the economy. It included a notion of geopolitics, where strong core-states support 'their' capitals, and core-like firms utilize differences in political regulation to their advantage (see Bernhold 2022 for a more detailed discussion). The WSA tradition often used Marxian language to bind these concepts together.

Like Dependency theory, the WSA represented powerful counter arguments to claims that became prevalent after the Second World War under US-hegemony, that all countries could achieve development. Such theoretical claims are best associated with W.W. Rostow's modernization theory. Rostow (1990) argued that all countries could move through linear 'stages of economic growth' given the correct policies and forms of global integration. WSA, including its CC approach, illuminated how such claims were more akin to ideology than rooted in a thorough historical political economic analysis of the development of capitalism.

Despite WSA's strengths, it suffered from various theoretical faults. Its failure to root the capitalist world system in the emergence and reproduction of historically specific class relations represented its foundational flaw from which other weaknesses sprang. As Robert Brenner (1977, 27) notes, WSA fails 'to take into account ... the way in which [capitalist] class structures themselves emerge as the outcome of class struggles whose results are incomprehensible in terms merely of market forces'. This limited conception of the specificity of capitalist class relations subsequently hampered its explanatory power, and arguably, made it easier for later GCC and GVC approaches to be mainstreamed.

The WSA's limited class-relational understanding of capitalism means that it theoretically prioritizes the structure of uneven exchange (rooted in market relations) between centre and periphery over the social relations of production. It comprehends capitalism as a system in which capitalists 'seek to accumulate capital *not via profit but via rent*' (Wallerstein 1988b, 103, emphasis added), that is, above-average profit enjoyed due to monopoly power. Thus, the focus lies on differential power relations *between trading firms* rather than on the *production AND distribution of surplus value*. In this vein, Wallerstein (2009, n.p.) emphasizes the centrality of monopolization to world capitalism:

> In a situation of perfect competition, it is absolutely *impossible to make significant profit*. (…) Any time the world-economy is expanding significantly, one will find that there are some 'leading' products, which are relatively monopolized. It is from these products that great profits are made and large amounts of capital can be accumulated.

This notion of monopoly-based profit in turn informs WSA's presentation of the world system as constituted, primarily, through a set of *exchange relations* that result in an international division of labour. Exchange relations are important under capitalism. But they are co-constituted by relations of production, and WSA prioritizes the former over the latter.

Wallerstein and Arrighi and Drangel are inspired by two elements of Schumpeter's (1987) political economy. First, his understanding of value in terms of rent. And secondly, his comprehension of capitalism as existing in a constant process of reshaping through innovation, which temporarily and unequally raises a small group of capitalists into economically powerful positions. Following Schumpeter, they ignore Marx's crucial insight, that ultimately capitalist profits (and the drive for innovation) derive from surplus value, generated by labour but extracted by capital, through the capitalist process of production (see Chapter 2).

There is a conceptual irony here. WSA elevates monopolization to primary explanator of 'real' profit and uneven capitalist development (and understands it as a constant feature through historical capitalism). However, WSA portrays monopolization one-sidedly as one or a few firms' capacity to outplay other firms by controlling scarce products and innovations. It misses, and fails to theorize the reasons for monopolization under capitalism, including firms' attempts to enhance competitiveness by increasing the rate of labour exploitation, that is, the surplus value relative to labour costs within and beyond their own enterprises. It also obscures the associated development of productive forces and tendencies towards the concentration and centralization of capital (explained in Chapter 2). Thus, WSA tends to assume rather than explain the existence of monopolies. While it presents competitive innovations as the drivers of socio-economic change, an even more foundational driver—capitalists' attempts to produce and sell goods more cheaply than their rivals through heightened labour exploitation (reducing the costs of labour power)—is not systematically accounted for. Consequently, the WSA/CC approach also curtails its own explanatory power of value production and distribution *within* particular chain links (i.e., between capital and labour) prior to its distribution amongst different capitalist firms throughout the chain.

This initial error generates other flaws that reduce further WSA's ability to grasp the developmentally dialectical relations between inter-class and inter-firm relations. For example, Wallerstein's (1974b) main attempt to incorporate labour into his analysis is via his concept of 'modes of labour control'. Here he identifies and explains how during the sixteenth century various modes of labour control existed within the world system. These ranged from free wage labour, self-employment, and sharecropping, to coerced cash cropping and slavery. Core economies, characterized by relatively capital-intensive production, high productivity rates, and a relatively integrated market for commodities (including labour power) are predominantly based upon relatively highly skilled wage labour. Peripheral economies, characterized by externally orientated economies, highly labour-intensive production (e.g., non-mechanized agriculture) and relatively weakly developed domestic markets are predominantly based upon slavery and coerced cash cropping (see Hopkins and Wallerstein 1982). The intermediate semi-peripheral economies, trading and interacting with core and periphery, are characterized by moderately capital-intensive and moderately labour-intensive production and are based on a wider range of labour systems but include the widespread use of sharecropping. Hence, just as the world system is stratified, so its stratification gives rise to a variety of modes of labour control:

> Free labour is indeed a defining feature of capitalism, but not free labour throughout the productive enterprise. Free labour is the form of labour control used for skilled work in core countries whereas coerced labour is used for

> less skilled work in peripheral areas. The combination thereof is the essence of capitalism.
>
> **(Wallerstein 1974b, 127)**

In other words, from a WSA perspective, historical capitalism is compatible with and often generative of a diverse range of what Wallerstein calls forms of labour control. WSA's critique of the functional and geographical division of labour in global capitalism is concurrently a critique of the miserable conditions under which most people work, above all, in the peripheries. We do not disagree with WSA here.

However, Wallerstein's attempt to explain the varying modes of labour control in the sixteenth century as a function of each state's positions in the world system is a deduction too far. In Chapter 2 we argued that class relations shape and re-shape profit-maximizing strategies that include forms of forced labour. In other words, different forms of labour control, which can vary historically within core and peripheral regions, are shaped by capitalist class relations, and they need to be understood through contested and evolving class relations, rather than as a function of their position within the international division of labour. However, while class struggle is not entirely neglected by WSA, the primary contradiction driving this approach is that between core and periphery or, in class-analytical terms, between core-capital and peripheral labour. Class struggle from below is then mainly conceived as a *political* struggle against exchange-based (geographically defined) exploitation. To be sure, production of higher or lower value-added goods present employers with decisions of whether to engage in strategies involving greater or lesser investments in labour and capital. However, to reduce working conditions and salaries to a question of the position in the world system is to ignore both the specificity of capitalist class relations and the complexity of social relations within which production always occurs.

Some limits to this approach are recognized from within the WSA tradition. As Beverly Silver, the most proficient labour analyst working from the WSA perspective notes, while WSA emphasizes the 'very real constraints that the totality imposes on the range of possible action open to local actors ... its weakness is that it excludes a priori a situation in which local action [for instance, decisions forced through by either capital or workers] significantly impacts local outcomes' (Silver 2003, 39). Such a recognition is a crucial element in explaining the possibilities for workers struggling for, and achieving, better pay and working, living and political conditions, and the relative shares of national income going to capital and to labour (see Chapter 9).

Global Commodity Chains Analysis

The Commodity Chain approach was transformed into Global Commodity Chain (GCC) analysis by Gary Gereffi and Miguel and Roberto Korzeniewicz (Gereffi et al. 1994), marking a step-change in its orientation. Crucially, while criticizing global power relations that prevent actors from upgrading, the approach de facto rejected the WSA/CC assumption that general upward mobility within the world system was a 'developmentalist illusion'. In contrast, the GCC approach promoted investigation of 'industrial upgrading by established exporters among the newly industrialized countries (NICs)' (Gereffi 1994a, 211) and how this generated diverse developmental outcomes.

Unlike WSA's concern with the historical emergence and dynamics of unequal exchange through commodity chains, GCC analysis was orientated towards detailing the *contemporary* effects of lead firm-led chain restructuring upon developmental processes in peripheral countries (Gereffi and Korzeniewicz 1994). As Daviron and Gibbon (2002, 141) noted, GCC research sought to address 'who controls global trade and industry, how they do so, and with what consequences for producers in developing countries'. The implication here was that global trade was neither free, nor simply 'managed' by lead firms but driven and dominated by the latter. Various GCC studies illuminated how lead firms used their market power to lower prices for goods or components, dictate standards, reduce labour costs via subcontracting and outsourcing, and shape overseas production networks by determining the terms and conditions of participation, even without having equity relations of any kind with contractors (see Gereffi 1994b on US retailers' control over industrial production in Asia). In this way the GCC approach provided important empirical insights into the workings of real-world markets.

Part of Gereffi et al.'s objective was to understand how dynamics of uneven development arise from and are organized through GCCs, and how consequently peripheral countries, regions, and firms face difficulties in upgrading. While jettisoning key elements of the WSA's critique of capitalism, Gereffi did establish useful conceptual categories for GCC scholars to deploy to analyse contemporary developmental dynamics. He suggested that every commodity chain can be analysed across four dimensions: (1) an input–output structure (where raw materials are transformed into final products); (2) a territoriality or geography; (3) a chain governance structure; and (4) an institutional context (Gereffi 1994b; Gereffi 1995; see Bair 2005).

While the GCC approach thus represented an important research agenda, these four dimensions identified by Gereffi obscure key elements of firms' attempt to pursue upgrading and the ensuing dynamics of uneven development. First and foremost, his conceptualization of production as an input–output structure misses (and perhaps deliberately obscures) the class relations that constitute these structures. Production in CVCs, however, is a political economic class relation rather than a technical relationship. It works through the production and circulation of commodities based upon exploitative (surplus value generating) relations. Gereffi's 'input–output' notion of production is not, per se, incompatible with a class-relational understanding of capitalism. But the way it has been deployed by him and later academics within the GVC mainstream is based upon conceptually externalizing class relations from production. This move clears the way for a relatively a-social conception of development, based upon inter-firm relations.

Gereffi introduced the concept of chain governance by lead firms to investigate how, in the context of the new international division of labour (Fröbel et al. 1978), such practices impacted upon dynamics of development in peripheral countries. Governance power determines 'how financial, material, and human resources are allocated and flow within a chain' (Gereffi 1994b, 97). The GCC notion of power was elucidated through its differentiation between 'buyer-driven' and 'producer-driven' commodity chains. In producer-driven chains, characterized by relative capital-intensity, 'large integrated industrial enterprises play the central role in controlling the production system' (Gereffi 1994b, 97; see Gereffi 1996, 430ff.; Raikes et al. 2000). Buyer-driven chains, characterized by relative labour-intensity, are those in which large retailers and brand firms set up 'decentralized production networks in a variety of exporting countries, typically located in the Third World' (Gereffi 1994b, 97). On the face of it, these conceptual innovations represented important contributions to understanding dynamics of uneven development.

As mentioned above, however, WSA was beset by the irony of simultaneously elevating, whilst failing adequately to explain, firm-level monopolization. This weakness was carried over and magnified further within the GCC approach. While it conceptually locates lead firms and their governance strategies at the centre of GCC research, it is ultimately unable to explain the political economic roots of lead firms' power to govern 'their' chains. Its non-class-relational focus upon relations between lead and supplier firms analytically excludes ways in which core-like capitals can increase the rate of exploitation of labour within, *and beyond*, 'their' nodes of the chain, and can capture surplus value produced by workers in other firms. Therefore, and quite ironically given the centrality of the concept of chain governance to GCC analysis, it analytically excludes the political economic basis of lead firms' power to govern global commodity chains.

The Value Chain Approach

Throughout the 1990s, GCC scholars placed increasing emphasis on the argument that 'regions, countries, and individual localities *can* improve their relative position in the global economy' through upgrading (Sturgeon 2009, 110, emphasis in the original). As part of this endeavour the Value Chain (VC) approach (Kaplinsky and Morris 2001) was formulated to provide greater specification of such possibilities, which it did through detailing a four-fold typology of upgrading: process, product, functional, and chain upgrading (see Humphrey and Schmitz 2000).

Process upgrading refers to firms' increased productive efficiency. It can take place within and between links, or nodes, of a chain. *Product* upgrading involves the introduction of new products or producing old products in a better way than rival firms. *Functional* upgrading enhances firms' competitiveness by changing the mix of activities conducted by a firm within a chain (for example, by shifting from manufacturing to design and branding). *Chain* upgrading involves moving into a new commodity chain altogether.

These notions of upgrading were influenced by Schumpeterian conceptions of rent-generating entrepreneurial innovations (understood as firms' control over scarce resources). Importantly for this way of conceptualizing capitalist competition, rents enable firms to insulate themselves partially from competition by other firms. Kaplinsky and Morris (2001, 28) differentiate between Schumpeterian rents (based on better technology, human resources, organization, and marketing), relational rents (arising from beneficial relationships), and rents external to the chain (policy rents, infrastructural rents, financial rents). Lead firms' governance of value chains, and their capture of the lion's share of value generated within those chains, was explained in terms of command over such rents—that is, high returns derived from control over/establishment of scarce resources.

Chain governorship itself—the power of lead firms to organize value chains and to maintain control over/establish scarce resources—is a key explanatory variable of the distribution of economic returns through the chain. It represents an important element of VC analysts' commitment to illuminating the 'growing disjuncture between the global spread of activities and incomes' (Kaplinsky and Morris 2001, 41).

However, whilst often illuminating the empirical reality of this disjuncture, VC's conceptualization of rents generates a circular explanation of lead firm power. This weakness was already apparent in the GCC literature and was carried over into the GVC approach (see below). On the one hand, the lead firms who have power control scarce resources and coordinate the chain to their own benefit. Governance power therefore determines 'how financial, material, and human resources are allocated and flow within a chain' (Gereffi 1994b, 97). On the other hand, power is supposed to accrue from the monopolization of scarce resources which again arise from 'governorship itself' (Kaplinsky 2000, 127). This tautological explanation is rooted in the failure to root value chains in the capitalist social relations from whence they spring: Power is conceived as arising from the control over scarce resources, and the control over scarce resources arises from power. What needs to be explained—the original control by lead firms over chain and scarce resources—is assumed, and the class relations upon which GVC power derives are obscured and ignored (see Bernhold 2022 for an in-depth discussion).

Global Value Chain Analysis

The Global Value Chain framework (Gereffi and Kaplinsky 2001; Gereffi et al. 2001) represented a merger between GCC and VC approaches (in part to achieve conceptual clarity between two very similar approaches). It drew upon Kaplinsky and Morris's (2001) categorization of upgrading to promote the framework as an explicit development strategy. In addition to the four types of upgrading noted above—process product, functional, and chain upgrading—Gereffi and Fernandez-Stark (2016) later expanded the notion to include the mere entry into value chains, and movements into larger end-markets. These authors also label upgrading a 'new paradigm for development' (Gereffi and Fernandez-Stark 2016, 24) that comprises the potential of firms shifting activities towards higher value-added activities within any industry, including agriculture (see Chapter 8). Upgrading is thus portrayed as a general development strategy, applicable to all supplier firms, provided the right institutional and business environment.

GVC practitioners' stated goal was to solve 'real-world policy problems' related to the widespread recognition that the gains from global capitalism are unevenly distributed within and between economies, and to:

> develop a theory that could help policymakers explain and predict governance patterns in cross-border production networks. With such tools in hand, our thinking went, interventions aimed at upgrading the position of local workers, firms, and industries within global scale production systems could be more finely crafted and effective.
>
> **(Sturgeon 2009, 112; see Sturgeon 2001)**

GVC research tends to focus upon the developmental implications of organizational features and governance structures in single chains. Whilst useful as a strategy for conducting studies into individual commodities and value chains, this conceptual narrowing down of analytical units nullified the strengths of its WSA heritage while introducing new weaknesses. As Henry Bernstein notes, the danger of this approach is that researchers 'lose sight of the entities from which the "slice" is extracted, how and where it fits into, and is shaped by, other elements of those entities' (Bernstein 2008, 128).

This tendency to abstract individual cases from their location within the wider capitalist economy generated further problems within the framework—including the fallacy of composition associated with the upgrading notion (see below), and interconnectedly, its increasingly apologetic account of lead firm power. As noted above, the GCC approach introduced the notion of lead firms' ability to 'drive' key developmental dynamics in commodity chains, in particular their control over resources and ability to capture value. As part of conceptual and political mainstreaming, the GVC approach dropped this observation in favour of a focus upon lead firms' 'coordinating roles' in value chains (Gibbon et al. 2008). In this move, lead firm power ceased to be conceptualized in terms of domination.

Gereffi, Humphrey, and Sturgeon (2005) draw upon Williamson (1979) to explain lead firm chain governance from a transaction cost economics (TCE) perspective. Where transaction costs are potentially high (caused, for example, by complex information) then corporations will assimilate or seek to organize/coordinate economic activities to reduce these costs. Reduced transaction costs through chain governance are portrayed as increasing allocative efficiency within and between firms, generating win–win outcomes for lead and supplier firms (and by implication for their workers).

Gereffi, Humphrey, and Sturgeon used this insight from TCE to establish a typology of forms of chain governance. At one end of the spectrum, 'relational' forms of governance entail high degrees of lead-supplier firm interdependence, requiring regular flows of tacit knowledge. At the other end, in 'captive' GVCs, suppliers are heavily dependent upon lead firms. In summary, unequal competencies of supplier firms enable, and require, lead firms to exert higher or lower degrees of control over them. Whilst there is no explicit discussion of how lead firms can deploy such power differentials to their advantage, such an outcome is at least recognized as a possibility in captive value chains.

However, this interpretation of inter-firm relations justifies lead firm power, ignores labour exploitation by capital, and veils lead firm strategies to capture as much value from 'their' chains as possible. These deleterious social and developmental relations are sidelined while lead firms' 'coordinating' role of their chains is conceptually brought to the fore and treated as a socio-developmental 'good'. It is hardly surprising then, that Gereffi et al. (2005) do not consider value capture strategies by lead firms from supplier firms as determinants of GVC governance practices. In contrast, as discussed in Chapter 2 of this book, our perspective emphasizes how participation in the production and distribution of the fruits of capitalist production is a question of (class-struggle over) the production of surplus value by labour, its seizure by the initial expropriating firm and the struggle over its subsequent distribution amongst other firms within the chain.

A Note on the Perils of the Ideal-type Methodology

There is a tendency within the mainstream GVC approach to explain different relations within and between GVCs (e.g., between lead and supplier firms) by establishing ideal type categories, or typologies of categories. The most influential example of this is the above-mentioned five-fold categorization of value chain governance types (markets, modular, relational, captive, and hierarchical/vertically integrated value chains). In another example of such typologizing, Gereffi and Lee (2016) identify six types of 'social upgrading' of workers conditions in GVCs: market-driven, corporate social responsibility driven, multi-stakeholder, labour-centred, cluster-driven, and public-governance paths (see Chapter 9).

It is undoubtedly analytically necessary and theoretically correct to recognize differences between and within CVCs. However, doing so by establishing typologies, as above, represents a form of description without an attempt at a foundational explanation. In fact, such categorizations are quite superficial.

This intellectual blind spot is reminiscent of the weaknesses of Max Weber's methodology of sociological ideal type construction. Ideal types, Weber argued, could illuminate social phenomenon, through the one-sided abstraction of features of these phenomenon (e.g., Weber's (2019) identification of key features of bureaucracy). However, Weber also recognized that such ideal types did not actually exist. Hence, the methodology was more descriptive—designed for comparative categorization—than explanatory. As Geoffrey Hodgeson puts it, Weber's ideal-type methodology 'was an attempt to interpret and to categorize, and thereby begin to explain, a complex reality, rather than to dig down and discover its allegedly fundamental building blocks' (Hodgson 2001, 122). While the ideal-type methodology can be useful for beginning to undertake *comparative* analysis, it is methodologically static and singular. There is no methodology within the notion of ideal-type construction to assess the relations between different cases/forms and their differential (co)evolution.

GVCs in the World Bank's World Development Report 2020

The most recent iteration so far in GVC mainstreaming is the 2020 World Development Report (WDR2020) (World Bank 2020, see Chapter 4 for an in-depth discussion). It marks yet another step-change in mainstreaming—where the unequal power relations that constitute the global economy are conceptually evacuated from the framework. It achieves this ideological feat by arguing that GVCs represent an outcome of, and function best when organized according to, the laws of 'comparative advantage'. Comparative advantage theory claims that gains from trade can be had by all trading partners according to their already-existing factor endowments. It analytically excludes power relations from its schema, as it is rooted in assumptions of arms-length market relations between firms which generate mutual gains. But the power of lead firms, for instance, to set prices, violates any notion of comparative advantage-based trade. In a sense, the WDR2020's notion of GVCs for development represents the end of the road for the GVC concept. As deployed by the World Bank, the GVC framework generates less a simplified (parsimonious) view of the world than a partial and propagandistic one, where key social economic relations, and their developmental outcomes are hidden from view.

3.3 GVC Mainstreaming: Two Critiques

GVC research can look back on a history spanning decades. It has produced numerous, useful, case studies of individual value chains. However, the main intellectual direction of travel has been one where research with a focus on upgrading as a development strategy has become dominant and mainstream. With each successive iteration of the GVC concept, exploitation, power relations, and the dynamics of uneven development that they generate have been ever-more filtered out of its framework. By contrast, capitalist markets are promoted increasingly as offering ever-greater developmental opportunities to poor world regions. This section delves deeper into two of the core concepts deployed by GVC analysis—its conception of upgrading and its notion of chain governance—to show how its mainstreaming undermines its ability to explain the political economic dynamics of exploitation.

As noted, the GVC concept of upgrading is influenced by Joseph Schumpeter, particularly his explanation of entrepreneurial innovation. However, the GVC mainstream has taken what is worst about Schumpeter's political economy—his non-recognition of the key social relations of capitalism and his reactionary social elitism—whist dropping his most important insight—that entrepreneurial innovations are bound up with dynamics of creative destruction and uneven development. This social elitism is reflected in mainstream GVC analysis' elevation of firm owners and managers to the status of primary agents of innovation, and thus, of wider economic development. This pro-capital perspective is bolstered by mainstream GVCs' incorporation of transaction cost economics into its notion of chain governance. The latter represents an ideological inversion of monopoly power into market efficiency. Whilst these moves have facilitated GVC mainstreaming they come at an intellectual cost—hindering the GVC mainstream from seeing how, below the pedestals of firm owners and managers, CVCs are mechanisms of enhanced labour exploitation, surplus value transfer, and uneven development.

Upgrading: Whither Creative Destruction?

The concept of upgrading stands front and centre of mainstream GVC analysis. According to this approach, supplier firm upgrading within GVCs represents the surest path towards sustainable local and national development for contemporary so-called developing countries.

However, as noted above the notion of upgrading suffers from a fallacy of composition—the assumption that if one firm can upgrade, so can all firms (Selwyn 2015; Bernhold 2022). This fact was initially recognized by Raphael Kaplinsky (1998, 33, emphasis in the original) who observed that '*production is upgraded in comparison to the achievements of competitors.* The very act of upgrading necessarily downgrades those who fail to match the innovation.' Consequently, CVC producers become locked into a competitive struggle:

> The challenge thus confronting producers everywhere is [to] upgrade by appropriating whatever categories of rent are within their grasp, but to do so more rapidly than competitors in the knowledge that a rate of innovation lower than the average will result in immiserizing growth.
>
> **(Kaplinsky 1998, 35)**

This recognition was carried over into Kaplinsky and Morris' (2001) influential *Handbook for Value Chain Research*, albeit with a subtle shift. While Kaplinsky had previously observed how upgrading simultaneously generated downgrading and immiserizing growth, in the handbook he and Morris offer a developmentalist way out of this conundrum by differentiating between 'low' and 'high' roads of global integration. This recognition does not, however, escape the fact (and Kaplinsky's earlier observation) that competition generates differentiating tendencies between firms—where upgrading by some generates downgrading for others. These observations caution against deploying the upgrading concept as a general development strategy.

As the GVC notion evolved and became increasingly developmentalist, however, observations like those by Kaplinksy became further marginalized. For example, Lee and Gereffi note the inequalities associated with GVCs, but explain them as arising out of the 'uneven distribution of upgrading opportunities' (Lee and Gereffi 2015, 319). This formulation obscures how the drive to upgrade *systematically* generates a few 'winners', and many 'losers' within CVCs. To understand the reasons why mainstream GVCs' notion of upgrading is beset by a fallacy of composition, it is necessary to go into some more detail about the origins and application of the notion.

As noted above, the upgrading concept is closely related—albeit in a conceptually watered-down way—to Joseph Schumpeter's (1987) notion of entrepreneurial innovation. These entailed introductions of new commodities, new sources of supply, new markets, and new organizational forms. Each innovation enabled entrepreneurs to produce and market new products or old products more cheaply than previously and/or to obtain prolonged monopoly rents.

When innovations cluster together, Schumpeter argues, they establish a leading sector—'new products with high demand, made with newer, cheaper forms of energy and distributed via newer, cheaper modes of transportation' (Schwartz 2018, 69; following Schumpeter 1987). Crucially, firms that deploy leading sector technologies can capture above-average profit (rents) which also enables them to monopolize sections of the economy.

In his conception of creative destruction—which he saw as intrinsic to capitalist competition—Schumpeter detailed how '[t]he new products and new methods compete with the old products and old methods not on equal terms but at a decisive advantage that *may mean death to the latter*' (Schumpeter 1987, 32, emphasis added). Schumpeter distinguishes between innovating entrepreneurs and normal businessmen (the latter who run non-innovating firms). Innovating entrepreneurs win the entrepreneurial profits—the 'difference between receipts and outlays', the latter of which are momentarily 'smaller per unit of product than for other businesses' (Schumpeter 1987, 73f.). 'Spectacular prizes ... are thrown to a small minority of winners' while the 'large majority of businessmen ... receive in return very modest compensation or nothing or less than nothing' (Schumpeter 1987, 73f.). The ability of firms to innovate, to keep innovating, and to control the innovation and technological diffusion process has big implications for whether firms win 'spectacular prizes' or 'nothing or less than nothing'.

For Schumpeter, creative destruction is, as the term suggests, eminently two-sided: creative on the one hand, destructive on the other. But mainstream GVC analysis has extracted and divorced conceptually Schumpeter's creative element of entrepreneurial innovation from its destructive element where non-innovating firms are thrown by the wayside. Put another way, the (normatively and developmentally) attractive elements in Schumpeter's model have been adapted while, unlike in WSA, his more critical observations about capitalist expansion have been dropped. This enables mainstream GVC proponents to advocate upgrading as a general development strategy, whilst portraying the negative effects of competition simply as the 'uneven distribution of upgrading opportunities'. But this is an ideological rather than theoretically sound move.

Entrepreneurial innovations, Schumpeter demonstrated, generate gales of creative destruction through centralizing capital, power, and wealth in ever fewer hands. Centralization of capital is also driven by mergers and acquisitions, whereby large firms (e.g., Google, Apple) swallow up smaller innovative firms that possess patented technologies (Blakeley 2021; Rikap 2021). Lead firms' centralization of capital is simultaneously driven by, and enables, new techniques of chain governance designed to further centralize capital.

In sum, the GVC concept of upgrading owes much to Schumpeter's notion of entrepreneurial innovation, but it drops any mention of the obverse of innovation—creative destruction. While this move is necessary to portray upgrading as a general development strategy, the intellectual cost is the generation of a contradiction right at the heart of mainstream GVC analysis. How can upgrading represent a general development strategy when it has both a competitive and a power-relational component (the establishment of barriers to entry and winning of rents) from which some firms can gain at the expense of others?

Chain Governance and Transaction Cost Economics: An Apology for Lead Firm Power

Throughout the history of the capitalist economy, thinkers have investigated and sought to theorize the increasing prevalence of monopolies and their relationship to capitalism. Their starting point was often a rejection of neoclassical assumptions about perfect competition. In his influential articles *The Nature of the Firm* and *The Problem of Social Cost*, Ronald Coase (1937, 1960) explained corporate integration (while eschewing any serious consideration of capitalism's monopolizing tendencies). He outlined how, as firms related to each other via product markets they incurred 'costs of using the price mechanism' (1937, 397) and 'costs of market transaction' (1960, 37). He then explained how vertical integration—where larger firms sought to integrate and/or to control their suppliers—was pursued as a strategy by the former to reduce the transaction costs of purchasing inputs on open markets, and to raise efficiency by producing them internally within that firm. These ideas were advanced by Oliver Williamson (1973) in his *Markets and Hierarchies*. He argued that the threat of opportunistic behaviour (e.g., lying) and market uncertainty could increase transaction costs, and, as Coase had argued, could be overcome through vertical integration. In short, Coase and Williamson explained (and justified) concentration and centralization of capital on grounds of efficiency.

The transaction cost economics (TCE) perspective has been described as a neoclassical apology for monopoly capital (Varman 2012) in at least two ways. First, it is based upon an essentialization, naturalization, and dehistoricization of capitalist markets, where, as Williamson puts it, 'in the beginning there were markets' (Williamson 1973, 21). Second, it assumes that firm hierarchies and wage-labour are voluntarily entered into by firms and workers for efficiency reasons (Ankarloo and Palermo 2004, 419).

However, the intellectual price of adopting the TCE perspective is a logical circularity (comparable to that generated in mainstream GVCs notion of lead firm power). As Foster, McChesney, and Jonna (2011, 28) put it, 'greater profits and accumulation are presumed to be indicators of efficiency and then justified because they are ... efficient'. From our reading, chain governance represents an outcome of historically secured class power of leading capitalists to outcompete other capitals in controlling the development of the productive forces, profiting from the exploitation of workers, and enhancing strategies to appropriate profits.

From this perspective, it is possible to understand in class-relational terms the attempts by larger firms to reduce transaction costs through forms of vertical integration, *and* the ways they seek to augment their power over and surplus value capture from subordinate firms to increase their profits.

3.4 Global Production Network Analysis: A Concept to the Rescue?

The Global Production Network (GPN) approach emerged, in part, in reaction to what its practitioners viewed as GCC, VC, and GVC's limitations, particularly their firm-centrism (Henderson et al. 2002; Taylor 2007). The central divergence between GVC and GPN approaches are that the former are conceptualized as 'essentially linear structures' and 'focus narrowly on ... governance and inter-firm transactions' whereas GPN approaches 'strive to ... incorporate all kinds of network configuration' and 'all relevant sets of actors and relationships' (Coe et al. 2008, 272; see Hess and Yeung 2006).

In contrast to the GVC mainstream, at its conceptual birth, GPNs stated commitment was to pay 'due attention to the issues of the reproduction of labour power' (Henderson et al. 2002, 444). More generally, it is a merit of critical GPN scholars to have illuminated how specifics of social, economic, and political geography matter to the formation, reproduction, and developmental dynamics of CVCs.

However, despite its critique of the GVC mainstream's firm-centrism, the GPN literature did not attempt an *explicit and consistent theorization of the class relations* upon and through which production networks are (re)produced. Consequently, relatively soon critics noted how GPN scholars had dropped earlier calls to include analyses of the capitalist labour process and systemic exploitation (Werner 2012, 405; see Cumbers et al. 2008).

In fact, the most popular iteration of the GPN approach—GPN 2.0 (Coe and Yeung 2015) has effectively sidelined, conceptually and empirically, the analysis of *systemic* inequality, exploitation, and uneven development (Werner 2019). This is unfortunate, as co-founder of the approach Neil Coe has done much to illuminate the fate of labour under GPN's (e.g. Coe 2013). In part this arises from these authors' aim to 'shed any remaining legacies of the world-systems theory that may linger in the literature on global production' (Coe and Yeung 2015, 169). In part it derives from their deliberately (and ideologically) restricted notion of development. They note, for example, how 'our focus here is on economic development, rather than development more generally', and that 'we see economic development as a process that results in the improvement of economic conditions within a particular territorial unit' (Coe and Yeung 2015, 167). Consequently, however, Siobhan McGrath (2018, 516) notes how Coe and Yeung's focus upon economic development 'represents a steadfast refusal to acknowledge the contested nature of development'.

GPN 2.0 starts from the (correct) recognition that diverse actors are involved in the making of production networks. However, given its conceptual 'shedding' of any notion of the social relations of production and structured hierarchies that constitute global capitalism, it is perhaps not surprising that GPN 2.0 finds it difficult to explain the structured reproduction of intense global uneven development.

Rather than investigating the dialectic of capitalist structure and agency, Coe and Yeung elevate agency above structure, and do not conceptualize agency as class agency in general, and capital's agency in particular. They seek to avoid a reduction of actors and localities to their functional position in the world-system by conceptualizing the global economy as a sum total of individual networks. GPNs are often presented, therefore, as conjunctural phenomena—as nodal points of social, political, and economic agents endowed with differentiated power. For example, they note how firms from different places, with different corporate cultures, and ownership structures (Yeung and Coe 2015, 53) adopt diverse strategic choices ('intrafirm coordination, interfirm control, interfirm partnership, and extrafirm bargaining') in response to different competitive pressures ('optimizing cost–capability ratios, sustaining market development, and working with financial discipline') (Coe and Yeung 2015, 32) There seems to be infinite combinations and possibilities of 'difference' in this approach.

In GPN 2.0, 'strategic coupling' plays the role that the notion of upgrading does in the mainstream GVC approach. Strategic coupling is defined by Henry Yeung as 'dynamic processes through which actors in cities and/or regions coordinate, mediate, and arbitrage strategic interests between local actors and their counterparts in the global economy' (Yeung 2009, 213; see MacKinnon 2012; Morgan 2018; Teixeira 2024). Strategic coupling has three key characteristics: (1) It is strategic in that 'it needs intentional and active intervention on the part of both regional institutions and powerful global production network actors to occur', (2) it is 'time-space contingent' (i.e., it is dynamic) as it represents a temporary coalition of local and extra-local actors, and (3) it transcends territorial boundaries 'as actors from different spatial scales interact' (Coe and Yeung 2015, 20). Regional assets, including human capital, knowledge, expertise, and skilled labour forces, provide the basis for regional development, but they must be harnessed by regional institutions to 'complement the strategic needs of lead firms in global production networks' (Coe and Yeung 2015, 20).

Under such scenarios local socio-economic benefits can result from complementarities between 'regional assets' and the global 'logics' of GPNs (Yeung 2015, 1). Coe and Yeung (2015) argue that it is possible to explain the developmental processes and outcomes of strategic coupling from an explicitly actor-centred perspective. Hence, varying results of strategic coupling emerge through 'the differentiated organization of global production networks in diverse industries and territories' (Coe and Yeung 2015, 202). The odds of these strategies generating inclusive development then depend on the agency of state and non-state actors involved.

It is undoubtedly necessary to recognize and investigate the above-noted diversities in inter-firm and extra-firm interactions to avoid creating a homogenizing image of CVCs (as admirably done by Pickles and Smith 2016). However, GPN 2.0 abstracts such diversity from capitalism's core social relations, and the structured hierarchies of exploitation that sustain them.

Consequently, GPN 2.0's anti-structural approach cannot but leave as undefined and un-theorized the relation between 'the economic', 'the social', and 'the state'. The differentiated power (and powerlessness) of actors to co-shape GPN development is never satisfactorily explained or theorized. Like the GVC notion of power, Coe et al. (2008, 276) argue that the relative power of actors within networks depends on the extent to which each possesses assets (or has access to them) sought by others.[1] But why do some actors have more assets, agency, and ability to influence the actions of actors, than others? GPN 2.0 has no answers to this question, because it fails to define capitalism and rejects any attempt of thinking about it as an uneven, unequalizing, and ultimately exploitative *structure*, produced and reproduced through international class relations.

Importantly, Coe and Yeung (2015, 189, emphasis added) recognize that global integration can generate tensions and 'dark sides':

> [T]he lack of indigenous technological capabilities and lead firms [have] compelled … regions to take the low road to industrialization and strategic coupling. While their coupling as assembly platforms can be considered

[1] In a similar manner, Coe and Hess (2013, 7) argue that the agency of labour is shaped by both GPN structures and the local labour control regimes in which it is embedded; however, the authors do not specify what they mean by structure.

> relatively successful, these regions exhibit a wide range of potential ruptures (for example, divestments, financial risks, and limited local linkages) and *frictions* (for example, external dependency, *labour exploitation*, and social and *class conflicts*) (emphases added).[2]

While the above observation acknowledges empirically labour exploitation and class struggle, it does not attempt to provide an integrated theoretical explanation for them. Such formulations generate limited (and limiting) conceptions of the relations between exploitation, class struggle, and diverse strategies and trajectories of capitalist development. For example, the class struggles waged by capital to establish and maintain cheap labour power are a key element of CVCs. However, the purposeful shaping and management of evolving class relations are excluded from notions of strategic coupling. Yet, such deliberate restructuring (in many cases worsening) of workers' conditions, imposed from above by international institutions, states, and local firms, may be central to the establishment of labouring classes as 'regional assets' prior to, or in the process of, strategic coupling (see the discussion of contemporary development in China in Chapter 5).

An additional problem with GPN literatures on strategic coupling is that it naturalizes the power of lead firms. Positive developmental processes generated by global integration are portrayed as arising from subordinate actors' cooperation with lead firms. The literature on strategic coupling rarely discusses the theoretical, practical, political, and developmental implications of moderating lead firm power, or eliminating it altogether, by for example, decreasing their ability to capture surplus value within global production networks through a fairer distribution of social wealth within and beyond GPNs.

3.5 Conclusions

This chapter has outlined the evolution of the GVC approach and has discussed the most popular iteration of the GPN approach (GPN 2.0). It shows that the currently dominant GVC approach is the product of a long process of intellectual mainstreaming—where exploitation and power relations have been sidelined and eventually excluded. The GPN (2.0) approach seeks to overcome GVCs' firm-centrism by establishing a more socio-spatially sensitive conception of change by including more non-chain actors. Its conception

[2] Other dark sides of strategic coupling include uneven resource allocation 'and the breakup of existing cultural, social and economic networks and systems' (Coe and Hess 2013, 134).

of strategic coupling also recognizes that certain forms of global integration may generate dynamics of exploitation and class struggles. However, it cannot operationalize these observations to explain the uneven development and structured hierarchies (of wealth and poverty) that characterize CVCs because it aprioristically rejects the notion that the capitalist world economy is intrinsically hierarchical. Like mainstream GVC analysis, it rejects a class-relational understanding of capitalist development. The next chapter discusses in greater depth the latest iteration of the GVC approach—the World Bank's *Trading for Development in the Age of Global Value Chains*.

4
The World Bank's Perspective on GVCs
An Immanent Critique

with Dara Leyden

> GVCs have contributed to lower inflation via downward pressures on labour.
>
> **(World Bank 2020, 106)**

4.1 Introduction

Ever since their inception in 1978, World Development Reports (WDRs) have sought to promote an ideology of inclusive global development. Framed in the mutual gains rhetoric of comparative advantage trade theory, they are pitched at the level of the *general interest*—as applicable to the entire international policy-making community. The WDR2020, *Trading for Development in the Age of Global Value Chains,* ('the Report') presents itself in the same light, confidently proclaiming that 'GVCs boost incomes, create better jobs and reduce poverty' (World Bank 2020, 3). Given the World Bank's promotion of neoliberal globalization, its argument is unsurprising.

Yet the report's own data undermines its claims. It provides evidence showing how Capitalist Value Chains (CVCs) depress wages (as noted in this chapter's epigraph), enable lead firms to squeeze suppliers, have contributed to reallocating value from labour to capital within national economies, and have accelerated destruction of the world's natural environment (see Chapter 10). For example, the report states that global value chains 'have contributed to lower inflation via *downward pressures on labour* through heightened competition across countries to attract tasks, in particular when low-wage countries are integrated in supply chains' (World Bank 2020, 106; see Andrews et al. 2018).

In this chapter we deploy an immanent critique methodology—taking seriously the claims set by a theory and highlighting its theoretical contradictions

Capitalist Value Chains. Benjamin Selwyn, Christin Bernhold with Dara Leyden, Oxford University Press.
 DOI: 10.1093/9780191994906.003.0004

as it attempts to explain the empirical world (see Bernhold 2022, 48ff.)—to undercut the Report's core claims. We juxtapose contradictory statements within the report (of which there are many), and we highlight its misuse of comparative advantage trade theory to explain CVC dynamics.

Comparative advantage trade theory assumes arms-length market transactions between firms with no power differentials. The existence of CVCs—where lead firms wield unprecedented economic power over suppliers—invalidates this key assumption. As Joan Robinson put it before the advent of CVCs, 'there is no branch of economics in which there is a wider gap between orthodox doctrine and actual problems than in the theory of international trade' (Robinson 1973, 14). This gap has been magnified by the World Bank's attempts to shoehorn GVCs into the categories and assumptions of comparative advantage trade theory. To attempt to explain CVCs via comparative advantage trade theory represents a false analogy (the application of qualities to one thing, that belong to another thing), or, as an economist might say, it is to compare conceptual apples with empirical oranges.

Comparative advantage theory, as we show below, is an ideological portrayal of a non-existent world. This should be self-evident under CVCs where lead firms effectively dictate supplier firms' actions. The notion is rooted in the exclusion of social relations and history. Many economists defend the notion as representing the formulation of a 'parsimonious' theorem that provides 'rule of thumb' guidance to trade and development policy-makers. As we show, comparative advantage trade theory is an ideological trope which legitimates the (enhancement of) power of internationally orientated sections of capital. Its ideological foundations make it incapable of shedding light on dynamics of trade and development through CVCs. While we are not surprised by the report's attempts to positively portray CVC-based development, we are somewhat taken aback by its foundational logical shortcomings.

In this chapter we show how in WDR2020's attempt to sustain its mutual-gains ideology, it deploys a multi-pronged strategy to obscure the anti-developmental outcomes for workers of CVC participation. It *ignores* evidence which opposes its good-news narrative (particularly regarding labour's agency) and it *misconstrues* various studies to support its claims. Where negative realities are undeniable, they are linguistically *inverted* as positives (for example, what this chapter categorize as relatively monopolized firms, WDR2020 refers to as 'superstar firms'). Finally, it does not reflect its own evidence in its overall recommendations.

WDR2020 is quintessentially capital-centric (Selwyn 2017). It conceives of private capital accumulation as the basis for the development of the poor, while it ignores both capitalist exploitation and workers' collective actions to ameliorate their conditions, and the developmental outcomes that these give rise to. This is reflected in the fact that even the relatively un-critical term 'social upgrading' is not mentioned (still less discussed), despite being central to three of the studies that are referenced within it, and despite its widespread use in the mainstream GVC literature (see Chapter 9). While the social upgrading concept differentiates between gains to capital and labour within GVCs, the Report conjures up a trickle-down image of GVCs where what is good for capital is good for labour.

Following this introduction, Section 4.2 outlines the Report's key claims. Sections 4.3 and 4.4 critique the Report's use of comparative advantage theory to explain the purported developmental gains generated by CVCs. Section 4.5 documents the Report's recognition that increased lead firm power has reduced supplier firms' margins. Section 4.6 details how the Report obscures ways in which workers in CVCs are exploited. Section 4.7 concludes.

4.2 What Does the World Development Report Say?

WDR2020 represents the culmination of almost two decades of pro-GVC ideological projection. It argues that

> participation in global value chains can deliver a double dividend. First, firms are more likely to specialize in the tasks in which they are most productive. Second, firms are able to gain from connections with foreign firms, which pass on the best managerial and technological practices. As a result, countries enjoy faster income growth and falling poverty.
>
> **(World Bank 2020, xii)**

The Report defines GVCs as where production takes place in a series of stages, with 'at least two stages conducted in different countries' (World Bank 2020, 265). According to this definition, by 2008, 52 per cent of world trade occurred under such arrangements. UNCTAD (2013, x), using a different recognition criterion, calculates that 80 per cent of world trade takes place in GVCs.

In a world of GVCs, according to the Report, so-called developing countries no longer need to establish entire industries. Rather, through linking up with lead firms they can access best-practice techniques and latest technologies, and match them with their comparative advantage 'factors of production' of cheap labour power and natural resources.[1] The Report emphasizes the benefits of 'relational' GVCs whereby 'durable firm-to-firm

[1] WDR2020 uses the language of developed and developing countries, which is reflected in this chapter's analysis (World Bank 2020, 86), although we do not agree that these are the right notions to describe a country's position within the structured dynamics of uneven capitalist development.

relationships promote the diffusion of technology and access to capital and inputs along chains' (World Bank 2020, 3).

In its promotion of GVCs for development WDR2020 draws upon a range of tropes from classical development theory. In its notion of hyper-specialization, the Report evokes Adam Smith's (1976) model of the beneficial effects of the division of labour. Smith articulated a model of development whereby expanding capitalist industry underpinned the growing wealth of nations through a dynamic feedback loop comprising market expansion, the division of labour, specialization, and productivity enhancement. In WDR2020, lead firms are said to accelerate benefits of the division of labour through knowledge and best-practice transfer, which assist suppliers to upgrade production. In short, the report portrays hyper-specialization as where supplier firms access advanced markets by focussing on the production of a limited range of (especially intermediate) components aided by lead firms.

The Report also draws upon W.W. Rostow's (1990) stagist notion of development. It disaggregates GVC trade into a four-tier value-adding hierarchy (World Bank 2020, 22): (1) commodities (basic goods and materials); (2) limited manufacturing (undertaken especially in Sub-Saharan Africa, Central Asia, and Latin America); (3) advanced manufacturing and services; and (4) innovative activities (undertaken primarily in North America, Europe, and East Asia). Notably, less than a quarter of its countries surveyed upgraded. The growth rate of GVC trade has stagnated since 2008 (see Figure 4.1).[2] While Smithian and Rostowian notions are supportive props

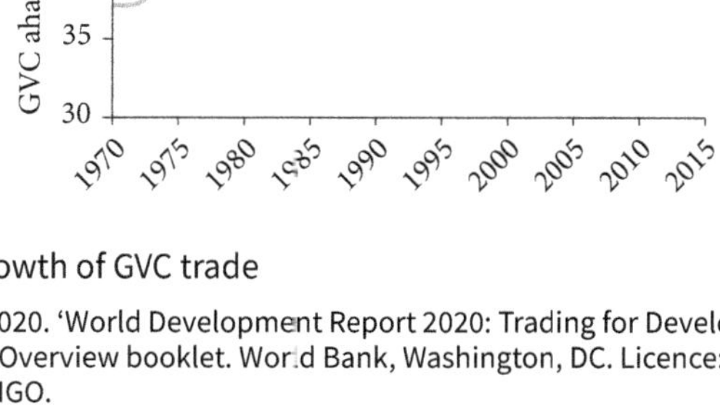

Figure 4.1 The growth of GVC trade

Source: World Bank 2020. 'World Development Report 2020: Trading for Development in the Age of Global Value Chains'. Overview booklet. World Bank, Washington, DC. Licence: Creative Commons Attribution CC BY 3.0 IGO.

[2] According to WDR2020, between 1990 and 2015 only 34 countries (23 per cent) upgraded out of its 146-country survey: 14 countries (including South Africa and Indonesia) upgraded from commodities into limited manufacturing GVCs, 11 countries (including China and India) upgraded from limited

for the Report, comparative advantage trade theory represents its intellectual guiding thread.

4.3 Comparative Advantage Theory and CVCs

The theory of comparative advantage dates to David Ricardo's classical argument that countries can benefit from trade even if they do not have an absolute advantage in producing any good, so long as they specialize in goods in which they have relatively higher productivity. If countries pursue their comparative advantage, then trade generates win-win outcomes whereby every country maximizes its income and enjoys cheaper goods (Mankiw and Taylor 2008).

WDR2020 uses the language of comparative advantage trade theory to assert that GVC-led development generates *mutual gains* for lead firms (concentrated in developed countries) and supplier firms (concentrated in developing countries), thus assumedly benefiting workers in both peripheral and leading countries alike:

> GVCs allow countries to benefit from the efficiency gained from a much finer international division of labour. GVCs exploit the fact that countries have different *comparative advantages* not only in different sectors, but also in different stages of production within sectors.
>
> **(World Bank 2020, 69, see also, e.g., pp. 36–39, emphasis added)**

Accordingly, this perspective shapes its policy recommendations:

> [B]ecause factor endowments matter, countries should exploit their comparative advantage by eliminating barriers to investment and ensuring that labour is competitively priced, by avoiding overvalued exchange rates and restrictive regulations.
>
> **(World Bank 2020, 161)**

WDR2020 deviates from previous GVC frameworks (some of which used the contrasting notion of *competitive* advantage), in that it does not contain an explicit notion of power. For example, Gereffi (1994b) and Kaplinsky (1998) drew upon Michael Porter's *The Competitive Advantage of Nations* (Porter 1990) which argues that nations must compete to enable their industries to occupy higher-value tiers of international trade:

manufacturing into advanced manufacturing and services, and 9 countries upgraded into innovative GVCs.

> National prosperity is created, not inherited. It does not grow out of a country's natural endowments, its labor pool, its interest rates, or its currency's value, as classical economics insists.
>
> (Porter 1990, 73)

To avoid theorizing the major power differentials between lead and supplier firms, the Report simply presents these power differentials as a positive by arguing that they facilitate knowledge transfer through GVCs.

However, although ideologically attractive to proponents of GVCs-for-development, models of comparative advantage trade theory bear little resemblance to the realities of GVCs. In fact, GVC trade is, essentially, the antithesis of the notion of comparative advantage trade. Put another way, the empirical reality of GVCs contradicts the core *assumptions* under which comparative advantage trade theory has theoretical validity. To understand why this is so, it is worth burrowing deeper into the disjuncture between the assumptions of comparative advantage theory and the realities of CVCs.

Fallacies of Comparative Advantage Theory

The deductive basis of comparative advantage trade theory (based upon assumptions rather than historical evidence) means that it is perilously difficult to apply it accurately to real world conditions. Indeed, models of the theory are only analytically valid under the assumption of 'perfect competition', and applicable only when market realities broadly adhere to it.

Perfect competition, according to mainstream theory, is a scenario where small price-taking economic actors transact in a competitive market. Because no power imbalances exist, prices merely reflect supply and demand, and liberalized markets ensure a fair distribution of value through arms-length transactions. According to this idealized scenario, suppliers receive a fair price, buyers earn 'normal' profits and workers receive a 'fair' wage.

However, this ideal of perfect competition bears no resemblance to the realities of CVCs (Table 4.1), in which powerful lead firms establish often exclusive relationships with suppliers, dictating many (sometimes all) aspects of production, and aggressively negotiating (often determining) prices. CVC trade is the antithesis of the notion of perfect competition.

As mentioned above, WDR2020 recognizes that 'suppliers are predominantly in developing countries' and that 'gains may be distributed unequally,

Table 4.1 Perfect competition versus CVC realities

Units and issues of analysis	Perfect competition assumptions	Realities of relational CVCs
Producers	Many producers operate in each industry	Lead firms dominate each industry, coordinating many suppliers
Counterparties	Anonymous buyers and sellers	Interdependent relationships between lead firms and suppliers
Power relations	Equal power between buyers and suppliers	Unequal power wielded by lead firms over suppliers
Coordination of transactions	Market forces	Governed by lead firms
Prices	Determined by balance of supply of demand	Outcome of unequal bargaining between lead firms and suppliers

Source: Reproduced from Selwyn and Leyden (2021, n.p.), Table 1.

even across countries in the value chain' (World Bank 2020, 141f.). It also recognizes GVCs as based upon exchanges between *connected* firms of *unequal* power, which it labels 'relational':

> [T]hese features of GVCs lead to a novel, relational conceptualization of GVCs that shifts the focus away from the mere allocation of value added across countries through *anonymous* spot exchanges of goods and services. Instead, the *identity of the agents participating in a GVC is crucial.*
>
> **(World Bank 2020, 3, emphasis added)**

These unequal power relations, once wrung through the ideology of comparative advantage trade theory, are presented as developmentally positive. This intellectual move, however, generates a cognitive dissonance between the theoretically based predictions of comparative advantage theory, and the evidence presented in the Report. Moreover, the attempt to retro-fit GVCs into comparative advantage theory represents an internally contradictory ideological move—the association of a set of qualities of one category (GVCs) that can only be associated with another category (the mythical notion of free market capitalism).

The dominant Heckscher-Ohlin (HO) version of the model reformulates comparative advantage based on 'factor endowments', that is, whether a country is relatively 'abundant' in either capital or labour. In this model, developed countries are capital-abundant and should focus on innovative high-tech production. Conversely, developing states should exploit their advantage in cheap labour power with labour-intensive production (Lin and Chang 2009). Poverty alleviation ensues through employment, and national income will be shared between capital and labour, with wages increasing in line with productivity. In this model, factor endowments are assumed to be immobile across borders, despite the evident mobility of capital (for example, through FDI). The Stolper-Samuelson (HO-SS) version of the model defines the two factors as low and high-skilled labour (rather than capital and labour) (see Table 4.2).

These models of comparative advantage rely upon *assumptions* which are not compatible with the contemporary reality of CVCs. These are that trade must occur in *competitive markets* and take place between *anonymous parties* with *equal bargaining power* (see Tables 4.1 and 4.2). In some of the literature cited in the WDR2020, the fact that CVCs contradict the theoretical foundations of the notions of perfect competition and comparative advantage is almost recognized. For example, the Report references an influential paper by Grossman and Rossi-Hansberg, which includes the following footnote:

Table 4.2 Comparative advantage trade theory versus CVC realities

Units and issues of analysis	Hecksher-Ohlin model assumptions (1)	Realities of relational CVCs
Markets	Perfect competition	(See Table 4.1)
Goods traded	Final goods	Intermediate goods
Technologies	Both countries have identical technologies	Developed countries protect their superior technologies
International factor mobility	Both factors are immobile	Capital is highly mobile, whereas labour is relatively immobile
Theorems	**Predictions**	**Realities of relational GVCs**
Factor–price equalization theorem	The return to labour relative to capital may fall in developed countries, but should rise in developing countries	The share of income going to labour has fallen in *both* developed and developing countries (2)
Stolper–Samuelson theorem	Inequality between skilled and unskilled workers may increase in developed countries, but should fall in developing countries	Inequality has increased in *both* developed and developing countries (3)

Source: Reproduced from Selwyn and Leyden (2021, n.p.), Table 1. Based on (1) Baldwin (2008), (2) Karabarbounis and Neiman (2014), (3) Meschi and Vivarelli (2009).

> We assume that factor markets are competitive so firms have no monopsony power. We might alternatively assume that firms can keep some of the benefits that result from a reduction in offshoring costs by using their monopsony power in factor markets. Similarly, we might assume that a reduction in offshoring costs enhances firms' market power. Then there would be an additional channel through which offshoring could affect wages. To keep our analysis as simple as possible, however, we maintain the assumption of competitive markets throughout the paper.
>
> **(Grossman and Rossi-Hansberg 2008, 1983)**

Put directly, the authors are conjuring up a fictional world to operationalize their theory. In the same vein, despite WDR2020's recognition that GVC trade is not based on arms-length market transactions (World Bank 2020, 32–34), it uses the language of comparative advantage to explain the benefits of GVC participation as trade-related specialization. Given this dissonance it should be no surprise that the empirical evidence from GVC trade diverges from predictions derived from models of comparative advantage (see Table 4.2).

Given the weakness of the prescriptive and predictive powers of comparative advantage theories, one might be forgiven for wondering why the Report's authors still deploy it? The notion of comparative advantage represents a liberal trope, or a myth, that is often used to bamboozle students of economics into believing in the mutual benefits of 'free' trade. It requires students to ignore power differentials between firms, and the exploitative international class relations that underpin them.

Comparative Advantage as Ideology Par Excellence of International Class Relations

Comparative advantage theory is best understood as an ideological justification, and guide to action, for the promotion of international class relations of exploitation and wealth transfer. The political attractiveness of Ricardo's theory is that it naturalizes capitalist social relations, within and between nation states. Every iteration of the theory—whether Ricardo's original formulation or Hecksher-Ohlin's reformulation—is deductive in that they start from economic assumptions that have been proven to be historically erroneous (see Tables 4.1 and 4.2). Furthermore, unlike Marx, Ricardo, and his followers assumed rather than explained the existence of capitalist and labouring classes and the subordination of the latter to the former. Similarly, Ricardo assumed rather than explained the existence of a fully globalized world economy to make his assumptions about the gains from free trade (see Pradella 2015). Marx, by contrast explained the historically unique social relations of capitalism, and the emergence of a globalized division of labour, as arising out of mercantile colonialism and 'primitive accumulation'. Consequently, 'capital comes [into the world] dripping from head to foot, from every pore, with blood and dirt' (Marx 1990, 926). As Harry Magdoff writes about the theory of comparative advantage: 'what is generally believed to have been natural and efficient when treated abstractly as a "pure" problem of international trade turns out to be historically created in the context of colonialism, war, nationalist rivalries, and military power' (Magdoff 1978, 158f.).

This illuminates the role of the theorem in fostering what Gallagher and Robinson (1953) label the imperialism of free trade. In an ingenious ideological twist, Ricardo argued that relative rather than absolute productivity determined gains from trade. This enabled his theory to predict that all countries could gain from trade, rather than only those that were more competitive. This intellectual move legitimated Britain's incorporation of large swathes of the globe into its imperial-centred division of labour, whilst enabling its advocates to portray such moves as developmentally benign.

Ricardo's classical example (where England produced wine and cloth less efficiently than Portugal) painted England as the weaker economic power. For over a century, however, England had presided over a superordinate relationship with Portugal, cemented through a series of Methuen treaties (starting in 1703) (Watson 2017). These treaties stipulated, amongst other things, that while England could impose import tariffs on Portuguese wine imports, Portugal could not impose tariffs on English textiles imports (Francis 1960). As a consequence, Portugal ran up a trade deficit with England. Just prior to Ricardo's formulation of the theory of comparative advantage, Britain liberated Portugal from Napoleon's rule (in 1808), subsequently incorporating it into its free trade-based sphere of influence.

As Joan Robinson (1977, 1336) observed, the free trade doctrine promoted through comparative advantage theory was 'a more subtle form of Mercantilism. When Britain was the workshop of the world, universal free trade suited her interests' while it 'ruined Portuguese industry'. By contrast, it boosted Portugal's winemakers, 'who occupied a position of strength within the domestic political structure, [and who] assented to this arrangement in the hope that it would provide them with something approaching monopoly conditions at some stage in the future' (Watson 2017, 265). As Matthew Watson (2017, 259) notes, Ricardo's original example 'strategically misdescribes in Panglossian liberal terms a deeply unequal trading relationship created through highly illiberal means'.

But there are still more disconcerting realities that Ricardo's theory obscured. The trade relations between England and Portugal were sustained not by mutual gains, but by debt and slave labour:

> The 'cloth' from 'England' in Ricardo's famous example simply could not be paid for alone by the wine exports travelling in the other direction. Brazil, a Portuguese colony at the time, was responsible for a massive 40 percent of the world's new gold reserves in the eighteenth century. It was this that was used to settle the trade deficit resulting from the inadequacies of the wine trade.
>
> **(Watson 2017, 261)**

Moreover:

> The newly hyper-powered Brazilian extractive industries were built upon slave labour.... The merchant ships that brought Brazilian gold to settle Portuguese commercial debts in Europe were simultaneously responsible for taking huge numbers of people from Portugal's African colonies to work in the gold mines as slaves.
>
> **(Watson 2017, 266, drawing on Magdoff 1978, 158)**

These tropes—comparative productivities, the benefits of international exchange, leading imperialist states acting benignly to the benefit of other regions—infuse subsequent theories of comparative advantage. They obscure the hierarchical internationally articulated class alliances between super- and sub-ordinate fractions of capital and the exploitative relations upon which they are based.

If comparative advantage theory is reconceptualized not as a theorem of the benefits of free trade but as a guide to action in establishing international class relations of exploitation and wealth transfer, it is possible to understand why it appeals to those promoting the GVCs-for-development ideology. In what follows we show how the WDR2020 provides sufficient evidence to illuminate how CVCs rest upon exploitative international class relations, which generate outcomes that contradict the assumptions and predictions of comparative advantage trade theory.

4.4 Lead Firms: Squeezing Suppliers

WDR2020 is keen to provide evidence of mutual gains under GVC trade, even though such trade is increasingly dominated by large corporations. GVC firms (which both import and export) account for only about 15 per cent of all trading firms in the world but capture about 80 per cent of total trade (World Bank 2020, 30f.). Following Autor et al. (2017), the report calls the biggest lead firms 'superstars'. It claims that GVCs accelerate development because 'relational' GVC linkages transmit gains from lead firms to supplier firms in developing countries and on to their workers. Irony rather than politically loaded admiration would have been more appropriate given that the lion's share of gains from GVC trade flow in the opposite direction. In fact, the Report itself documents that GVCs have inflated the profitability of lead firms at the expense of the profitability of supplier firm capitals.

The rise of GVCs has ushered a profit bonanza especially for US lead firms, who have secured continually rising markups over costs of production. WDR2020 notes that 'GVCs have boosted superstar firms that earn superstar profits and may dominate the market' (World Bank 2020, 84). The Report references De Loecker and Eeckhout's (2018) analysis of the financial accounts of 70,000 firms across 134 countries, which found that profits have risen substantially since 1980, particularly in the United States and Europe, with average mark-ups over costs of production rising from 1.1 to 1.6 by 2016.

Crucially, supplier firms in countries lower down in the imperialist chain do not profit in the same way, and the workers they exploit do not profit at all (on the latter, see Section 4.5). De Loecker and Eeckhout (2018, 7) find that supplier firms have seen markups stagnate or decline. WDR2020 acknowledges that:

> Large corporations that outsource parts and tasks to developing countries have seen rising markups and profits, suggesting that a growing share of cost reductions from GVC participation are not being passed on to consumers. At the same time, markups for the producers in developing countries are declining.
>
> **(World Bank 2020, 3)**

In contrast to 'superstar' firms, the Report finds that when supplier firms integrate into GVCs they earn *lower* markups:

> The implications of GVCs for the emergence of superstar firms huge in scale, high in market power, and large in profit rates are exacerbated by the disproportionate

> bargaining power that these large lead firms may have over their suppliers.... Although buyer firms in developed countries are seeing higher profits, supplier firms in developing countries are getting squeezed.
>
> **(World Bank 2020, 85)**

The distributive effects of intensifying lead firm power are neither theorized in WDR2020, nor is it presented as a barrier to supplier-level regional development. Rather, problems of enduring poverty and lack of development are presented as having nothing to do with lead firm value-capture strategies. Instead, they are attributed to the slowing of globalization, and to incorrect policies by developing countries. The solution? WDR2020 recommends further liberalization, deeper trade agreements and enhanced intellectual property protection for lead firms (e.g., World Bank 2020, 5, 7, 36). These policies are likely to buttress, rather than challenge, the power of these lead firms.

The closest WDR2020 gets to considering the extent of lead firm power are cursory mentions of 'market power', mainly to describe anti-competitive behaviour of digital platform firms (World Bank 2020, 145). The term is not defined in the Report, but it appears to adopt orthodox economics' definition of firms' ability to raise consumer prices. Remarkably, the 294-page Report only mentions monopoly in two restricted contexts; (i) to critique 'inefficient public monopolies' or (ii) to discuss how cartels raise prices for consumers (another ailment which is apparently best addressed by enhanced trade agreements) (World Bank 2020, 169, 249).

Unlike WDR2020, concentrated lead firm power has been investigated by various academics, although not from a class-relational perspective. For example, as Strange and Newton (2006, 184) put it, a partial consequence of the centralization of lead firms' economic power is that powerful buyers can 'push down the prices of supplies to marginal cost and thus extract the full profits from the sales of the final goods....' William Milberg (2008, 429) calls this the 'mark-up effect ... [through] which the lead firm in the global value chain is able to raise the mark-up over costs ... through the control of input costs'. For example, significant import price declines (of over 40 per cent between 1986 and 2006) have benefited US firms engaged in computers, electrical and telecommunications products, clothing, footwear, textiles, furniture, chemicals, and miscellaneous manufacturers (including toys) (Milberg 2008, 433).

One consequence of intensified lead firm concentration within GVCs is a rising share of national income going to capital rather than labour. De Loecker and Eeckhout (2018, 10) find that:

> higher markups lead to higher profits.... This further confirms the fact that the increase in markups brings about a distributional change with more of the surplus going to the owners of the firms and less to the workers.

Further still, lead firms have wielded their power to construct a global institutional environment in their favour—such as through the global intellectual property regime (TRIPs). The latter was integrated into the WTO's constitution in 1994 following aggressive lobbying led by a small cabal of US lead firms (Stiglitz 2007; Drahos and Braithwaite 2017). Durand and Milberg (2020) explain how the monopolization of intangibles was a key strategy of lead firms to generate 'information rents' and crystallize their market power, contributing to the uneven distribution of value along CVCs, and transfers from peripheral countries to leading capitalist countries.

Indicative of the Report's ideological bias is its non-engagement with UNCTAD's 2018 Trade and Development Report *Power, Platforms and the Free Trade Delusion.* While WDR2020 portrays giant 'superstar' firms as innovative actors spreading developmental opportunities through their value chains, UNCTAD (2018), citing many of the same sources as WDR2020, shows how in a world of giant, lead-firm driven GVCs the 'winner takes most'. The latter report argues that lead 'superstar' firms themselves are partially responsible for accelerating global inequality.

Unsurprisingly, this recognition has no impact on WDR2020's perspective (comparative advantage trade theory), its developmental outlook (mutual gains derived from GVC participation), its policy proposals (designed to enhance lead firms' power), or its conception of labour (as a factor of production).

4.5 Labour's Fate in WDR2020

WDR2020 sees the world from the perspective of capital and invites its readers to do the same. It heralds lead and supplier firms as dynamic and innovative actors while workers are portrayed as 'comparative advantage factors of production' to be deployed by developing countries to attract foreign direct investment. It claims that GVCs boost incomes, create better jobs, and reduce poverty. The evidence, however, is against it.

In fact, WDR2020 admits that GVCs have exerted 'downward pressures on labour through heightened competition across countries to attract tasks, in particular when low-wage countries are integrated in supply chains' (World Bank 2020, 106). This recognition is based, in part, upon an OECD study which notes how stronger GVC integration 'can put downward pressure on wage growth through the use of foreign workers embodied in inputs who thus become more direct competitors to domestic workers' (Andrews et al. 2018, 21). However, this recognition is brushed aside as the WDR resumes its celebration of GVCs' developmental dynamism.

The Report relies upon four propagandistic techniques to conceal the anti-developmental outcomes suffered by workers from exploitation by lead and supplier firms. As mentioned in the introduction, these are: (i) ignoring evidence (particularly of labour's agency), (ii) misconstruing studies, (iii) inverting negatives into positives, and finally, (iv) recognizing remaining problems (together with progressive proposals) but failing to make meaningful redistributive recommendations.

Ignoring Evidence

The case study of Samsung's new factories in Vietnam runs throughout the Report. Its opening lines wax lyrical about Vietnam's successful integration into electronics CVCs, recounting how

> Samsung makes its mobile phones with parts from 2500 suppliers across the globe. One country—Vietnam—produces more than a third of those phones, and it has reaped the benefits. The provinces in which the phones are produced, Thai Nguyen and Bac Ninh, have become two of the richest in Vietnam, and poverty there has fallen dramatically as a result.
>
> **(World Bank 2020, xi)**

The Report ignores Samsung's record of labour rights violations in Vietnam (AMRC 2013). In 2018 UN inspectors found widespread maltreatment of its mainly female workforce:

> Researchers reported testimonies of dizziness or fainting at work from all study participants and high noise levels that violated legal limits. Miscarriages were reported to be common and workers reported pain in their bones, joints, and legs which they attributed to standing at work for 70 to 80 hours a week.
>
> **(UNHR 2018, n.p.)**

There is, by now, a burgeoning literature charting exploitation in CVC firms. Even where workers earn higher wages than before being employed in these firms, these wages are often earned through working excessive overtime and in health-damaging conditions (Chan 2013; Mezzadri 2016; Ruwanpura and Hughes 2016, Alessandrini 2022; see Chapter 7 on immiserating growth-regimes). Such dynamics reflect the often difficult, sometimes desperate, attempts by workers to establish viable livelihoods. However, rather than address these contradictory processes WDR2020 misattributes improved earnings to GVC employers rather than to workers' survival strategies.

Ignoring Labour's Agency

The Report credits lead firms for implementing 'voluntary codes of conduct' that improve working conditions within their supply chains (World Bank 2020, 89). It also celebrates campaigns by benevolent Western consumers and NGOs. But it veils worker's own attempts to improve their pay and conditions. For example, it claims that: 'In response to demands from international buyers, and learning from international best practices, Bangladeshi producers are increasingly recognizing that they must not only improve their practices, but also ensure that improvements can be independently verified by third parties' (World Bank 2020, 67). Empirically, however, militant strike action was instrumental in securing permanent pay rises in Bangladesh's CVCs:

> Bangladesh's official wage board has approved a 77 percent rise in pay for the region's garment workers from December [2013] after the world's second largest clothing exporter was crippled by strikes and the Rana Plaza disaster.... In September this year, thousands of garment factory workers in Bangladesh protested over low wage rates, resulting in the closure of many factories.
>
> **(Brinded 2013, n.p.)**

At the hands of the Report, workers in Indonesia, Vietnam, and China (World Bank 2020, 89, 79, 80) amongst others, suffer the same fate of agential negation. For example, the better wages that the Report identifies as an outcome of China's successful upgrading from limited manufacturing into advanced manufacturing and services (World Bank 2020, 1, 41, 80) are not a simple effect of entry into higher technology/value-added activities. From the early 2000s onwards, combinations of labour shortages, mass labour struggles, and central state policy (in part in response to these struggles) led to rising wages (often of double-digits) in one after another of China's CVC sectors (Friedman 2014b).

Misconstruing Evidence

The Report is keen to argue that '[n]ot only do GVC firms employ more people, but they also pay better' (World Bank 2020, 79). So keen in fact, that it presents a highly selective, or even misleading, interpretation of the evidence. It states that 'across a sample of developing countries, firms that both export and import pay higher wages than import-only and export-only firms and nontraders' (World Bank 2020, 80). It supports this statement, citing an article by Ben Shepherd and Susan Stone (2012), claiming that their findings are that 'firms with the strongest international linkages—export, import, and foreign-owned—pay higher wages' (World Bank 2020, 95).

However, the purpose of Shepherd and Stone's study is to provide 'evidence on the links between Global Value Chains (GVCs) and labour markets, focusing on developing economies, particularly the OECD's Key Partner countries (Brazil, India, Indonesia, China, and South Africa)' (Shepherd and Stone 2012, 3). These countries account for a large proportion workers employed in CVCs (Suwandi 2019, 47). Shepherd and Stone do find a positive link with wages for a large sample of 108 countries. Crucially, however, when they focus on these five developing economies they find: 'no discernible impact of international linkages on wage rates in these data for the key partner countries ... the effects of GVCs may be primarily felt in emerging markets through increased employment rates rather than higher wages' (Shepherd and Stone 2012, 15). In summary, they discern no association between GVC employment and higher wages in these countries.

In a later section, WDR2020 reiterates that 'firms operating in GVCs tend to pay higher wages than firms operating in direct trade only' (World Bank 2020, 198), referencing two further literature surveys. Again, this is a selective, or misleading, representation of the evidence. For example, the cited survey by Margaret McMillan and Íñigo Verduzco-Gallo (2011) does present several studies that have identified higher wages in foreign firms, but they continue:

> However, these wage gaps can be due to other factors. For example, if foreign firms attract more productive workers, then it would be reasonable to expect that these workers would demand higher wages to compensate for their higher productivity. In that case, the wage gap between wages in foreign and domestic firms would be explained by differences in the characteristics of the type of workers they hire. This seems to be the case; after controlling for firm and worker characteristics, the wage premium paid by foreign firms drops significantly.
>
> **(McMillan and Verduzco-Gallo 2011, 45)**

Further, the conclusion of their literature review on offshore outsourcing is that: 'overall, the effects of production offshoring on labour market outcomes in developing countries are likely to be mixed, and we still know too little about this issue' (McMillan and Verduzco-Gallo 2011, 47). They also analyse a large international dataset to investigate the connection between trade liberalization and labour market outcomes, and conclude that 'at least in the aggregate, trade liberalization is *not correlated* with changes in real wages or employment' (McMillan and Verduzco-Gallo 2011, 55, emphasis added). None of this is reflected in WDR2020.

Inverting Adversities

WDR2020 claims that GVCs are inclusive and provide 'better jobs' (World Bank 2020, 3, 80, 196). However, the widely observed realities of job insecurity and inequality throughout GVCs are too ubiquitous to be ignored or misconstrued (Barrientos 2008; Anner 2012; Newsome et al. 2015). An important example is the higher prevalence of women amongst the lowest-paid and most precarious jobs within GVCs, with some of the worst conditions (Barrientos 2008). Women, working under gendered exploitative relations, are often perceived by employers as easier to discipline (Elson and Pearson 1981; Baglioni 2018). Aspects of gender-related wage inequality are recognized in the Report, but only after it celebrates GVCs' inclusivity and how they contribute to the 'broader development benefits of higher female employment', thus 'improving their livelihoods and those of their families' (World Bank 2020, 3, 68).

Widespread inequality within CVCs is sometimes recognized by those who promote the GVCs for development agenda. In an earlier co-authored paper, for example, Pinelopi Goldberg—the World Bank's chief economist at the time of the Reports' publication—observed a 'contemporaneous increase in globalization and inequality in most developing countries' (Goldberg and Pavcnik 2007, 76–77). However, the Report does not mention this prior observation. On the one hand it claims that 'GVCs are, on the whole, inclusive' (World Bank 2020, 196), and that there is a 'lack of a systematic relationship between GVC participation and growth in income inequality for developing countries' (World Bank 2020, 82). On the other hand, it also recognizes, that GVCs have 'increased wage inequality in low- and middle-income economies' (World Bank 2020, 87). This contradiction is circumvented by arguing, and celebrating the fact that, GVCs disproportionately reward higher-educated and higher-skilled workers (World Bank 2020,

3, 68, 87). This is scant comfort, however, to the workers that are heavily exploited throughout CVCs.

The Shift of Produced Wealth from Labour to Capital: Recognition but No Reparation

Considerable evidence shows that the share of national income in developed countries has shifted from labour to capital since the early 1980s (Elsby et al. 2013). Studies have attributed the trend both to the rise of 'superstar' firms (Autor et al. 2017), rising lead firm profits (Barkai 2020), and GVC participation (Dao et al. 2017; Parteka and Wolszczak-Derlacz 2020). Contrary to the predictions of Heckscher-Ohlin model of comparative advantage trade theory (see Table 4.2) this has occurred in both countries further up and lower down in the imperialist chain (Karabarbounis and Neiman 2014). As UNCTAD's 2018 report puts it:

> [T]he rise in the profits of top TNCs accounted for more than two thirds of the decline in the global labour income share between 1995 and 2015. Therefore, although the rising share of the profits of top TNCs has come at the expense of smaller enterprises, it has also been strongly correlated with the declining labour income share since the beginning of the new millennium.
>
> **(UNCTAD 2018, 57)**

Faced with this growing consensus, WDR2020 acknowledges that

> In 63 developed and developing economies, GVC integration as well as other domestic within-industry forces, such as technology or markups, contributed significantly to the reallocation of value added from labour to capital within countries between 1995 and 2011.
>
> **(World Bank 2020, 86)**

In any objective analysis, this fact would have serious implications for the purported potential of GVC-led development. Not so for WDR2020. It fails to consider whether the shift of national income from labour to capital across many countries might be caused by these countries' changing capital–labour relations, which are often impacted by CVCs—particularly the augmented power of lead firms. By contrast, Alexander Guschanski and Özlem Onaran include capital–labour relations in their extensive econometric study of what they call emerging economies (Guschanski and Onaran 2021). They find that labour's share of income was negatively impacted by a reduction in workers' bargaining power following GVC integration.

Despite this partial recognition, no meaningful redistributive proposals are suggested in the Report. Quite the contrary, it recommends policies such as 'deep preferential trade agreements' and stronger 'intellectual property rights protection' for lead firms (World Bank 2020, 36, 161, 172, 230). But, given the income-distributive dynamics of CVCs, such policies would be expected to amplify the continuous flow of profits to 'superstar' firms (Durand and Milberg 2020; Rikap 2021).

One potentially redistributive mechanism that is mentioned in the Report is the implementation of higher minimum wages. However, what it gives with one hand it takes with the other: While it mentions minimum wages and even living wages (World Bank 2020, 198) it cautions immediately against meaningful wage increases: 'In some countries, distortions in the domestic market may drive a significant wedge between a living wage for workers and the wage at which firms can remain competitive in international markets' (World Bank 2020, 199). Where 'competitive' wages are below living wages, WDR2020 shifts the responsibility onto the state to provide wage-subsidies (effectively, subsidies to firms) (World Bank 2020, 200, 202, 204).

On labour policy, some more progressive suggestions are put forward in WDR2020. It references the ILO's better work campaign and recommends adopting the ILO's core conventions on labour standards (World Bank 2020, 195, 202). However, the overarching suite of policy recommendations aligns with the previous WDR on *The Changing Nature of Work* (World Bank 2019), which portrays capitalist globalization and technological change as certain, arguing that governments should not, therefore, burden employers with troublesome workers-rights and protections. Instead, WDR2020 argues that the state should promote a 'flexible' labour market (making it easier for firms to hire and fire):

> Because GVC employers need to compete in absolute terms in global markets, restrictive labour market policies can be a barrier to investment. To balance inclusion and competitiveness, countries may combine greater labour market flexibility (that is, limiting labour regulations that significantly restrict employers, while maintaining adequate protection of workers) with highly supportive social protection and complementary social insurance.
>
> **(World Bank 2020, 202)**

Rather than recommending progressive taxation on capital/profits to fund these protections, WDR2019 instead argues that value-added taxes should be prioritized for raising the necessary domestic public revenues (World Bank 2019, 132). Such taxes are widely understood to be regressive because they penalize the poor, who spend a higher proportion of their income of consumption (Tamaoka 1994).

4.6 Conclusions

On the face of it, WDR2020 signifies the apogee of mainstream GVC analysis. Over several decades, the approach has gone from academic sub-discipline to a primary concept in development theory and policy. However, while WDR2020 represents the zenith of influence of the GVC for development approach it also embodies its intellectual low point. WDR2020's key messages and conclusions do not follow from its own evidence: Whilst the Report claims that 'GVCs boost incomes, create better jobs, and reduce poverty', its own evidence suggests that they concentrate wealth, repress incomes and create many bad jobs. The report selectively *ignores* evidence which opposes its good-news narrative, and it *misconstrues* other studies to better support its claims. Wherever the negative realities are undeniable, they are linguistically *inverted* as positives, and it does not reflect its own evidence in its overall recommendations.

The Report claims that GVCs generate mutual gains for lead and supplier firms, while its evidence suggests increasingly unequal gains for lead firms. It recognizes that buyer firms in developed countries reap higher profits while supplier firms in developing countries are squeezed through GVC participation but nevertheless promotes such participation as a development strategy for the latter. While it claims that workers benefit from employment in supplier firms, it ignores well-documented evidence to the contrary. It erases any scent of workers' agency when explaining improvements to their conditions.

The WDR's long-standing commitment to the assumptions of mutual gains derived from comparative advantage theory generates a GVC framework devoid of power relations. The attempts by the authors of the report to explain GVCs via comparative advantage trade theory represents a false analogy—the association of a set of qualities of one category (GVCs) that can only be associated with another category (the mythical notion of free market capitalism). While such an error is common in tabloid journalism, most academics would attempt to avoid such a mistake. The consequences of this forced marriage of incompatibles—of GVCs and free market theory—is that even when the Report recognizes problems of GVC participation caused by the exercise of lead firm power, these are externalized from its pre-determined deductive narrative. This creates a simplified, inaccurate, and ideological image of the world. In short, WDR2020 is an intellectual failure of epic proportions.

5
Making CVCs
The Role of Geopolitics

> The road to the free market was opened and kept open by an enormous increase in continuous, centrally organized and controlled interventionism.
>
> **(Polanyi 2001, 146f.)**

5.1 Introduction

What do states have to do with Capitalist Value Chains (CVCs)? Karl Polanyi's observation, in this chapter's epigraph, that capitalist states play a significant role in maintaining the operations of the 'free market' undermines the myth that the latter is 'self-regulating'. Rather, it highlights how the historically and geographically differentiated configurations of capitalism's social relations—endless competitive capital accumulation predicated upon exploitative surplus value extraction from labour—are enabled and often put into place by states. CVCs—historically specific configurations of capitalist production, based upon and reproduced through international class relations—are no exception.

Capitalist states institutionalize and enforce capital's ability to extract surplus value from labour. Their relative autonomy from capital accumulation implies that—dependent on the class interests represented within them and on their strengths within the imperialist chain—states can, to a greater or lesser extent, play more coordinating economic roles than most individual firms. These include playing decisive roles in determining patterns of investment, and establishing rules and norms under which capital accumulation occurs. Such actions influence, and are influenced by, class and geopolitical relations. This chapter provides an overview of how key states—the United States and China—established core technologies and political economic frameworks in which CVCs emerged. It details how they promoted 'their'

Capitalist Value Chains. Benjamin Selwyn and Christin Bernhold, Oxford University Press.
 DOI: 10.1093/9780191994906.003.0005

firms, and how these developments simultaneously represent continually evolving geopolitical relations.

Key to understanding such dynamics are our class-relational notions of the imperialist chain (see Chapter 2) and core technologies, that is, state of the art means of production that allow powerful firms to control significantly how capitalist production and thus, exploitation, occurs. Such core technologies are often dual-use—serving economic and military competitiveness. Firms and states that facilitate the development of, and control over, core technologies attain economic and political advantages over their rivals.

Rafael Reuveny and William Thompson (2001, 691) note how core technologies 'are fundamental to attaining global political-military leadership. The profits from pioneering economic innovation fund the development of military instruments and networks of global reach'. Furthermore '[S]ystemic leadership is made possible by the spatial concentration of key resources in the leader's country' (Reuveny and Thompson 2001, 695). From iron production, steam engines, and railroads during Britain's nineteenth-century pre-eminence, to electricity and automobiles during the United States' rise in the twentieth century—core technologies and leading political economic status are closely related (Reuveny and Thompson 2001, 696).

Contemporary core technologies—digitalization, micro-electronics, semiconductors and aerospace, big data, AI, and machine learning—facilitate the existence and proliferation of CVCs. It is not just firms such as Microsoft, Google, Amazon, and Apple at the technological frontier for whom such technologies are key, but most lead firms in CVCs that rely upon them to 'govern' and coordinate their value chains. Such technological developments are driven forward by capital's endless quest to increase surplus value extraction from labour (a dynamic ignored by WSA, GCC, and GVC approaches, but central to this book's comprehension of capitalism) and competitive capital accumulation.

Clearly, it is not only the United States and China that determine the political framework within which CVCs evolve. Other states as well as the supranational EU have also implemented rules that shape international class relations. However, given the limited space here, we focus in this chapter on the United States and China due to their influence in making CVCs and the growing significance of geopolitical rivalries between them. Further, the emphasis on geopolitics is to be read in the context of the entire book: geographic restructurings of CVCs need to be analysed from the vantage point of domestic and international class relations.

In the remainder of this chapter, Section 5.2 details the role of the US state in facilitating the development of core technologies that underpin CVCs, and in helping US lead firms to gain dominant positions in these chains. Section 5.3 discusses how CVCs have been institutionalized globally in ways that augment the power and profits of firms that control core technologies. Section 5.4 provides an overview of China's integration into CVCs. We show how state policies in China effectively created the political framework to become the workshop of CVCs—attracting unprecedented volumes of Foreign Direct Investment (FDI) which used China as a global assembly and export platform. More recently, however, state policies are assisting Chinese firms to upgrade and to compete directly with high-tech US firms in CVCs and in the production of dual-use core technologies. Section 5.5 concludes.

5.2 The United States: Making CVCs and Supporting US Lead Firms

The US response to the 1970s crisis—at home and abroad—proved decisive in making CVCs. The US state and many of its (would-be) leading firms increasingly engaged in geographic expansion in and through CVCs. By re-organizing the spatiality of global capitalism—through neoliberal globalization—the United States' firms and other firms in leading capitalist states were able to establish new socio-geographic arenas for capital accumulation and new hierarchical relations with subordinate firms. These global transformations—combined with Chinese state policies—also facilitated China's rise (see Section 5.2).

Although the origins of CVCs can be traced further back, decisive moments can be identified in the 1970s and 1980s. In the 1970s, in response to the 1973 oil embargo implemented by Arab states against allies of Israel, the breaking of the dollar–gold link, and world economic slowdown, leading imperialist states with the United States at the fore formed the G7. The organization facilitated free trade policies through establishing close links between core economy heads of states, finance ministers and central banks, centred around the US Treasury, and the US federal reserve (Baker 2006). This involved:

> [C]oordinating with other states the adoption of legal frameworks for market-making and guaranteed property rights to sustain the international mobility of capital and integrated production and trade, as well as disciplining states in their application of these 'rules of law'.
>
> (Panitch and Gindin 2019, 13)

The principles of openness to foreign capital and sanctity of property rights were codified into a global common sense. Such principles were rigorously reinforced and extended by the 'Washington Consensus' institutions—the IMF, World Bank, and WTO (Gill 1998; Gowan 1999).

The US's Military Industrial Complex has been referred to as its hidden 'developmental state' (Block 2008) and its National Security State (Wade 2014; Weiss 2021). Under the guise of defence expenditure the US state played a crucial role in establishing core technologies—semi-conductors, computing, and software, GPS, communication satellites, the internet, and autonomous vehicles—that help US firms occupy the most profitable positions within CVCs (see below). As Linda Weiss (2021, 153, emphasis added) puts it:

> Sustained geopolitical rivalry motivated Pentagon planners to pursue high-tech supremacy as a national security imperative. That strategy imbued a cluster of national security agencies with a mission to pursue trail-blazing innovations and a tolerance for costly long-term investments. It is those efforts, the result of concerted national security policymaking, which have spawned numerous *radical general-purpose technologies* that not only underpin *US military primacy*, but also *power the modern economy*.

A key moment here was the Soviet Union's launch of the Sputnik satellite in 1957, suggesting its potential to rival US technological development. Sputnik 'triggered an abrupt discontinuity', transforming the US state [through various agencies] into 'self-conscious promoters, not just of technological change but of perpetual technological revolution' (McDougall 1982, 1011). Following Sputnik, the federal government founded the Defense Advanced Research Project Agency (DARPA) and the National Aeronautics and Space Administration (NASA). DARPA supported the research that led to the development of the internet and continues to support cutting-edge research on electronics. Military procurement represented a significant source of demand for DARPA-related activities and firms such as Fairchild Semiconductor (Mazzucato 2018). As Margaret O'Mara (2019, 260) noted, defence-related spending in the 1980s 'remained the big-government engine hidden under the hood of [Silicon] Valley's shiny new entrepreneurial sports car'.

As one-time free market champion Francis Fukuyama has belatedly recognized: '[m]any of the foundational technologies of our era, including computers, radar, semiconductors, integrated circuits, and, most famously, the internet all started out as government-funded military projects' (Fukuyama 2021, n.p.).

These moves to leverage US firms into prime global position were aided by the US states' interventions in the global monetary system. The 1985 plaza accord effectively devalued the US dollar (USD) against the Japanese Yen, the UK Sterling, the French Franc and the German Mark, increasing the competitiveness of US exports and decreasing the ability of its rivals to penetrate the US domestic market. Although this was driven largely by protectionist pressures, it had a significant role in the emergence of CVCs. One consequence of this realignment of currencies was the move by Japanese firms out of Japan and into mainland China in the search of cheaper labour power (see Section 5.4).

The US state, and its control over the USD, is central to the financial architecture that facilitates the operation of CVCs. Production in CVCs is fragmented across national borders (with different currencies) and integrated through lead-firm governed value chains, underpinned by a USD-centred financial system. US lead firms gain a crucial advantage from having the USD as their home currency in accessing finance, lowering transaction costs, and reducing currency risks. At the time of writing, the role of USD in global trade has never been higher (Johnson and Tanzi 2023), even as emerging economies seek to reduce their reliance on it.

The substantial financing required to bring about globally integrated industrial production—including through FDI, mergers and acquisitions, and joint ventures between international and domestic firms—is eased by expanding markets for USD, myriad financial services, and a growing array of financial intermediaries (Bonizzi et al. 2022). Mega trade finance intermediaries (such as Citibank) have facilitated the expansion of giant lead firms. Lead firms' relative freedom to operate in, and shape, globalized capitalism has been underpinned by state actions, in particular by the United States.

Geopolitical Management of Global Capitalism

Following the dissolution of the Soviet Union in 1991, the US state's objectives were to incorporate the remaining quarter of the world economy under its leadership. As Tom Stevenson (2023, n.p.), author of *Someone Else's Empire: British Illusions and American Hegemony*, puts it:

> The US has military superiority over all other countries, control of the world's oceans via critical sea lanes, garrisons on every continent, a network of alliances that covers much of the industrial world, the ability to render individuals to secret

> prisons in countries from Cuba to Thailand, preponderant influence over the global financial system, [and] about 30 percent of the world's wealth. . . . US foreign policy has … the aim of pre-empting the emergence of any potential challengers to its primacy.

While calling the United States an 'empire' risks underplaying the specificity of capitalist social relations (Rosenberg 1994; Wood 2016) and evolving geopolitical rivalries, the above quote does highlight the United States' *dominance* over other capitalist states. It is true that the extent of the endurance of US *hegemony* is debatable (Wallerstein 2003; Callinicos 2009; Panitch and Gindin 2015; Starrs 2019). This does not mean, however, that it has lost its economic and military *dominance*. While the formation and expansion of CVCs have enabled China's economic rise, this has increased the importance of US military dominance to its global leadership.

In 2020, based on its position as the world's strongest military power with capacity to intervene at great geographical distances (globalfirepower.com), the United States accounted for 40 per cent of all global military expenditure, spending more than the next 10 highest-spending nations combined (see Figure 5.1), and operating approximately 750 overseas military bases across 80 countries (Vine 2021). Furthermore, in 2020, 45 out of the Top 100 arms-producing and military services companies were US firms (SIPRI Arms Industry Database). Such overwhelming capacity for violence clearly extends beyond the needs of domestic security. However, China is increasing

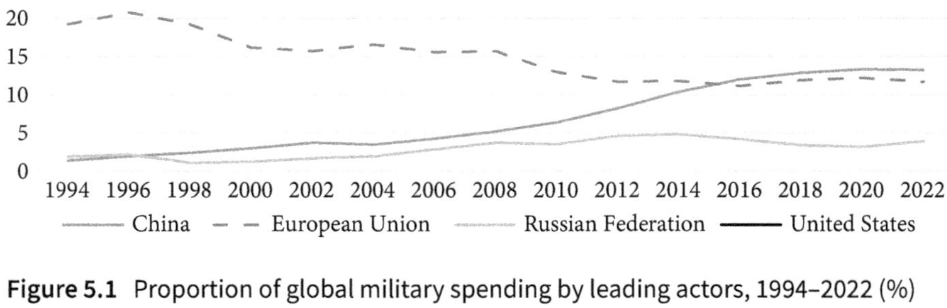

Figure 5.1 Proportion of global military spending by leading actors, 1994–2022 (%)

Source: Own elaboration based on World Bank (2024) data on military expenditure in current USD. Chart displays percentages of total global military expenditure. Series code MS.MIL.XPND.CD.

its military expenditure, in large part through investments in cutting edge technologies (see below).

Mainstream GVC and GPN scholarship emerged during the 1990s and early 2000s following the temporary elimination of any visible, however partial, challenge to US geopolitical power. This, perhaps, explains why conceptions of geopolitics, as a constitutive feature of CVCs, were largely excluded from these theoretical frameworks, and why some authors now argue that geopolitics have 'returned' in the context of the US–China trade and tech war (Yeung 2023). However, geopolitics have always shaped CVCs. For instance, the global electronics industry: from its Cold War origins to the development of East Asian supply chains, the US–Japan rivalry of the 1980s, and the recent US–China geopolitical rivalry (see Glassman 2011). Yet, the GPN 2.0 framework, which uses electronics as its main case study, conceptually excludes geopolitics (see Chapter 3).

In contrast to the GPN 2.0 approach, based on our class-relational understanding of the imperialist chain, we recognize that contemporary CVCs are underpinned by politics, diplomacy, and ultimately military power. From George Bush's declaration of a New World Order to his son's administration's proclamation of 'full spectrum dominance', to the contemporary attempt to contain China's technological and military development—the US state has always been ruthless in promoting its firm's economic advantages. During the establishment of CVCs, the United States was clear about its military might in re-enforcing its political-economic dominance. In its 1998 report entitled *Long Range Plan*, US Space Command outlined how:

> The United States will remain a global power and exert global leadership. Widespread communications will highlight disparities in resources and quality of life, contributing to unrest in developing countries. The global economy will continue to become more interdependent. Economic alliances, as well as the growth and influence of multinational corporations, will blur security agreements. The gap between 'have' and 'have-not' nations will widen, creating regional unrest. The United States will remain the only nation able to project power globally.
>
> **(United States Space Command 1998, 1ff.)**

The doctrine of 'Full Spectrum Dominance' was developed prior to the 9/11 attacks on the World Trade Centre in New York, but was deployed to guide US political, economic, and military actions thereafter, as part of George W. Bush's Project for a 'New American Century' (see, e.g., National Defence University 2000). While the doctrine focussed upon US military predominance, it complemented the US state's objectives of achieving what Peter

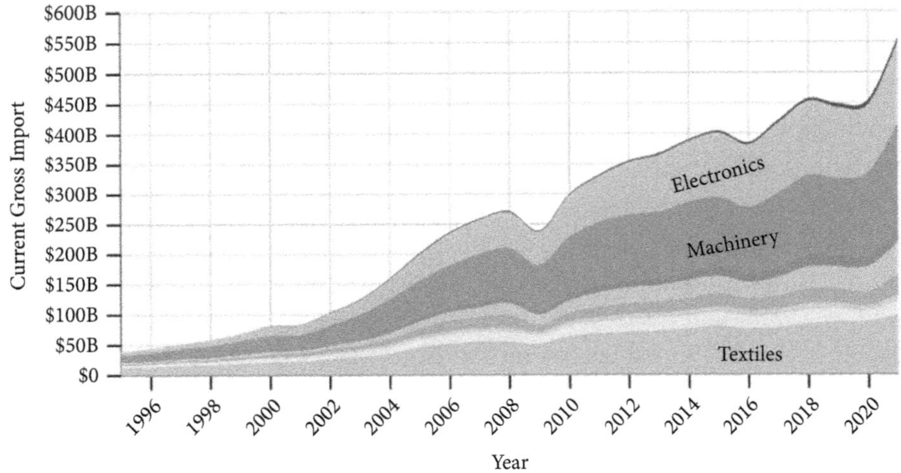

Figure 5.2 US goods imports from China, by industry, in USD billions, 1995–2021

Source: The Growth Lab at Harvard University. The Atlas of Economic Complexity. http://www.atlas.cid.harvard.edu.

Gowan (1999) labelled 'World Dominance' in the economy and through international institutions (see Section 5.3). Part of the US's attempts to maintain its global pre-eminence—its position in the imperialist chain—involves facilitating the continued expansion of CVCs and the associated ability of key sections of the US capitalist class to control resources, trade routes, and key means of production beyond its borders.

Such relations and structures do not change easily. At the same time, however, nothing in global capitalism is static. China's growth was long based on the position of Chinese firms within CVCs as ultra-cheap outsourcing locations for US and other firms and as cheap producers of wage goods for export to Western capitalist countries (see Figure 5.2). The former would boost US corporations' profits and the latter would provide material concessions to US workers, partially compensating for their stagnant wages. In this vein, President Bill Clinton claimed that China's accession to the WTO was an 'opportunity that comes along once in a generation' (Jefferies 2021, 300). More recently, however, Chinese firms have started to compete directly with US-firms in high-tech militarily strategic CVCs (see Section 5.4).

Disciplining Domestic Labour

Offshoring—a key mechanism of establishing CVCs—had a dual element: (1) enabling emerging lead firms to access cheap labour power abroad, while

(2) weakening US labour. Both aspects were carried out with support from the US state. One of the defining features of the US domestic political economy since the 1980s has been a fierce class-struggle from above—by capital against labour. The 1970s profitability crisis and political upheavals increasingly panicked large sections of the US ruling class (Harvey 2005a). The state, together with elite intellectuals, supported capital in a long-term restructuring of class relations, seeking to establish neoliberal social relations—what Adolph Reed terms 'capitalism without a working-class opposition' (Reed 2014, 67).

Restructuring class power entailed restoring profitability to capital and increasing workers' reliance upon market-based forms of social reproduction. Trade unions were beaten back—exemplified by the Reagan government's breaking of the Professional Air Traffic Controllers Organization (PATCO) strike in 1981—discouraging them from mobilizing their members. In 1999, an IMF report on the US economy observed how non-wage benefits—from healthcare to unemployment payments—fell throughout the 1980s, as did labour's share of national income (IMF 1999). Indebtedness skyrocketed—with household debt tripling between 1980 and 2005 (Harvey 2010, n.p.). These regressive social dynamics have continued. For example, between 1979 and 2021 productivity in the United States rose by 64.6 per cent while hourly pay only increased by 17.3 per cent. That is, productivity has grown 3.7 times as much as pay (see Figure 5.3)—an example of how, under capitalism, the development of (core) technologies that raise productivity serves the interests of capital, above all.

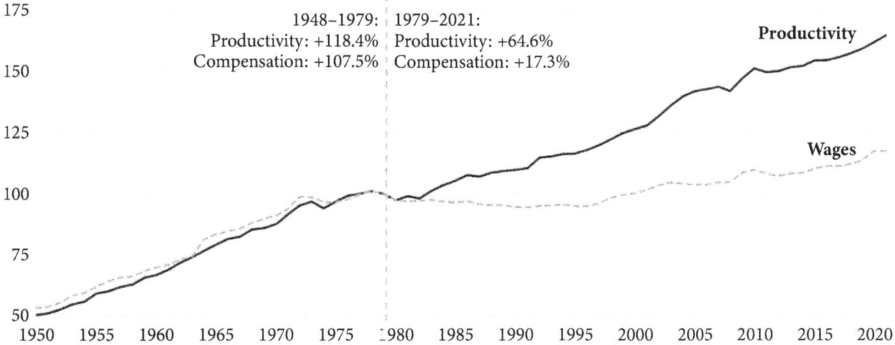

Figure 5.3 US productivity growth versus private-sector wages (Index, 1979 = 100)

Data source: Economic Policy Institute (2022, n.p.).

Workers were effectively forced to respond to these heightened pressures by working longer hours. Between 1983 and 1997 mothers in married families increased their number of annual wage working hours by 223 hours (six weeks) and fathers by 158 hours (four weeks) (Harman 2001). Stephen Roach (1996, n.p.), then chief economist of Morgan Stanley, wrote at the time how:

> The American restructuring model has three attributes: massive headcount reductions, real wage compression, and outsized currency depreciation that took the value of the dollar down 50 percent from the early 1985 highs. And the US system of flexible labour is the glue that holds the whole thing together.

The US state's leadership in weakening (flexibilizing) US labour in relation to capital provided much of the social bedrock upon and through which emergent lead firms would rise. Strengthened—institutionally, through rising profits, and facing decreasingly effective opposition from labour—sections of US capital could seek out ever-more ambitious strategies for establishing US and world markets in their own image.

5.3 Institutionalizing CVCs

If US high-tech firms benefitted from combinations of state largesse and strategic guidance, they were aided further by the establishment of the WTO. As mentioned above and in Chapter 1, CVCs emerged as major firms sought out novel accumulation strategies in response to the crisis of profitability in the 1970s. Such strategies were institutionalized through private property rights for capital, public policies supporting global capital mobility through trade and investment, and fiscal and monetary policies that favour international as opposed to domestic capital (see Gill 1998; Cammack 2006). These rights were reinforced further by the establishment of the WTO, and its rules that enhanced the power of lead firms in relation to national states. In fact, some US lead firms lobbied directly for WTO agreements that would favour them (see below). In important respects, the WTO projected globally the interests of US lead firms (Gowan 1999).

Since its formation in 1948, the General Agreement on Tariffs and Trade (GATT) sought to lower barriers to trade worldwide. By the time of the Uruguay Round, which led to the establishment of the WTO in 1995, not only had the numbers of countries subscribing to GATT increased (from 23 at its origin, reaching 123 by 1994), but so too had its remit. From a focus on shallow integration—reducing 'at the border' trade barriers (such as tariffs)—the WTO shifted towards deeper integration, entailing more rigorous rules governing production behind states' borders (Shadlen 2005a).

Promoters of the WTO presented it as a new 'grand bargain' between so-called developed and 'emerging' economies—where the former would reduce trade barriers to the latter, while the latter would increasingly harmonize their industrial policies in accordance with regulations formulated by advanced countries to facilitate greater foreign investment. By effectively constraining the industrial policy space of countries lower down in the imperialist chain, WTO agreements contributed to persuading policymakers in these countries to subordinate previously nationally owned firms to lead firms' accumulation strategies: to move away from establishing entire industries oriented at domestic supply to facilitate, instead, component production for CVCs. Such policies facilitate lead firm strategies of cost-reduction through giving them access to an expanding world of suppliers, the latter competing amongst themselves by employing cheap labour power.

WTO agreements augment lead-firm power in various ways. As Robert Wade puts it, two of its key agreements, TRIMS (Trade Related Investment Measures) and GATS (General Agreement on Trade in Services), 'limit the authority of developing country governments to constrain the choices of companies operating in their territory'. The WTO's third core agreement, TRIPS (Trade-Related Aspects of Intellectual Property Rights), 'requires the governments to enforce rigorous property rights of foreign (generally Western) firms' (Wade 2003, 621). However, the rise of lead firms in China joining the WTO demonstrates that domestic capital is not *necessarily* suppressed by WTO agreements (see below).

Lead firm's control over CVCs is enhanced by the commodification and privatization of knowledge. The WTO's TRIPS agreement was lobbied for by lead firms such as Merck, Microsoft, Pfizer, and IBM. The agreement enabled these and other lead firms to increasingly monopolize core technologies, ideas, and knowledge required for production itself (Drahos 1995, 2003; Drahos and Braithwaite 2017). International payments of royalties and licensing fees for the use of intellectual property amounted to approximately $300 billion in 2014, a ten-fold increase over 1990. The biggest patent holders are US, European, and Japanese firms, which account for 82.5 per cent of patents registered at the world's three major patent offices (Standing 2017, 57, 62).

WTO membership reduces countries' abilities to apply and provide economy-wide tariffs or subsidies while providing leeway for targeted industrial policies. Linda Weiss (2005) characterizes the organization as an upgrading club for advanced capitalist countries. It effectively reduces the capacity of countries lower down in the imperialist chain to deploy infant industry protection strategies—which could entail restrictions upon foreign capital—associated with prior successful late development strategies. Simultaneously it facilitates governments' support for their own fledgling industries higher up the imperialist chain (see Henderson et al. 2002; Sell 2003).

The WTO does not do away with policy space and industrial policy per se, but reforms it—making export subsidies and blanket economy-wide protection more difficult for countries lower down the imperialist chain (see Amsden 2005), and increasing the costs of technological transfer, as noted by Wade (2003) above.

WTO agreements act as a ratchet effect, pushing increasing numbers of countries to reduce nationally orientated industrial policy in favour of lead firm-driven global integration. This was furthered through the use by leading capitalist states of regional and bi-lateral investment agreements and treaties. Regional agreements proliferated throughout the 1990s and 2000s (Figure 5.4). For the United States, the 1994 North American Free Trade Agreement (NAFTA) and the 2006 Central American Free Trade Agreement (CAFTA) complemented 20 bi-lateral Free Trade Agreements (FTAs). The EU, whilst expanding eastwards, also negotiated 30 FTAs, and Japan

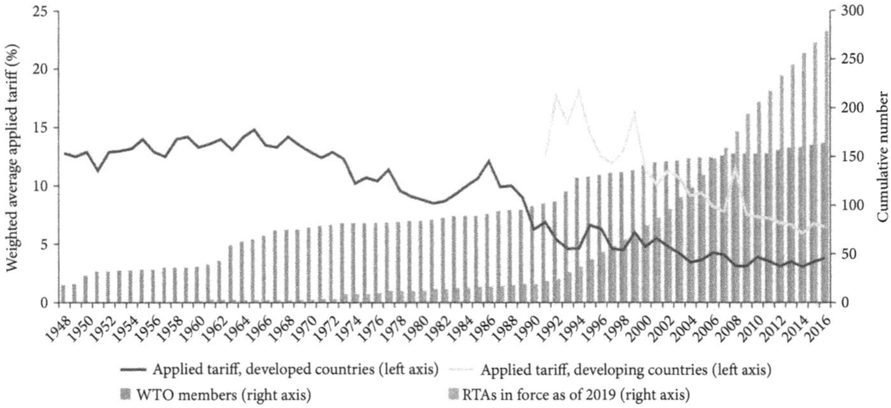

Figure 5.4 Number and average tariffs, developed and developing countries, 1948–2016

Source: World Bank. 2020. 'World Development Report 2020: Trading for Development in the Age of Global Value Chains'. Overview booklet. World Bank, Washington, DC. Licence: Creative Commons Attribution CC BY 3.0 IGO.

agreed 14 (Mayer and Phillips 2017, 139). The US and EU have also pursued bi-lateral investment treaties (BITs)—the former agreeing 40 and the latter 52 by 2017 (ibid.). These often entail even stricter limitations on the scope of peripheral countries to pursue industrial policies in exchange for deeper integration into the core economies (Gruber 2001; Shadlen 2005a, 2005b).

Whilst FTAs and BIT's lower trade barriers, they have neither eliminated nor sought to eliminate them. Rather, FTAs and BITs represent the geopolitical management of trade. Wallerstein's (2011b) observation that free trade imperialism is an enduring characteristic of historical capitalism is apt here (see Chapter 2). Rules of origin and local content requirements specify the quantity of a good that must be produced in a single country for firms producing it to enjoy the benefits arising from trade agreements. Such rules generate tendencies towards regional-based concentration and centralization favouring already-dominant firms. In addition, countries at the top of the imperialist chain include tariff escalation policies in many of their trade agreements—where they apply low or zero tariffs for primary goods (such as raw materials and agricultural goods), but the tariffs then rise as the product involves increased processing (for example, from soybeans to biofuels) (Mayer and Phillips 2017, 139f.; see Elsby 2020).

Crucially, global, regional, and bi-lateral trade agreements have minimal real concern for the protection of environmental and labour standards, enabling labour power and nature to be more easily accessed for exploitation through international class relations (and see Chapter 10).

As already noted however, while it limits economy-wide industrial policies that were used historically to diversify industrial production, the WTO *does* permit state investments and subsidies for research and development, regional development, and 'environmentalism' (Amsden 2005, 221). This is especially important when considering China's rise. In the early days of China's ascension to the organization, in its endeavours to modernize its science and technology base, it 'combined science parks and national R&D projects, tax breaks and subsidized credit' (Amsden 2005, 221).

Contemporary complaints, principally from Washington, that China is 'distorting' markets by state-intervention, represent historically myopic and politically bad-faith misinterpretations of China's industrial policy—as if vested-interest-policies were not previously, and are not currently, deployed by the US state and its allies. As two free-trade proponents note: 'China does not violate WTO rules more than any other WTO member. And when it is told by WTO judges that it has violated international rules, it takes appropriate measures to correct its domestic rules' (Mavroidis and Sapir 2021, viii). The reason for disquiet in Washington is that China's industrial policies have contributed to establishing high-tech leading industries that are beginning to compete directly with US CVC lead firms, with potentially significant future economic and military consequences (see Section 5.4).

5.4 China: From CVC Workshop to 'Challenger'?

'Cheap labour' power and 'Labour repression', wrote Alice Amsden, are the 'basis of late industrialization everywhere'. However, she also noted how '[d]evelopmental differences among late industrializers are best explained in terms of the discipline imposed on big business, not labour' (Amsden 1990, 18). This observation is also true in present-day China. This section shows how, from the outset of the reform period in the late 1970s, the Chinese state directed investments into industry and fashioned the largest working class in world history. These moves underpinned China's position, first as CVC workshop, and more recently as potentially challenger to some US CVC firms.

The Chinese state has distinguished itself compared to prior 'developmental' states. The latter—from Post WW2 Japan to the East Asian 'Tigers' between the 1960s and 1980s—had it quite easy, operating under the relatively generous GATT system and with significant US largesse. China, by contrast, has pursued its industrial policy under and through the relatively more stringent WTO where lead firms are empowered vis-à-vis states by the organization's rules (Wade 2003). Under these circumstances the Chinese state has formulated industrial policies to facilitate technological transfer and to stimulate innovation in increasingly high-tech CVCs. China's industrial policy success is in no small part an outcome of the state's innovative institutional arrangements. National (state and private) and multinational capital has been shoved and shaped towards investments that complement the state's longer-term objectives of technological development.

The extent to which China's industrialization underpins CVCs is indicated by one simple fact: that by the late 2010s 70 per cent of all products sold by Walmart, the leading US supermarket chain, and the largest corporation in the world by revenue, were sourced from China (Chan 2011, 4; Fortune 2024).

China's economy grew, on average, by 10 per cent per annum between the late 1970s and 2011. At market exchange rates, China's GDP overtook Germany's in 2007 and Japan's in 2009 (EIU 2015, 3, cited in Jenkins 2018, 13).

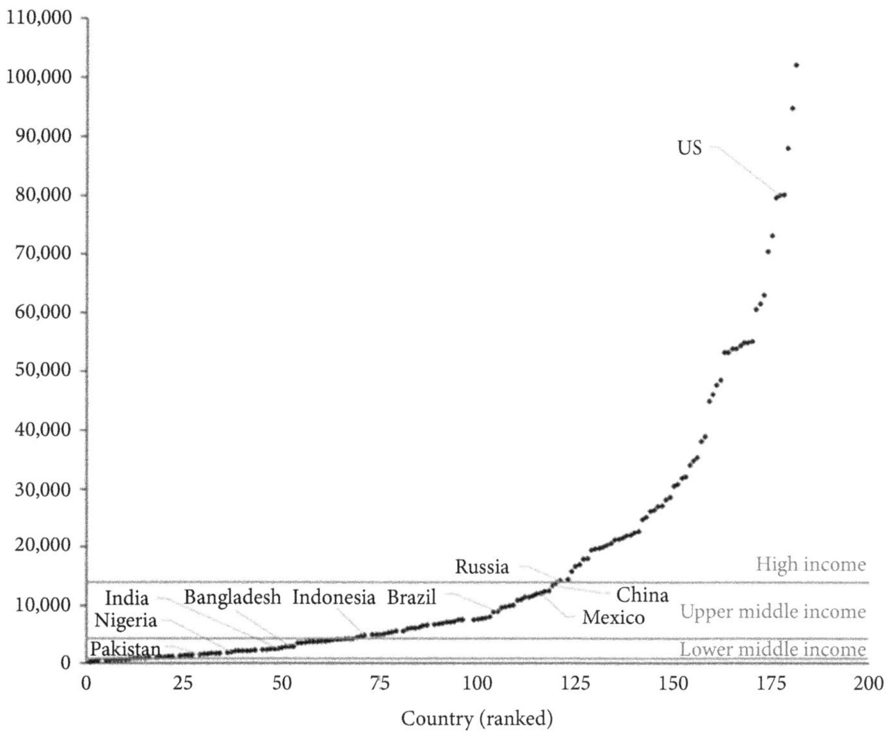

Figure 5.5 Countries' average income per capita in USD, 2023

Source: Data from World Bank (2024) 'World Development Indicators': GNI per capita, Atlas method, in current USD. Series code NY.GNP.PCAP.CD. Overlaid with World Bank country income categories. The ten most populous countries are labeled.

There was much hype in the 2010s about its immanent catch-up with the US economy. However, its growth rate slowed after 2014, and then flatlined in the early 2020s (Sharma 2022). Washington warns its allies about the dangers of China's rise: although in per capita terms, the income gap between the two countries is still sizeable (Figure 5.5), it is narrowing. More significantly, however, from the perspective of US strategic planners, China's technological upgrading is beginning to challenge some US CVC firms in the production of high tech means of production.

The following overview highlights key policy elements that have contributed to the transformation of Chinese firms within CVCs. From the outset Deng Xiaoping and other leaders of the Chinese state aimed to establish 'a country that would be producing cutting-edge technology' (Mavroidis and Sapir 2021, 90). This was brought about by a combination of purposeful state action, China's attractiveness as a global investment location, and fortuitous historical conjuncture (including political revolution and relative independence from US dominance). It benefitted from capital inflows from the ethnic Chinese community in the broader East Asian region (and later investments from the US and other countries), currency manipulations (in particular, the Plaza accords which increased the cost of export manufacturing in Japan and, indirectly, encouraged Japanese investment in China), and the broader neoliberal moment of capitalist globalization.

The Chinese State: Making Cheap Labour Power, Establishing the CVC Workshop

Over the last four decades, the Chinese state has, through CVC integration, generated a historically unique set of relations between itself, foreign and domestic capital, labour, and the world market (see, e.g., McNally 2012). In doing so, and in achieving rapid catch-up industrialization, the Chinese state has also altered the position of its firms in CVCs, and its position within the imperialist chain, much to the chagrin of Washington.

Over four decades into its reforms process, the Chinese state has successfully maintained its political economic guiding capacities by establishing a 'cadre-capitalist class' (So and Chu 2012) which 'use their prerogatives to create ties with ... foreign capital seeking access to China and Overseas Chinese; while private players team[ed] up with party cadres to thrive as businessmen' (van der Pijl 2012, 508).

The Chinese state used the attractiveness of its vast cheap labour force to engage lead firms in joint ventures with local firms obtaining 'technology on a scale unprecedented for a developing nation' (Shenkar 2005, 24), whilst maintaining a tight grip over, and direction of, investments (Naughton 2007).

These investments were channelled by the state into export-orientated economic sectors—starting with primary product manufactures but rapidly evolving towards high-tech manufactures that would become crucial to China's increasingly competitive position within CVCs (see below). Investments were guided by an evolving state policy, such as its 'dual track' system, where 'processing trade' (importing raw and other materials and components, processing, and re-exporting them) was incentivized over 'ordinary trade' (imports for consumption) (Jenkins 2018).

FDI was attracted to China's rural-to-urban migrant workforce. Rural-urban migration was stimulated by agrarian reforms that boosted agricultural productivity and increased the provision of basic foodstuffs to urban areas (Ye 2015). Deng began dismantling agricultural communes to 'free' rural labour (Rolf 2021, 100; see Hughes 1998; Aglietta and Bai 2014).

State industrial policy aimed to increase China's attractiveness to foreign investment, while establishing national firms that could compete in high-tech CVCs. In the late 1990s, under the state's strategy of 'grab the large, let go of the small' many State Owned Enterprises (SOEs) were privatized ('let go of the small'), generating over 50 million unemployed workers alone by 2000 (Naughton 2007). The remaining SOE's ('grab the large') occupied an increasingly strategic position in the evolution of China's CVC firms, effectively subsidizing the latter by providing them with cheap inputs. The Chinese state maintains control of enterprises in sectors such as mining and energy production and distribution, which are heavily reliant upon a minimum (and often below minimum) wage migrant labour force. This ownership structure 'subsidises the cost of Chinese manufacturing' contributing to the latter's low-cost competitive advantage (Bayari 2018, 4). The state specifies sectors in which FDI is prohibited, restricted or encouraged (OECD 2005, 82; Breslin 2010).

The United States eased this process by lowering tariffs for Chinese manufactured exports. As the US state facilitated a shift in its domestic economy towards high-tech CVC nodes such as research and development 'knowledge', and professional services, it relied increasingly on importing cheap manufactured goods from China which were often produced under the control of, or for, Western firms (Rolf 2021, 105).

Cheap Labour Power and Labour Repression

China's transformation—from the workshop of CVCs to a challenger to some US firms in high-tech CVCs—has been based upon a profound 'transformation of the context in which its workers find, experience and are remunerated for their labour' (Cantin and Taylor 2008, 52). It is a commonplace that the country possesses vast quantities of cheap labour power. It is less common to hear about how such enormous numbers of hard-working labourers were made available for CVC firms. The notion of the labour regime, discussed in Chapter 2, suggests the importance of explaining how workers are made available, recruited, mobilized, and disciplined in production.

The lynchpin of China's rise is its *hukou* system—roughly translated as household registration system. It is a circular migrant-labour regime which manages the 'largest migration in world history' (Walker and Buck 2007, 39). While the hukou existed in ancient China—as a form of family registration system—its current form originates with the formation of the People's Republic of China. It has been deployed by the Chinese state as part of its development strategy in general, and to provide millions of workers for CVC industries in particular. By 2023 there were approximately 297 million migrant workers[1] and the UN estimates that by 2050 another 292 million rural dwellers will have moved to cities (UN 2014, 12).

Every Chinese citizen must be registered at birth with the local hukou police to qualify for and receive their personal identity, which includes the key categories of non-agricultural (urban) or agricultural (rural). Government authorization is required to change hukou location permanently and hukou category from rural to urban (Wang 2010). Pervasive policing enables the state to effectively shift labour from one region or sector to another at relatively short notice. For example, following the 2008 global financial crisis, approximately 27 million migrant workers lost their urban-based jobs and were forced back to the countryside (Wang 2010).

It is widely argued that China's integration into CVCs 'has provided jobs for large numbers of low-skilled workers, helping drive economic growth and reducing poverty' (Dollar 2019, n.p.). Arguments that poverty in China has fallen are, for the most part, based upon the World Bank poverty line (IPL). As noted in this book's introduction, however, this measure does not indicate whether such levels of consumption meet their basic needs (Pogge and Reddy 2006; Selwyn 2017). More recent evidence suggests that the state's commodification and marketization of increasing elements of social life increased the numbers of the Chinese population unable to afford their basic needs (see below). This made available to CVC firms hundreds of millions of workers who could be subject to immiserating exploitation (see Chapter 7).

In pre-reform China, the costs of basic needs were much lower than in contemporary China. Jean Drèze and Amartya Sen describe the limited degree of marketization of subsistence requirements in the pre-reform period:

> The network of health services introduced in post-revolutionary China in a radical departure from the past—involving cooperative medical systems, commune clinics, barefoot doctors, and widespread public health measures—has been remarkably extensive. . . . Similar [considerations] hold in the distribution of food through public channels and rationing systems.
>
> **(Drèze and Sen 1989, 209)**

In addition to health provision, the state also controlled prices to maintain low-cost subsistence provision to the mass of the population. As Sullivan et al. note, the 'share of retail prices set or guided by the state declined from close

[1] https://www.statista.com/topics/1540/migrant-workers-in-china/, accessed 15 October 2024.

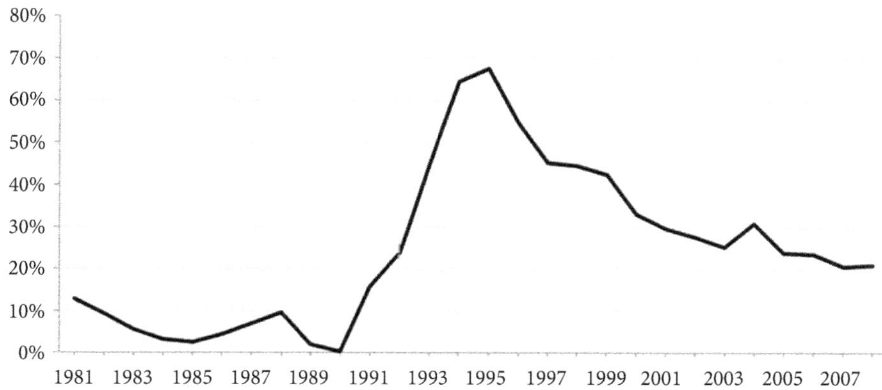

Figure 5.6 China, share of population unable to afford subsistence basket, 1981–2008
Source: Data from: Moatsos (2021) and Sullivan et al. (2024).

to 100 per cent in 1980, to a nadir of 10 per cent around 1993' (Sullivan et al. 2024, 4). The reform period downgraded the state-organized welfare state (of the iron and clay rice bowls). This increased the populations' market-dependency and their costs of meeting subsistence.

The share of the population unable to purchase a subsistence basket rose during the early 1990s, peaked in the mid-1990s, and declined thereafter (see Figure 5.6). However, even as its declined, it did not fall to the relatively low levels of the 1980s. The fall in numbers in poverty from the mid-1990s onwards was achieved by workers increasing their labouring hours (see Figure 5.7). It also reflected the effects of mass struggles by workers to improve their pay and conditions (see below). The huge numbers of workers ready to labour for extremely long hours underpinned China's rapid expansion.

The institutionalization of long working hours, driven by below subsistence pay has been documented in China's electronics factories, for example:

> The wage and employment system is designed to extract extensive overtime work. The base wage, usually near the local legal minimum wage, is low and provides not more than 50% of workers' regular incomes. Workers achieve the larger part of their wages through extensive overtime work and bonuses for personal performance and disciplined behaviour. Workers are housed in factory dormitories and eat in canteens, usually at very low cost or free. The dormitory regime has become the hallmark of this system; it plays a central role in maintaining social control and stability in the factories.
>
> **(Lüthje and Butollo 2017, 224)**

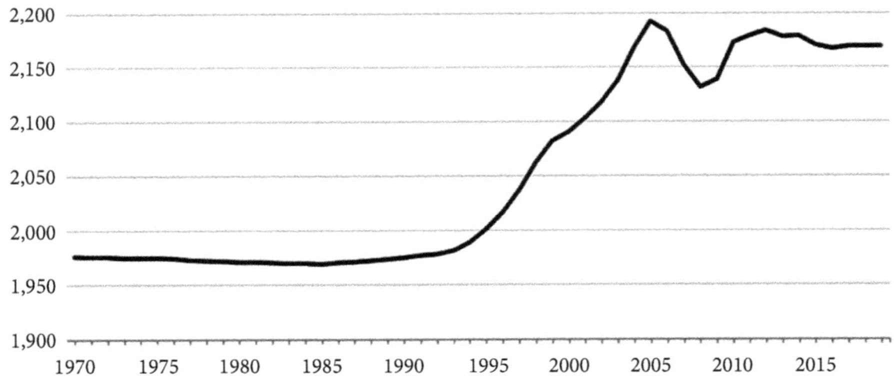

Figure 5.7 Annual working hours per worker, China, 1970–2019

Source: Data from Penn World Table version 10.0, see: Feenstra et al. (2015), available for download at https://www.rug.nl/ggdc/productivity/pwt/pwt-releases/pwt100.

Hours are also very long in China's high-tech sector, into which the state has channelled high levels of investment. Some of China's high-tech firms are now competing directly with US lead firms in CVCs (Li 2023).

From Workshop to Challenger

Prior to and priming its accession to the WTO in 2001, China's state industrial policies included (a) compulsory technology transfer requirements imposed on large foreign investors; (b) a company law (1994) that enabled SOEs to retain profits while the state maintained ultimate control; and (c) direct financial support from a newly established state-supported banking sector (Nolan 2001). Such policies were part of a broader strategy described by Steven Rolf as an ability to insulate 'frontier industries such as digital technologies from integration with the predominant US multinationals' (Rolf 2023, 132). Through such measures the Chinese state impelled domestic firms to adopt and innovate core technologies.

While WTO rules effectively outlawed blanket industrial subsidies to exports and reduced protective tariffs (Gallagher 2005), it permitted state investments and subsidies for research and development, regional development, and environmentalism. Following its entry into the WTO, Alice Amsden noted how:

> The State Planning Commission [rolled out a policy of building] approximately one hundred national key laboratories (analogous to corporate central R&D

> laboratories) in selected field [sic] of basic science in which Chinese capabilities already excelled. 'S&T' [Science and Technology] enterprises were spun off by city, provincial or national governments to commercialise the knowledge of public labs.
>
> **(Amsden 2005, 229)**

The Chinese state guided university and research institutions to focus on technological development and its transfer to (potentially) leading tech firms (Xiwei and Xiangdong 2007). Recently, in its attempts to increase R&D investments, the Chinese state cut corporation income tax (from 25 per cent to 15 per cent) for firms that classify as High and New Technology Enterprises. Such firms must be Chinese-registered and own the intellectual property of their core technology, which itself must be classified by the state as strategic (Hopewell 2020; Zhou 2023).

As part of its acceleration of high-tech investment, innovation, and production, the Chinese state and leading tech firms such as Baidu (Artificial Intelligence), Alibaba (cloud computing and digital media), and Tencent (Video Streaming) established joint labs for research and development (Lucas 2018).

China's rapid high-tech industrial development, which includes Chinese firms operating in CVC links producing state of the art means of production, and its increasing challenge to Western firms, is exemplified by the rise of Huawei. Established in 1987, by 2012 it had overtaken Ericsson to become the world's biggest telecommunications equipment manufacturer, and in 2018 it overtook Apple to become the second largest smartphone producer in the world (Wen 2020). Huawei's rise is, increasingly, predicated upon collaboration with state-backed companies such as Semiconductor Manufacturing International Corporation (SMIC), which is producing near cutting-edge computer chips (Liu 2023). While the technological gap between US and Chinese chip producers remains substantial, it is closing, and the Chinese state has created the political economic framework within which this became possible. For example, at the time of writing, SMIC is currently manufacturing chips using older-generation process technologies but is narrowing the gap to cutting-edge processes.

In Washington, the perceived consequences of China's technological advance are at least two-fold. First, if Chinese firms equal or better US chip manufacturers, it would begin to undercut US global military superiority as, according to the Washington-based thinktank *The Centre for Strategic and International Studies*, 'all major US defence systems and platforms rely on semiconductors' (Shivakumar and Wessner 2022, n.p.). Second, as Robyn Klingler-Vidra and Steven Hai (2024, n.p.) put it, 'Beijing's ascent to the technological frontier would mean an economic boom for China and bust for the US.'

In 2015, the governments 'Made in China 2025' policy specified that industries to receive strong governmental support include 'aerospace, bio tech, information technology, smart manufacturing, robotics manufacturing, advanced rail, electric vehicles, biomedicine, and pharmaceuticals' (Li 2023, 193). Central to these objectives are large-scale investments in space technology, Artificial Intelligence, and quantum computing. As Goswami (2023, n.p.) puts it:

> China will launch both an observer and an impactor spacecraft in 2025. While one spacecraft will study the asteroid, the other spacecraft will collide with the asteroid to deflect it. . . . Dual nature application is rather obvious; used for military purposes, the same technology can crash into satellites and 'deflect' them.

Under Xi Jinping military spending more than doubled between 2012 and 2021—stimulating and stimulated by developments in high-tech. It now has the largest military in Asia, although its defence budget is currently only one third of the United States' (Davidson 2022). The above-noted high-tech innovations, with potential military application, represent a step-too-far in China's technological development as far as US state planners are concerned (and see Chapter 6). This fast-moving situation may change again soon, and we do not attempt to predict the future of US–China relations.

In summary, from CVC workshop, Chinese firms have become a challenger to increasing numbers of US CVC firms. The story of China's rise includes the establishment of the largest working class in world history and its intense exploitation, the state elite's extraordinarily adept deployment of industrial policy, and rising geopolitical tensions as the country's firms became increasingly important players in high-tech CVCs.

The relative success of China's CVC integration means that over the last decade, increasing numbers of its CVC firms have begun challenging US CVC firms. This late-development success, however, represents a growing tension in the constitution of the US dominated imperialist chain. The United States, as noted, has responded by attempting to re-draw geopolitical relations (see also Chapter 6).

5.5 Conclusions

One of the defining characteristics of much mainstream GVC research is its firm-centrism—where large chunks of the international political economic system are conceived of as 'external' to, or merely as part of, the 'institutional environment' within which GVCs operate. This chapter, by contrast, focusses upon how states—in particular the United States and China—have established and guided CVC expansion.

Our class-relational conception of core technologies, informed by our comprehension of the imperialist chain, illuminates these dynamics. Following the USSR's launch of the Sputnik satellite in 1957, the US state responded by establishing a national system of innovation for dual use—military and commercial—technologies to secure its long-term position at the pinnacle of the imperialist chain.

Our notion of the imperialist chain denotes a hierarchical structure maintained by leading powers. It contains the conceptual space for understanding how China has pursued catch-up development and, in the process, has disrupted the organization of the chain. We show how following the beginning of its reform period from 1979 onwards the Chinese state forged a path—first of low-tech labour-intensive industrialization through integration into CVCs, and later of increasingly high-tech development—which, by the 2010s was concerning US state planners.

As we show in the following chapter, in response to China's relatively successful catch-up development, US state planners have sought to contain and to roll back China's technological rise. These developments occurred in a broader neoliberal historical moment, as the US state began rolling back prior socio-economic gains made by labour. The breaking of the wage-productivity link for increasing numbers of workers channelled ever-greater sums into the coffers of big firms. The dissolution of US labour's organizational power increased the capacity of firms to formulate and implement increasingly exploitative capital–labour relations.

US firms were emboldened and empowered by their state to pursue CVC-based globalization. They were enabled yet further militarily, and by the global institutions that it shaped, such as the WTO. However, the Chinese state—with its unique relationship to domestic and international capital—took full advantage of flexibilities in WTO rules. It used these, plus the attractiveness to international capitals of its vast, cheap, and disciplined labour force, to attract enormous volumes of FDI and to expedite a long-term programme of technology transfer and innovation.

China has evolved from the workshop of CVCs, via technological innovation, to become a challenger to increasing numbers of US high-tech CVC firms. But this is unsettling the US-dominated imperialist chain. While it constituted the workshop—particularly the mass production of cheap wage goods for an American working class experiencing long-term downward pressure on their pay packets—its development was consistent with US interests. However, as Chinese catch-up development became increasingly orientated towards breaking into and competing in high-tech CVC links, the US state has ramped up its geopolitical attempts to contain and even to reverse China's technological development (and see Chapter 6 on Resilience).

6

The Supply Chain Resilience Agenda

Unveiling Its Geopolitical and Class-Relational Dynamics

> The United States needs resilient, diverse, and secure supply chains to ensure our economic prosperity and national security.…
>
> **(Then US President Joseph Biden, cited in The White House 2021b, n.p.)**

6.1 Introduction

As the Covid-19 pandemic expanded across the world in early 2020, it generated the 'first global supply chain crisis' (Feltri 2020, n.p.) and the first 'great lockdown' (Gopinath 2020, n.p.). This event disrupted capitalist value chains (CVCs), and it was common to hear predictions, for example from the International Monetary Fund (IMF), that the 'global economy would suffer its worst blow since the 1930s' (Giles 2020, n.p.). In response, the notion of supply chain resilience gained widespread popularity. It has been defined by the World Trade Organisation (WTO) and Asian Development Bank (ADB) as 'the ability of these chains to anticipate and prepare for severe disruptions in a way that maximizes capacity to absorb shocks, adapt to new realities, and re-establish optimized operations in the shortest possible time' (Xing et al. 2021, 154).

While in debates about global value chains (GVCs) the notion of resilience emerged in the early 2000s—especially in response to the 2008 world economic crisis (see Ali et al. 2017 for a review)—it gained added impetus in the context of the Covid pandemic. In the popular literature it is often referred to as 'supply chain resilience' but in this chapter we use the terms GVC, CVC, and VC resilience as appropriate and in accordance with the rest of this book. The advocacy for GVC resilience has become increasingly widespread, and vocalized by the US state, as it deploys the notion as part of its broader geopolitical objectives of containing China's technological rise (see Chapter 5). The subject matter of this chapter—efforts to strengthen CVCs in the context of

Capitalist Value Chains. Benjamin Selwyn and Christin Bernhold, Oxford University Press.
 DOI: 10.1093/9780191994906.003.0006

crisis—follows previous chapters which dealt with the political economic and geopolitical frameworks in which CVCs were established. As with the previous chapters, our main focus is upon (a) a critique of mainstream GVC research and (b) US–China relations, without discounting the importance of other states, supranational institutions, and organizations.

In this chapter, we make four main points. First, the mainstream literature on GVC resilience ignores the class relations upon which, and through which, resilient supply chains are constructed. Second, while the literature offers its advice as representing the general interest of all CVC actors—it appears to be articulating the interest of a minority of well-resourced lead firms. Third, and consequently, it fails to discuss how the resilience agenda may increase lead firm control over supplier firms, and dynamics of concentration and centralization amongst lead firms. Fourth, and as indicated by then President Joseph Biden's quote at the head of this chapter, it underplays how the notion of supply chain resilience is being deployed geopolitically by the US state.

Following this introduction, Section 6.2 outlines the emerging notion of resilience as formulated within the mainstream GVC policy and academic community. Section 6.3 shows how many CVC firms have enhanced their resilience by increasing labour exploitation. Section 6.4 discusses how the notion of resilience relies upon digitalization, but occludes how digital technologies are being used to enhance capital accumulation (by heightening the rate of exploitation) and capital's power over labour. Section 6.5 argues that the mainstream resilience agenda fails to conceptualize lead firms' differential resources and capacities to implement resilience strategies, with the potential outcome of heightened monopolistic control by lead firms over suppliers. Section 6.6 identifies the geopolitical dynamics of resilience, focussing on the White House's (2021a) report *Building Resilient Supply Chains, Revitalizing American Manufacturing, and Fostering Broad-Based Growth.* Section 6.7 concludes.

6.2 Resilience in GVCs

The expansion of global trade through CVCs was at its most rapid in the near two decades between the collapse of the former Eastern bloc in 1991 and the 2008 crisis (Eichengreen 2024, see Chapter 5). At the time of writing there is some re-routing of trade and investment. For example, in the context of the US–China rivalry, the US state has introduced policies to encourage greater inward/domestic investment and so-called 'near' or 'friend' shoring,

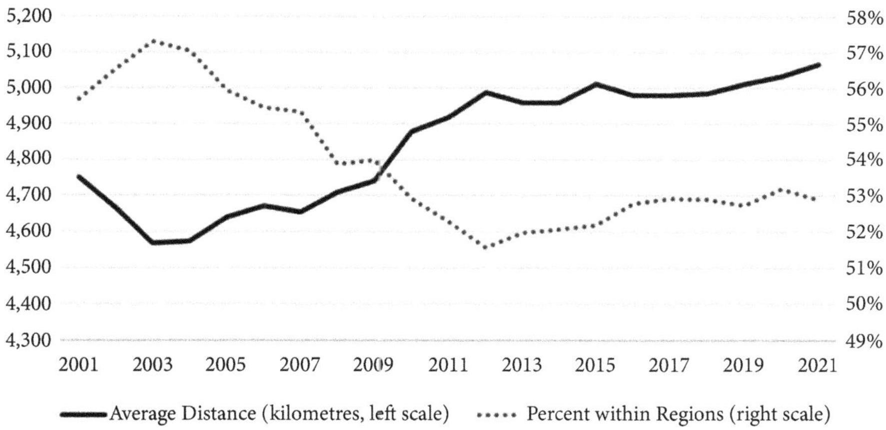

Figure 6.1 Average distance and regional concentration of world trade, 2011–2021
Data source: Altman and Bastian (2022, 67).

and some firms have rerouted investment away from China (Alfaro and Chor 2023). These shifts notwithstanding, global trade continues to expand (see Figures 4.1 and 6.1).

In this context, discussions of 'deglobalization' are premature. Instead, attempts are occurring by capitalist firms and leading imperialist states to maintain globalization, including through the continued expansion of CVCs, while containing China's technological rise. The notion of resilience, and relatedly 'friend' and 'near' shoring, are part and parcel of this containment agenda.

The GVC community's response to the Covid-19 pandemic has been to call for greater value chain resilience. As Gereffi et al. put it: 'At the firm level, resilience can be strengthened by enhancing the capabilities of lead firms, suppliers, and other partners through strategies that improve risk management, flexibility, and agility to respond to and recover from disruptions and vulnerabilities.' They also identify the importance of institutional support for such strategies: '[w]ith sophisticated firm-level capabilities and complex GVC configurations, more direct participation of the state is crucial in the quest for recovery' (Gereffi et al. 2022, 48, 61; see Xing et al. 2021).

A key vector of the debate about enhancing resilience revolves around the trade-off, or relationship between 'risk' and 'resilience'. The former is a consequence of just-in-time production (JIT), which was immensely profitable to firms during the expansion of CVCs via decreased inventory costs and increasing the flexibilization of employment. However, the benefits of JIT are potentially complicated or undermined by supply disruptions. JIT magnifies so-called bullwhip and ripple-effects—situations where small disturbances at one node in the CVC generate increasingly large disruptions further up or down the chain (see Selwyn 2008). As Peter Hasenkamp—former director of Tesla's supply chain strategy—noted: 'It takes 2500 parts to build a car, but only one not to' (cited in McGee and Edgecliffe-Johnson 2020, n.p.).

In response to heightened risks, firms are advised to increase their supply chain resilience by introducing:

- New production processes—which enable easier replacement of standardized inputs and the establishment of buffer stocks;
- New forms of chain governance—through risk analysis of places and suppliers; and
- Resilience monitoring—by assessing recovery time required by suppliers in response to shocks in the chain (Miroudot 2020, 124).

Multilateral agencies and consultancies have operationalized these concepts into specific recommendations for CVC managers. This is captured in a two-pronged strategy outlined in a World Bank publication by Qiang et al. (2021). On the one hand, the deployment of new technologies will be essential:

> Plant shutdowns and the consequent labour shortages have rippled through industries from food processing to automotive manufacturing. Firms are increasingly looking to robotics to augment locked-down employees, support health and safety measures, and tap into new opportunities or salvage their operations.
>
> **(Qiang et al. 2021, 201)**

On the other hand, new dynamics of outsourcing are posited as enabling cost-efficiencies.

> By geographically broadening their supplier bases, MNCs are more likely to cut production costs by offering more competitive wages at the local level and more likely to better serve local customers by tailoring products to their demands.
>
> **(Qiang et al. 2021, 204)**

In a widely cited report, the McKinsey Global Institute (McKinsey 2020b) provides a generic list of actions that firms can undertake to enhance resilience. These include strengthening risk-management, reshoring production, reducing product complexity, building capacity to flexibilize production across myriad sites, improving supply chain transparency, and building redundancy into the supply chains (by, for example, using multiple suppliers for each part, maintaining low-capacity utilization and holding extra inventory). At the high point of the Covid pandemic, in mid-2020, a McKinsey survey of CVC executives across different industries found that 93 per cent aimed to enhance their supply chain resilience, and that 90 per cent aimed to increase the use of in-house digital technologies to do so (McKinsey 2020a, n.p.).

In addition, CVC mapping is increasingly posited as a necessary strategy for lead firms. A *Harvard Business Review* article highlights how it 'entails going far beyond the first and second tiers and mapping your full supply chain, including distribution facilities and transportation hubs', to identify suppliers' capacity to withstand shocks (Shih 2020, n.p.). Intrinsic to notions of supply-chain mapping is enhanced surveillance by lead firms over supplier firms, as an additional aspect of lead-firm governance strategies. Even mainstream global supply chain commentators note how such dynamics may generate 'a rather paradoxical co-evolution of surveillance and collaboration wherein companies will be more watchful of their suppliers' actions and capabilities while collaborating with them to strengthen their capabilities' (Panwar et al. 2022, 14). As Sébastien Miroudot notes:

> Large multinational enterprises (MNEs) develop 'control towers' and information systems that give accurate real-time information on production networks, and these tools allow for an efficient management of risks, independent of production and length of supply chains.
>
> **(Miroudot 2020, 123)**

In short, then, the mainstream notion of resilience implies cheapening wages, flexibilizing employment, and deploying new technologies in novel geographic settings to enhance firm-level competitiveness (including heightened lead firm surveillance of suppliers).

6.3 CVC Resilience—through Class Struggle from Above

During the Covid pandemic it was reported widely that corporations were using the crisis to 'restructure' employment relations at the expense of workers (Wall 2021). These observations, however, are absent from the mainstream resilience literature. This is noteworthy since the first response to the pandemic and to lockdowns by many firms and states was to seek ways in which to increase labour exploitation in key CVCs. They did so through handing state (public) subsidies to big corporations while presiding over dangerous conditions, wage suppression, or deployment of heightened degrees of coercion in the wage–labour contract. What looks like supply chain resilience to lead firms may well look like the establishment or deepening of immiserating growth regimes to workers (see chapter 7).

At the height of the pandemic in April 2020, US and UK governments (among other countries) pushed through legislation forcing workers in some industries to labour in unsafe working conditions. For example, then US president Donald Trump deployed the Defense Protection Act to enable meat processing companies to stay open amid fears of shortages. The act, supported by Tyson—the US's largest meat processing company—reduced companies' liability to their workers for remaining open and potentially exposing the latter to the Covid-19 virus during the pandemic (Sevastopulo et al. 2020). In the UK, thousands of Eastern European migrant workers were flown in on charter flights to work in the fruit and vegetable sector under the 'Pick for Britain' scheme. In a legalized contravention of the then society-wide social-distancing rules, they were housed, up to four per room, in temporary accommodation (Salyga 2020).

The pandemic illuminated myriad cases of how CVC firms deployed outright wage suppression, heightened degrees of labour coercion and presided over dangerous conditions to maintain their operations. For example, a study of garment workers in Ethiopia, Honduras, India, and Myanmar found sharp declines in working conditions and an 11 per cent average decline in pay. Income loss occurred due to 'less opportunity for overtime; not being paid the appropriate overtime rate; unfair deductions from wages; unpaid work; late wages; severance pay theft for workers who have been terminated; and unpaid wages for workers who have been temporarily suspended' (LeBaron et al. 2021, 21). In Bangladesh over a million workers were fired or furloughed by mid-2020 as buyers cancelled orders and refused to compensate suppliers (Anner 2020, 2). According to the Clean Clothes Campaign (2020b), garment workers globally had lost approximately $6 billion in unpaid wages by mid-2020.

The provinces of Bac Ninh and Bac Giang, located east of Hanoi, are the centre of Samsung's operations in northern Vietnam. In early 2020, in the early days of the pandemic, Vietnamese electronics exports boomed as the country appeared to have implemented successfully a zero-Covid strategy. However, by May 2020 cases began to spike, and worryingly for the government and for exporters, to cluster in industrial districts. In response, the government told manufacturers to either shut down operations, or find ways of maintaining them by isolating workers from the wider population. Samsung Vietnam formulated a 'three-on-site' containment policy, where workers worked, ate, and slept in the same area. Lam Le reported what this arrangement meant for a worker called 'Nam':

> [Workers] were moved onto the factory's premises. The lines between their workplace and home evaporated. For nearly three weeks, Nam slept with a blanket on a mattress in a warehouse alongside around 100 other male colleagues, moving between there, the company canteen and the production line in what felt like a twilight of unending work. His life revolved around screens.
>
> **(Le 2021, n.p.)**

Supplier firms used compulsory redundancies to attack trade unionists and workers they considered less productive. As a Bangladeshi worker producing for H&M testified to the Clean Clothes Campaign:

> The factory management is very hostile to its workers. Last year, they sacked more than 500 workers in the name of order cancellations. However, most of the sacked workers were elderly like me and were involved with a workers' union.
>
> **(Clean Clothes Campaign 2021, 23)**

Some companies responded to the skyrocketing demand for personal protective equipment (PPE) during the pandemic by forcing workers to labour. Malaysia and China were two important locations of PPE production, both presiding over increased incidences of what the US Bureau of International Labour Affairs calls forced labour, entailing practices such as debt-bondage. The majority of the almost two billion examination gloves used across (mostly core states) during the first six months of the pandemic were sourced from Malaysia. According to the bureau:

> Forced labour predominately occurs among migrant laborers from Bangladesh, India, Myanmar, and Nepal working in more than 100 rubber glove factories throughout Malaysia. Reports indicate that there are an estimated 42,500 migrant workers employed in the Malaysian rubber glove industry. Workers are frequently subject to high recruitment fees to secure employment that often keeps them in debt bondage; forced to work overtime in excess of the time allowed by Malaysian law; and work in factories where temperatures can reach dangerous levels. Additionally, laborers work under the threat of penalties, which include

> the withholding of wages, restricted movement, and the withholding of their identification documents.
>
> (Bureau of International Labor Affairs 2024, n.p.; see also Hughes et al. 2023)

Lead and supplier firms have a common interest in increasing labour exploitation throughout their supply chains. However, the former used their overwhelming power to shift the burdens of the pandemic onto supplier firms, which in turn deployed strategies of enhanced labour exploitation. From cancelled orders that result in wage suppression and mass unemployment, to lead firms' structural power which compel suppliers to adopt novel strategies to maintain production—labour power is maintained as cheap and often expendable. These dynamics are empirically and conceptually absent from the mainstream GVC resilience literature.

6.4 Digitalization and Resilience

As we discussed in Chapter 2, capitalism is a technologically dynamic system. However, new technologies are deployed, overwhelmingly, for the purposes of increased capital accumulation rather than the betterment of workers' conditions. Much of the resilience agenda aims to accelerate and deepen these dynamics.

Common to all mainstream discussions of enhanced GVC resilience are the purported opportunities and imperatives of digital technology deployment, whether in 'smart factories', or through increasingly widespread 'remote work' (see below). As president of the European Central Bank (ECB) Christine Lagarde put it, '[g]reater use of digital technology makes it easier to better match jobs with skills across Europe—especially in the face of limited labour mobility' (ECB 2020, n.p.). While Lagarde notes the dangers of rising rates of unemployment generated by the uptake of digital technology, she portrays such technologies as representing an opportunity to foster sustainable growth across Europe (and by implication, across the world). She does not dwell upon the implications for employed workers' conditions (ECB 2020).

Digital technology provides new opportunities for capital to increase the rate of labour exploitation—by increasing work intensity and the amount of surplus value producing labour—while simultaneously countering labouring classes' attempts to resist such moves. Lead firms are investing heavily in robotization and automation to achieve these objectives. In the global warehouse sub-sector, for example, the automation market is projected to increase from $15bn in 2019 to $30bn by 2026 (O'Connor 2021). Amazon is at the forefront of these innovations that seek ever more to subordinate workers to machines. As Sarah O'Connor reports in the *Financial Times*:

> Chuck is an autonomous robot trolley which leads a human picker through a warehouse from one shelf to the next. 6 River Systems, which sells or rents the robots to warehouse operators such as DHL, XPO Logistics and Office Depot, says the technology relieves strain on workers because they no longer have to push a trolley around. But Chuck also sets a relentless pace... A 6 River Systems 'business case' report says workers who set their own pace 'travel only half as fast as when they follow Chuck [and] their speed without Chuck also fluctuates wildly'.
>
> **(O'Connor 2021, n.p.)**

As noted in Chapter 2, while technological development could be used to lighten workers' toil, when deployed to enhance capital accumulation it often has the reverse effect. In a survey of 145 workers at an automated Amazon warehouse on Staten Island, 66 per cent experienced physical pain while working (in their shoulders, hands, back, ankles and knees) and 42 per cent continued to experience pain outside work (Jabsky and Obernauer 2019). As Sarah O'Connor notes 'humans are being crunched into a robot system working at a robot pace' (O'Connor 2021, n.p.).

An element of the resilience agenda is capital's heightened surveillance in 'traditional' working environments such as factories, and in the so-called gig-economy. The number of digital labour platforms have increased five-fold since 2010 (ILO 2021). As lead firms intensively focussed upon their 'core competencies' they contracted out non-core activities, which are now increasingly undertaken by individualized workers employed through digital labour platforms (Scheiber 2015). Such platforms have facilitated remote working (often labelled 'cloud', 'crowd', or 'micro' work) for tasks such as translation, data collection, processing, image identification, audio and video transcription, transcription, annotation and content moderation (Srnicek 2017; Berg et al. 2018). Simon Joyce (2020) observes how the growth of the platform economy is based, in part, upon a huge expansion of piece-work payment systems. In Capital vol.1 Marx (1990, 697f.) described piece work as 'the form of wages most in harmony with the capitalist mode of production' because:

> it is naturally the personal interest of the labourer to strain his labour-power [exert maximum effort] as intensely as possible; this enables the capitalist to raise more

> easily the normal degree of intensity of labour. It is moreover now the personal interest of the labourer to lengthen the working-day, since with it his daily or weekly wages rise.
>
> **(Marx 1990, 695f.)**

As Joyce (2020, 548) notes, much of contemporary platform work is 'unadorned by any accretion of legal rights, management accountability or employment and social protection' and brings 'no additional benefits. No pension. No training or promotion ... No security. In some countries, not even health care.'

Remote work boomed during the covid pandemic, although it has partially been reversed since, as increased numbers of 'white-collar' workers began working from home. These workers are subject to so-called 'algorithmic management': 'continuous tracking of workers' performance, automated decision-making about tasks and evaluations of client feedback'—whilst undertaking a range of unpaid tasks that are essential to their jobs (Roberts 2022, 176). Antonio Aloisie and Valerio de Stefano note the proliferation of surveillance technology at the disposal of employers:

> *Activtrack* surveils the programs used and tells managers if the employee is distracted, wasting time on social media. *HubStaff* combines performance anxiety and control freaks, routinely taking snapshots of the personal computer screen every five minutes. *TimeDoctor* and *Teramind* keep track of every effort conducted online. *Interguard* compiles a minute-by-minute timeline that considers every data such as web history and bandwidth utilization and sends a notification to the managers in case workers pick up anything suspicious. It notifies when an employee completes a combination of flagged behaviours. *OccupEye* compulsively records when and for how long someone is away from their workstation.... *Sneek* continuously takes photos of colleagues to generate a timecard and circulates them to keep the team's mood up. *Afiniti* pairs customers with agents according to demographic data. *Pragli* synchronizes professional calendars and music playlists to create a sense of community; it also features a facial recognition feature that could display a worker's real-world emotion on their virtual avatar's face.
>
> **(Aloisi and Stefano 2022, 298)**

In the USA, the *Harvard Business Review* hinted at how digital technology has enhanced capital's power over labour, whilst generating dynamics of capital concentration:

> [T]he length of the average workday increased by 48.5 minutes during lockdown in the early weeks of the pandemic. In highly productive organizations, employees have capitalized on new technologies to stay connected with customers and co-workers during this time. We estimate that the best organizations have seen productive time increase by 5% or more.
>
> (Garton and Mankins 2020, n.p.)

In addition to enhanced surveillance possibilities for capital over labour, digitally-enabled remote work enhanced employers' power (Haynes 2021). It offloaded building maintenance, energy, and in some cases equipment costs, and it increased the number of hours worked. For example, in the UK during the covid pandemic, home-workers undertook almost double the amount of unpaid labour (six hours a week) than those who never work from home (3.6 hours) (Office for National Statistics 2021).

6.5 Intra-Capital Dynamics of Resilience

In a World Bank publication, Qiang et al. noted how the pandemic exacerbated capitalism's inner tendencies of monopolization:

> COVID-19 could cause a further rise in corporations' market power because large corporations are in the best position to withstand the economic downturn and deploy new technologies... In the past three recessions, the share prices of US firms in the top quartile across 10 sectors rose by an average of 6 percent whereas the share prices of those in the bottom quartile fell by 44 percent. The same divergence has been evident since the start of the COVID-19 outbreak.
>
> (Qiang et al. 2021, 202)

The power disparities between many giant lead firms and their suppliers means that the resilience agenda will likely enhance the power of the former over the latter.

On the surface, mapping value chains to improve the efficiency of inter-firm interactions and reduce risk makes sense for lead firms. It represents a ramping-up of their governance and surveillance capacity, increasing their panopticonic power over suppliers. However, it is easier said than done. A key dynamic that underpins CVCs—hyperspecialization in the context of capital accumulation and competition between firms—complicates the possibilities of risk-mapping as a comprehensive resilience strategy. Hyperspecialization has increased the scale and complexity of CVCs and, under these conditions, complex tacit knowledge is an ever-more important element in production. Consequently, it is jealously guarded by firms. The possibilities of sharing knowledge along chains are limited not just by the complexity of these chains, but also by capitalist private ownership of the means of production.

There is also a tension in the feasibility of lead firms conducting supply chain mapping exercises *and* undertaking *new rounds of supplier diversification*. Incorporating new suppliers promises to complicate existing supply chains, and renders risk-mapping as a general strategy somewhat myopic. As Elizabeth Braw writes in *Foreign Policy*:

> [N]o CEO actually knows his or her companies' complete supply chain ... suppliers are just the first tier of the supply chain. [They] have suppliers of their own, who may, in turn, even have a third layer of suppliers ... a multinational company such as Volkswagen has 5000 suppliers (the so-called tier-one suppliers), each with an average of some 250 tier-two suppliers. That means that the company actually has 1.25 million suppliers—the vast majority of whom it doesn't know.
>
> **(Braw 2020, n.p.)**

As Foster and Suwandi (2020, 552) note '[u]sually, the financial centers and procurement officers in corporations know their first-tier suppliers, but not their second-tier ... much less the third- or even fourth-tier suppliers'. Part of the reason for these limits to informational flows—even though chain governance is meant to reduce such transaction costs (see Chapter 3)—is that firms are unlikely to share this information with each other, as it is a key source of competitive advantage.

In practice, the costs and labour requirements to undertake value chain mapping and risk assessment are often prohibitively expensive. As Willy C. Shih (2020, n.p.) notes in the *Harvard Business Review*, '[e]xecutives of a Japanese semiconductor manufacturer told us that it took a team of 100 people more than a year to map the company's supply networks deep into the sub-tiers following the earthquake and tsunami in 2011'. (The fragmentation of CVCs through hyperspecialization is also often used by lead firms as an excuse for their limited ability to influence workers' pay and conditions at the supplier end.)

Two consequences flow from this fact. First, because risk-mapping is an expensive, complex and labour-intensive innovation to lead firms' governance strategies, it can only be successfully undertaken by a minority of well-resourced lead firms. Smaller, less-resourced CVC firms will not be able to undertake such risk-mapping exercises, or will do so less effectively. Second, such mapping requires, and generates, the attainment of more and better information by lead firms about their suppliers' activities. The concentration and ownership of information about activities by and within other firms is part and parcel of the emergence of intellectual monopolies (Pagano 2014; Rikap 2021). Practices imposed by lead firms upon their suppliers, such as requiring the latter to open their books (Miller 2013) are being used to augment lead firm power and to exert further control throughout the supply chain by, for example, determining from whom and at what prices suppliers source inputs, rather than, for example, to ensure better quality working conditions.

So, rather than supply chain mapping representing a general strategy for supply chain resilience, it is perhaps better interpreted as a particular strategy for highly concentrated lead firms to increase further their already unprecedented power over suppliers. To the extent that supply chain mapping becomes an increasing and exclusive core competence of a few lead firms, it is likely to exacerbate the continuing trend of concentration and centralization in CVCs.

In addition to supply chain mapping, advocates of GVC resilience recommend that, under certain circumstances, lead firms pursue strategic forms of re-shoring and localization (engendering a supplier base closer to, if not in the same country as, lead firms) in conjunction with the deployment of new technologies (Phillips et al. 2022). Even prior to the pandemic, and in response to rising wages in and geo-economic rivalry with China, these strategies were discussed widely by CVC managers. They were also part and parcel of Donald Trump's Make America Great Again promise—to bring back industries that had relocated production to China, Mexico, and other low-wage production zones. Implicit in his promise was that such firms' restarting of operations in the USA would entail the proliferation of good jobs and working conditions.

However, his agenda attracted few global firms (back) to the United States—unsurprisingly, given global wage differentials in which wages in China are still a fraction of US wages (Suwandi 2019). For example, in 2017 Trump hailed Foxxcon's plans to invest $10 billion in Wisconsin, generating 13,000 blue-collar jobs. By 2021, the Taiwanese electronics giant had reduced its investments to under $1 billion with fewer than 1500 expected new (mostly white-collar) jobs, blaming relatively high US labour costs (Shepardson and Pierog 2021). As the *Financial Times* noted, 'coronavirus-induced "reshoring" is not happening' (Beattie 2021).

In the mainstream GVC resilience literature, notions of re-shoring are often presented in abstract terms—where such dynamics could combine new technologies with 'domestic' workers to enhance competitiveness as compared, for example, to Chinese manufacturing based upon cheap labour power and less advanced technologies. So-called 'smart factories' are presented as representing such a pathway to reshoring, where digital technology and labour are integrated in novel ways (Kagermann et al. 2013). Smart factories are digitalized manufacturing facilities that use

> connected devices, machinery and production systems to continuously collect and share data. This data is then used to inform decisions to improve processes as well as address any issues that may arise.... Smart factories connect the digital and physical worlds in order to monitor an entire production process, from supply chain management to manufacturing tools and even the work of individual operators on the shop floor.
>
> **(TWI 2021, n.p.)**

However, the possibilities of reshoring and localization are often abstracted from the material reality of capitalist production—whether the costs and complexities of building smart factories and establishing supporting labour regimes, or of writing off the massive sunk costs of already-existing infrastructures in CVCs. For example, China's emergence as the workshop of the world after its 2001 WTO entry was preceded by more than two decades of infrastructure development and local capital formation.

Much of the reshoring narrative is based upon an assumption that firms (supported by states) in low-wage zones of the world economy will *not* pursue similar technological upgrading. However, as Florian Butollo (2021, 265) notes, 'it seems counter intuitive to suggest that a surge of automation would support tendencies towards reshoring given that catch-up automation in emerging economies could also have the effect of lowering unit labour costs of producers if productivity-enhancing automation equipment is deployed'. Indeed, China has 'become main buyer of automation equipment since 2013, with a share of 30% of sales in 2016'.

Even if re-shoring and the proliferation of smart-factories occurs, the consequences for labour cannot be assumed to be positive, as hinted at in Donald Trump's Make America Great Again politics. Rather than a re-shoring of many 'good jobs', it will very probably be accompanied by, on the one hand, a renewed mix of high-tech relatively good jobs for high-skilled workers, and on the other hand, an expansion of precarious low-wage employment (Butollo 2021).

6.6 Resilience as Geopolitics

The US state is deploying the notion of GVC resilience as part of its long-term strategy of containing China's rise through economic and geopolitical means, discussed in Chapter 5. This agenda includes encouraging firms to diversify away from excessive reliance upon Chinese production, often referred to as the 'plus one' strategy (Enderwick 2011; Roberts 2023).

US capitals benefit from access to the China's labour force. However, as noted in Chapter 5, China's state-managed integration into the world economy, first as an export-assembly platform but increasingly as a producer of high-tech products, has accelerated the formation of its capitalist class and strengthened the Chinese state. Together these dynamics are modifying US dominance in Asia and potentially beyond.

This began to worry US policymakers who, at least since then President Barack Obama's 'pivot to Asia', have formulated political, economic, and military strategies to contain China's rise (Foster 2021). This containment strategy represents an attempt to maintain China in what Minqui Li calls a semi-peripheral position in relation to the USA, by forestalling its attempts at becoming an economic and technological rival to the latter. As Li puts it,

> although China has developed an exploitative relationship with South Asia, Africa, and other raw material exporters, on the whole, [it] continues to transfer a greater amount of surplus value to the core countries in the capitalist world system than it receives from the periphery.
>
> **(Li 2021, n.p.)**

Maintaining this pattern of surplus value transfer and limiting China's regional influence is part and parcel of US containment strategy. While much US–China trade is complementary (Starrs 2014, 2019), the numbers of Chinese firms competing directly with US firms are growing. China's rise is interpreted increasingly in parts of the US state, policy and academic communities as representing a threat to US global dominance (Mirrlees 2024).

While many observers were greatly relieved by Joe Biden's victory over Donald Trump in the 2020 presidential election, in relation to China there was more continuity than change between these administrations. As John Mearsheimer notes, Biden 'embraced containment and has been as hard-nosed toward China as his predecessor was, pledging "extreme competition" with China shortly after taking office' (Mearsheimer 2021, 55). Following

Starrs' observations above, however, under Biden, such extreme competition was not meant to prevail over the mass-production and sale of cheap wage goods—where China leads the world and plays an important role in keeping down the cost of wage goods in the USA. It was meant to apply to high-tech sectors—such as microchips and digital technologies—which leading US policy makers fear may one day facilitate a military challenge by China to the USA (and see Chapter 5).

For example, early in his term then President Biden invoked the notion of resilience, arguing that:

> The United States needs resilient, diverse, and secure supply chains to ensure our economic prosperity and national security.... Resilient American supply chains will revitalize and rebuild domestic manufacturing capacity, maintain America's competitive edge in research and development, and create well-paying jobs. They will also support small businesses, promote prosperity, advance the fight against climate change, and encourage economic growth in communities of colour and economically distressed areas.
>
> **(The White House 2021b, n.p.)**

Four months later, The White House published its report entitled 'Building Resilient Supply Chains, Revitalizing American Manufacturing, and Fostering Broad-Based Growth' (The White House 2021a). The report expressed concern that the US economy was potentially vulnerable to supply chain shocks in four key industries—rare earth minerals for telecommunications and other core electronics sectors, semiconductors, active pharmaceutical ingredients and advanced batteries for large-scale utilities and electric vehicles—and proposed a range of measures to enhance supply chain resilience. It emphasizes how US vulnerability is exacerbated by China's direct control over, and/or access to, key resources.

The US Innovation and Competition bill—which had formerly been called the Endless Frontier Act—labelled China 'the greatest geopolitical and geo-economic challenge for United States foreign policy' (cited in Mearsheimer 2021, 55). It was integrated into the CHIPS and Science Act, passed by US Congress in summer 2022, committing around US$280 billion to fund research and development of semiconductors in the USA. As Robert Wade put it, the aim of these acts was 'to choke China's access to crucial technologies while limiting the reach of Chinese tech and telecommunications companies in foreign markets' (Wade 2023, 2).

In words that could have been uttered by Donald Trump, Biden argued that:

> The United States does need to get tough with China. If China has its way, it will keep robbing the United States and American companies of their technology and intellectual property. It will also keep using subsidies to give its state-owned enterprises an unfair advantage—and a leg up on dominating the technologies and industries of the future.
>
> **(Biden 2020, n.p.)**

Biden argued that, following the relative isolationism pursued by Trump, the United States must 'build a united front of U.S. allies and partners to confront China's abusive behaviors' (Biden 2020, n.p.). According to Gregory Allen, from the Centre for Strategic and International Studies in Washington, the Biden administration's objectives were of 'actively strangling large segments of the Chinese technology industry—strangling with an intent to kill' (Allen 2022, n.p.). Jake Sullivan, then President Biden's national security advisor, advocated a combination of engagement, competition with, and containment of, China. His notion of a 'small yard' with a 'high fence' implied that the United States will attempt to wall-off from China a small but strategic element of its domestic technological development:

> Our export controls will remain narrowly focused on technology that could tilt the military balance. We are simply ensuring that U.S. and allied technology is not used against us. We are not cutting off trade. In fact, the United States continues to have a very substantial trade and investment relationship with China. Bilateral trade between the United States and China set a new record last year [2022].
>
> **(Sullivan 2023)**

In the White House's 'Building resilient supply chains' report, China's rise was interpreted in strict geopolitical terms:

> China was estimated to control 55 percent of global rare earths mining capacity in 2020 and 85 percent of rare earths refining. The United States must secure reliable and sustainable supplies of critical minerals and metals to ensure resilience across U.S. manufacturing and defense needs.
>
> **(The White House 2021a, 9)**

The US state openly interprets value chain resilience in geopolitical terms:

> [T]he United States has a strong national interest in U.S. allies and partners improving the resilience of their critical supply chains in face of challenges—such as the COVID-19 pandemic, extreme weather events due to climate change, and

geopolitical competition with China—that affect both the United States and our allies.

(The White House 2021a, 12)

The political-economic implications of Biden's response to the global supply chain crisis was to signal the American state's willingness and ability to undertake gigantic investments in R&D, infrastructure (sea ports, air ports, highways, and logistics infrastructure including warehouses and transport terminals), and directly in manufacturing. Federal state investments of 'tax payer's dollars' will be dedicated to revamping the foundations of private-capital dominated global supply chains—another huge public subsidy to the private sector (Arriola et al. 2020).

This book was finished as Donald Trump won the 2024 US presidential election. His victory fuelled speculation about the future of trade, supply chains, geopolitics, and globalization. As noted above, there has been much continuity between the Biden and the previous Trump presidency of 2017–2021. However, during the 2024 election campaign Trump proposed imposing 60 per cent tariffs on goods from China and 10 per cent on goods from other countries. Such moves may accelerate 'friendshoring'—where investment moves away from China to countries that are more influenced by the USA, like Mexico (Martinez and Terrazas-Santamaria 2024)—thus re-drawing the global geography of CVCs.

One difference between Biden and Trump, however, is that the former aimed to isolate China through the United States' hegemonic network of alliances. The latter's 'America First' agenda, by contrast, appears to discard the importance of such relationships, whilst promising the augmentation of US power resulting from its independence from international agreements (Panitch and Gindin 2019). In sum, speculation about the future of CVCs under a Trump presidency will likely continue for a while.[1]

Unfortunately, it is not just politicians who deploy Sino phobic imagery to support a geopolitical resilience agenda. Academics too, are buying into and promoting this narrative. Ignoring the long-history of catch-up development—entailing all kinds of trade 'distortions'—of which the USA was the perhaps the best example (Chang 2003), Panwar et al. (2022, 10) report how the above-noted White House report raises concerns about

[1] Trump's Make America Great Again agenda purports to care for American workers who have experienced a decades-long decline in their take home pay. Yet, he is avowedly anti trade-unionism, advocates greater labour market flexibility (bosses' ability to fire workers), and preaches that minimum wage rates should be determined by states, rather than federally. Further, cutting off the principal source of cheap imports (from China) through tariffs may increase consumer prices (Armstrong and Reiter 2024).

'aggressive industrial development policies of other countries, especially China'.

Central to much mainstream GVC commentary on resilience is a notional commitment to free trade. For example, during the tail-end of the Covid pandemic Gereffi et al. (2022, 65) warned how 'nationalistic policies that restrict trade and investment flows could have a deleterious impact on companies that operate in the hyperconnected global economy'. Richard Baldwin and Simon J. Evenett (2020, 2) argued that 'in the 21st century, open trade routes and international supply chains are critical to controlling and defeating the pandemic'. They highlight the dangers of protectionism and extoll the virtues of the free market in responding to the pandemic whereby 'a liberal world trading system gives health ministries, hospitals, and other medical service providers a wide range of suppliers to choose from' (Baldwin and Evenett 2020, 16).

Although Gereffi et al. (2022, 64) note how policies such as vaccine export controls 'that give primacy to domestic interests could jeopardize global public health concerns' (see also Baldwin and Evenett 2020, 9), they fail to mention, theorize, or still less critique, how global trade regulations such as the WTO's TRIPS agreement contributed to dominant pharmaceutical oligopolies' ownership of Covid-vaccine patents. As the People's Vaccine campaign (2022) details, while the latter paid out vast shareholder dividends, they effectively blocked poor countries' attempts to develop generic vaccines. Making CVC's more resilient would not address these injustices in global production and trade.

While the reshoring narrative is big news, at the time of completing this book it appeared to represent an inflated concept. As the DHL Global Connectedness Index (Altman and Bastian 2022) notes, company interest in reshoring rose sharply in 2020 during the covid pandemic, fell the following year and rose again with the onset of the Russia–Ukraine war. Even if reshoring does become a general trend, its materialization will be generations long. A Bloomberg report estimates, for example, that it would take eight years for Apple to move 10 per cent of its iPhone production capacity out of China (Baschuk et al. 2022).

6.7 Conclusions

The mainstream GVC literature promotes resilience as a strategy reflecting the general interest of all lead firms, nations, and their populations. In this chapter we have argued that this notion of resilience is limited—in explanatory and in policy terms—in four ways. First, the literature obscures the capital–labour dynamics inherent in the resilience agenda, as well as ample evidence that suggests that digital technologies are being deployed to increase labour exploitation through enhanced productivity under conditions of precarity. The literature also excludes from its notion of resilience capital's age-old strategy of making workers' pay for crises through pay cuts, increased hours, wage-theft, and worsened conditions.

Second, the high costs entailed in enhancing supply chain resilience suggests that only a minority of relatively well-resourced lead firms will be able to implement comprehensive forms of resilience upgrading. Third, it ignores how CVC mapping represents an agenda and a strategy for increased buyer control over suppliers. These dynamics will, likely, generate new rounds of concentration and centralization of lead firm capital, as successful lead firms are able to enhance their competitiveness through greater surveillance and control over their suppliers.

Finally, the emergent literature underplays how resilience is interpreted and deployed geopolitically by the US state. The heightened geopolitics associated with, and underpinning, CVCs means that it is increasingly difficult to claim that resilience represents a general, rather than a specific, interest. For these reasons, we argue that the resilience strategy will likely contribute to heightened labour exploitation, greater concentration, and centralization amongst CVC firms, enhanced lead firm control over suppliers, and the sharpening of geopolitical tensions.

7

CVCs and Poverty

Immiserating Growth-Regimes

> As human beings are also animals, to manage one million animals gives me a headache.
>
> **(Terry Gou, chief of Foxconn, cited in Chan et al. 2020, 57)**

7.1 Introduction

A recent legal case exposed how Burmese migrant workers in Thai factories, producing jeans for the mega UK retailer Tesco, experienced sub-minimum wages and abusive working conditions. Between 2017 and 2020, these workers made jeans, denim jackets, and other clothes for VK Garment factory (VKG). They are suing Tesco—the UK's biggest retailer, and the world's ninth-largest by revenues—for alleged negligence and unjust enrichment (Dugan 2022a). Workers typically laboured from 8 a.m. to 11 p.m. with one day off a month. Sometimes they were forced to work for twenty-four hours a day to fulfil large orders. While the Thai minimum wage at the time was £7 for an eight-hour day, most workers received less than £4 a day. Workplace injuries and abuse by managers were common. The migrant workers relied upon VKG for their immigration status, increasing their vulnerability to managerial bullying and wage theft. VKG accommodation was dirty and overcrowded. When one woman asked to be paid the Thai minimum wage, managers called her a dog and told her: 'If you don't want to work at the factory anymore, you can get out.' Tesco made profits of over £2 billion in 2020 (Dugan 2022b).

This case is just the tip of the iceberg of capitalist value chains (CVCs). The expansion of CVCs has been based upon the proliferation of similar cases in countries lower down and higher up the imperialist chain. CVCs have expanded through a generalized, though geographically differentiated, increase in labour exploitation globally. As outlined in Chapter 2, CVCs enable capital to heighten exploitation by combining absolute and

Capitalist Value Chains. Benjamin Selwyn and Christin Bernhold, Oxford University Press.
 DOI: 10.1093/9780191994906.003.0007

relative surplus value extraction—lengthening the working day and deploying advanced technologies in production—through international class relations. We also noted how capitalists attempt to increase labour exploitation by pushing down wages. This chapter focuses upon the latter—through specific CVC case studies—and its human developmental impacts. Terry Gou's quote in this chapter's epigraph—that he considers workers to be like animals—encapsulates the practical devaluation of workers' lives in and through CVCs. The GVC mainstream, however, deploys a range of techniques to sidestep such inconvenient interpretations.

As noted in this book's introduction, much mainstream GVC analysis deploys extremely frugal conceptions of poverty and based on these calculations, claims that employment in GVC firms lifts workers out of poverty. The reality is that in numerous cases the wage for a normal working day in CVC supplier firms does not suffice to cover their and their family's social reproduction costs—more commonly in countries lower down in the imperialist chain, but also in leading countries. Consequently, they need to work health-damaging levels of overtime, multiple jobs, and/or rely on other sources of income.

Such examples highlight how capitalists—in their never-ending quest for amassing greater quantities of surplus value—attempt to reduce workers' wages. Often, they do so to such low levels that the only ways for workers to make ends meet is to labour for longer hours and reduce their consumption (and see Chapter 2). In this chapter we use the notion of the living wage to (a) illuminate how miserly is the World Bank's definition of poverty, and to (b) establish a basic benchmark for comprehending where CVC employment is predicated upon and reproduces impoverished labour forces (and see below). Where workers do not earn sufficient wages in a normal working day to sustain their and their family's social reproduction costs, we comprehend such dynamics as arising from *immiserating exploitation* organized through *immiserating growth regimes.*

Lead and supplier firms often work in concert with national states to construct labour regimes—more comprehensively in countries lower down in the imperialist chain—where CVC firms can benefit from the existence of, and access to, vast pools of low-cost labour power. The concept of immiserating growth regimes (IGR) facilitates enquiry into, and explanation of how, such pools of cheap labour power are (re)produced through systematic poverty pay.

Following this introduction, Section 7.2 outlines how we conceptualize IGRs. Section 7.3 discusses the relationship between wages, productivity, and worker poverty in CVC firms. Section 7.4 provides case studies of IGRs—Cambodian garments, Chinese electronics, Eastern and Central European footwear production, and UK garments. Section 7.5 concludes.

7.2 The GVC Mainstream and Poverty Analysis

Mainstream arguments about the causes of poverty often portray it as an outcome of insufficient integration into capitalist markets. For example, the World Bank claims that:

> [G]lobal economic integration has supported poverty reduction and should not be reversed. But the world economy could be much more inclusive: the growth of global markets must not continue to bypass countries with 2 billion people. The rich countries can do much, both through aid and trade policies, to help the currently marginalized countries onto the path of integration that has already proved so effective for the new globalizers.
>
> **(Collier and Dollar 2002, xi; see Wade 2004 for a critique)**

Much of what passes for poverty analysis adopts the World Bank's international poverty line (IPL)—$2.15 per day (for what it labels as low-income countries), $3.65 (lower-middle-income-countries), and $6.85 (upper-middle-income countries). This IPL is unfit for the purpose of measuring, still less explaining, global poverty (Sumner 2007, 2020; Hickel 2019). As noted in Chapter 1, it cannot detect the generation of in-work poverty where workers may consume above the value of the IPL but still consume insufficient calories. It says nothing about the number of hours workers need to labour for to afford to consume sufficient calories. Nor does it say anything about social reproduction costs—of bringing up children, of education, health, accommodation, or transport to work (Selwyn 2017, see Chapter 2).

In this chapter, our conceptual dividing line between poverty and non-poverty pay is the notion of the living wage as formulated by the Asia Floor Wage (2022), itself rooted in the United Nation's Declaration of Human Rights (1949), article 23 on the right to work. It stipulates a standard working week of no more than 48 hours, allows for a worker to buy food for themselves and their family, pay the rent, for healthcare, clothing, transportation, education, and to be able to have a small amount of savings.

We deploy this definition of non-poverty pay to critique notions of poverty derived from the World Bank's poverty lines. We view a living wage, compared to poverty wages, as a *basic demand* for workers' betterment. It does not, however, imply a good living or an end to workers' exploitation by capital. Contrasting the GVC mainstream's notions of non-poverty pay against this definition of a living wage represents part of our immanent critique of the GVC mainstream (Bernhold 2022, 48ff.). Quite simply, it highlights that many jobs in CVCs cannot secure the reproduction of individual CVC workers' labour power.

The question of the quantity and quality of working hours is vitally important. A recent study by the World Health Organisation highlights how longer working hours have deleterious impacts upon workers' health. Working over 55 hours a week is associated with a 17 per cent higher risk of heart disease and 35 per cent greater risk of a stroke, compared to working 35–40 hours a week. The numbers of people working long hours is increasing globally. Long working hours led to 745,000 deaths from stroke and coronary heart disease in 2016, a 29 per cent increase since 2000 (Pega et al. 2021, n.p.).

If the above conception of a living wage is deployed to investigate the relationship between employment in CVC firms and worker poverty, then much of what is labelled as GVC-based development needs to be re-thought. When workers in CVCs do not earn living wages, as defined above, the broader political economic context should be labelled IGRs.

Immiserating Growth Regimes

Much mainstream GVC analysis explains workers' poverty wages as a consequence of their employment in low productivity industries (see below). In this chapter we show that productivity in CVC supplier firms in countries further down the imperialist chain is often equal to or higher than in similar industries in leading countries. Yet, wages are often so low that they constitute poverty wages.

The notion of *social* reproduction costs—that is, the cost of the goods and services that are deemed necessary for all society's members to have—implies a 'moral element' in the definition and calculation of poverty (Marx 1990, 275). These costs are determined in part by socially accepted or enforced norms governing workers' living and working conditions, which are ultimately a question of class relations and struggles. The relationship between social reproduction costs and wages is, this chapter argues, co-determined by the balance of class power in given contexts (including sectoral specificity, state formation, social policies, and state's positions within the imperialist chain). The proliferation of CVCs has been rooted in the establishment of an institutionally weak and divided world working class. Under such circumstances, in numerous cases lead and supplier firms have been able to employ workers under conditions where they do not earn a living wage within a 48-hour working week. These dynamics have generated what we call immiserating growth regimes. *An IGR is one in which workers are kept poor to increase capitalist profit and extend capital accumulation.*

The idea of IGRs represents an elaboration upon the concept of the labour regime (see Chapters 2 and 9). To recall, the labour regime denotes 'the set of social relations and institutions that shape and construct exploitation at multiple scales and through different spheres across the global economy' (Baglioni et al. 2022b, 82). The supporting notion of *immiserating exploitation* specifies where capitalist exploitation is organized around the objective of securing high profits by granting workers so little of the value they produce, that they do not earn a living wage within a 48-hour working week. In the remainder of this section, we discuss commonalities and differences between our and other useful notions of immiserating growth.

In the early days of GVC analysis, Raphael Kaplinsky (1998) observed that 'in previous eras, participation in industrial segments of the value chain provided the source for sustainable income growth. But, increasingly, in a globalising economy these industrial niches have become highly competitive, raising the spectre of immiserising growth' (Kaplinsky 1998, 31). For Kaplinsky, immiserising growth represents a situation where growing 'participation in industrial activities—reflected in the level of industrial activity, the growth in physical trade and the increase in industrial employment ... become associated with *declining overall standards of living*' (Kaplinsky 1998, 4, emphasis added). While some firms can successfully upgrade, the general trend across the world economy is one of:

> declining real wages and declining real incomes in those countries specialising in rent-poor products.... The challenges thus confronting producers everywhere is to upgrade by appropriating whatever categories of rents are within their grasp, but to do so more rapidly than competitors in the knowledge that a rate of innovation lower than the average will result in immiserising growth.
>
> **(Kaplinsky 1998, 34, emphasis added; see Knorringa and Pegler 2006)**

Another attempt to comprehend the relationship between CVC inclusion and workers' poverty is Nicola Phillips' (2011) notion of 'adverse incorporation':

> [I]t is often the case that poor people are not in fact excluded from markets or indeed societies, but rather are included on adverse terms in ways that either

> perpetuate conditions of chronic poverty or heighten their vulnerability to transient forms of poverty, as particular forms of employment or work offer few or no prospects for accumulation.
>
> **(Phillips 2011, 390)**

Furthermore, 'destitution and poverty are associated respectively with a person's absolute or partial loss of control over assets and income, and specifically, in the case of the poor, over their key asset of labour'. The author characterizes forced labour as the most extreme case (Phillips 2011, 392). She also posits that '[e]xploitation of other forms—that is, systematic violations of workers' rights—similarly leads to the loss of control and heightened vulnerability that define adverse incorporation' (Phillips 2011, 392). Phillips identifies 'top-down' and 'bottom-up' dynamics of adverse incorporation, the former shaped by states and capital, the latter by 'local conditions' including poverty, vulnerability, and labour informality.

A third contribution to the immiserating growth literature is Paul Shaffer, Ravi Kanbur, and Richard Sandbrook's (2019) notion of immiserizing growth. They define it as 'situations when growth fails to benefit, or harms, those at the bottom' (Shaffer et al. 2019, 3). Within this broad notion, they note the importance of setting rigorous criteria/metrics by which to identify and measure the incidence of immiserizing growth. These include poverty lines, norms about consumption (covering basic needs, health, education, and access to clean drinking water and sanitation), and the importance of workers' subjective criteria such as degrees of vulnerability, happiness, and dignity (Shaffer et al. 2019, 6).

Shaffer et al. distinguish between failed inclusion and active exclusion. An example of the former is a situation where remote communities are inadequately incorporated into processes of income generation. An example of the latter is a situation where communities are forcibly dispossessed of their land (ibid., 10). They argue that active exclusion is a process associated with deliberate harm imposed by one actor upon another. Both are widely observed when countries integrate and expand participation in CVCs.

The contributions of Kaplinsky, Phillips, and Shaffer et al. are necessary rebuttals to the simplistic argument that poverty is an outcome of insufficient world market integration. Kaplinsky identifies a fallacy of composition in policies designed to maximize CVC inclusion—where what might be developmentally positive for one firm can be developmentally negative for many firms because of what he identifies as excess competition at the supplier node of the chain. Phillips notes how 'top-down' forces (development policies and competitive strategies by states and firms respectively) may contribute to incorporating workers into CVCs in ways that increase their vulnerability and poverty. Shaffer et al.'s insistence that aspects such as the denial of workers' dignity should be considered as part of immiserizing growth, enables researchers to transcend ideological notions of poverty such as the dollar-a-day approach.

However, these contributions miss how the exploitative dynamics at the heart of the capital–labour relation themselves generate (diverse forms of) worker poverty. For example, Kaplinsky's insights into immiserising growth rests upon a questionable double-assumption. First, it generates an image of declining *overall* standards of living, where it assumes that labour *and* capital lose out from immiserising growth. While uneven development implies that peripheral capitals lose out against lead firms in the distribution of value, such an assumption blurs the mechanisms and social relations that enable employers to cream off surplus value from their labour forces at the expense of the latter. Second, it reproduces the assumption that upgrading is the only rational development strategy, even while it recognizes that such strategies are themselves beset by a fallacy of composition.

More generally, in all three examples of immiserizing growth above, the specificities of capitalist exploitation—capitals' ability and ceaseless quest to extract surplus value from labour—are conceptually bracketed out of these analyses. Note, for example, Phillips' (2011, 392) definition of exploitation as the 'systematic violations of workers' rights', and how this presupposes non-exploitative scenarios defined by employers' respect for worker's rights.

Our conception of IGRs advances the notion of immiserating growth in at least two ways. First, by approaching IGRs from a class-relational perspective we keep in view the core social relations that underpin their formation and reproduction. Second, whilst the noted conceptions of immiserating growth interpret it as a sub-optimal outcome of firms' accumulation strategies and processes, we explain why it can be seen as the opposite: immiserating growth is an optimal outcome of CVC development used by capitalist firms to increase the exploitation of workers, and an optimal development strategy from the perspective of many supplier firms and local institutions.

7.3 Wages, Productivity, and Poverty in GVC Analysis

As noted above, the World Bank's international poverty lines facilitate claims that globalization in general, and CVC integration in particular, is reducing poverty. One of the more prominent advocates of such claims is Jeffrey Sachs, President of the UN sustainable development solutions network. He argues that 'sweatshops are the first rung on the ladder out of extreme poverty' (Sachs 2005, 11). Sachs deploys commonplace arguments about productivity to explain/justify Bangladeshi apparel workers' extremely low wages:

> Some rich-country protesters argued that Dhaka's apparel firms should either pay far higher wage rates or be closed, but closing such factories as a result of wages forced above worker productivity would be little more than a ticket for these women back to misery.
>
> **(Sachs 2005, 12)**

Sachs' arguments represent the consensus within mainstream GVC analysis (OECD 2014; Taglioni and Winkler 2016). For example, economists in the Employment Trends Unit of the International Labour Office assert a link between a national society's productivity and wealth levels. They contend that:

> As higher levels of productivity facilitate higher average earnings from labour, there is a *direct link* between labour market outcomes—in terms of both the quantity of available jobs and the productivity of the workforce—and the middle class standard of living enjoyed by the majority of people in the developed world.
>
> **(Kapsos and Bourmpoula 2013, 12, emphasis added)**

Similarly, as outlined in Chapter 4, in its 2020 World Development Report, the World Bank claims that GVCs 'allow firms to raise productivity and income, rendering GVC trade more powerful than traditional trade in supporting growth and poverty reduction' (World Bank 2020, 14). The mainstream GVC consensus assumes, or simply posits, that low wages in poor country supplier firms are caused by low productivity.

The Productivity-Wage Relationship in CVC Supplier Firms

Arguments that low wages in firms in so-called developing countries reflect these firms' low productivity levels are problematic for several reasons. First, they often fail to differentiate between national average productivity and the productivity of firms integrated into CVCs. It is likely that national average productivity in such countries will be lower than that in leading countries. However, the opposite is often the case in larger CVC supplier firms operating in peripheral countries. In such workplaces, firms adopt advanced technologies to meet world market quality requirements at low cost. Here, worker productivity may be comparable to, if not higher than, that in similar firms in leading countries, while their pay may be 10, 20, or 30 times less than that of workers in peripheral countries (Ness 2016, 10ff.). Second, the productivity–wage relation is determined primarily by labour's social reproduction costs and by the balance of power between capital and labour rather than by firm-level productivity. Where social reproduction costs are low firms will find it relatively easy to pay workers poverty wages.

Third, it is wrong to assume that workers are rewarded according to the value they produce, or in mainstream GVC terms, their contribution to value-added. Rather, capitalists seek to maximize profit by extracting as much surplus value as possible from workers. Whether workers receive a greater or lesser share of the value they produce is dependent upon the balance of power between capital and labour, often instituted by states.

Global wage differentials reflect less in-firm productivity levels than (1) the socially determined costs of wage-labour force reproduction, (2) labour market institutions (that do or do not link wage rates to productivity), and (3) the ability of labouring-class organizations to achieve 'progressive' wage settlements (Mosley 2008). Where the first variable is very low, the second pro-capital and anti-labour, and the third weak, and where firms utilize relatively advanced technologies, they can benefit from higher productivity levels than those in leading countries whilst paying poverty wages, facilitating increasing surplus value extraction and appropriation (Ali 2016). As we show below, such dynamics are present even in leading imperialist countries, where low wages are the norm in some economic sectors.

Table 7.1 provides calculations of productivity in autos and textiles by value (dividing worker value-added by their wages) from the early 2000s. It shows that Mexico and India had higher productivity rates than the United States and Germany in autos and that Brazil, Thailand and Mexico had higher productivity rates than the United States and Germany in textiles (Kerswell 2013). The implications are that barriers to enhancing workers' wages and conditions are not low productivity but (supplier and lead) firm's capital accumulation strategies.

The relationship between productivity and wages is, thus, multi-determined. In his analysis of the trajectory of development in Mexico, Gabriel Palma (2005) shows how, between the late 1970s and late 1990s, real wages fell while workers' productivity increased. Workers were certainly exploited prior to the 1980s, and it would be mistaken to portray this period as a golden age for Mexican labour. However, the relative class compromise between capital and labour, mediated by the state, ensured that workers in technologically advancing industries shared, to some degree, in the benefits

Table 7.1 Country productivity ranking (automobiles and textiles)

Country	Year	Value added per worker (annual US$)	Wages per worker (annual US$)	Average Productivity (Worker Value Added\Wages per worker)
Automobiles				
Mexico	2000	102,000	11,700	**8.69**
India	2003	22,817	4,575	**4.99**
US	2002	231,729	54,157	**4.28**
Thailand	2000	13,555	4,680	**2.85**
Germany	2003	89,117	56,425	**1.58**
Textiles				
Brazil	2004	12,353	3,584	**3.45**
Thailand	2000	6,583	2,318	**2.84**
Mexico	2000	14,983	5,292	**2.83**
US	2002	66,483	27,223	**2.44**
Germany	2003	43,881	30,974	**1.42**

Source: Reproduced from Selwyn (2019, 13).

of rising productivity (Hesketh 2017; Crossa 2022). But in response to the 1982 debt crisis and with the roll-out of neoliberalism in Mexico, that relative class compromise was dismantled. Rapid productivity increases brought about in part by foreign direct investment (FDI) and the import of advanced technologies were combined with falling wages and rising levels of immiserating exploitation. Gabriel Palma notes how '[i]n manufacturing ... the average wage had only just recovered its 1976 level [by 2000] while productivity had increased by about 80%' (Palma 2005, 974; see Parnreiter 2007, and see Figure 5.3 in Chapter 5 for a comparable dynamic in the United States). Complementarily, Doug Henwood (1995, 33) shows how in the 1990s US firms in the Mexican maquila sector were 85 per cent as productive as their US-based counterparts but paid their workers only 6 per cent of the wages of the US-based workers undertaking comparable tasks.

In their study of the Mexican auto industry Crossa and Ebner (2020) show how the cost of a basic food basket for the average family in Mexico in 2017 was US$417 per month, while the average monthly income of workers in the industry was US$314. These wages covered only 77 per cent of a family's nutritional needs, excluding other essential costs such as health care, transport, or housing. As Claudia, an assembly line worker, recounts 'in order to make ends meet, I work a double-shift five days a week' (cited in Crossa and Ebner 2020, 1232).

The above dynamics are not exclusive to the Mexican economy but are common throughout CVCs. In her study of US lead firms' overseas investment strategies, Mona Ali (2016, 1014) documents how '[t]he rising insecurity of workers ... is reflected in across-the-board increases in labour productivity ... alongside declining wage shares'. In 2010, Lowell Bryan of the *McKinsey Quarterly*, noted how:

> Any company sourcing its production or service operations in a lower-wage emerging-market country ... can save enormously on labour costs.... Even today, the cost of labour in China or India is still only a fraction (often less than a third) of the equivalent labour in the developed world. Yet the productivity of Chinese and Indian labour is rising rapidly and, in specialized areas (such as high-tech assembly in China or software development in India), may *equal or exceed* the productivity of workers in wealthier nations.
>
> **(Bryan 2010, 4f., emphasis added)**

7.4 Case Studies

This section provides empirical examples of immiserating exploitation and IGRs in industries integrated into CVCs, focussing on Cambodian garments, Chinese electronics, Central and Eastern European footwear production, and garment production in the UK respectively. It shows that workers in these sectors: (1) are highly productive; (2) receive base wages that are insufficient to meet their individual, let alone their dependents' social reproduction requirements; (3) are required by firms (sometimes by force) and by economic necessity as a consequence of insufficient base wages to undertake large amounts of overtime; and (4) as a consequence of 1–3 are physically and emotionally degraded.

Cambodian Garments

Following the end of the Cold War, and under the leadership of the Cambodian People's Party, economic development in Cambodia was predicated upon attracting FDI to stimulate export-led growth, based upon cheap labour power. The garment industry expanded, from next to nothing in 1994, to a situation where by 2015 699 firms produced footwear and garments for giant global retailers (see Arnold 2013b; Better Factories Cambodia 2016; Arnold 2017; Salmivaara 2018), with employment in the sector reaching over half a million (Kashyap 2015, 1). Lead firms such as Levi's, Nike, H&M, and GAP sourced clothing and footwear from Cambodia. Supplier firms include firms such as 8 Star Sportswear Ltd and A & J Carter (Cambodia) Ltd. By 2014 the sector was responsible for around $5billion in output, constituting 80 per cent of Cambodia's total manufacturing and total exports, and one-third of its GDP (Better Factories Cambodia 2016; Chang 2022). The sector is predominately owned by Asian capital. Chinese capital has the largest presence (around 33 per cent), followed by investors from Taiwan, Hong Kong, and South Korea, whilst Cambodian ownership is around 3 per cent (Better Factories Cambodia 2016).

Around 90 per cent of workers in the garment sector are rural-urban migrant women (Arnold 2013b, 4). A large and expanding reserve army of labour has been established as the Cambodian state granted land concessions to (primarily foreign) capital at the expense of small-scale farmers and rural workers, who have been dispossessed of (access to) land and pushed towards the cities. By 2015, around 2.2 million hectares of arable land (out of a total of 3.9 million hectares) had been leased to private companies, mostly specializing in export sugarcane, logging, mining, and rubber production, or for the construction for the tourism sector. These concessions have impacted negatively upon between 400,000 and 700,000 people, the largest percentage of which are indigenous (Pen and Chea 2015; Chang 2022). Protestors are met with state-led armed intimidation, including surveillance, imprisonment, and shooting (Salmivaara 2018).

The 1997 Labour Law guarantees a minimum wage. It defines overtime as work more than the normal eight-hour working day, limits it to 12 hours a week, and states that such practices can only be deployed 'exceptionally' (Salmivaara 2018, 334). These stipulations are not a reality for most workers in the garment sector.

Overtime, which is often compulsory (i.e., forced), characterizes the sector. A 2013 survey by Better Factories Cambodia found 94 per cent of factories deploying overtime as a regular rather than 'exceptional' strategy, and 74 per cent requiring workers to undertake more than two hours overtime per day or 12 hours per week. Many workers in large Cambodian textile factories work between three and five hours overtime a day (Kashyap 2015, 58).

Historically, workers' wages have been low, and prone to downward pressures. They declined by 22 per cent between 2001 and 2011, before rising substantially due to increases in the minimum wage (Workers Rights Consortium 2013). A recent ILO report on wages in the garment and footwear sector argues that 'the increase in the minimum wage, and by extension, in final take home pay appeared to benefit garment workers of all union statuses' (ILO 2018, 7). The report did not mention how the engine driving up workers' wages have been waves of mass strikes and protests (Arnold 2017). Nor did it mention how the Cambodian government responded to these protests by simultaneously raising minimum wages (albeit below worker's demands for a living wage) while cracking down on workers' protests, and on democracy more generally (Chang 2022, and see below). Most fundamentally, however, it does not discuss the long-term trend of declining pay preceding the wage increases in the garment sector noted above.

From 2010, workers in the garment sector struck and protested more vigorously against their low pay and poor working conditions. Strikes and protests continued throughout the decade, quadrupling in 2012 alone (Arnold 2013a), and pushed the government to increase the minimum wage from US$100 to US$140 a month (ILO 2018) between 2014 and 2016. In his study of Cambodia's development model, Dae-Oup Chang, quoting garment sector workers, notes:

> Garment workers organised mass rallies in major cities. Even though employers strived to stop their employees from joining by 'locking them up in factories', many workers 'managed to escape from the factory' to join the rallies or simply did not come to work and attended the rallies.
>
> **(Chang 2022, 63)**

Rather than signifying an unambiguous improvement for workers, however, these wage increases have been met by employers with work intensification and cutting non-wage benefits.

There are two principal employment categories in the sector: undetermined duration contracts (UDCs) and fixed-duration contracts (FDCs). Up until the mid-2000s, most workers in registered garment factories were employed under UCDs—with entitlements to benefits such as sick and maternity leave, paid holidays and regular, albeit very low, wages. Since then, across the sector, fixed duration contracts became increasingly widely deployed whilst shortened from six to three months (Arnold 2013b, 11; Fair Action 2015).

Employers have also offset wage increases through reduced overtime payments, from double-time to only 30 per cent above the normal working time wage rate (Kashyap 2015, 3). Whilst productivity targets were always high, they were intensified still further since the wage increases of 2014–2016. Factories reduced the size of work teams whilst requiring that workers meet the same daily task targets. In one example, workers produce 1200 'difficult design' and 2000 'simple design' garments in an 11-hour shift (Kashyap 2015).

Workers labour under poor conditions, ranging from a lack of health and safety provision to overly hot working conditions. One consequence of these pressures are high numbers of workplace faintings, reaching approximately 1,806 in 2015 across the garment and footwear industry (Human Rights Now 2018) In part, these mass faintings derive from insufficient calorie intake caused by inadequate pay and excessive overtime.

To lead a healthy life, workers conducting physically demanding labour over extended durations and under tough conditions (such as very hot working environments) require 3000 kilocalories per day. A report by Labour Behind the Label identified that 'the average worker currently ingests just above half the amount required to perform the physically demanding work of a factory' (McMullen 2013, 11). Moreover, the protein intake was found to be well below half of what should be ingested for a healthy body (McMullen 2013, 11).

According to the World Health Organisation, a body mass index of less than 18.5 is underweight, and may indicate eating disorder and\or malnutrition. A survey of 95 garment workers in the Phnom Penh region in late 2012 and early 2013 found that 33 per cent of participants had a BMI of between 16.00 and 18.49 ('underweight'), and 3 per cent had a BMI of under 16.00 ('severely underweight') (McMullen 2013, 11). This is not to say that garment workers' conditions are worse than elsewhere in the economy. It does say that employment in the sector exposes workers to significant health risks and dangers.

Because of their very low pay, rent is relatively high, while living conditions are poor:

> A cleated gangplank runs from the alleyway up to the raised dilapidated shelter that houses all 11 members of the immediate family. A covered area, opened on one side to the outside, provides a gathering space for cooking and washing. Behind, two adjoining rooms sleep eight in one room, three in the other. There is power, as the hysteria of wires running through one room attests. There is no running water. A damp thickness of refuse carpets the ground below, nuzzled at the moment by an enormous rat … Neang pays a monthly rent of $30 (U.S.) for the shanty. The monthly utilities total 75,000 riels, or about $18.
>
> **(Jennifer Wells, cited in Cambodian Center for Human Rights 2014, 15f.)**

In response to mass demonstrations by workers demanding higher wages in December 2013, and to fortify its cheap-labour development strategy, the Cambodian state attacked the demonstrations, killing six and wounding many others (Kashyap 2015, 40). Dennis Arnold (2017, 30) observes how:

> The military police attacked protesters with electric batons, smoke grenade, slingshots and finally AK-47 rifles with live ammunition. The military fired at unarmed protesters at around 2 a.m. on 3 January. Five garment workers were killed and 25 protesters suffered bullet wounds, while another 13 had other types of serious injuries.

Arnold notes how the government's strategy combines aggression with attempts to buy off workers with (limited) concessions, albeit ones designed to maintain Cambodia's garment sector as an IGR. 'Following the violence, arrests and numerous court cases an unprecedented 28% wage increase, from $100 to $128/month plus allowances and bonuses was confirmed in November 2014—still short of calls for a living wage' (Arnold 2017, 30). Dae-Oup Chang broadens the analysis to account for the characteristics of the Cambodian state and its IGR:

> Cambodia's transition to outright authoritarianism has been accelerated since the violent suppression of protesting garment workers in 2014. In 2016, the Trade Union Law was revised … [and] introduced tighter regulations over the establishment of trade unions by requiring a higher number of affiliations to create union federations and confederations… [it] forbade labour activists with lower educational backgrounds and criminal records from becoming union leaders. The legal procedure for strike actions was also made difficult for unions as they were required to hold a secret ballot in which more than half of members need to vote and more than half of those voting need to support strike action for a legal strike.
>
> **(Chang 2022, 64)**

In September 2017, the *Cambodian Daily* newspaper was shut down by the government, and its last front-page headline was 'Descent into Outright Dictatorship' (Chang 2022, 64).

It might be argued, by mainstream GVC proponents, that such conditions may exist in countries such as Cambodia because their supplier firms are producing relatively basic consumer goods, characterized by low entry barriers and therefore poor wages and conditions. Such arguments, presumably, would prioritize upgrading into higher-tech industries which can yield better wages and conditions. However, when we look at China's booming electronics industry, we find more similarity than divergence with the poor conditions suffered by Cambodia's garment workers.

Electronics in China

High-tech electronics such as laptops, iPhones, and iPads, represent icons of CVCs, as their globally dispersed production and sale integrates workers, firms, and consumers across the world, with China representing the world's electronics assembly platform. Giant firms like Pegatron and Foxconn supply Apple and other lead firms. Taiwanese-owned Foxconn is China's largest exporter of high-tech electronics consumer products, employs over one million workers across China, and rose to infamy in 2010 after a spate of worker suicides at its factories (SACOM 2010). It exemplifies the capacity of CVC firms to combine advanced technology and low wages. Its level of technology is not so different from that which would be available in the United States, but the conditions of labour exploitation are far more extreme (Norfield 2011).

China's transformation into the world's electronics assembly platform has been based on its circular migrant-labour regime, underpinned by its *hukou* system, where rural workers migrate to urban areas albeit without enjoying rights of registered urban residents (see Chapter 5). This 'floating population' comprises up to 70 per cent of workers in the manufacturing sector (Foster and McChesney 2012; Friedman 2014a). In Foxconn's Pearl River Delta plants, for example, between 75 per cent and 80 per cent of workers are rural-urban migrants (Pringle 2011; Pun and Koo 2015; Ren et al. 2016; Lüthje and Butollo 2017, 225).

The electronics labour force is mostly male, as female infanticide (in response to China's one-child policy) skewed the gender ratio towards males (Chan et al. 2013). Migrants' wages are a fraction of those of registered urban workers, and in partial consequence, 'neither can they depend on wages alone to live a decent life in cities, nor can they obtain sufficient subsistence resources from their hometown villages' (Feng 2017, 608).

Apple stands at the pinnacle of the global electronics sector. Its value chain governance strategy includes direct intervention in supplier firms' labour processes. Even after the suicides at Foxconn it required that its 'suppliers achieve an average of 95 percent compliance with our maximum 60-hour week' (Apple 2014, 4). This contrasts with the International Labour Organization's Convention C030 on work hours, which recommends upper limits of 48 hours per week and eight hours per day respectively (Fuchs 2016).

While workers' base wages in the electronics sector are insufficient for their individual reproduction requirements, workers do attain these through overtime. Meanwhile, they are subject to health-damaging working conditions (China Labour Watch 2014b, 2015a). For example, workers at Compeq 'need to apply dangerous chemical agents including copper sulfate, sulfuric acid, nitric acid, paint, cleaning-machine solvent, thinner, industrial alcohol and gold-coating agent'. Many workers 'suffer skin problems such as rashes' (SACOM 2008, 29; see China Labour Watch 2011). The documentary film *Complicit* highlights the proliferation of occupational Leukemia in China's electronics industry.[1]

Indicative research provides estimates about the discrepancy between monthly minimum wages and workers' social reproduction requirements in two cities in Guangdong in 2017. In Guangzhou, the minimum wage of 1895 Yuan was only 50 per cent of the social wage of 3755 Yuan. In Dongguan, the minimum wage of 1510 Yuan was only 44 per cent of the social wage of 3439 Yuan (GoodElectronics 2018)[2].

During the 2010s the Chinese state and local municipalities raised minimum wages, in part as a response to growing labour unrest and labour shortages, and to expand the domestic market (Hung 2015). Electronics manufacturers responded to these, and other wage-inflating pressures, by further intensifying the labour process. Pun and Chan (2012, 400) quote a group of young workers responsible for processing cell phone casings in the Foxconn Shenzhen factory saying that 'production output was set at 5,120 pieces per day in the past, but it has been raised by 20 percent to 6,400 pieces per day in recent months'. At Pegatron Shanghai workers had to assemble 450–500 motherboards per hour. Over half of its employees worked over 90 hours overtime a month because 'their base wages ... cannot meet the local living standard' (China Labour Watch 2015a, 2). In the Donngguan Chenming Electronic Company, which assembles PC shells and cases, task targets were 2,000 products per day (China Labour Watch 2016b, 14).

Foxconn's engineers 'study the entire manufacturing process in minute detail ... [t]he posture of workers sitting or standing is monitored no less rigorously than the work itself'. One worker describes their job as '[t]ake a motherboard from the line, scan the logo, put it in an anti-static bag, stick on a label, and place it on the line. Each of these tasks takes two seconds. Every

[1] https://javafilms.fr/film/complicit/, last accessed 31 October 2024.

[2] Note: These calculations are based on the assumption of two working adults and one dependent child. Hence, they are more conservative than the Asian Floor Wage conception of a living wage noted in Section 7.2.

ten seconds I finish five tasks' (Chan et al. 2020, 60). Another worker explains how:

> Now we must use both hands at work to increase efficiency and productivity. Not a hand is left idle for a moment ... [f]or example, I hold an electric screwdriver with my right hand, and fix the screws with my left hand. Then, I pick up another printed circuit board. I screw the screws without a break.
>
> **(Chan et al. 2020, 60)**

The intensity with which such techniques are deployed at Foxconn physically harms workers. They are facilitated by the broader labour regime, which includes cramped on-site dormitories to make workers ever-ready for last-minute production drives; deliberately low state-mandated minimum wages that are designed to extract vast overtime hours from workers; and a state-controlled national trade union which actively seeks to supress workers' collective actions. Above-all, the *hukou* system divides the national workforce into rural and urban dwellers, denies the former the rights enjoyed by the latter, increasing their vulnerability to the payments below living wages.

In addition to labour process intensification, some manufacturers cut workers' overall compensation. Following the government of Shanghai's increase of the minimum wage from $304 to $330 in April 2015, Pegatron followed suit. But, to offset the increase, it cut worker subsidies, made them liable for paying workplace insurance, and implemented other changes to the remuneration structure. Workers that worked 40 regular hours per week plus 40 weekend overtime hours per month were US$24.5 worse off, whilst without overtime they were US$60.9 worse off than prior to the increase of the minimum wage (see Table 7.2).

Foxxon and Pegatron house workers in their 'dormitory labour system' on and off factory grounds (Pun and Smith 2007). In the former, workers typically number up to eight per room. In the latter, a China Labour Watch investigation describes accommodation comprising 'a four storey building with 43 rooms on each floor and 14 beds to a room' (China Labour Watch 2015b, 20). Whilst such conditions are often considered degrading (by workers and by investigators), workers tend to favour them over the often-unaffordable alternative of private sector renting (Pun and Chan 2012).

In another attempt to reduce costs, firms have found new ways to access very cheap labour power. Up to nine million interns were working in China's manufacturing and other industries in 2010, many of whom are channelled into the electronics sector by their schools (Hodal and Bengtsen 2017; see

Table 7.2 Pegatron workers' income before and after the 2015 minimum wage increase (in US$)

	Busy Season (assuming 40 regular hours per week and 40 weekend overtime hours)		Offseason (assuming no overtime)	
	Before the wage rise	After	Before the wage rise	After
Base Wage	304.3	349.5	304.3	349.5
Overtime Pay	244.9	281.2	0.0	0.0
Food Subsidy	42.2	0.0	42.0	0.0
Performance Bonus	7.5	0.0	7.5	0.0
Seniority Pay	42.5	42.5	42.5	42.5
Skill Allowance	22.6	22.6	22.6	22.6
Meals	−60.3	−60.3	−60.3	−60.3
Accommodation fee	−24.1	−24.1	−24.1	−24.1
Insurance	0.0	−56.4	0.0	−56.4
Total	**582.3**	**557.8**	**337.5**	**276.6**
Change after the raise	**0.0**	**−24.5**	**0.0**	**−60.9**

Source: Reproduced from Selwyn (2019, 13).

Smith and Chan 2015). Vocational schools benefit financially from these arrangements, as they may deduct commissions from interns' salaries or get paid directly by factories. In some cases, interns can make up most of the labour force (Hodal and Bengtsen 2017). Interns earn less than regular workers. China Labour Watch reports wages as low as one-fifth of a regular workers' starting salary and the payment of 'living expenses' instead of wages, as low as US$7 a month. Some of these interns are as young as 15 and therefore classify as child labour (China Labour Watch 2014a).

If we adopt the World Bank's international poverty line approach, then the Foxconn model is no bad thing. It has enabled rural migrants to find relatively well-paid urban jobs and to consume above the value of the IPL. If, on the other hand, we use the living wage approach, we see something very different. Foxconn (and large sections of China's economy) have institutionalized poverty wages. Simply put, basic wages are insufficient to provide a worker and their family with a dignified existence. The labour process (intense specialization of tasks) and the labour regime (dormitory systems, health-damaging overtime, and institutionally segmented labour forces) represent a core component of China's competitive advantage as a CVC supplier region. Extreme hard work and health-threatening overtime are part and parcel of the IGR supporting China's electronics sector.

Immiserating Growth Regimes in Eastern and Central European Footwear Production

Following the dissolution of the Eastern bloc, Eastern and Central Europe (ECE) emerged to become a major supplier region for western European fashion lead firms, including Benetton, Esprit, and GEOX. Selwyn et al.'s (2020) research on export footwear production in ECE shows how sub-living wage payments to workers are the norm rather than the exception across the footwear sector.

As part of the project of constructing relatively flexible labour markets, ECE states, in conjunction with international financial institutions and the EU, have established low wage floors. The legal minimum wage in many countries is less than 60 per cent of the average wage (the relative poverty measure in many countries) (Table 7.3).

Across the sector, workers recounted how they found it impossible to regularly pay for utility bills, that they often missed their rent payments and that they could not afford a family holiday. Many workers recounted how they relied upon family and friends for loans, and for free or very cheap agricultural goods. They noted how they rarely, if ever, were able to afford medical (especially dental) check-ups, that they suffered from poor hygiene, and that

Table 7.3 Legal minimum wage as a percentage of estimated living wage (2016)

Country	Legal Minimum Net Wage in Shoe Industry[a]	Estimated Minimum Living Wage for a family of four[b]	Legal Minimum Wage as a Percentage of Estimated Living Wage[c]
Albania	144€	588€	24%
Bosnia-Herzegovina	164€	859€	19%
Macedonia	145€	726€	20%
Poland	318€	1000€	32%
Romania	156€	706€	22%
Slovakia	354€	1360€	26%

[a] Official government statistics.
[b] Based on interviews with workers.
[c] Calculation based on interviews with workers.

Source: Selwyn et al. (2020, 394).

they could not afford school uniforms and school supplies for their children. A Romanian worker recounted how her family relied upon remittances from their parents:

> We are renting a flat in the city and the most difficult thing is to pay for heating in winter. I am afraid to look at the bill. If we fail to pay for more than two months, we get cut off. Our parents, who work in Spain, send us money every few months and that's how we get by.
>
> **(Selwyn et al. 2020, 394)**

Access to land, loans, and other forms of financial assistance, in addition to help from extended family are frequently mentioned as representing coping mechanisms. Another Romanian worker recounted:

> We have to spend everything we have on daily needs and sometimes run out of money before the end of the month. Luckily, the local shop owners know us well and let us get products for free if we run out of money, allowing us to pay them later. We don't want to borrow money, and my husband had to take 5 months' leave from his factory job to work in construction in Germany.
>
> **(Selwyn et al. 2020, 395)**

She also noted how access to land, for agricultural production, was necessary to provide her family with sufficient food:

> We have a garden and some animals. If I had to buy meat, like chicken breast from the shop, I would not be able to afford it. So we must also take care of our animals every day because they are some of the only food we can afford. Sometimes my sister comes in to feed the animals when both my husband and I are away for work.
>
> **(Selwyn et al. 2020, 395)**

The above cases exist in a broader situation where rates of immiserating exploitation (measured as the gap between real and living wages) in the same economic sector are higher in ECE than across much of Asia (Table 7.4).

At the end of the Cold War and with the dissolution of the Eastern bloc it was common to hear claims that free market capitalism would enrich these countries' populations. In the case of export footwear production, at least, we see something quite different. The establishment and expansion of ECE's export footwear sector has been based upon the presence of a highly exploitable, predominantly female, labour force. As this chapter notes, such dynamics are increasingly prevalent across CVCs, to the extent that related processes also exist in leading capitalist countries.

Table 7.4 Legal minimum wage vs living wage: Eastern Europe and Asia compared

Eastern Europe (including Turkey)	Minimum Wage as a Percentage of Living Wage	Asia	Minimum Wage as a Percentage of Living Wage
Slovakia	21%	India	26%
Ukraine	14%	China	46%
Romania	19%	Bangladesh	19%
Moldova	19%	Cambodia	21%
Georgia	10%	Malaysia	54%
BiH	25%	Sri Lanka	19%
Macedonia	14%	Indonesia	31%
Bulgaria	14%		
Croatia	36%		
Turkey	28%		

Source: Clean Clothes Campaign (2014, 34).

Immiserating Growth in the UK Clothing Sector

CVCs have generated, and been built upon, a vast global labouring class, divided along numerous lines. Segments of workers in countries higher up the imperialist chain are pitted against workers further down the chain, with the latter's wages and conditions representing a competitive cost baseline. In the United Kingdom, impoverishment caused by poverty wages expanded during the 2000s.

In-work poverty has proliferated because of factors ranging from Conservative Party government austerity policies to rising costs of living. Prior to the Covid pandemic, a 2018 report by the Joseph Rowntree Foundation found that '[s]ince 2004/05, the number of workers in poverty in the UK has increased at a faster rate than the total number of people in employment' (Barnard et al. 2018, 33). The report estimated that four million workers live in poverty. Some of this in-work poverty is caused by underemployment (insufficient hours of work), but it is also caused by systemic low pay, so that even when workers labour for a full working week, they are unable to afford a basket of basic goods.

In June 2020, while the Covid pandemic was still a prime concern of most people, news stories broke across the UK media about highly exploitative working conditions at garment factories in the city of Leicester. Many of these factories were supplying the fast-fashion label *Boohoo*, were engaged in paying below minimum wages to their workers, and were forcing the latter to labour in unsafe conditions (Labour Behind the Label 2020).

Boohoo is a UK-based online fast-fashion retailer aimed at teenagers and young adults. It has over 30,000 own-brand products. By 2019 it had sales worth almost £900 million and profits of almost £60 million. Its success is based, in part, on selling its products very cheaply. A red dress, for example, retailed at £4 in mid-2020 (Labour Behind the Label 2020, 11). *Boohoo* sources approximately 60 per cent to 70 per cent of its production from Leicester (Labour Behind the Label 2020, 3).

The fast-fashion industry specializes in rapid product innovation (as opposed to the traditional four-season styles) facilitated by quick design, production, and store delivery. The industry has received much criticism for its deleterious environmental impacts, but this time the media stories were concerned about workers' appalling conditions in the UK, which it was also speculated, might have contributed to a regional spike in Covid-19 infections across Leicester.

As a Labour Behind the Label Report notes, 'Garment manufacturing is a major industry in Leicester with over 1000 known sites, excluding home-working. Most factories in Leicester are small workshops, often housed in dilapidated buildings with little investment in building safety and modern ventilation' (Labour Behind the Label 2020, 3).

The workforce in Boohoo's supplier factories is predominantly made up of Black, Asian, and Minority Ethnic individuals, with around one-third being immigrants from India, Pakistan, and, increasingly, Eastern Europe. Many don't have documented resident status and are particularly vulnerable to deportation by the Home Office (Sullivan 2022).

During the Covid-19 lockdowns *Boohoo* was sourcing 300,000–400,000 units per week from Leicester workshops at very low unit prices. For example, it paid £1.90 for a pair of cycling shorts (which retailed at between £3 and £10). Wages of £2–£3 per hour were commonplace (Labour Behind the Label 2020, 4). The Boohoo case is not exceptional. A 2015 report by Leicester University's Centre for Sustainable Work and Employment Futures (Hammer et al. 2015) found that:

> There is considerable evidence that the ... business strategies are associated with severe violations of work and employment rights. Throughout the Leicester case-study, most widespread is the under- or non-payment of wages at the National Minimum Wage (NMW), the absence of employment contracts, late payment of wages, and the official declaration of a portion of wages only. Employers often consider welfare benefits as a 'wage component' and force workers to supplement wages below the NMW with welfare benefits. These problems are endemic in the industry: reports consistently put the average wage at £3 per hour and state that

> this applies to 75–90% of jobs in the sector. A conservative estimate on the above evidence would put the underpaid wage sum in apparel manufacturing within the East Midlands at £1 million per week.

Further:

> Management practices have created a segmented workforce that works under different price/quality/social compliance parameters. Sketched broadly, the highest, and smallest segment, consists of workers who do not have an employment contract but, overall, are paid at NMW rates. This is followed by a much larger segment of mostly female workers whose language and/or socio-cultural capabilities are too limited to work in other industries. These workers earn around £3/hour, are forced to complement their wages with welfare benefits and work under the conditions described above. Finally, migrants on student or visitor visas as well as undocumented migrants who no longer have the legal right to work and remain in the UK constitute the most vulnerable groups. These groups often work for even lower or no wages, work night shifts, and are dismissed at will, amongst other potential issues.
>
> **(Hammer et al. 2015, 10f.)**

In sum, the Boohoo case study illuminates how workers are subject to immiserating exploitation in parts of the UK. Such dynamics are not caused by the employing firm alone, but have been institutionalized through the government's immigration regimes, which reproduces workers vulnerable to immiserating exploitation.

7.5 Conclusions

The predominant argument within the GVC mainstream is that workers benefit from employment in GVCs. Many of these claims are based upon conceptions of poverty/non-poverty derived from the World Bank's IPLs. But these IPLs represent arbitrary measures. They have not been designed, and cannot be used, to assess whether individuals can survive, still less meet their individual and familial basic needs, at the poverty lines' specified levels of consumption. These poverty lines' focus upon individual consumption do not address the kinds of labour workers must undertake to afford to consume at, or above, the poverty threshold. If a poverty measure based upon workers' individual and familial social reproduction requirements is deployed to investigate the relationship between employment in CVCs and poverty generation/alleviation, then a different, and often negative, image emerges—of widespread immiserating growth. This chapter uses the concepts of immiserating exploitation and IGRs to highlight (a) how capitalist firms will, when they can, pay workers below living wages, and (b) that such employment strategies—of maintaining workers' in poverty to boost profits—are buttressed by (supplier and lead) firms in concert with national states.

As noted in Chapter 2, the concepts of IGRs and immiserating exploitation contribute to the labour regime research agenda by providing a vantage point to assess ways in which such regimes are based upon/reproduce relatively impoverished labouring classes. Such research can be advanced further by tracing relations between countries and firms' position in the imperialist chain and in CVCs, and the extent and form of such poverty. In this way a sharper geographical focus would complement this chapters' political economy approach.

As discussed theoretically in Chapters 1 and 2, and as acknowledged empirically by the World Bank, CVC firms place downward pressure on labour. Immiserating exploitation in one part of the world, and the profits deriving from it, exacerbates pressures upon capitalists in other parts of the world to adopt such strategies of accumulation. States often facilitate such accumulation strategies by institutionalizing poverty pay.

This is not to say that improvements to workers' wages, conditions, and livelihoods are impossible under CVCs. As Chapter 9 (Social Upgrading) shows, workers' collective actions are essential to the winning of improvements in wages, conditions, and livelihoods. It is to say that capitalist value chains are vehicles for immiserating exploitation and that they are widely associated with, and in many cases are causes of, immiserating growth regimes.

8

Economic Upgrading through Class Differentiation

The jungle needs ants but it must also have elephants and giraffes.

(El Agro's[1] then president, naturalizing class differentiation, cited in Bernhold 2022, 294)

8.1 Introduction

In mainstream GVC literature upgrading is presented as a development strategy.[2] It would be more accurate to state that upgrading, when it occurs, re-shapes the dynamics of uneven development—where some firms gain at the expense of other actors. But this would, of course, change the attractiveness of the upgrading for development paradigm. This chapter provides an example of how, rather than representing a 'win–win' strategy, upgrading occurs through class differentiation, including the concentration and centralization of capital. Economic upgrading strategies are based on and shape class and power relations. They imply the restructuring of capitalist social relations and thus shifting patterns of control over means of production and labour power. In short, economic upgrading is achieved not just by technological or organizational innovations, but by (re-)shaping the exploitative relations of production.

To examine these processes, this chapter uses an in-depth case study of agribusiness in Argentina. After the 1990s agro-industrial chains gained heightened importance in Argentina's political economy. The harvested area for grains (wheat and maize) and oilseeds (soybeans and sunflower seeds) more than doubled from approximately 14.5 million hectares (ha) in 1990 to nearly 32 million hectares in 2019, with significant productivity gains achieved with biotechnology and agrochemicals, among other innovations.

[1] The names of the company and all its representatives and employees are changed due to anonymization.

[2] This chapter is adapted from Bernhold and Palmisano (2022).

Capitalist Value Chains. Benjamin Selwyn and Christin Bernhold, Oxford University Press.
 DOI: 10.1093/9780191994906.003.0008

A large part of this area (41.63 per cent) was planted with soybeans. This export crop and its derivatives alone accounted for a quarter of Argentina's total exports in 2018. In this regard, Argentina has emerged as a key global player. Currently, it is the third-largest producer of raw soybeans, following Brazil and the United States. Additionally, the country has built a robust processing industry for these oilseeds. In 2020, companies based in Argentina processed 38.8 million tons of soybeans (of the 48.8 million tons of soybeans produced), completing at least the initial stage of industrial processing domestically (Bernhold 2022, 12).

This expansion, however, was accompanied by a notable de-diversification of Argentina's industry, giving rise to the concept of a 'reprimarization' of the country's political economy (Teubal 2006, 79, own translation; see Azpiazu et al. 2011; Schorr 2013). Nonetheless, Argentinian GVC scholars have posited that upgrading in agribusiness has opened a 'window of opportunities' (Anlló et al. 2013a, 13, own translation) for development that can be best utilized through further upgrading.

In contrast to this optimistic view, this chapter illuminates the interrelated dynamics of economic upgrading, capital concentration, and class differentiation, within Argentinian agribusiness. In the above-described context of agro-industrial development, some local companies have managed to grow significantly, producing grains and oilseeds on enormous scales (see below). They have integrated their investment activities across agro-industrial value chains, including technology development, the production and sale of agrochemicals, the provision of financial and other agro-related services, the commercialization of crops, and the operation of processing plants.

In doing so, these actors have reshaped the dominant model of capitalist farming in the Pampean region. Throughout much of the twentieth century, before agriculture became increasingly capital intensive, the region was characterized not only by large-scale farmers but also by so-called *Chacareros*—'traditional' capitalized farmers who owned the machinery required for production and relied heavily on family labour for both subsistence and market production. Until the mid-twentieth century, many of them leased-in (rented) land. Later, they gradually acquired land property through market purchases or colonization policies (Muzlera 2021; see Archetti and Stölen 1975; Balsa 2007).

With the neoliberal restructuring of class power, and especially from the 2000s onwards, production became increasingly controlled by large agribusiness firms. The 1990s saw the emergence of a distinctive Argentine feature that would later play a crucial role in the new millennium: *Pools de siembra* (sowing pools) proliferated. Similar to trusts, these pools were mostly organized around agricultural companies, which pooled finance from all over the world to invest in soy production (Fernández 2012a, 103). Managing soy production on over 100,000 hectares or more, these firms outsourced rural labour (such as sowing and harvesting) to labour service providers (so-called *contratistas*) and leased-in land—often from former *chacareros*, the latter who ceased to be profitable as independent farmers and became small rentiers.

However, after international soy prices dropped and leasing prices rocketed, some companies further adjusted their strategies, so that land, machinery, and other resources are often no longer simply leased at fixed rates. Instead, small producers, landowners, labour service providers, and other actors are formally integrated, under the effective direction of large agribusiness firms, as network partners, receiving a share of the harvest rather than a fixed payment for rents or services.

These developments have entailed a profound transformation of the social structure in rural areas, which includes processes of class differentiation. Our notion of class-differentiation emphasizes two aspects. First, class is a relational concept that defines the positioning of groups of actors towards each other in and through exploitative capitalist relations of production. While the latter are based on and dominated by the capital–labour relation, class dynamics entail a myriad of social groups. These include intermediate classes (which in this chapter refer to petty commodity producers and self-employed managers, see below). Second, dynamic processes of capitalist development, including economic upgrading trajectories, entail shifts within the social (class) structure. That is, members of a social class can (be forced to) change their location in the class structure.

This phenomenon is evident in the case study below: an agribusiness production network controlled by El Agro—a figurehead company in Argentina that has pioneered process upgrading (raising productivity) and restructuring agriculture into a high-tech production network. The company also exemplifies what GVC scholars describe as functional upgrading (taking on higher-value functions within agro-industrial chains), offering a range of agricultural and financial services, among other things.

However, this development is not a story in which elephants, giraffes, and ants all come out winners—to pick up the metaphor in this chapter's epigraph, that naturalizes capitalist social differentiation. Instead, we show how—besides CVC-integration—El Agro's economic upgrading involves: (a) the centralization of capital through the acquisition of other companies; (b) ties created with smaller capitals, intermediate classes and (outsourced) labour in a process of class differentiation; and (c) El Agro's power to profit from these relations by appropriating surplus value at different points of the value chain. In that sense, El Agro's initiatives have influenced the operational landscape by reshaping the relations of production. Capital concentration pushed many farmers out of the market over recent decades, but some of these farmers have been re-integrated into agribusiness in new class positions—and El Agro profits most from these relations.

In comparison to previous chapters of our book, to analyse upgrading through class differentiation in its various facets we focus in detail on one case. While the re-shaping of the social relations will likely be different in other CVC cases, we argue that its analysis must be part and parcel of CVC analysis. The GVC mainstream, however, lacks the conceptual tools to recognize, or conceptualize, such transformations.

Following this introduction, Section 8.2 briefly discusses how mainstream GVC literature has analysed economic upgrading in agriculture, with a particular focus on Argentina. Section 8.3 then provides a theoretical overview of concepts linking capitalist dynamics of economic upgrading, class differentiation, and capital concentration. Although these dynamics shape agribusiness networks in Argentina, they are omitted by the mainstream literature. Section 8.4 notes the degree of concentration and centralization in agriculture in the Pampean region, Argentina's heartland of agribusiness. Section 8.5 zooms into the case study. Section 8.6 concludes.

8.2 Schumpeter in Argentina? The GVC Mainstream on Upgrading in Agriculture

The GVC mainstream posits that economic upgrading can work as a 'new paradigm for development' in any industry, including agriculture (Gereffi and Fernandez-Stark 2016, 24). While different perspectives exist in the literature on economic upgrading in agricultural value chains (Ponte and Ewert 2009, 1637), mainstream scholars adopt a distinctly modernist approach to economic upgrading, conceptualizing it as advancement towards higher value activities (Fernandez-Stark et al. 2012). Here, proposed policies include technical assistance, knowledge transmission and skill improvement, support for local producers to gain market access and competitiveness (e.g., through product upgrading into fair trade agriculture), and the promotion of processing in situ (Stamm 2008; Fernandez-Stark et al. 2011; Farole and Winkler 2014). John Humphrey (2006, 584ff.) argues explicitly that donors intervening in agriculture GVCs should align their agendas with lead firm interests and avoid undermining them. 'If the goal is poverty reduction', this may involve 'allowing small farms to decline and focusing instead on improving conditions for waged employees' (Humphrey 2006, 588).

The GVC mainstream in Argentina echoes this sentiment, emphasizing the state-of-the-art technology driving soybean, maize, and wheat production, and highlighting the role of domestic industrial processing as an engine of development (Bisang 2007; Anlló et al. 2013b; Campi 2013). According to these writers, Argentinian agribusiness has undergone profound changes in the past decades, a path that they say must be further developed. This includes the ongoing refinement of biotechnology, agrochemicals, and no-till farming, high-tech machinery, and patterns of organizing production that have changed from the vertical integration of small farming entities to a network model that strongly relies on (labour) subcontracting.

Anlló et al. (2013a) have asked the rhetorical question whether Joseph Schumpeter has been visiting the Pampean region, the main hub of Argentina's grain and oilseed production. Adopting his idea of creative destruction, they argue that old production schemes have been replaced by new entrepreneurs who readily take the risk of implementing new technologies, form new, network-like organizational patterns of agricultural production, and hence 'push the economic cycle towards a positive phase' (Anlló et al. 2013a, 28; see Chapter 3 on creative destruction).

In this view, production networks, characterized by a separation of machinery/land ownership and control over production, allow for a rapid economic and territorial expansion of agricultural companies, since they do not have to fix capital in land or equipment. Instead, labour service providers (so-called *contratistas*) own the necessary machinery and hire workers (Anlló et al. 2013c, 193). As a result of these changes, Argentinian agribusiness 'operates at the vanguard of the so-called biological revolution' (Bisang and Campi 2013, 92).

Existing inequalities are recognized by these authors. They acknowledge 'adverse events', such as land conflicts, enduring economic crises among small producers, rural poverty, and a concentration of tacit knowledge and technologies in the hands of large biotech corporations (Anlló et al. 2013b). For example, the biotechnology for genetically modified organisms (GMO's) is largely controlled by Monsanto/Bayer (Bernhold 2022, 171). However, Anlló et al. (2013a, 28) posit that such adverse events are normal in early stages of creative destruction, and that *they can be overcome by further economic upgrading* in situ. For example, Bisang et al. (2008) argue that existing asymmetries are conducive to innovation: they have their 'productive counterpart in the form of adopting and adapting innovations' (Anlló et al. 2013c, 198f., own translation). Accordingly, it depends on 'the Argentinians' whether they 'seize this window of opportunity' and 'work intensely on a new generation of innovations' (Anlló et al. 2013b, 352, own translation).

This notion of economic upgrading abstracts from class relations in general, and from specific agricultural dynamics that impact those who produce grains and oilseeds in the fields. For example, many rural wage workers contend with temporary unemployment due to the seasonal nature of the labour process. But these social relations are not factored into, or theorized within, notions of the benefits of economic upgrading and creative destruction in the Argentinian Pampas in any meaningful way. This sidelining of social dynamics reflects a reluctance amongst proponents of economic upgrading to analyse how the exploitative social relations of production both shape and are re-shaped by the development of agro-industrial value chains.

By contrast, this chapter analyses how firm-level upgrading is grounded in re-shaped exploitative relations and capital concentration in Pampean agriculture. Before delving into the empirical material, the next section introduces the concept of class differentiation, which we employ to make sense of these developmental dynamics.

8.3 Class Differentiation and (Agrarian) Social Change

Critical agrarian political economy advocates a class-analytical understanding of agricultural value chains (Bernstein and Campling 2006). While a substantial body of scholarship has analysed different forms of exploitation in global capitalism (Campling et al. 2016), racialized and gendered social segmentation (Werner 2012; Bair et al. 2013; Werner 2016), and the fragmentation of the working-class along both the functionally divided labour process and labour markets (Jha and Chakraborty 2016; Butollo 2021; Howson et al. 2022), this chapter underscores the role of *class itself* in dynamics of differentiation.

As outlined in Chapter 2, our analysis of class is concerned with the social relations through which surplus value is produced (by labour), appropriated (by capital), and distributed. However, the ways in which unpaid surplus labour is squeezed from the direct producers, and surplus value is distributed, takes myriad forms. As Marx (1991, 927 f.) puts it, class relations display 'endless variations and gradations in its appearance'. Both capital and labour are internally differentiated, and there are intermediate classes (Projekt Klassenanalyse 1974, 67).

Capital is not only differentiated by size. Within the division of labour, particular (groups of) capitalists also perform specific functions such as the commercialization of commodities (Marx 1991, 379). As *productive capital*, investors make profits that are based on the extraction of unpaid labour directly from the workers. Others participate thereof in form of an *interest* (finance capital), *commercial profit* (commercial capital), or *ground rent* (landowners) (Projekt Klassenanalyse 1974). The case study below shows how El Agro has, through wide-ranging functional upgrading, managed to expand into all these capital functions, enabling it to increase its profits by appropriating surplus value across various points in the value chain.

In class-analytical terms, labour is differentiated along these lines as well. Marx observes how 'just as the labourer's unpaid labour directly creates surplus-value for productive capital, so the unpaid labour of the commercial wage-worker secures a share of this surplus-value for merchant's capital' (Marx 1991). Labour is further differentiated by qualifications, which are linked to the functional division of labour (Projekt Klassenanalyse 1974, 215). Below, we show how El Agro has shaped its network in a way that makes some qualified management and commercial workers appear as equal business partners—a relation that has even led them to do some of their work without remuneration, as they do not perceive themselves as employees.

Workers are not always in a direct relation with capital, they can also be employed, for instance, by petty capitalist producers who belong to the intermediate classes. The latter own (at least some) means of production that they employ themselves, such that they combine the positions of capital and labour (Projekt Klassenanalyse 1974, 177f.). For example, while El Agro profits from the labour performed in the soybean fields, these workers are directly employed by labour service providers, many of which are petty capitalist producers.

The notion of class differentiation does not imply that capital and labour change beyond recognition. On the contrary: 'the totality of class', the fact that those who essentially control the means of production appropriate the fruits of others labour, is itself 'reproduced through intra-class differences' (Das 2017, 17). The ways in which unpaid surplus labour is squeezed from the direct producers, and surplus value is distributed, undergo historical changes, generated by evolving dynamics of capitalist growth, class struggles, and capital strategies. Marx notes how, 'uniformity or similarity of reproduction—the repetition of production under the same conditions does not exist. Productivity itself changes and changes the conditions [of production]' (Marx 1989, 517). In David Harvey's (2017, 115) words, 'capital is innately revolutionary ... because it is value in motion under conditions of continuous growth and technological innovation'. Such dynamism is intimately related to changing class structures and relations.

In this chapter we focus upon two facets of how capitalism's 'revolutionary' dynamism involves changes within the social structure. First, the systematic efforts to increase the extraction of surplus value entail ongoing transformations in systems of production, and individual capitals' increased control over means of production. Especially, advances in high-tech production require the investment of ever larger amounts of capital (Altvater 1975, 149). Capitalism's dynamism thus implies the concentration and centralization of capital. As outlined in Chapter 2, these notions highlight the tendency, and private property-based capacity, to appropriate surplus-value continuously and on an expanded scale, either directly from workers or from other capitals. To recap, concentration refers to the reproduction of capital on growing scales and to the related control over means of production and labour power by individual capitalists. Centralization describes the 'transformation of many small into few large capitals', where one capitalist 'strikes down many others'.

Second, economic concentration and new organizational processes that are more efficient for capital (such as new models of sharecropping, or the organization of rural labour via contractors, see below) imply changes within the social/class structure. In this way members of a social class (can be forced to) change their location in the exploitative class structure (for instance, when they cease to be competitive as capitalist farmers and are reintegrated into agribusiness networks in new social positions). This process can also imply a further centralization of (intangible) means of production, for example, when the knowledge of these former farmers comes to be deployed on behalf of big agribusiness capital in such networks.

Agrarian Political Economy and Class Differentiation

Dynamics of class differentiation apply *in general* to capitalist development. An important body of agrarian political economy literature explores and theorizes how such processes occur *in agrarian industries* (e.g., Byres 1997; Bernstein 2010). This literature illuminates historically, and conceptually, the diverse forms that capital concentration and social structures take as part of the development of agrarian capitalism.

For example, Terry Byres' (1997) analysis of the rise of agrarian capitalism in England illuminates how dynamics of relatively open, militant and often violent class struggle occurred over centuries. In the fourteenth century, the great plague and mass peasant rebellions eroded the structures of feudalism.

For a while peasants experienced a 'golden age', gaining relatively independent control over land and production compared to prior feudal practices of exploitation. However, between the sixteenth and eighteenth centuries, a new agrarian class arose. The enclosure movement—driven forward by the emergent agrarian capitalist class—simultaneously concentrated land under its ownership while displacing former peasants. The new landed class rented its new property out to tenant farmers, who in turn employed the emergent rural wage labour force that had been dispossessed of its access to land (see Brenner 1982).

Byres then shows how other countries, in Europe and beyond, transitioned to capitalism in different ways, depending on their constellations of class relations. He, and Cristobal Kay (2002) also note how in many Latin American countries, feudal oligarchs effectively transformed into large-scale agrarian capitalists. As we discuss below, Pampean agriculture had been dominated by capitalist farms of different sizes throughout the past century, many of which worked with family labour in direct production for both subsistence and the market. However, the class structure in Pampean agriculture has changed over the last few decades. Through processes of concentration and centralization of capital—reinforced by upgrading strategies—while some farmers have expanded, many farmers have ceased to be competitive. Some have been re-integrated into agribusiness networks in new class positions, from which they relinquish parts of the fruits of their labour and of the surplus value that they initially appropriate.

Central to Byres', Brenner's, and Kay's class-relational accounts of divergent agrarian capitalist development is a comparative political economy approach. Whilst eminently useful, this downplays international dynamics. Bernstein (1988, 2010) therefore advocates a conceptual framework that, whilst maintaining the insistence upon the class dynamics of capitalist agriculture, places it in the context of the global political economy. His framework considers geographically specific class relations (as, in our example, in Argentinian agribusiness) in the context of global agrarian political economy (considering, for example, the fact that the demand for soy, for example by Chinese or European meat companies, impacts upon investment decisions in Argentina).

Under conditions of global class dynamics of agrarian transformation generated by, and underpinning capitalist agriculture, Bernstein (2010) argues against assuming the ongoing existence of peasants or farmers as homogenous social groups. Beyond (internationalized) big agribusiness capital and rural labour, Bernstein (2010, 104) identifies the social positions of (a) emergent capitalist farmers who reproduce themselves as capital on larger scales; (b) petty commodity producers who reproduce themselves as capitals on the same scale; and (c) those who are struggling to reproduce themselves, becoming subject to a 'simple reproduction squeeze'.

However, for the purpose of this chapter, Bernstein's theoretical classification requires some moderations. First, in today's agro-industrial CVCs, *petty commodity producers* and other intermediate class actors (such as self-employed managers) are not necessarily peasants or farmers. In Pampean agribusiness, they are often integrated into agribusiness networks by taking on just one task, such as the provision of labour services, or commercial management. Second, there are *capitalist farmers* in the Pampean region who remain in business despite capital concentration—but they are not 'emergent' capitalists. Some of those who emerged decades ago to produce on fields larger than a few hundred hectares now face increasing challenges producing independently at these scales.

We therefore classify as *medium-capitalized producers* those who own the means of production (and/or have the capital to buy the services and inputs) necessary to control production on average scales (see the discussion about the development of farming units and their sizes, Table 8.1). They participate in productive labour, mainly assuming coordinating tasks, but also *systematically* exploit wage labour. We refer to *petty commodity producers* as those who own some means of production, which they deploy themselves, employing minimal, if any, wage labour.

With these conceptual modifications of Bernstein's approach in mind, the common thread is that class differentiation takes different forms, over particular lengths of time, in specific political economic contexts within CVCs.

8.4 Economic Upgrading and the Concentration and Centralization of Capital in Pampean Agriculture

Agriculture has been increasingly integrated into industrial capital circuits. This occurs as agricultural producers become dependent upon inputs (such as fertilizers, pesticides, herbicides) and other means of production (such as high-tech farming machinery). It also occurs through ever-greater integration into downstream logistical, processing and retail networks. At both ends of agribusiness CVCs, the concentration and centralization of capital have accelerated and deepened. Agriculture in the Pampean region is no exception.

The cultivation of grains and in particular of soybeans and maize has increased significantly in Argentina over the last three decades. The production of soybeans, wheat, maize, and sunflower seeds rose from roughly 30 million tons in 1990 to 135.4 million tons in 2019. Soybeans alone accounted for 55.3 million produced tons in 2019, compared to 10.7 million tons in 1990. Today, Argentina is the third largest producer of soybeans behind the USA and Brazil (Bernhold 2022, 179). This growth is due to an increase in land devoted to agribusiness, and to process upgrading and a resulting increase in productivity. In the case of soybeans, average yields rose from 2.2 tons/ha to 3.3 tons/ha between 1990 and 2019, and maize yields increased from 3.5 tons/ha to 7.9 tons/ha (Bernhold 2022, 180f.). These improvements in productivity were achieved through the introduction of a 'technological package' employing the biotechnology-agrochemical complex with no-till sowing, as well as of other innovations such as precision farming technology (Leguizamón 2014, 151; Berndt and Bernhold 2018, 37).

The most recent National Agricultural Census (NAC) data published by the Argentinian National Statistics Institute (INDEC) illuminate that ever-fewer farming units (FU) control economic expansion in this sector (Bernhold and Palmisano 2022). Between 1988 and 2018 the number of farming units smaller than 100 ha declined by 62.7 per cent, while farms bigger than 5000 ha increased by 32.9 per cent (see Table 8.1).

The NAC data also reveal a process of land use concentration in big farms (see Table 8.2).[3] While the share of the area cultivated by the smallest farming units has decreased by 61 per cent, those bigger than 5000 ha have expanded their share in land use by 41 per cent. Today, the latter control 22.1 per

Table 8.1 Variation in number of farming units in the Pampean region according to size

Farming Units (ha)	1988	2002	2018	Variation 1988–2018 (%)	Variation 2002–2018 (%)
Up to 100	83,591	49,469	31,179	−62.7	−37.0
100–500	70,11	50,763	36,604	−47.8	−27.9
500–1000	14,226	13,658	11,478	−19.3	−16.0
1000–5000	10,725	11,417	10,474	−2.3	−8.3
More than 5000	882	1,031	1,172	32.9	13.7
Total	179,534	126,338	90,907	−49.4	−28.0

Source: Bernhold and Palmisano (2022: 346).

[3] The total land used for agriculture production has shrunk in the context of increasing urban growth (Bernhold and Palmisano 2022: 346).

Table 8.2 Share in land use among farming units in the Pampean region according to size

Farming Units (ha)	1988		2002		2018	
	Million ha	%	Million ha	%	Million ha	%
Up to 100	3.53	6.1	2.20	4.0	1.36	2.7
100–500	16.37	28.1	12.34	22.2	9.09	18.1
500–1000	9,95	17.1	9.63	17.3	8.13	16.2
1000–5000	20.55	35.2	22,09	39.7	20.57	40.9
More than 5000	7.88	13.5	9,37	16.8	11.09	22.1
Total	58.28	100	55,63	100	50.24	100

Source: Bernhold and Palmisano (2022: 346).

cent of the land used in Pampean agriculture, while the former only control 2.7 per cent.

Furthermore, the parameters of what constitutes a medium-sized producer are growing in the wake of economic upgrading and concentration. For example, Fernández (2013, 95) calculated in 2009, for soy plantations, that only around 11 per cent were then smaller than 600 ha (down from over 40 per cent in 2002). In part, this is because increasing capital-intensive production is reducing the profitability and viability of smaller-scale production (Fernández 2012b).

Reflecting and reinforcing these dynamics, large firms' economies of scale generate extra profits. Growing production volumes and the ability to purchase in bulk enables large firms to acquire inputs relatively more cheaply than smaller firms (Fernández 2013). Large firms also benefit from a better access to finance and means of speculation, such as global futures markets (Sosa Varrotti 2019).

State policy has further accelerated capital concentration. For example, during the 1990s, President Menem (1989–1999) liberalized trade, and the Convertibility Plan (1991–2002) pegged the Argentine Peso (ARS) to the US dollar. This policy benefitted big agrarian capital over family farms, as it cheapened imported means of production compared to living expenses (Peretti 1999; Azcuy Ameghino 2000). Despite redistributive changes in socio-economic policy, the neo-developmentalist government of Cristina Kirchner (2007–2015) ultimately also fostered agribusiness concentration (Lapegna 2017), for instance, by levying export taxes on big corporations and petty commodity producers in equal percentages to the disadvantage of the latter (Teubal and Palmisano 2010; Fernández 2013).

8.5 Economic Upgrading, Capital Concentration, and Class Differentiation in Pampean Agribusiness

Not all farmers that cease to be competitive cease to exist entirely. However, their reproduction as farmers is often contingent on dependent relations with large agribusiness companies. The latter's value capture strategies are, in turn, based upon presiding over networks of smaller actors who lease-out land and buy inputs and services. Furthermore, some indebted farmers who were forced (or who opted) out of agribusiness were reabsorbed in new—dependent—ways, transformed, for instance, into labour service providers (*contratistas*) (Acosta Reveles 2008; Gras and Hernández 2013). The following examines these processes, showing how class differentiation is shaped by, and in turn affects, the capacity of big agribusiness to concentrate and centralize capital.

El Agro's Diversified Investment Strategies

As mentioned, El Agro is one of the most well-known agribusiness corporations in Argentina that increased its annual sales by a factor of 60 to more than one billion USD between the early 1990s and 2012–2013. The company was formed out of an older family business in 1984, inheriting 3500 hectares of land and storage facilities. Ever since, agriculture-related activities have remained at the core of its strategies, but it has also changed its strategies of accumulation through functional upgrading. It has integrated itself into agribusiness CVCs with a variety of acquisitions and investments as productive, finance and commercial capital, enabling it to capture surplus value at different points of production and circulation.

As *productive capital*, it operates in agriculture, processing, agrochemical production, precision farming and other services, as well as technology development. It became one of the biggest soybean cultivators in Latin America at the beginning of the 2000s, farming over 250,000 ha of land in Argentina and neighbouring countries in the 2009–2010 season. Later however, as described in the introduction, big agrarian capitals, including El Agro, developed a sharecropping model, where various actors are formally integrated as network 'partners', receiving a share of the harvest at the end of the season. This way, El Agro can control land while outsourcing a part of the risk: As one of its managers explains, 'when the harvest isn't good, you avoid things going wrong only for you'.[4]

[4] Interview with Carla, commercial manager of El Agro, 15 June 2016.

In its operation as productive capital, El Agro maintains a flexible approach to direct soy production. In the 2015–2016 season, it produced soy on 20,000 ha (55,000 ha when including sharecropping). After former President Macri won the election in 2015 and reduced export taxes on grains, production was increased to 80,000 ha (100,000 when including sharecropping).

An important reason to stay in primary production is that it secures fruitful contacts with potential clients who can be drawn into El Agro's network of services. The provision of services (including engineering and marketing consultancy, and logistics) has become an important business in and of itself, sprouting more stable profits than agriculture itself. In words that are familiar to the mainstream GVC community, El Agro's former president explains that today, 'we are a "one-stop shop"'. The agricultural producer 'needs an ecosystem around him that is more and more sophisticated and specialized. A seed supplier ... an agrochemical supplier, a precision farming service, a financial service, logistics, risk management, cutting-edge technology and management practices, consulting, and so on'.[5] However, the notion of a one-stop shop captures only superficially what the corporation has become. It's assumption of various capital functions illuminates how its investments signify its entry into, and increasing domination of, a range of operations, the better to capture part of the value produced in other firms and ultimately from workers in the network.

The company also operates as *commercial capital*. It trades seeds and agrochemicals, and it commercializes grains and oilseeds. Because primary producers buy seeds and agrochemicals independently of the outcome of the harvest, operating as commercial capital means profiting from agriculture even when primary producers lose money. At the same time, El Agro circumvents the problem of fixing capital in agriculture where the labour process pauses during the plants' growth. As manager Carla explains figuratively, El Agro is harvesting all year: clients always need a service, to buy inputs, or to sell grains.[6]

This is also true for El Agro's function as *finance capital*. Marx points to the credit system as another 'mighty weapon in the battle of competition' (Marx, 1990, 778), and El Agro has taken advantage of its power in this capacity. It acts through a company-owned Reciprocal Guarantee Society (SGR, in Spanish), which earns interest for providing bank guarantees that grant small and medium enterprises (SMEs) access to credit.[7] By providing finance, the corporation widens its network of clients: Usually, managers reinforce the

[5] Interview with Santiago, former president of El Agro, 21 August 2014.
[6] Interview with Carla, commercial manager of El Agro, 15 June 2016.
[7] Interview with Ana, manager of El Agro's SGR, 28 April 2015.

expectation that SGR-clients buy other things from the one-stop-shop. Especially smaller clients must prove that they are customers worth financing. As one El Agro-manager explains: 'We consider the reciprocity ... whether they bought the inputs and delivered grains. If not, that can obviously influence future decisions.'[8]

El Agro's evolution into a one-stop shop for its network of clients represents a paradigmatic case of how functional upgrading works through class differentiation, including capital concentration. While the GVC mainstream emphasizes the former element (functional upgrading and the purported, and often assumed, developmental benefits arising from it) the class relations of such processes illuminate exploitative and unequalizing social dynamics.

Relations to Smaller Capitals and Intermediate Classes

El Agro's business—and upgrading—model encompasses links with other capitals of varying sizes, and myriad actors in intermediate class positions, including petty commodity producers and remunerated management service providers who work on a mainly (pseudo) self-employed basis.

(Small) Capitalist Clients, Petty Commodity Producers and Differentiated Value Capture

Associations with other capitalist producers establish business opportunities for El Agro by buying goods and services from the 'one-stop shop.' For example, one of its clients is itself a merger of agrarian family businesses who together owned 3000 ha of land and joined forces to buy high-tech machinery. They also lease in several thousand hectares for cultivation. Relations with this client enabled El Agro to expand its business as commercial capital as the client firm sells 65 per cent of its grains to and buys 70 per cent of its inputs from El Agro.

The smaller their property base, the more the clients tend to act in favour of El Agro. For example, a medium-capitalized producer reports that he usually closes most of his deals in agrochemicals, services, etc. with El Agro, often even in cases when he could get better prices elsewhere. This is to maintain a positive relationship with the firm mainly due to the financial services he can receive.[9]

[8] Interview with Ana, manager of El Agro's SGR, 28 April 2015.
[9] Interview with a medium-capitalized producer, 14 July 2016.

In the following we give two examples of how members of a social class can (be forced to) change their location in the class structure. In the first case, through his relations to El Agro, Darío keeps his head above water, but he has started to resemble a dependent rentier rather than the medium-capitalized producer he used to be. Second, Federico is a petty commodity producer (and a labour service provider to El Agro).

Darío is a good example of how the centralization of capital has affected farmers. He used to breed cattle on 1500 ha of land owned by various family members. By 2016, this land was mainly dedicated to grain and soy production in association with El Agro, as livestock farming lost profitability and the family now lacks capital and know-how for independent farming. Darío hires two workers. When only considering the land ownership, he may appear a medium-capitalized producer, but as most of the land is now de facto controlled by El Agro via the above-described association, he rather resembles a dependent rentier in the sense that his role is largely limited to contributing land. The SGR (the Reciprocal Guarantee Society) advances money for Darío's running costs, and he reasons that he is therefore 'ethically obliged to sell them my grains. I could not ask them for money [from the SGR] ..., then go sell my grains somewhere else.'[10] Minus the fee he pays for the financial service, he feels he has a moral duty to support El Agro.

Federico is an example of a petty commodity producer whose family has experienced a downward trajectory in the class differentiation process. They used to own some land they had to sell in the 1990s. Today, he co-manages the production of grains on 200 to 400 ha of leased land. In addition, he owns a fumigation machine which he runs himself, because he does not have the capital to pay a worker. Sporadically, he fumigates crops for El Agro as a salaried service provider. Instead of being paid a fixed salary, he receives a previously determined share of the harvest. This means relatively good pay in times of good harvests, but also insecurity, for example, in the event of adverse weather conditions. For someone like Federico, a local crop shortfall means a bigger slump than for a company with investments as large and diversified as those of El Agro. However, he explicitly perceives himself as a partner, not as an employee.

In the end, these actors form parts of El Agro's value capture strategies. However, although the narrative of network partnership blurs existing class differences, their socio-economic position determines their form of attractiveness as clients for El Agro, their dependency upon it, and whether they are de facto exploited. The closer their socio-economic position to that of

[10] Interview with Darío, rentier and petty commodity producer, 7 July 2016.

capital, the more these companies are attractive for El Agro as commercial clients on equal footing—enabling it to continue expanding commercially and capturing shares of the produced surplus value. Petty producers like Federico qualify as 'network partners' only under stricter requirements. They are more dependent on El Agro—especially due to the SGR—and tend to act to the company's advantage. Some tend to be so loyal to the company that they voluntarily transfer a greater part of the surplus value to it than what is formally required.

Manager's Dependent Self-employment

As part of its one-stop-shop-strategy, El Agro has professionalized its management. Beyond a structure of permanently employed top-managers and white-collar workers, there are area managers who have become a centrepiece of El Agro's accumulation strategies. They work close to the clients and coordinate production or commercial branch offices. However, although they de facto work for El Agro, most of them are not paid fixed salaries. They are de jure independent entrepreneurs and sell a service as formally self-employed 'partners'. One of El Agro's permanently employed office managers explains that this is because the company wants to have investment flexibility. It always maintains ties to area managers 'to be able to scale-up production quickly'. Yet when it reduces primary production, it does not have to pay a fixed staff. This way, it can also outsource risks.

Area managers receive forms of pay, such as a share of the harvest, which tend to mystify the fact that they de facto work for El Agro. For the company, this has the advantage that the labour time is only paid insofar it is successfully embodied in a commodity, and not on a regular basis. Furthermore, the managers tend to be strongly committed to work, because their earnings do not come with a regular paycheck but depend on the business performance.

One example of this kind of relation is Juan Manuel, who is responsible for attracting customers in one of the company's commercial offices. He charges a commission for the crops he buys and the inputs he sells. Besides this role, he sells logistics services to El Agro with his own trucks. Juan Manuel portrays his position as follows: 'I officially belong to the network, not directly to the company. I am outside and inside the company at the same time.'[11]

This relation shows how the social boundaries between petty capitalists, remunerated service sellers and top qualified workers are fluid. It establishes a relationship where managers that de facto work for El Agro appear as de jure partners. The related promise of ascendance influences the commitment to El

[11] Interview with Juan Manuel, self-employed trade manager of El Agro, 1 July 2016

Agro to the extent that they would sometimes even work without asking for remuneration. One of them considers some jobs that involve lengthy travel 'like participating in an NGO ad honorem'.

This notion of belonging is further reinforced by the fact that many area managers have a very small—formally defined—business with which they cultivate grains in association with El Agro. Thus, even though they almost completely reproduce themselves as area managers, the additional existence as petty commodity producers influences their identities and strengthens the sense of partnership to El Agro.

El Agro has benefitted from this situation in another way. The business plan offered to the area mangers implies that they—although they lost control over their means of production—keep working in the areas that they had known for decades. Their knowledge and the personal ties they developed to other actors (landowners, contratistas, etc.) are intangible means of production now employed on behalf of El Agro. For the latter, these locally produced ties are crucial to win over customers. Relations that are built by locals are more familiar and confidence-building than those that can be built by a big alien corporation.

In sum, the relation between El Agro and these area managers implies a centralization of productive relations that are now put at the service of big capital. Especially in times of good harvests, they say that this relation has secured them a good living. However, in contrast to El Agro, they have not accumulated capital but maintained their disguised relation of qualified labour. At the same time, El Agro avoids fixed salaries and outsources economic risks to managers, who are nevertheless committed enough to do some of their work without asking for pay.

Outsourced Wage Labour

Lower down in the class hierarchy, among the workers who have nothing to sell but their labour power, are those who do the seeding and harvesting in the fields (mainly agricultural equipment operators). As outlined above, El Agro has partly shifted its source of profits away from extracting surplus value directly from workers, as it has outsourced the hiring of agriculture labour. *Contratistas* (labour service providers) oversee organizing the direct production in the fields. The class relations and labour conditions have thus much to do with big agribusiness corporations, even if the latter do not hire workers directly (for an in-depth analysis of labour in Pampean agribusiness, see Villulla 2015).

The relative proletarianization in Pampean agribusiness that has accompanied capital concentration is noteworthy. On the one hand, the demand for labour has been reduced considerably with increasing labour productivity, leading to competition among workers and heightened dependency by the latter on the jobs that exist. On the other hand, the *proportion* of wage labourers among those who still work in the sector has increased: A growing share of the work is commanded by capital and done by wage labourers who produce a surplus value that does not remain in their own hands. For example, the Population Census shows that 'the share of wage workers among the economically active population in Pampean agriculture grew by 11.9 percentage points from nearly 47% in 1991 to nearly 59% in 2010; the remaining share consists of self-employed and family labour, and of farm owners' (for an in-depth empirical consideration, see Bernhold 2022, 382).

This was paralleled by growing job insecurity, among other things, due to the seasonality of agriculture: the share of wage workers who are only temporarily employed by *contratistas* (compared with permanent workers) rose from 37.2 per cent to 47.4 per cent in the same period (Bernhold 2022, 389).

The re-organization of the social relations of agricultural production through economic upgrading is key here. The process of relative proletarianization is directly linked to the outsourcing of labour to *contratistas* as a strategy of flexibilization. This allows firms to reduce labour costs and related risks in an increasingly competitive and concentrated environment by reducing permanent employment (Neiman 2010; Sánchez Enrique 2016). It allows firms like El Agro to control production without employing workers directly and paying them off season.

This form of organizing production tends to conceal exploitation, for it defines capital and labour without them being in direct contact with one another (Villulla 2015). Instead, *contratistas* appear as the direct exploiters. In these labour relations, workers are not just geographically scattered (on individual machines as well as on distant fields), they are also socially dispersed in terms of whom they work for. The fact that they are not directly related to firms like El Agro blurs class differences both objectively and subjectively. Indeed, petty capitalist *contratistas* and their workers are often acquaintances and share the physical work in the field. The social difference between them is often much smaller than with El Agro or similar firms. This is also one of several factors that complicate local labour struggles,[12] for instance, for higher

[12] There is no single reason for the absence of collective labour disputes in Pampean agribusiness; instead there is an array of economic, practical, and political-cultural constraints to both organizing and the development of class solidarity. A conjunction of (a) the locally specific social relations of production, (historical) domination and disciplining of labour, (b) the organization of the work process, (c) the type of activity, (d) technological changes, (e) a responsible labour union that has supported neoliberal policies and (f) questions of culture and identity together constrain the possibilities to translate a need for change into actual political class formation (see Villulla 2015).

salaries—which have not increased correspondingly with the growing labour productivity in agribusiness. Hourly wages are low, and workers often spend three or more months on the road, working up to 16 hours per day. They sleep in trailers in the fields where they are available around the clock, thus often spending 24 hours per day at work (Villulla 2015).

8.6 Conclusions

This chapter illuminated the dynamics of CVC economic upgrading, capital concentration and class differentiation. It exemplified how whilst economic upgrading is promoted by the GVC mainstream as both a firm-level competitive objective and as a developmental strategy, it is achieved through class differentiation—by (re-)shaping the exploitative capitalist relations of production. In this process means of production and labour power are combined and controlled in class-constellations that encompass differentiations within both capital and the working class, as well as intermediate classes.

The case study showed how El Agro's economic upgrading involved (i) capital investments in various links of agribusiness value chains; (ii) centralization of capital through the acquisition of other companies; (iii) ties created to smaller capitals, petty commodity producers, self-employed managers, and outsourced labour in a process of class differentiation; and (iv) the power of big capital to profit from these relations by appropriating surplus value at different points of the value chain.

The analytical and theoretical considerations made in this chapter rest upon a particular case study, and the geographically particular web of social relations analysed here cannot be transferred to other historical and geographical contexts; class differentiation is not the same everywhere and many determinants mediate between tendencies in CVCs and local class dynamics.

However, this study can facilitate the investigation and analysis of other constellations of economic upgrading through changes to the class structure. Future CVC research needs to analyse how economic upgrading and capital concentration go hand in hand with shifting social relations across broader CVC geographies. In other words, the geographies of 'economic upgrading through class differentiation', from workplace to the international level, are part and parcel of the future CVC research agenda.

9
Social Upgrading from Below?

with Dara Leyden

> [I]f we fight, we won't always win. If we don't fight, we will always lose.
> **(attributed to Bob Crow, British Trade Unionist)**

9.1 Introduction

Does employment in Capitalist Value Chains (CVCs) benefit workers? And if so, how? In previous chapters we have explained how CVCs are structures that benefit capital, and lead firms in particular (see Chapter 2).[1] Yet, the mainstream GVC framework emphasizes the developmental potential of GVCs for workers, particularly in peripheral countries (see Chapter 3). This chapter will explore attempts by GVC authors to understand how such workers benefit from GVCs. It does so by foregrounding a developmental dynamic that has been largely neglected in GVC scholarship and articulated by Bob Crow in this chapter's epigraph—workers' struggles to improve their own conditions.

In economic history, it is taken for granted that workers fought to win minimum wages, weekends, holidays, working hour limits, health and safety provisions, sick pay, social insurance, and various other protections and entitlements (Thompson 1968; Roediger and Foner 1989; Darlington 2023). Working-class organizations took many forms, such as trade unions, political movements, and social campaigns. But during the intellectual and political left's 'retreat from class' (Wood 1998) from the 1980s onwards, theories of economic development tended to exclude labour as an agent of development. The GVC framework was no exception (Selwyn and Leyden 2022).

As we note in Chapters 1–3, the GVC framework is poorly equipped to analyse workers' conditions due to its narrow focus on *inter-firm* relations, that is, the distribution of value between lead firms and suppliers,

[1] This chapter is adapted from a PhD Thesis by Dara Leyden (2024), School of Business and Management, Queen Mary University of London.

Capitalist Value Chains. Benjamin Selwyn, Christin Bernhold with Dara Leyden, Oxford University Press.
 DOI: 10.1093/9780191994906.003.0009

and its lack of analysis of how value is produced by workers and distributed between firms and workers. Nevertheless, evidence of immiseration in GVC sweatshops compelled GVC authors to explain, rather than assume, how workers benefit from employment in GVCs (Raworth 2004; Raworth and Kidder 2009, see Chapter 7). Subsequently, therefore, the GVC framework was augmented with the concept of 'social upgrading', which was defined as improvements in the rights and entitlements of workers as social actors (Barrientos et al. 2011).

An important contribution of the social upgrading framework was its identification of 'social downgrading' in GVCs—that is, the worsening of workers' wages and conditions—particularly for vulnerable groups of workers (Rossi 2013). Despite this observation, the concept of social upgrading prioritizes *inter-firm* relations, and under-theorizes *capital–labour* relations. For example, it attributes improvements in workers' conditions primarily to measurable standards, such as voluntary corporate social responsibility (CSR) 'codes of conduct' that lead firms impose on their suppliers, rather than workers' collective actions. As we will argue, the concept of social upgrading's analysis of improvements in workers' conditions in GVCs is at best partial, due to its under-theorization of class relations.

As part of our critique of the notion of social upgrading, and our exposition of an alternative way of conceiving of workers' betterment in CVCs, we discuss three alternative approaches that take seriously the agency of workers in globalized production. Firstly, the Labour Geography approach studies how different groups of workers assert agency in the diverse global contexts connected by CVCs (Herod 1997). The Labour Geography approach has yielded many rich and valuable insights. However, we also identify how it suffers from a predicament—despite labour agency being its central concern, labour geographers have not coherently defined or conceptualized labour agency—which limits the analytical contributions of their studies. We locate this predicament in Labour Geography's deprioritization of Marxist conceptualizations of the unequal structural basis of capitalist class-relations (Herod 1997, 7–13; see Das 2017).

The second approach we explore defines labour agency in explicitly class-relational terms. The 'power resources approach' (PRA) is rooted in the dialectic between labour struggles and the reshaping of CVCs (Silver 2003; Schmalz et al. 2018). It reveals how 'just-in-time' supply chains have provided strategically positioned groups of workers, such as in logistics, with enhanced 'structural power' that they can assert through strategic actions to win socio-economic improvements (Newsome et al. 2015). However, we note how the PRA tends to abstract from the more general constraints that workers face, which undermines its strengths. In particular, the approach does not adequately address ways in which capital–labour relations and class politics are constituted not only within the CVC, but are also shaped by economic, political, and cultural dynamics at the national level (Fox-Hodess 2019; Nowak 2022).

The final approach explored in this chapter transcends the PRA's weaknesses by recognizing how workers in CVCs are located in particular 'labour regimes'. These are context-specific relations and institutions that shape and constrain work, exploitation and struggle. Baglioni et al. (2022a) make a significant contribution to the labour regime approach by applying it to CVCs. We outline the strengths of this approach, while also suggesting that its analytical specificity about how labour regimes change over time could be enhanced further through the inclusion of workers' power resources and our concept of international class relations (see Chapter 2).

The boundaries between these approaches are often fluid, and authors move in between them. For example, Labour Geographers have worked with the PRA approach. However, we address these approaches separately for the sake of clarity.

Finally, we turn to the title of this chapter, to discuss the possibility of 'social upgrading from below' in CVCs. We illuminate the concept by drawing upon a case study of struggles by garment CVC workers in Honduras who successfully fought against the largest employer in the country to win sustained social upgrading (Anner 2011, 2013, 2021, 2022). Whilst recognizing the importance of such cases—for the workers, and conceptually for notions of more progressive developmental dynamics within CVCs—in our conclusion we caution against dangers of 'fallacies of composition', that is, the notion that because some workers can secure improvements, similar improvements are possible for all workers in CVCs.

9.2 Economic Upgrading with Social Upgrading?

As Chapter 3 explained, the mainstream GVC framework analyses global capitalism as a structure of *inter-firm* relations, primarily between lead firms and suppliers: the important agents are firms, and agency is conceptualized as economic upgrading (Gereffi 1994b; Gereffi et al. 2005). In the early days of the GVC framework it was implicitly assumed that supplier upgrading benefits workers in peripheral countries, but the framework contained no theory of how, or why, gains from economic upgrading would be shared with workers.

Case studies soon revealed that, conversely, supplier upgrading was often accompanied by the heightened exploitation of workers (Raworth 2004).

For example, in an extensive study of the apparel and fresh produce GVCs, Raworth and Kidder (2009) revealed that lead firms' requirements for speed, flexibility, and low-cost exerted commercial pressures upon supplier firms. In turn, these suppliers pursued upgrading by transferring the pressures onto workers, resulting in flexibilization, low wages, long hours, and insecure contracts.

In response to increasing numbers of such observations, Barrientos, Gereffi, and Rossi (2011, 324) distinguished between the 'economic upgrading' of firms and 'social upgrading' of their workers. They defined the latter as 'the process of improvement in the rights and entitlements of workers as social actors, which enhances the quality of their employment'. Barrientos et al. argue that economic upgrading can be pursued either through higher-quality production, which is more likely to lead to social upgrading, or through flexibility and cost-reduction, which can lead to 'social downgrading'.

Two components of social upgrading were defined: 'measurable standards', such as health and safety standards, and 'enabling rights', such as freedom of association (Barrientos et al. 2011). The authors recognize that standards are often the outcome of bargaining, which are enabled by rights. They nevertheless focus upon standards, noting that future research should focus on workers as 'social agents with rights' (Barrientos et al. 2011, 336).

To test the connection between economic and social upgrading, institutional economists Thomas Bernhardt and William Milberg (2011) developed a quantitative method using country-sector statistics, based on indicators of economic upgrading (rising unit export prices) and social upgrading (increased employment) (Rossi 2019, 275). Based on these restricted measures, they found that economic and social *downgrading* were more common than previously thought within the mainstream GVC literature.

The lack of empirical and analytical clarity on the relationship between economic and social upgrading begged the question, repeatedly, of how the former is translated into the latter. This question was taken forward by the *Capturing the Gains* ('CTG') research programme. CTG analysed 34 country-sector case studies across four GVC sectors to identify the links between economic and social upgrading (Goger et al. 2014, 33).

CTG studies yielded important insights. It illuminated how lead firms' procurement practices exacerbate social downgrading among their suppliers via employment casualization and excessive overtime. It attributed these outcomes to two main factors: firstly, buyers' monopolistic strategy of playing their suppliers off against each other to push down suppliers' prices (Milberg and Winkler 2013); and secondly, buyers' practices of placing large orders with suppliers with very short deadlines (Barrientos et al. 2011).

The former suppresses wages and the latter encourages suppliers to construct flexible workforces such that workers can be pressured to do excessive overtime to fulfil orders and then dismissed once the orders are completed. Such casualization is frequently pursued through labour contracting, disproportionately affecting women and racialized groups (Barrientos 2008; Christian et al. 2013).

CTG studies identified that growing lead firm power is related to enhanced concentration in GVCs since the 2008 global financial crisis (Milberg and Winkler 2011). In mobile phones, for example, higher concentration among lead firms has enabled them to suppress suppliers' prices. Due to thin margins, the latter sought economies of scale, expanding to become large 'contract manufacturers', such as Foxconn. This mutually reinforcing concentration of lead firms and suppliers has accelerated the geographical concentration of production in China. At the same time, CTG authors identified how the concentration of GVC workforces in a few producers and locations 'provides a fertile ground for the rise of strong labour activism' (Lee and Gereffi 2013, 22; Lee et al. 2013; see also Appelbaum 2008; Kumar 2020; and see Chapter 2).

Similar dynamics—of a dialectic of capital concentration and enhanced workers' organization—were identified in garments GVCs. For example, a study of garment workers in Bangladesh by Ahmed and Nathan (2014) identified dynamics of economic and social upgrading. While social auditors attributed improvements in workers' conditions in Bangladesh's garments factories to greater compliance with buyers' labour standards, the authors argue that buyer's audits are generally 'perfunctory' and are not undertaken in the second-tier suppliers where the worst working conditions exist (Ahmed and Nathan 2014, 17).

Conversely, Ahmed and Nathan (2014) find that buyers squeeze their suppliers hard on prices, resulting in thin margins, which cascades down to lower-tier suppliers, thus suppressing workers' wages. Therefore, wage increases did not result from buyers' standards, but from the formation of garment workers into a politically assertive class, enabled by their dense concentration in industrial areas. Women workers formed independent labour organizations, and mass protests and wildcat strikes secured significant wage increases (see also Arnold 2013b on mass strikes for higher wages in Cambodian garment GVCs).

In Morocco, Rossi's (2013) seminal study of social upgrading identifies divergent social upgrading and downgrading for different groups of garment workers within the same factories. Rossi argues that employers use segmentation as a strategy to manage the tension between, on the one hand, volatile short-term orders from buyers, and on the other hand, buyers' insistence on compliance with their labour standards. Suppliers manage this tension by segmenting their workforce into two groups: firstly, regular skilled workers whose entitlements comply with the buyers' standards; and secondly, irregular workers hired flexibly to meet the buyer's deadlines. Economic upgrading led to social upgrading for the former, but social downgrading for the latter (see also Godfrey 2013 on garments in South Africa).

Rossi (2013) thereby challenges simplistic notions of a causal relationship between economic and social upgrading. However, Rossi attributes the contradictory dynamics of social upgrading alongside social downgrading to *inter-firm relations* in GVCs—specifically, the tension between buyers' standards versus buyers' commercial requirements. She does not explicitly conceptualize the importance of *capital–labour relations* in GVCs as determining differential developmental outcomes of employment within these industries. For example, Rossi does not consider how employer practices of workforce segmentation are deployed to supress workers' collective action (contra Martinelli 2022, see Section 9.4).

Rossi's prioritization of standards over capital–labour struggles was also reflected in the conclusions of the CTG programme as laid out in a report by Goger et al. (2014). The report focussed primarily on the effects of standards, rather than analysing the various workers' struggles that were identified through CTG case studies. The overarching claim of the CTG conclusions was that a virtuous path of combined economic and social upgrading can be achieved through improved skills-training, infrastructure, rights, and standards (Rossi 2019, 278ff.).

Labour standards are important. However, CTG's prioritization of standards over workers' struggles is surprising given that its studies were generally critical of private standards, while providing many examples of workers organizing and fighting to secure social upgrading (Arnold 2013b; Staritz and Morris 2013; Ahmed and Nathan 2014).

This conceptual tension can be traced to the theorization of social upgrading by Barrientos et al. (2011). Despite attempts to observe and comprehend the relationship between workers' employment and their conditions within GVC firms, the social upgrading approach under-theorizes capital-labour relations. The authors' distinction between economic and social upgrading recognizes that gains for firms in GVCs are sometimes shared with their workers, and sometimes not. In other words, social upgrading depends on relations between capital and labour. While the GVC framework conceptualizes relations *between firms*, social upgrading required a conceptualization of relations between *employers and workers*. However, the notion of social upgrading prioritizes the *inter-firm* analytical lens of the GVC framework. This resulted in CTG's conclusions prioritizing the benefits of standards transmitted through GVCs, rather than workers' struggles against capital to improve their own conditions (Selwyn 2013b).

The under-theorization of *capital–labour* relations in the concept of social upgrading is evident in its under-theorization of the complexities and dynamics of capital–labour relations, particularly the labour process—evident in its typology of work (Barrientos et al. 2011, 332). Its five-fold typology of work is based upon five different GVC sectors. It posits that higher-skilled forms of work exist in greater proportions in GVCs of higher technological sophistication. The authors argue that upgrading towards GVC sectors or segments with higher proportions of higher-skilled work influences the prospects for improved standards, and thus, social upgrading. For example, the typology counterposes 'low-skilled' work in apparel versus 'high-skilled' work in electronics (Barrientos et al. 2011, 333).

However, Barrientos et al.'s (2011) typology of work did not incorporate a rigorous comparative analysis of the labour process within the five sectors, their differing capital–labour relations, how their labour processes have been transformed by CVC restructuring, or how workers have responded to these transformations. Consequently, the typology's predications are inconsistent with empirical research. For example, rigorous studies of electronics CVCs show how large suppliers meet the requirements of lead firms by *deskilling* the labour process, which enables employers to informalize work and suppress wages. As a result, most of the global electronics workforce are not employed in high-skill roles, but *low-skill* roles with poor wages and limited protections (Chan and Pun 2010; Lüthje et al. 2013; Raj-Reichert 2016).

Beyond its limitations in investigating and comprehending capital–labour relations in CVCs, the concept of social upgrading's emphasis on the positive developmental effects of measurable private standards is challenged by studies showing how CSR standards tend to be weakly and inconsistently enforced in supply chains (Locke 2013; Siegmann et al. 2014). Audits of private standards are typically commissioned and controlled by lead firms, exclude worker representation, and lack transparency. The motivation for establishing private standards usually stem from lead firms' need to protect their brands. Accordingly, as Mark Anner (2012) documents, improvements tend to be concentrated in hazard-prevention, rather than wages or rights. Codes of conduct rarely promote the fundamental ILO conventions of freedom of association and collective bargaining (Egels-Zandén and Merk 2014). In their cross-sector study of 139 GVC suppliers in Brazil and Kenya, Graz et al. (2022) found no evidence that private standards supported these basic rights.

One such private standard is the Electronics Industry Code of Conduct (EICC[2]), which emerged from an investigative report by NGOs revealing widespread labour abuses in electronics supply chains (CAFOD 2004; Raj-Reichert 2016, 139). However, the EICC was criticized for failing to prevent the suicides of 14 migrant workers at Apple's main Chinese supplier Foxconn in 2010. Both Apple and Foxconn were reportedly members of the EICC and public exposés about Foxconn's labour abuses had existed since 2006 (Watts 2006; GoodElectronics 2010; Chan et al. 2020). The EICC has also been criticized for being non-legally binding (SOMO 2012; Lüthje et al. 2013, 169). As with other private standards, membership is voluntary, such that employers often 'opt-out' during economic downturns while they cut wages and jobs. For example, during the global recession in 2009, seven out of the EICC's 45 members reportedly chose not to renew their membership (GoodElectronics 2010).

Responding to mounting criticism of private standards, CTG authors Gereffi and Lee (2016, 29) acknowledge that:

> it has become clear that the CSR compliance model alone is woefully inadequate to fully address labor issues in global supply chains … also … the model generally does not allow suppliers and workers in developing countries to provide meaningful input.

Theoretically, one way of addressing this limitation would have been for these authors to incorporate a rigorous conception of capital-labour relations into their theoretical framework. However, rather than doing this, Gereffi and Lee (2016) create another typology, of 'synergistic governance'. Within this rubric, they broaden the range of actors that may contribute to social upgrading through 'public', 'private', and 'social' forms of governance, whereby the latter includes labour unions as one stakeholder in Multi-Stakeholder Initiatives (MSIs).

The new typology outlines six potential 'paths' to social upgrading, each driven by different primary actors and mechanisms. The inclusion of a 'labour-centred path', which includes labour unions, bargaining, and strikes, does at least acknowledge worker agency as a potential mechanism of social upgrading (Gereffi and Lee 2016, 35). The authors specify this pathway by referencing Selwyn's (2013b) labour-centred argument, but without

[2] Now part of the Responsible Business Alliance (RBA).

incorporating its class-relational conceptualization. Thus, while the authors recognize the need for workers to struggle for improvements, they conceptually exclude capital–labour relations from their approach. Consequently, the motivations of the various actors in the six pathways, and how their interests relate to each other, are not theorized, such that the categorization remains largely descriptive, static, and abstract (and see Chapter 3 for a critique of Gereffi's and other mainstream GVC authors' tendency to deploy ideal types to explain complex dynamics, rather than delving deeper into the social relations that generate such complex processes in the first place).

The notion of 'synergistic governance' failed to resuscitate the social upgrading agenda and its influence gradually faded (see Alford 2020). For example, social upgrading was not mentioned once in the World Bank's (2020) 270-page World Development Report on GVCs. In their analysis of how the concept of social upgrading has been used by experts and policymakers, Fridell and Walker (2019, 1) argue that discourses of social upgrading shifted from criticizing the limits of GVC-led development towards promoting top-down CSR standards as part of a 'neoliberal market fantasy'.

While the concept of social upgrading proposed to analyse workers as 'both productive and social agents within production networks' (Goger et al. 2014, 4), its prioritization of *inter-firm* relations inhibited a *class-relational* analysis of how workers' agency influences social upgrading. In contrast, we turn next to an approach that explicitly foregrounds the agency of workers.

9.3 Foregrounding Workers' Agency: Labour Geography

The Labour Geography research agenda was initiated by Andrew Herod (1997, 2) to explicitly foreground the agency of workers. Herod analytically prioritized worker agency by rejecting overly structuralist interpretations of class relations in Marxism in which, according to Herod, capital defines production and labour merely *reacts* to exploitation. Herod called for case studies to demonstrate how the (pro)active agency of workers shapes their economic geographies.

Labour Geographers subsequently compiled a rich body of research on diverse forms of work and agency across varied contexts (Lier 2007; Peck 2018). However, Herod's partial de-anchoring of labour agency from class relations risked fetishizing agency by disarticulating it from structural features of class exploitation. One consequence is that recent Labour Geography analysis has not developed a shared definition or conceptualization of labour agency. This predicament has tended to generate theoretical and empirical eclecticism rather than strategic analytical insights on how workers act to improve their shared conditions (Coe and Jordhus-Lier 2011, 2023; Das 2012).

Early Labour Geography studies intentionally analysed capital-labour struggles in order to generate insights for labour activists in CVCs. Studies revealed successes by local trade unions in defending workers' conditions and resisting offshoring of jobs (Cumbers et al. 2008). Herod's (2001) seminal case-study of US automotive workers revealed how the impact of local strikes was amplified by GM's just-in-time supply chain. The strikes shut down nearly all of GM's North American plants and affected 117 of its international suppliers, thus forcing GM to agree to workers' demands for improved conditions.

While these early studies generated useful insights about labour struggles in CVCs, they were criticized for focussing on unionized workers in Euro-America (Lier 2007). As a corrective, Labour Geographers refocused on more diverse workforces in CVCs (Knutsen et al. 2015). However, this empirical step was also accompanied by a theoretical shift, away from theorizing labour agency in class-relational terms.

Labour Geography's 'diversity turn' focussed more attention on large globalized workforces, such as in garments and electronics CVCs, that are constituted largely of young women in peripheral countries who migrate from rural areas to work in urban factories (Jepson 2005; Pike 2007). In these locations, context-specific gender relations are leveraged by employers to recruit rural women into factories under authoritarian control, where they suffer low pay, long hours, and poor conditions. Important studies preceding Labour Geography had revealed how the construction of these feminized workforces benefitted local subcontractors, but the lion's share of surplus value was captured by foreign lead firms (Elson and Pearson 1981; Ong 1987, 1991).

As well as studying the diversity of workforces, Labour Geographers sought to diversify forms of worker agency beyond tradition unionization. For example, Padmanabhan's (2012) study of women workers in Kerala, India revealed how workers resisted social downgrading of their conditions that occurred when their garments factories were integrated into CVCs. The women workers acted outside of traditional trade unions, as unions are heavily politicized in the patriarchal context of the study. Instead, the women workers formed an informal association, forged strategic coalitions and staged large wildcat strikes to win improved wages, conditions, and the abolishment of compulsory overtime.

Labour Geographers identified how local gendered norms facilitate the establishment of context-specific constraints to women workers' agency, including their 'double-burden' of work and social reproduction (Silvey

2003). For example, in Pakistan's football industry, Lund-Thomsen (2013) highlights how women are concentrated in home-working, enduring the lowest wages and largest constraints to collective action (and see Section 9.5).

As these examples demonstrate, Labour Geography's diversity turn yielded rich insights about context-specific varieties of work and agency. Nevertheless, Coe and Jordhus-Lier (2011) identified a growing predicament in Labour Geography whereby it lacked a coherent definition or theorization of labour agency. They note that agency is a hollow concept unless defined in relation to relevant 'structural constraints'. As Castree (2007, 858) explains:

> paradoxically, agency is both under-theorized and under-specified in most labour geographers' analyses of it. The term agency, to my mind, has become a catch-all for any instance in which some group of workers undertake any sort of action on behalf of themselves or others.

To address this predicament, Coe and Jordhus-Lier (2011) promote Cindy Katz's (2004) distinction between resistance, reworking, and resilience ('the 3 Rs'). Labour Geographers use of the 3 Rs tended to reframe labour agency away from collective resistance towards everyday forms of resilience and survival (Cumbers et al. 2010). For example, the 3 Rs were deployed to analyse *individual* acts of resilience by diverse workers, such as migration for work (Rogaly 2009). Carswell and De Neve's (2013) study of garment GPNs in South India identified how workers' everyday acts of individual agency forced capital to accommodate demands for flexible work and enabled some Dalit caste migrants to improve their lives.

However, while some individual acts, such as sabotage or refusal, can indeed undermine exploitation (Naylor 2017), others, such as resilience or changing employer, can serve to reinforce structures of exploitation. As Carswell and De Neve (2013, 69) recognize in their case study, individual agency 'does not challenge the basic status quo between capital and labour within the industry'. Further, 'particular interests and individualized tactics is precisely what curbs their ability to engage in collective action'.

Labour Geography's increasing focus on diverse and local expressions of worker agency expanded its empirical research agenda, albeit at the expense of conceptually deprioritizing capital–labour relations. Consequently, it under-theorized forms of agency that may challenge the structures of exploitation. In other words, efforts to diversify conceptions of *worker agency* did so by neglecting what is socially specific about *labour* agency.

Labour Geography's failure to conceptualize labour agency is puzzling, since the answer lies in its name. *Labour* agency should be understood in the same manner as *labour*—by its position in social production relations. If 'agency' is given meaning in its relation to a structure—if indeed they are 'ontologically and methodologically inseparable' (Coe and Jordhus-Lier 2023, 6)—then labour agency is defined in its dialectical relation with capital. While a worker's everyday agency can be represented by practically any human action, *labour agency* has a specific meaning derived from workers' responses to exploitation.

Labour Geography's predicament can be traced back to its partial rejection of Marx's conceptualization of the structural relation between capital and labour (Das 2017, 87; Herod 1997). According to Marx (1990), capital's ownership of the means of production means that it has primacy over labour in organizing production (see Section 2.6). In contrast, Herod (1997, 17) states: 'Capital is not the only actor actively shaping the geography of capitalism *or even, in some places and times, the most significant one*' (emphasis Herod's).

The notion that labour can have the same, or more, influence than capital in shaping the economic landscapes of capitalism, for example in establishing new industrial estates, is problematic. Even if workers are proactive in influencing economic geographies, they have not done so under conditions of their own choosing. Rather, they do so within the system of capitalism, a system within which labour is the exploited class. As Raju Das notes:

> Are capital and labour equally powerful in creating the landscape of capitalism? If that were the case, capital would not be capital, and labour would not be what it is: labour. The fact of capital's dominance does not exclude labour's agency.
>
> (Das 2017, 144)

Recent Labour Geographer's studies conceptualize structural constraints to labour agency in globalized production as arising not from capital–labour relations, but from 'vertical' GVC/GPN relations *combining* with local 'horizontal' social relations. Examples include Carswell and De Neve's (2013) study of garment GPNs in South India and Lund-Thomsen's (2013) study of football stitching GPNs in Pakistan. Yet, local 'horizontal relations' remain vaguely defined.

Labour Geographers have addressed the latter by adopting the concept of 'intersectionality' (McDowell 2008; Valentine 2007; Strauss 2020; Zampoukos 2021; Jordhus-Lier and Coe 2024). The concept of intersectionality asserts that multiple forms (or 'axes') of oppression intersect to be experienced as more than the sum of their parts, as informed by the specific discrimination experienced by African-American women in the US (Crenshaw 1989). Before the academicized term 'intersectionality' was coined by Crenshaw, the Combahee River Collective (CRC) (1983, 267) had famously asserted: 'We find it difficult to separate race from class from sex oppression because in our lives they are most often experienced simultaneously.'

This approach can help to identify complex oppressions, exclusions, and representation deficits. However, as a social theory, intersectionality is problematic (Rutherford 2010; Ferguson 2016; McNally 2017; Russell 2018; Vogel 2018; Lütten et al. 2021). The CRC (1983, 268), in seeking to resist the co-optation of their struggle by elite white feminists, emphasized their subjective experiences and called for the development of Marxist theories to incorporate the 'specific class position of Black women who are generally marginal in the labor force'. It remained unclear how exactly different forms of oppression interrelate, and what their social basis is—but unlike later academic debates on intersectionality, the CRC combined their approach with a socialist agenda (Lütten et al. 2021, 20). However, as Martha Gimenez documents, the later, academic notion of intersectionality, became a 'floating signifier' that increasingly marginalized class and blurred its fundamental structuring role in capitalism (Giménez 2019, 107).

Gimenez's (2019, 96) review of intersectionality literature concludes that there is 'no specific and widely accepted intersectional theory', and that feminist scholars are referencing the concept in ways in which 'intersectionality lacks explanatory power' because it cannot 'account for the existence of the "axes of inequality", the nature of the processes that bring them together, the processes leading to identity formation, and the resulting complex, rather than unitary, nature of identity it postulates'. Gimenez's review suggests that intersectionality does not offer a resolution to Labour Geography's predicament regarding its conceptualization of labour agency.

Labour Geographers' use of intersectionality—where a description of axes of oppression substitutes for an analysis of the relation between capitalist exploitation and oppression—manifests as an unsatisfactory conceptualization of structural constraints to workers' agency as the interaction of local 'horizontal' intersectionalities with 'vertical' GVC/GPN relations. This double-weakness impairs Labour Geography's ability to analyse labour agency. As Das notes:

> Labour is there in the literature. But labour in relation to capital, its exploitative other, (and in relation to the capitalist state which acts as a most coercive force with respect to labor), is more or less left out. This type of work is oblivious of

> the fact that 'capital presupposes wage-labour; wage-labour presupposes capital. They reciprocally condition each other's existence' (Marx 1977, 724).... What Marx calls in Capital vol. 1 the hidden abode of production remains, more or less, hidden.
>
> **(Das 2017, 142)**

In contrast, Marxist scholars theorize oppressions not as intersections of static and spuriously universalized identities, but as arising from dynamic processes of struggle in different contexts over who works and who profits (Roediger and Esch 2012; Robinson et al. 2022; Schling 2022; Knox and Kumar 2023). As Jennifer Bair (2010, 224) notes:

> The gendered organization of transnational production is not simply a reflection of the specific meanings and practices through which social difference is manifest at particular sites on the global assembly line; it is, rather, an ongoing process in which these forms of difference are brought within a particular social relation, which is capitalist production, and mobilized for a specific purpose, which is the creation of profit.

In summary, while Labour Geography has enriched our understanding of the diversity of workforces and forms of agency across varied production contexts, its gradual deprioritization of structural class relations has inhibited its ability to conceptualize labour agency. This predicament limits the insights it can offer on how workers act to improve their shared conditions in CVCs. The following section turns to approaches that conceptualize labour agency explicitly in dialectical relation to capital in CVCs.

9.4 Critical Approaches to Labour Agency in CVCs

Critical analyses of CVCs take seriously *capital–labour* relations (Campling et al. 2016; Campling and Selwyn 2018). In what follows, we explore scholarship that analyses labour agency and its structural constraints in CVCs in explicitly class-relational terms, demonstrating how this can overcome the aforementioned predicament of Labour Geography. We will discuss the strengths of the 'Power Resources Approach' (PRA) approach (Schmalz et al. 2018), but also identify limitations stemming from its somewhat narrow focus on sectoral conflicts. This guides us to a final approach that we outline in Section 9.5.

Critical GVC scholars reveal how workers have forced employers to improve wages and conditions by asserting different forms of power, particularly 'structural' and 'associational' power. Structural power is where small groups of strategically positioned workers can inflict wider disruptions on capital to secure improvements for themselves or the wider workforce. Examples include localized strikes at crucial links in production processes or CVCs. Associational power is where workers form collective organizations to challenge capital. Examples include trade unions or national labour movements (Wright 2000). The foregrounding of workers' 'power resources' contrasts with social upgrading's tendency to emphasize top-down measurable standards (Schmaltz et al. 2018).

Selwyn's (2013b, 87) early critique of the social upgrading agenda noted that it lacked a coherent theorization of capitalist exploitation, due to its under-theorization of capital–labour relations. Consequently, the concept leans on idealistic notions of institutionalism, which assumes that when the right institutions are selected by policymakers, then capital will not systematically exploit labour. Institutions are not, however, the result of nonpartisan policymaking, but state-mediated outcomes of past struggles between capital and labour.

Selwyn's study of horticulture CVCs brought to the fore how workers in Brazil successfully combined structural and associational power to secure improvements in their conditions. Demand by supermarket retailers in the Global North for high quality standards and tight delivery timetables for fresh produce provides workers at Brazilian suppliers with enhanced structural power, because the produce is rejected if quality processes are not completed, or will perish if deliveries are delayed. As a result, strikes become powerful threats. This structural power was realized through the associational power of a rural worker's union to negotiate a collective convention providing better security, pay, benefits, and conditions. Selwyn concludes that the ability of workers 'to transform their structural power into associational power in order to extract concessions from capital constitutes a core determinant of the relationship between economic and social upgrading' (2013b, 84; see Selwyn 2012a, 2012b).

Although national restructuring into CVCs may have increased the structural and associational power of some workers, it has diminished the power of many others. In neighbouring Argentina, Bernhold (2021, 2022) shows how the restructuring of soybean CVCs affected associational power differently for workers located at different value chain nodes. In primary processing of soybeans, workers have been fragmented through a process of economic upgrading based on class differentiation (see Chapter 8), which contributed to a near absence of workers' associational power. In contrast, in the downstream node of vegetable oil processing, workers benefitted from enhanced structural and associational power realized through the actions of assertive trade unions. Through strategic strike action in an economically and geographically highly concentrated industry, where strike action can paralyse a delicate part of Argentina's export economy, oil processing workers have negotiated wage increases and protections against work outsourcing, among other things. The two groups of workers have experienced very different outcomes: although their wages were roughly equal in 2008, by 2018 the oil processing workers' wages were twice as high as those of primary processing workers (Bernhold 2021, 247).

Capital responds to labour agency in CVCs through its own counter-strategies. Beverly Silver (2003) shows how this dynamic reshaped the global automotive industry between 1930 and 2000, whereby companies continually relocated their production sites to escape waves of labour militancy: from the United States, to Europe, and then to the Global South. Silver explains that in each new location mass production enabled strong labour movements to emerge, and every time this occurred, capital relocated to new non-unionized sites of production.

> On the one hand, the expansion of capitalist production tends to strengthen labor and, therefore, brings capital (and states) recurrently face to face with strong labor movements. The concessions made to bring labor movements under control, in turn, tend to drive the system toward crises of profitability. On the other hand, efforts by capital (and states) to restore profits invariably involve breaking established social compacts and intensifying the commodification of labor, thereby producing crises of legitimacy and backlash resistance.
>
> (Silver 2003, 20)

Silver's study aligns with this book by disclosing how capital–labour dialectics drive the socio-spatial development of capitalism. According to Silver, diverse groups of workers deployed structural and associational power to pursue social upgrading via outbreaks of labour unrest, using innovative and contextually relevant tactics to secure unionization, higher pay, better security, and improved conditions. In electronics, a similar story is told by Cowie (1999), who describes how, between the 1920s and 1990s, RCA relocated five times within the United States and then to Mexico in part to escape labour militancy (see also Peet 1983, 130).

The concepts of structural and associational power therefore enable a dialectical analysis of struggles vis-à-vis structures in globalized production. In CVCs, Kumar (2020) argues that the growth of oligopolistic garment suppliers, and the dependence of lead firm buyers upon them, has provided workers with enhanced structural power that could be asserted through union bargaining. Kumar, Silver, and Cowie also recognize that employers' counter-strategies are similarly creative and adaptive.

A powerful counter-strategy by capital is the fragmentation and segmentation of workforces to suppress their structural and associational power (Hammer and Riisgaard 2015). In their study of the automotive manufacturer Maruti Suzuki in India, Jha and Chakraborty (2016, 409) describe how capital's restructuring through CVCs entailed the outsourcing of work to tiers of suppliers, enabling lead firms to squeeze costs while offloading risks onto precarious workers located at lower-tier suppliers. They identify an increasing segmentation of the workforce, similar to how the authors of social upgrading identified how employers use contract workers to manage flexibility in GVCs, for example in Rossi's (2013) social upgrading study of garment GVCs in Morocco. However, Jha and Chakraborty deploy a class-relational analysis that pinpoints very different (i) motivations for segmentation, and (ii) mechanisms of social upgrading.

The motivations for segmentation identified by Jha and Chakraborty (2016) include not just managing commercial volatility in CVCs (as argued by Rossi 2013), but crucially, suppressing the associational power of workers. They describe how lead firms redesigned, automated and deskilled the labour process, such that minimal training was required for new contract workers to operate the machinery. Then, permanent staff were replaced with contract workers who lack the right to unionize, thus weakening the union's associational power (Jha and Chakraborty 2016, 405).

The mechanisms of social upgrading revealed by Jha and Chakraborty (2016, 404) can be understood as workers asserting structural and associational power to defend against social downgrading. In 2011, workers conducted three strikes, as well as factory occupations and 'go-slows', and were supported by solidarity strikes at other plants. Eventually they achieved improved working conditions and the abolishment of labour contracting.

The recognition that GVC restructuring can enhance the structural power of workers in particular locations or industries implies that such industries could become new loci of labour struggles. In their edited collection on 'Labour Process Theory' (LPT), Newsome et al. (2015, 16) show that in many GVCs, just-in-time supply chains create vulnerabilities that workers at particular nodes can exploit with bursts of strike action (Taylor et al. 2015). The logistics sector is identified by the authors as a particularly vulnerable 'choke point' in increasingly complex supply chains (Newsome 2015). LPT researchers subsequently focussed upon the logistics and transport industries as the potential epicentre of labour conflicts in CVCs, due to workers enhanced structural power (Alimahomed-Wilson and Ness 2018).

There is a risk, however, that focussing narrowly on workers' structural power within particular CVC nodes or sectors, can neglect the wider political-economic relations that condition labour agency. For example, Jörk Nowak (2022) criticizes the notion that logistics workers automatically acquire enhanced structural power in CVCs. Nowak uses a case-study of a large but ultimately unsuccessful truckers' strike in Brazil in 2018 to argue that truckers could block the flow of goods to ports but could not crystallize their gains, because of structural constraints in the wider political economy such as state capacity, industrial relations, hegemonic ideologies, infrastructure, and GVC/GPN dynamics.

Similarly, Katy Fox-Hodess (2019) criticizes the abstraction of structural power from socio-political contexts by comparing two dockworker disputes in Chile and Colombia in the 2010s in which dockworkers had ostensibly similar structural power but experienced different outcomes. In Chile, facilitative regulations enabled dockworkers to strike at strategic ports such as Mejillones to secure a national sectoral collective bargaining agreement with the support of left-wing political parties and the International Dockworkers Council. In Colombia, however, dockworkers in Buenaventura faced repressive conditions involving port privatizations, labour subcontracting and state-sanctioned violence. The Colombian unions were weakened by blacklistings and were unable to strike or gain state protection. In summary, Nowak and Fox-Hodess show that workers' ability to assert structural power is not determined only by their position in CVCs, but also by the situated class relations and institutions of their contexts.

Class relations at the scale of the national political economy strongly influence the prospects for workers to win improvements. A comparative study of four GVCs across six countries by Teipen and Mehl (2021, 232) concludes that:

> Social upgrading trajectories thus crucially depend on the level of associational and institutional power that trade unions can exercise in transformation processes vis-à-vis the state and business interests. Brazil and South Africa are examples for—albeit limited—social upgrading paths, while social downgrading tendencies prevail in countries with weak trade unions such as India, Bangladesh and Vietnam.

To address these weaknesses, the concepts of structural and associational power were augmented with other 'power resources' that extend beyond workplaces to the wider political economy (AK Strategic Unionism 2013). Various contributions by researchers on trade union strategies coalesced into the 'Power Resources Approach' (PRA). In addition to structural and associational power, the PRA includes 'institutional power', which includes legal rights won in past struggles, and 'societal power', which includes strategic alliances with other actors as well as discursive forms of ideological power (Schmaltz et al. 2018).

The broadened PRA responds to the criticisms of labour scholars from the Global South, who noted that earlier versions tended to assume that a Western-style industrial relations framework applied in all contexts (Coe and Hess 2013; Nathan 2013; Bieler and Nowak 2022). For example, in contexts where strong union frameworks did not develop, Edward Webster (2015) argues that workers have relied more on societal power through national campaigns and 'social movement unionism'.

The expanded PRA recognizes how workers can leverage additional alliances and institutions, but it doesn't theorize how struggles interact with evolving production structures and the political economies of particular contexts. Nowak (2022, 8) remains critical of the broadened PRA for retaining a focus on sectoral conflicts, rather than considering how workers are often confronted by 'capitalism-as-a-whole'. In other words, the ways in which labour agency is constrained by wider class relations, structures of historical production relations, and politics and cultures of capitalist social formations. In focussing somewhat abstractly on sectorial conflicts, the PRA is therefore also vulnerable to fallacies of composition, that is, the notion that because workers in a CVC successfully asserted power resources in one context, they can do so in all contexts.

In summary, the LPT and PRA approaches possess relative strengths over the social upgrading approach and recent Labour Geography studies in how they theorize labour agency in an explicitly class-relational manner in CVCs that is sensitive to capitalism's structural features. However, they do not adequately situate constraints to labour agency in the wider relations of the international political economy. We turn next to a recent approach that has the potential to resolve the weaknesses of the LPT and PRA approaches while retaining their strengths.

9.5 Situating Labour Agency: The Labour Regime Approach

The recognition that class struggles take place within particular 'labour regimes'—that is, context-specific relations and institutions that shape work, exploitation, and struggle—is the basis of labour regime analysis. Historically, scholarship on labour regimes was limited to within national boundaries, but a recent edited collection by Baglioni et al. (2022a) titled *Labour Regimes and Global Production* (LRGP) has developed a multi-scalar approach for researching diverse sites of work connected through CVCs. This section introduces the LRGP approach and outlines its strengths over the social upgrading and Labour Geography approaches. We also suggest that comprehending dynamics of change in labour regimes can be advanced further through our concept of international class relations.

Marxist scholars understand exploitation as a social relation, rather than a moral category. Accordingly, class struggle and labour disciplining are processes that extend beyond the boundaries of the workplace to the ways in which workers are constructed into exploitable workforces in, for instance, the national political economy. For example, CVC capitals are attracted to China not just for low wages, but for the distinctive qualities of its labour regime, as described by Martin Hart-Landsberg (2013, 52):

> It is not just low wages that attract transnational corporations to China, it is also the broader work environment, an environment that offers corporations maximum freedom to mobilize and direct the work effort of their employees. The New York Times, in discussing why Apple relies on China-based production for its products, offered the following story: One former [Apple] executive described how the company relied upon a Chinese factory to revamp iPhone manufacturing just weeks before the device was due on shelves. Apple had redesigned the iPhone's screen at the last minute, forcing an assembly line overhaul. New screens began arriving at the plant near midnight. A foreman immediately roused 8,000 workers inside the company's dormitories, according to the executive. Each employee was given a biscuit and a cup of tea, guided to a workstation and within half an hour started a 12-hour shift fitting glass screens into bevelled frames. Within 96 hours, the plant was producing over 10,000 iPhones a day. 'The speed and flexibility is breathtaking', the executive said.

The core concept of the LRGP approach is exploitation: what enables it and how it is contested. In a central chapter in the edited collection, Baglioni et al. (2022b) outline their LRGP framework, which defines four analytical spheres. The framework starts in the sphere of *production* with an analysis of exploitation in the labour process (Braverman 1974) and the mechanisms of labour control, coercion and consent at the workplace (Burawoy 1985). It recognizes that exploitation in the workplace is supported by disciplining processes that span the *recruitment and reproduction* of workforces, in the sphere of social reproduction (Baglioni 2018, 2022; Bair 2022). The role of competition and value chain subcontracting in heightening exploitation is considered within the sphere of *circulation* (Newsome 2010). Finally, the ecological basis of, and limits to, capitalist exploitation are analysed in the sphere of *ecology* (Baglioni and Campling 2017, see Chapter 10 for an in-depth discussion).

According to Baglioni (2022, 449): 'Whilst labour exploitation corresponds to capital extraction of value from the labour process, labour disciplining includes all those mechanisms that mitigate, contain and prevent the conflict inherent to production and is therefore a crucial ingredient in the making and remaking of workers.'

In this manner, Baglioni et al.'s (2022b) LRGP framework centres exploitation as the key relation and structuring logic. This analytical consistency means that the LRGP approach does not encounter the predicament of many Labour Geography contributions—the under-theorization of labour agency in relation to capital—because labour agency and its structural constraints are analysed in class-relational terms, whereby different dynamics across the four spheres impact upon the strategies of capital and labour vis-à-vis exploitation. In addition, LRGP's analysis of structural constraints is intrinsically multi-scalar (see Smith et al. 2018), which contrasts with Labour Geography's additive approach to combining 'vertical' GPN structures with often vaguely defined 'horizontal' social relations. LRGP also overcomes the sectoral narrowness of the PRA by incorporating context-specific relations and institutions that shape and constrain labour agency. This reveals, for example, how labour organizing in varied contexts often emerges from households and communities rather than workplace unions (Doutch 2022).

In another chapter, Campling et al.'s (2021) study develops a key attribute of the LRGP framework: its ability to analyse capital-labour relations at multiple scales. This enables the authors to analyse the impact of EU free trade agreements on labour regimes in South Korean automotive and Moldovan clothing GPNs. In the former, workers' worsening conditions were driven by a profitability squeeze resulting from enhanced competition with German supply chains, while in the latter, it was driven by a cost squeeze imposed by powerful lead firms on Moldovan suppliers. The authors conceptualize labour regimes as 'composed of nested scales, institutionalized formally in organizations with codified rules but also informally in relational norms and habits' (Campling et al. 2021, 142). In the process, they highlight the geopolitical underpinnings of such trade arrangements and the historically formed national labour politics that influence labour's ability to defend against immiseration in CVCs.

Anner's (2015) analysis of labour control regimes in apparel GPNs identifies how different regimes are associated with different labour agency patterns. In *authoritarian state control regimes*, exemplified by Vietnam, a strong state controls unions and represses activism, driving workers towards wildcat strikes. In *despotic market control regimes*, exemplified by Bangladesh, a weak state provides limited regulations for easily replaceable workers who instead use mass protests and appeal to international regulations. Finally, in *repressive employer control regimes*, exemplified by Honduras, violence and a lack of state protection means that workers rely on cross-border campaigns. Anner's study demonstrates how labour regime analysis overcomes the weaknesses of the PRA, as identified by Nowak and Fox-Hodess, by analysing how the labour regime constrains and shapes workers' power resources.

A separate study of apparel GPNs by Wickramasingha and Coe (2022), deciphers how differences in labour regimes derive from their historical development. In turn, this shapes the integration of states into capitalist value chains, resulting in different labour struggles and outcomes. The authors historicize how class formation in Bangladesh and Sri Lanka resulted in divergent institutional structures. As a result, Sri Lanka's centralized state maintained stronger labour regulations due to the prior struggles by trade unions to resist deregulation, and its suppliers had more power vis-à-vis lead firms to upgrade to high-quality niche production. In contrast, Bangladesh's decentralized authorities competed to court capital based on the repressiveness of their labour regimes, such that workers in Bangladesh experienced worse conditions and a lack of representation (Wickramasingha and Coe 2022; see Ruwanpura 2022).

As these examples demonstrate, the labour regime provides a powerful framework for analysing how labour agency can secure improvements at different scales and spheres in CVCs. There is also scope, we suggest, for the approach to develop a more dynamic theory of social change. While exploitation, and the struggles against it, are the fabric of LRGP, the approach has not yet clarified how such struggles in turn re-shape the labour regime. For example, why do labour regimes in different contexts diverge or converge over time? And how do outcomes of struggles in one sphere/scale impact upon relations in other spheres/scales? (López 2023, 47).

One way forward is to be more analytically specific about the mechanisms by which labour struggles unfold, in terms of the strategies and counter-strategies that labour and capital assert in different spheres and at different scales. A major strength of LRGP is its panoramic analysis of struggles against exploitation that extend beyond the workplace (Baglioni 2022). For example, it highlights how workers often organize in their communities. However, as yet, LRGP is less explicit than the PRA about how workers actually develop and assert power in the different spheres, and how both capital and labour learn from and adapt to each other's strategies.

Similarly, at the scale of the international political economy, the LRGP approach could go further in theorizing how labour regimes are shaped through international class relations and struggles. We explain in Chapter 5 how the offshoring that created capitalist value chains emerged from economic crises and class struggles in the United States in the 1970s, and in turn, how this offshoring enabled the dismantling of hard-fought labour protections in the US labour regime. Meanwhile, the conditions that attracted US capital to offshore production sites in East Asia were outcomes of prior class struggles from above, among other dynamics, resulting in repressive labour regimes (Gray 2015). In this manner, the reshaping of labour regimes in lead firm countries, such as the United States, and the reshaping of labour regimes in supplier firm countries, such as China, were mutually connected and internationally articulated.

The LRGP approach benefits from its intrinsic multi-scalarity (Campling et al. 2022). This complements our book's concept of international class relations (see Chapter 2), which could be incorporated to help analyse how class struggles at the international scale shape domestic labour regimes.

For example, the development of electronics CVCs in India demonstrates how international class relations contribute to shaping labour regimes in particular states. As part of plans to expand iPhone production in India, Apple and Foxconn have reportedly lobbied the state of Karnataka to change its labour regime to allow young women to work night shifts (Reed and Hille 2023). At the same time, Indian workers are resisting the imposition of a Chinese-style labour regime. For example, thousands of Indian workers destroyed an iPhone factory in Karnataka belonging to the Apple supplier Wistron in 2020 (Krishnan et al. 2022b). Workers' grievances included low pay, unpaid wages, overtime hours, labour contracting, unsanitary living conditions, and unsafe food. Wistron subsequently decided to exit India due to problems with its 'work culture' (Hsiao 2023).

9.6 Social Upgrading from Below?

The merits of a multi-scalar labour regime approach that incorporates workers' power resources are demonstrated by Mark Anner's (2011; 2013; 2021, 29; 2022) study of struggles by garment CVC workers in Honduras. Anner is a contributor to the LRGP edited collection (Baglioni et al. 2022a). He analyses how Honduran workers organized themselves and forged coalitions at multiple scales to achieve sustained social upgrading. Such gains are relatively rare in garments CVCs, but were possible because of the specificities of Honduras' labour regime and workers' particular strategies.

Anner's (2011) study reminds us that workers' struggles against exploitation are constant under capitalism, but the forms these struggles take are always historically and contextually specific. For example, struggles to unionize garments factories were more successful in Honduras than in neighbouring El Salvador. Honduras' history of strong labour organizing dates back to a wave of worker militancy in the banana sector in the 1950s. In contrast, the labour movement in El Salvador had experienced violent repression by US-backed military governments.

Nevertheless, successes in unionizing garment factories in Honduras during the 1990s were negated by CVC firms' strategy of relocating production to un-unionized sites. Anner (2013, 28) notes that:

> the weak structural power of apparel workers eventually undermined these successes. With time, each unionised factory with a collective bargaining agreement closed and moved elsewhere. The hyper-mobility of capital in the apparel global value chain trumped the ... power of labour.

This situation began to change from the 2000s, as competition in garments CVCs led to growing capital concentration, which increased the structural power of workers at some Honduran' producers. These producers expanded their operations to incorporate more capital-intensive textile production, associated with direct ownership by lead firms, thus reducing capital's mobility. An important example for this case study was Russell, which became the largest private employer in Honduras, operating several large factories. Russell is part of Fruit of the Loom (FOTL), a major supplier of university-branded clothing in the United States that is owned by Warren Buffet's Berkshire Hathaway Group (Anner 2013).

Workers at a Russell-owned factory, Jerzees Choloma, sought to build their associational power by forming a trade union. They received support from a labour federation operating at the national scale in Honduras to organize the factory workers and register the union. Management reacted by intimidating the organizers and dismissing 145 workers in 2007. In 2008, Russell closed the factory, relocating its workers to another factory in Honduras, Jerzees de Honduras (Anner 2013).

At the new factory, workers encountered abusive treatment. They responded by organizing a union to represent 1800 workers, thus forcing management to participate in a collective bargaining process. However, harassment of union members continued, and in October 2008 Russell announced that it was closing the plant for 'economic reasons' (Anner 2013).

Acknowledging the difficulties of confronting the country's largest employer, the unionists decided to develop their associational power by forming a transnational coalition with US-based labour activists. They strategically selected the Worker Rights Committee (WRC), which had waged powerful anti-sweatshop campaigns in the past and had strong connections with the United Students Against Sweatshops (USAS) movement.

Anti-sweatshop campaigns leverage lead firms' vulnerability to negative publicity. This power arises from the lead firms' competitive strategy in CVCs of establishing strong consumer brands, which provides them with power over their suppliers (Anner 2013, 34).

WRC's investigation found that the factory closure was motivated by management's desire to eliminate the only trade union at Russell factories in Honduras (Anner 2013). This finding motivated USAS to launch a campaign to force Russell/FOTL to re-open the factory, including three major speaking tours where the dismissed unionists visited US universities. As a result of the campaign, 110 universities terminated their licensing agreement with FOTL (Anner 2022).

The campaign pressured an industry CSR association, the Fair Labor Association (FLA), into investigating Russell's treatment of its labour force. The FLA is a corporate-influenced body that has established a top-down industry code of conduct and works with lead firms to monitor their CSR commitments in their supply chains. Its chosen social auditor concluded that workers were not dismissed for their union activity (Anner 2013).

The workers' union rejected the social auditor's report and were supported by complaints from a national union federation in Honduras and US-based allies. The complaints highlighted how workers felt unable to speak honestly about their treatment because they were accessed through management and were interviewed in groups inside the factory. The FLA was compelled to engage an ILO consultant to re-examine the case. The consultant conducted a detailed investigation into Russell's treatment of its labour force and sided firmly with the workers. The FLA was forced to place FOTL/Russell under review, but still failed to recommend re-opening the factory (Anner 2022).

Other US-based union federations and labour NGOs sensed that Russell/FOTL was vulnerable and joined the campaign. Coordinated pressure by this transnational coalition forced Russell/FOTL to sign a 'Washington Agreement' with the union in 2009 that included re-opening the factory, re-hiring the fired workers, good-faith collective bargaining and respect for freedom of association rights at all of its factories in Honduras. The first collective bargaining agreement (CBA) at the factory was signed in 2011 and included a 19.5 per cent pay rise for workers (Anner 2021, 2022).

The Washington Agreement's stipulation of non-harassment of labour organizers enabled workers at four other Russell factories in Honduras to successfully fight for unions and CBAs by 2021. These CBAs covered the full workforces, and included investments in new machinery, whereby productivity gains are shared with workers in the form of increased wages and benefits (Anner 2022).

The successes by Russell workers inspired a wave of unionization drives and collective bargaining across Honduras' garments CVCs. A follow-up study by Anner (2022, 4) identifies '22 CBAs in the export assembly sector covering 50,625 workers. Of these, 45,737 workers are in the garment export sector, which represents 44% of the 105,000 garment workers in Honduras'.

Anner's follow-up study undertakes a detailed review of these CBAs combined with a survey of 387 workers, covering both CBA and non-CBA factories in Honduras' CVC export sector. The study concludes that:

> compared to workers who do not have a CBA, Honduran garment workers with CBAs are 67% more likely to always have the choice as to whether or not to work overtime, 82.1% more likely to always have a lunch subsidy, 93.6% more likely to have access to a company savings and loan account, 56.3% more likely to have free transportation to work, and 83.1% more likely to find that work intensity is not increasing over time.... Workers not covered by a CBA are 20.3% more likely to face verbal abuse, and female workers who are not covered by a CBA are 10.7% more likely to face sexual harassment on the job when compared to workers who are covered by a CBA. Notably, female workers covered by CBAs are 119.8% more likely to have a valid mechanism at work for addressing gender-based violence and harassment in the world of work. Most workers covered by CBAs also receive various maternity and paternity benefits, including extend leave time.
>
> (Anner 2022, 4)

Anner's (2022, 5) survey also identifies clear benefits of worker-driven bargaining over lead firms-driven voluntary CSR initiatives. The survey revealed that 'workers with CBA coverage at the workplace earned, on average, 7% more than workers with CSR inspections but no CBA coverage'.

In summary, Anner's study reveals how garment CVC workers in Honduras developed power resources at multiple scales to achieve sustained 'social upgrading from below'. These successes were a direct result of the workers' strategies, which leveraged the particularities of garments CVCs by targeting lead firms' vulnerabilities to brand damage, and the particularities of the regional labour regime in Honduras, with its historical legacies of labour organizing institutionalized in state laws protecting unionization and collective bargaining. The case demonstrates powerfully how capital and state actors engage meaningfully in multi-stakeholder initiatives that benefit workers when forced to by worker-led struggles.

A major strength of Anner's study is its recognition of how historically formed international class relations affect exploitation in Honduras through, for instance, the history of US interventions and the impact of capital concentration on CVC firms' strategy of relocating unionized factories—thus demonstrating the importance of centring international class relations in the theorization of CVCs, as we lay out in Chapter 2.

9.7 Conclusions

Returning to our critique of social upgrading in Section 9.2, we have explored and developed tools for an alternative analysis of improvements in workers' wages and conditions in CVCs. Like the Labour Geography agenda, our approach takes seriously the agency of workers, but foregrounds the structural features of class exploitation in CVCs.

We have turned to critical scholarship that conceptualizes the 'power resources' of workers to analyse their struggles for improvements in an explicitly class-relational manner. The PRA connects the restructuring of CVCs with changes in workers' structural and associational power, thus conceptualizing labour agency in a more dialectical manner. However, the PRA tends to abstract from structural constraints within particular political economies and 'labour regimes'.

We argued that the recent LRGP framework by Baglioni et al. (2022b) has the potential to address these weaknesses in the PRA, and we have identified how it could do so by resolving two gaps in the current LRGP framework: the inclusion of power resources to clarify how struggles connect different scales and spheres together, and the inclusion of our concept of international class relations to clarify how broader class struggles shape CVC formation and participation. Together, these concepts help specify dynamics of labour regime (re)construction.

The example of struggles by garment CVC workers in Honduras, based on Anner's (2022) detailed studies, demonstrates how an augmented LRGP approach can be deployed to analyse instances of 'social upgrading from below'. This contrasts with the focus on 'top-down' measurable standards in the concept of social upgrading. Instead, it analyses labour agency in terms of workers' struggles for improvements against counter-tactics deployed by CVC employers. In that sense, we aim for a research agenda that takes workers' power seriously, while also accounting for the structural constraints of the broader labour regime, and considers the conditions for labour struggles in the context of international class relations and geographically uneven development.

While Anner's case study helps to showcase the strengths of the augmented LRGP framework for analysing how improvements in workers' wages and conditions result from struggles that unfold within specific labour regimes, care must be taken not to extrapolate isolated cases into a generalized emancipatory potential. The ability of some workers to achieve improvements in CVCs does not mean that such improvements are possible for all workers—still less that exploitative relations between capital and labour could be overcome in CVCs. Indeed, in 2025, Russell announced that it was closing its unionized factories in Honduras. The announcement was made during a period in which it has increased its sourcing of garments from suppliers in other low-wage countries such as Bangladesh[3].

Throughout this chapter we have highlighted the risks of fallacies of composition—that is, assuming that what can be achieved by some workers in some places can be achieved by all, within CVCs. Rather, genuine emancipation for workers would require overcoming exploitative relations of production. To the extent that such struggles widen to challenge structures of exploitation, such as CVCs, they may constitute part of such a transformation.

[3] Fruit of the Loom Turns Rotten on Worker Rights. Worker-Driven Social Responsibility Network, 14 February 2025. Available online at: https://wsr-network.org/fruit-of-the-loom-turns-rotten-on-worker-rights/

10
CVCs and Nature Destruction

> GVCs ... offer opportunities to support environmentally sustainable production models.
>
> **(World Bank 2020, 204)**

10.1 Introduction

Although it is widely understood that climate change has dire consequences, the ongoing extraction and consumption of fossil fuels continues apace (Armstrong McKay et al. 2022; Malm 2016, see Figure 10.1). The first human-induced mass extinction is in full swing, and several planetary boundaries have already been overstepped (Steffen et al. 2015; Persson et al. 2022). It is no exaggeration to say that Capitalist Value Chains (CVCs) are contributing directly to environmental depletion. CVC hyper-specialization entails an increase in production, transportation, and energy use—accelerating climate breakdown and mass environmental ruin.

Even those intellectuals and organizations who most ardently support the expansion of CVCs recognize (some of) their deleterious environmental impacts. However, such recognition does little to dampen their enthusiasm for continued CVC-expansion. Rather, as this chapter's epigraph highlights, the World Bank sees GVCs as potentially contributing to environmentally sustainable production. Relatedly, many mainstream GVC scholars acknowledge that 'economic upgrading' does not unconditionally translate into ecological sustainability. However, they then proffer the notion of 'environmental upgrading'—where firms reduce their ecological footprint—as a viable solution to CVC's disastrous impact upon nature (see Section 10.3).

Many critical scholars have used theoretical and empirical evidence to argue that 'green capitalist growth' is an oxymoron with no historical precedent (see, e.g., Foster et al. 2010; Stache 2017; Foster and Clark 2018, 4; Hickel and Kallis 2020). We argue that mainstream GVC analysis is unable to understand, or is politically oriented towards obscuring, the root causes of systematic capitalist and CVC destruction of the natural world. Mainstream

Capitalist Value Chains. Benjamin Selwyn and Christin Bernhold, Oxford University Press.
 DOI: 10.1093/9780191994906.003.0010

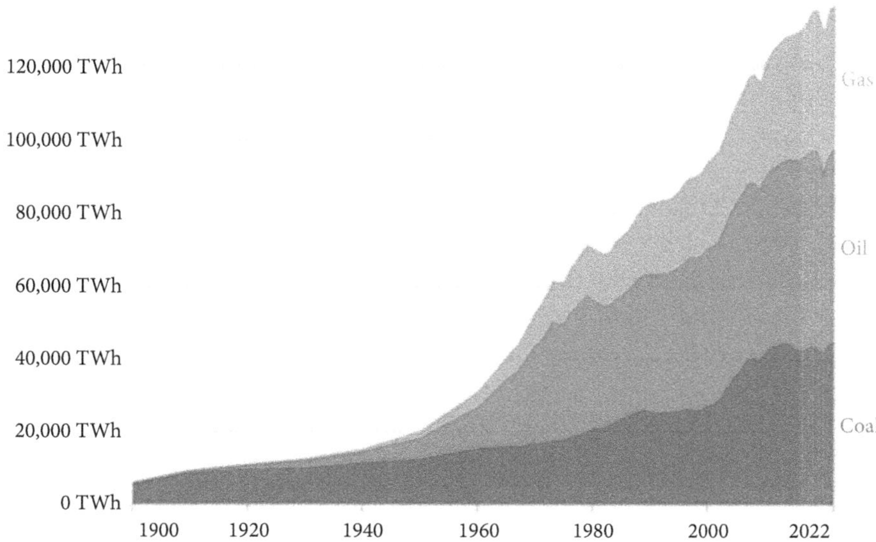

Figure 10.1 Global fossil fuel use, 1900–2022

Reproduced from Hannah Ritchie and Pablo Rosado (2017): 'Fossil Fuels', published online at 'https://ourworldindata.org/fossil-fuels' under Creative Commons licence CC BY 4.0, using data from Energy Institute—Statistical Review of World Energy (2024); Smil (2017)— with major processing by Our World in Data.

GVC research's prime focus upon chain governance and upgrading effectively brackets out the social relations of production underlying capitalisms' interaction with, dependence upon, and ultimately destruction of nature.[1] Furthermore, mainstream GVC analysis' methodological singularism—the empirical focus upon, and theoretical extrapolation from, the vantage point of single firms and/or value chains—generates a perspective suggesting that if one firm can develop 'greener' innovation, this can be generalized.

However, one of the aspects that mainstream GVC analysis overlooks in this context is research on Jevons' Paradox. This 'paradox at the heart of modernity' (York 2010, 6) illuminates how potential per-unit increases in efficiency through enhanced technology are voided by resulting capitalist growth, which not only offsets any ecological gains achieved through such technology, but actually exacerbates environmental devastation (see Malm 2012). While advocates of environmental upgrading portray increased technological efficiency as part of the solution, under capitalism efficiency

[1] We conceive of nature as having its own 'natural history', which is mediated through historically specific social relations. While aware of the differences between the notions of 'nature' and 'environment', we alternate the terms, first, for literary reasons. Second, the term 'environment' does not allow for an adequate description, for instance, of the appropriation of sentient animals.

gains tend to generate the opposite outcome—yet more resource use. Some 150 years ago Jevons described this paradox. He noted, for example, that improvements in engines and efficiency of coal use

> 'will only accelerate anew the consumption of coal. Every branch of manufacture will receive a fresh impulse—hand labour will be still further replaced by mechanical labour, and greatly extended works will be undertaken by aid of the cheap air-power, which were not commercially possible by the use of the costly steam power.
>
> **(Jevons 1866, 132f., see Figure 10.1)**

In other words, capitalist firms systematically use savings achieved by more efficient technologies to increase investment and accumulation, and to maximize profits—generating yet further growth (Clark and Foster 2001). Thus, the relationship between capital accumulation, technological change, and environmental degradation cautions against technocratic solutions to natural resource depletion.

We explain the economic dynamics that give rise Jevons' Paradox through the notion of the 'metabolic rift' (Foster et al. 2010). This concept illuminates how, while humans are intrinsically a part of nature, societal–nature relations under capitalism generate cumulative natural destruction. As capital exploits labour, it appropriates nature, subordinating its cycles and reproductive needs to the dynamics of capital accumulation (Stache 2017).[2] The latter's systemic reproduction generates, thus, an 'irreparable rift in the interdependent process of social metabolism' (Marx 1991, 949) between human (capitalist) society and nature.

Given the conceptual contradictions at the heart of much mainstream GVC research, a growing body of literature addresses the anti-ecological basis of value chains. These include approaches influenced by the notion of uneven ecological exchange[3] and Jason Moore's (2015) world ecology (see Werner 2022). While these literatures represent correctives to the myopia generated

[2] We understand appropriation in terms of a 'class-exploitative appropriation of nature by capital' (Burkett 1997, 168). While the exploitation of labour and the exploitative appropriation of nature differ qualitatively, 'it is appropriate to describe capitalism as exploiting nature insofar as it treats nature as a material condition for the extraction and realization of surplus value' (Burkett 1997, 179). Both the exploitation of labour and the exploitative appropriation of nature are parts of the socio-economic process of capitalist production.

[3] Uneven ecological exchange 'can most simply be defined as the net transfer of ... resources from one part of the world-system (usually the periphery) to another (usually the core) by means of market transactions' (Malm 2012, 151). The debate also embraces waste products and environmental pressures such as pollution, land transformation, and resource depletion that are suffered in the periphery but arise from activities that benefit the capitalist centres (Muradian et al. 2002, cited in Malm 2012, 152). We agree with Malm in that 'a better theory should concentrate not only on trade (...), but just as much—perhaps even more—on investment, thus saving the moment of production from oblivion' (Malm 2012, 152).

by much of the GVC mainstream, we discuss them critically in the next section.

Following this introduction, Section 10.2 outlines our understanding of capitalism's destruction of nature and how we apply it to the CVC-environmental depletion nexus. Section 10.3 introduces and critiques the mainstream GVC notion of environmental upgrading. Section 10.4 discusses and critiques the World Bank's techno-optimism. Section 10.5 uses the animal feed-meat CVC as an example of the mass natural destruction caused by CVCs. Section 10.6 summarizes and concludes the chapter.

10.2 Capitalist Accumulation and CVC-Exacerbated Nature Destruction: A Class-Relational Perspective

As argued in Chapter 2, CVCs are historically specific socio-spatial configurations of capitalist production and trade. Mainstream scholars have usefully focused on the organization of inter-firm market relations along value chains, but they have largely ignored the capitalist social relations of production upon and through which chains operate. For example, Gereffi (1994b, 96f.) subsumes the sphere of production into his relatively a-social notion of the input-output structure of GVCs, which he defines as 'a set of products and services linked together in a sequence of value-adding economic activities'.

Consequently, in much mainstream literature, two elements are usually ignored in the discussion of GVCs' relation to the environment. First, the capitalist relations of production encompass both the spheres of *production* and circulation (not just exchange relations between firms). In David Harvey's (2017) words, capitalist production is 'value in motion', implying a process of surplus-value production to which the reproductive capacity of non-human nature is subordinate. Second, that capitalist production is 'value in motion' implies that it expands continuously. CVCs necessarily entail ever-growing scales of production and, thus, ever extended scales of nature appropriation and environmental destruction.

The mainstream GVC approach is predicated upon the assumption of continuous expansion, and its core notion of economic upgrading encourages competitive growth. However, this assumption is neither theorized in and of itself (within the economic upgrading literature), nor is it integrated into the literature's attempts to advance a theory of environmental upgrading (and see below). Consequently, mainstream GVC analysis cannot explain why capitalist development systematically, rather than contingently, destroys nature.

The remainder of this section elaborates upon three elements of our approach in greater detail. First, we posit that capitalist production abstracts, dangerously, from the qualities and reproductive needs of non-human nature. Second, we specify our consideration of capitalist nature relations from a class-relational perspective. Third, we illuminate how our approach explains the relationship between CVCs and their accelerating effects on ecosystem damage. We also discuss Jason Moore's (2015) notion of commodity frontiers. A book-length treatment of the subject would make it necessary to further analyse various issues from a class-relational perspective, including the uneven geographies of nature-destroying production and trade, unequal ecological exchange, the role of state policies, hegemony and cultures of consumption, and uneven environmental risk. However, our main objective here is to provide the theoretical tools necessary to understand the role of nature in capitalist production and to critique the technological fixes proposed by mainstream GVC research.

Capitalist Growth, Metabolic Rift, and the Abstraction from Nature's Qualities

The disrupted planetary metabolism is caused by the relations between capital on the one hand and labour and nature on the other (Burkett 1999; Burkett 2009; Foster et al. 2010; Stache 2017). Every economy has a particular metabolism, meaning that all 'bearers of production' interact with, and use, non-human nature in the labour process (Marx 1991, 957). Under capitalism, the form of social labour mediating this metabolism 'is shaped according to the imperatives of capital accumulation under the directive of the ruling class' (Rackwitz 2022, own translation). This generates ecological destruction in at least two ways.

First, while capitalist commodity production involves nature-transforming work, and produces useful things, the production of these use values, and thus the satisfaction of human needs, is not its prime purpose. Rather, the actual usefulness of a commodity as well as its natural basis are only a means to the end of the production of surplus value and profitable sale. Consequently, the functioning of ecosystems, the wellbeing of animals, and the reproductive capacity of non-human nature in general are subordinate to the drive for profit.

Second, given that competitive capital accumulation is endless and that it occurs on an ever-expanding scale, so too, then, is the transformation and destruction of nature. Production on ever-extended scales brings with it a constantly growing mass of commodities and their transport. Therefore,

Capital's 'passionate chase after value' (Marx 1990, 254) leads to a systematic overuse of natural resources. It abstracts repeatedly and on an ever-greater scale away from the qualities and reproductive needs of non-human nature (Stache 2017, 444f.). The ruinous result of capital's 'specific antagonism towards nature' (Burkett 1999, 19) is what Foster et al. (2010, 45), call the 'metabolic rift'—the 'rift in the metabolic exchange between humanity and nature'.

This does not mean that it is impossible to create greener niches in some CVCs. But the full prevention of ecological destruction is incompatible with the capitalist profit motive and competitive accumulation. Environmental upgrading cannot, by definition, solve this problem. Marx (1991, 318) notes how the progressive development of the social productivity of labour is demonstrated precisely by the fact that 'the same number of workers', in the same time, 'sets in motion ... an ever-growing mass of means of labour', including 'raw and ancillary materials'. Economic expansion (which upgrading implies) thus entails the transformation of ever-more non-human nature into means of production (and, as a corollary, its use as a sink). Even when per-unit increases in environmental efficiency are achieved through process upgrading, they are voided by the systematic expansion of CVC production. Under capitalism, productive forces constantly turn into 'destructive forces' through the systematic appropriation of nature (see Stache 2017, 485).

Capital's Socio-ecological Contradiction with Labour and Nature

Not all humans account equally for the current environmental devastation. Workers might drive SUVs, eat meat, and fly on vacation, if their salaries allow them to do so (see, for instance, Stache and Bernhold 2021 on material concessions and hegemony formation in connection with meat). But they do not decide upon the systemic destruction of nature through controlling and directing the continual expansion of profit-orientated production. Rather, the appropriation of nature works through the exploitation of labour. Based on the historical privatization of the means of production, capital exploits workers and appropriates nature as part of the very same process. While workers interface directly with natural resources or animals in production (through, for example, mining lithium or slaughtering cattle), they do not control such processes. The separation of workers from the technological, organizational, and natural means of their reproduction—and consequently the coercion to sell their labour power—entails their alienation from nature.

As noted in Chapters 1 and 2, in the capital–labour relation, capital and labour appear to be nominally equal—wage workers can (more or less) 'freely' decide to which capitalist they sell their labour power for which they receive a salary. Exploitation occurs through economic means, through the appropriation of surplus value. By contrast, Capital's relation to non-human nature, including animals, is one of private property and direct appropriation (Stache 2020a; Stache 2020b).[4] However, while wage labour and nature are thus each integrated into capitalist social relations in different ways, the exploitation of workers and appropriation of non-human nature are both necessary parts of the same production process. On that basis, Burkett (1999) and Stache (2017) have argued that there is a socio-ecological antagonism between capital on the one hand and labour and nature on the other.

Unlike capital, which is augmented through production, wage workers come out of the production process as they entered it: without means of production and without control over the labour process or the social wealth they produce, other than their wages.[5] Nature on the other hand is monopolized as a 'free gift' and integrated in the productive process in ways that existentially contradict the reproductive logics of ecosystems, animals, and other parts of nature.

While capital's pursuit of growth is boundless, nature's capacities to cope with the effects of it are not. While the working class can potentially fight for its interests, nature cannot prevent capital from destroying it. Unless capital's destruction of nature becomes a fundamental problem for further accumulation—or unless non-human nature becomes an object of class struggle from below—natural appropriation and destruction will continue apace.

Global Chains, Global Rifts

With the growing importance of CVCs at the end of the twentieth century, the metabolic rift has increasingly globalized—geographically affecting more

[4] This does not necessarily imply that capital can completely control nature. As Baglioni and Campling (2017, 2441) note, 'whereas some natural resource industries like oil, gas and mineral extraction face the challenge of more pervasive geological and biophysical conditions, others like agriculture, fishing and forestry can achieve a more extensive control of the biological process. But even in these sectors, capitalist subsumption of nature is never fully achieved: "natural conditions" always shape and fetter the circuit of capital. For example, the life cycles of plants and animals can be accelerated but never annihilated; hence, idle-time cannot be totally eliminated.'

[5] As we argued in Chapter 8, both capital and labour are internally differentiated, and, furthermore, there are intermediate classes. Small capitalist farmers, for example, appropriate nature as a means of production. However, they often do so in direct dependence on big agribusiness capitals–as in the example of feed production discussed below.

regions and socially working through an ever-larger labouring class. Much contemporary planetary destruction happens in and through CVCs. Indeed, 'the history of global value chains in capitalism is a history of enterprises appropriating ... nature at ever-increasing scale and pace' (Baglioni et al. 2017, 315). For instance, the organization of CVCs requires the expansion of infrastructure (roads, railways, air- and seaports, buildings, server hubs), heightened energy use, and enhanced intangible commodities (services and knowledge deployed through computers and software).

Different CVCs are constituted by firms of different sizes, economic power, and orientation, and they contribute to metabolic rifts of varying extents. Powerful lead firms have a greater influence on conditions of production and trade than small capitals, and upon the intensity of the metabolic rift generated in and through CVCs. As we shall see below, the environmental upgrading literature also argues that in some lead firms, corporate managers establish 'greener' forms of production or can introduce socio-technological innovations to the extent that an increase in sustainability has become a competitive advantage due to consumer pressure. However, lead and supplier firms produce commodities on ever-expanding scales, and natural resources are used in the production of all these commodities necessary for capital to expand and circulate in CVCs.

A case in point is what Andreas Malm (2016) labels 'fossil capital'—an essential enabler of hyper-specialized production and trade. Fossil energy has been deployed by capital to enable its rapid global expansion and to reach vast pools of cheap labour power (Malm 2012, 153f.). The existence and deployment of increasingly large volumes of fossil fuels are a prerequisite for CVCs—enabling the mass production of commodities (including parts and components) and their transport.

The logistics sector—crucial to the expansion of CVCs—is imposing an ever-greater toll on the world's environment. The use of gas, oil, and coal has vastly contributed to the rise of CO2 emissions from 22 billion tons in 1990 to over 36 billion tons by 2019 (see Figure 10.1).[6] The shipping industry is central to the functioning of CVCs. About 90 per cent of all globally traded goods are ferried by sea. Between 1990 and 2021, the volume of seaborne trade increased from 4 billion tons to nearly 11 billion tons (UNCTAD 2023). Merchant ships burn approximately 300 million metric tons of dirty fossil fuels each year, emitting 1billion metric tons of carbon dioxide in the process—roughly equivalent to the annual carbon emissions of Japan (Stone 2021). The logistics of CVCs have generated vast quantities of maritime litter, the

[6] https://ourworldindata.org/emissions-by-fuel

influx of toxic substances and heavy metals into the bio- and geosphere, the transportation of invasive species, the destruction of marine environments, and a loss of biodiversity (Stenmanns and Ouma 2021, 270ff.).

A Note on Jason Moore's Commodity Frontiers Thesis

Unlike the GVC mainstream, a growing body of literature seeks to examine the relationship between CVCs and nature from a perspective critical of capitalism. While several approaches including political ecology and theories of unequal ecological exchange have influenced this debate, the critical GVC community has increasingly referred to Moore's (2015) world ecology and his notion of 'commodity frontiers' (see Baglioni and Campling 2017; Stenmanns and Ouma 2021; Werner 2022).

Moore starts from the premise that capital must 'ceaselessly search for, and find, ways to produce, Cheap Natures: a rising stream of low-cost food, labour-power, energy, and raw materials to the factory gates' (Moore 2015, 53). He posits that these 'Four Cheaps'[7] are socially constructed through power and knowledge as 'others' at the 'frontiers of appropriation' (Moore 2015, 87).

Moore highlights how his use of the notion of appropriation differs from that of Marx who, he says, deployed the term 'more or less interchangeably with the exploitation of wage labour' (Moore 2015, 17). For Moore, the term refers to 'those extra-economic processes that identify, secure, and channel unpaid work [of "women, nature, and colonies" (Moore 2015, 216)] outside the commodity system into the circuit of capital' (Moore 2015, 17). Unlike the exploitation of wage labour that lies within the circuit of capital, Moore conceives of appropriation (e.g., of nature) as lying 'outside that circuit but within reach of capitalist power' (Moore 2015, 118, see p. 87). One of his key arguments is that without these 'frontiers of appropriation', capitalism could not survive. Hence, he argues that '[t]he law of value in capitalism is a law of cheap nature' (Moore 2015, 53). In essence, he presents a theory of historical capitalism's sustenance and expansion through extra-economic violence that takes place at the frontiers of capitalism, for instance, where ongoing primitive accumulation occurs.

Critical GVC research has adopted this approach to highlight 'contemporary capitalism's ever-shifting organizing and pursuing the appropriation

[7] In 2017, Moore extended this to seven Cheaps together with Raj Patel (Patel and Moore 2017). However, this expansion reflects an additive approach rather than fundamentally changing his original position.

and transformation of nature' (Baglioni and Campling 2017, 2438; see Stenmanns and Ouma 2021). For example, Liam Campling (2012), who applies a class-relational approach in his work, deploys Moore's approach to show how lead firms push into new commodity frontiers. He argues that lead firms appropriate natural resources and cheap labour until the socio-ecological environments are exhausted, for instance, through the extraction of fish from the ocean. Furthermore, he posits that this extraction happens to a degree that undermines the possibilities of further accumulation. Over time, 'ecological surplus' deteriorates (Campling 2012, 256). Accordingly, seeking new frontiers becomes a vital condition for capitalism to survive (see Werner 2022).

We agree that primitive accumulation, including dispossession and the commodification of nature, occurs constantly under historical capitalism. However, rather than being the driving force, it is itself an outcome of the capitalist pursuit of surplus value. As noted in Chapter 2, it is the historically specific capitalist relations of production that shape different power relations in historical capitalist societies, including to nature.

Whilst Moore would no doubt disagree with us here, we think that his approach—which combines a World-Systems Analysis notion of an appropriation-based economy with a social-constructivist notion of the Four Cheaps—downplays the specificity of capitalist class and societal-nature relations. He recognizes exploitation and valorization in the circuit of capital, but his theory shifts the analytical focus away from this key social relation of production towards extra-economic, political processes at the frontiers of capitalist expansion. Thus, he also theoretically de-emphasizes the role of non-human nature *within* capitalist production. However, the appropriation of non-human nature is always an indispensable part of the socio-economic relation of exploitation *in* capitalist production. In our example of the feed-meat chain below, we show how animals—and other parts of non-human nature, such as soils—are appropriated as means of production *within* these capitalist relations of production. Based on these dynamics, soy production in Argentina has been intensified productively, *and* the soy-frontier has been expanded geographically. The appropriation of nature cannot, therefore, be reduced to extra-economic power relations in frontier-struggles.

Moore also contends that society and nature develop through each other as 'capitalism-in-nature/nature-in-capitalism' (Moore 2015, 78). He criticizes Marxists such as John Bellamy Foster as operating with a dualist mindset when they juxtapose society to nature (Moore 2011). In doing so, however, he obscures the historically specific relations between capitalist society and nature. Natural history is *relatively* independent of human social history.

However, through the class-relational severance of the mass of producers from the natural conditions of production, capitalism *creates* a novel, historically specific, separation of humanity and nature. While relations between humans and nature are always socially mediated, today's dominant mode of production leads to a capital-led 'degradation of natural processes and life' (Foster and Angus 2016).

In short, considering the nexus between class-based exploitation and the appropriation of nature, we advocate that critical value chain scholarship focus on the relation to—and the use of—nature as a political-*economic* (not just an *extra*-economic) process occurring in and through capitalist production, rather than only at its frontiers.

The GVC mainstream does recognize, partially, the deleterious impacts of CVCs upon the environment. It posits environmental upgrading as part of the solution. The following section shows that this notion suffers from many of the same problems as mainstream GVCs' core concept of economic upgrading. This includes the fallacy of composition (the error of assuming that what can be achieved by one firm or chain can be achieved by all firms and chains) derived from methodological singularism (the abstraction of single firms and chains from capitalism).

10.3 Environmental Upgrading: Limits, Gaps, Contradictions

In recent years, GVC scholars have discussed the barriers to, and possibilities of, environmental upgrading (De Marchi et al. 2019; Ponte 2019; Krishnan et al. 2022a; De Marchi and Gereffi 2023). Stefano Ponte (2019, 211) critically notes how '[s]ustainability management has become a key element of contemporary capitalism, in addition to cost, flexibility and speed'. Corporate actors have discovered that 'going green' (De Marchi et al. 2019, 310) can be a source of competitive advantage. However, most of the environmental upgrading research links environmental upgrading to the established notions of economic upgrading, with all its limitations discussed throughout this book.

The notion of environmental upgrading refers to changes that results in the reduction of firms' ecological footprints (De Marchi et al. 2019, 312f.). Firms can transform 'internal processes by redesigning them based on new environmental standards or goals', meaning greater eco-efficiency (environmental process upgrading). They can produce greener products within the same chain (environmental product upgrading), which are more competitive through eco-branding (e.g., shifting from genetically modified (GM) to non-GM crops). They can take on new environmentally friendly activities within the chain (environmental functional upgrading) to enhance their corporate image. Moving into the production of new, environmentally friendly products, is an example of environmental chain upgrading (De Marchi et al. 2013, 66).

De Marchi et al. (2019) do acknowledge that environmental upgrading is not straightforward. Firms' strategies of environmental upgrading in one activity may be based, or at least be coterminous with, environmental downgrading, defined as 'negative outcomes on the natural environment', in another activity. For example, reduced emission outputs by farmers in the biofuels sector are often 'offset by destruction or damage of high-biodiversity areas' (De Marchi et al. 2019, 320; see Dauvergne and Neville 2009).

Importantly, De Marchi et al. (2019, 310) also recognize that environmental upgrading is not 'sufficient to tackle global sustainability challenges'. Yet, this observation neither tempts, nor pushes these authors to provide a systemic analysis of the CVC-environmental destruction nexus, nor to consider the capitalist dynamics of CVCs. Rather, they chose to 'pragmatically focus on a narrower set of strategies at the unit of analysis of the value chain, in the context of a broader and much more complex picture'. Such methods are vulnerable to fallacies of composition.

Despite the above-noted caveats, some of these scholars endorse quite emphatically the expansion of export production via GVCs. They portray lead firms as important actors in reversing 'humanity's path toward destroying essential planetary boundaries' (De Marchi and Gereffi 2023, 156). In their study of the shipping industry, De Marchi et al. (2019, 318) even claim that 'energy efficiency enhancement represents a win–win for business (in terms of cost savings) and the environment'.

De Marchi and Gereffi (2023, 152) argue that 'green supply chain management' and sustainability have become mainstream concerns, and the problem is only that the 'pace of improvements is lagging the urgency'. This outlook facilitates De Marchi et al.'s (2013, 62) claim that firms are 'improving their environmental performances and promoting green strategies to transform environmental constraints into new drivers of competitive advantage'. De Marchi and Gereffi (2023, 154) recommend that GVC analysis should include the role of the state, as well as how activities are governed and distributed across key actors. According to them, identifying the 'best practices to manage GVCs to tackle environmental problems' requires incorporating various actors—from firms to states to NGOs—and also honestly accounting for possible contradictions among them. (This idea of synergistic governance imbues the weaknesses of the social upgrading approach discussed in Chapter 9.). These authors nevertheless advocate lead firms and GVC expansion as central 'in the fight to address climate crisis' (De Marchi and Gereffi 2023, 154, 156). In this way they are advocating continued capitalist expansion and are providing an environmental fig leaf for firms pursuing it.

By contrast, Stefano Ponte (2020, 2019) and Aarti Krishnan et al. (2022a)—although they are partly co-authors of the previously quoted articles—provide useful examples of how sustainability management in GVCs works well for 'green capital, but does not address brown environments', (Ponte 2019, 212) meaning that, in the end, it does not benefit nature enough, if at all. Ponte (2019, 2020), especially in his single-authored texts, provides a more nuanced and highly insightful analysis about how concepts such as 'green capitalism' have been employed to 'argue that capitalism can be leveraged to solve the pressing environmental issues that arise from its very logic' (Ponte 2019, 213). He shows how the spatial, organizational and technological fixes used by corporate actors to address sustainability issues are designed to facilitate continued profit-maximization. Such strategies by lead firms often include what he calls a 'sustainability-driven supplier squeeze' (Ponte 2020, 78). Lead firms deploy certification criteria at low cost and impose new demands upon suppliers to appropriate value from smaller GVC firms. Consequently, 'in the name of sustainability, a massive transfer of value is taking place from the Global South to the Global North' (Ponte 2019, 133).

One example Ponte uses to illustrate his argument is IKEA's supply chain management strategy. The firm provided advice (e.g., on materials), technical and organizational support, and financial assistance to suppliers in China and South East Asia, to facilitate the sourcing of certified wood and the reduction of emissions. This green upgrading had at least two implications that flow from the dynamics of concentration and centralization of capital noted in Chapter 2. First, IKEA strategically reduced the number of its suppliers such that only firms that (a) would sell 60–70 per cent of their production to IKEA and (b) could implement IKEA's standards on quality and sustainability, became the lead firms' strategic partners. Second, supplier-upgrading implied the capacity to expand production under environmental specifications (Ponte 2019, 144ff.). As a result of these strategies, production became cheaper, but a large share of the profits subsequently generated were 'captured by IKEA itself', such that green upgrading paid 'handsomely for the company' (Ponte 2019, 146).

In another example, Krishnan et al. (2022a) show how UK supermarkets have required Kenyan horticultural suppliers to comply with environmental requirements, such as organic production and the use of waste for energy (Krishnan et al. 2022a, 38). However, farmers and local communities experienced environmental degradation arising out of the expansion of large-scale export monocultures, for example, when they are required to grow crops in non-indigenous ways that cause soil depletion, biodiversity loss, and decreased uncontaminated freshwater availability. When soils are exhausted, supermarkets and exporting firms switch to new locations instead of providing farmers with support to mitigate environmental effects (Krishnan et al. 2022a, 41ff.). Here, UK supermarkets' strategies of environmental upgrading in CVCs not only lead to wider environmental downgrading, but also to a trend towards lower margins for farmers and 'increasing and direct value appropriation' by exporting firms (Krishnan et al. 2022a, 41). Furthermore, lead firms did not contribute to the mitigation costs to farmers arising out of problems such as erosion management.

Ponte (2019, 215ff.) advocates stronger and greener state policies, including the pricing or taxation of environmental impacts and the provision of 'incentives and infrastructures to align private and public interests'. He argues for pursuing sustainability through public–private–civil society partnerships, in which social movement and public demands are tailored to push lead firms in more sustainable directions. However, this approach assumes that the socio-economic relations that underpin the destruction of the natural world could be *politically* changed within capitalism if market forces, power, and inequality can be contained.

Ponte (2019, 223) does acknowledge that 'reformist tweaks can only go so far'. Ultimately however, he argues for 'rethink[ing] the current organization of the global economy' but not its capitalist form—by reforming GVC governance. He also recognizes, however, that this is insufficient to address the CVC-environmental destruction nexus (Ponte 2019, 222).

Ponte's analysis of how handling ecology from a 'green capitalism angle can indeed pay handsomely' for lead firms—while consumers are delivered 'feel-good-content' (Ponte 2019, 216)—is insightful and represents a useful avenue for further analysis. He sees capitalism's continuous expansion as a problem to which technological fixes cannot be a solution. However, capitalist socio-ecological relations and the *systemic* drive towards the destruction of nature remain marginal in his analysis. Notably, however, in some of his co-authored work, Ponte appears to buy into the mainstream environmental upgrading agenda (De Marchi et al. 2019).

In sum, the approaches discussed in this section range from pro-lead firm approaches to those more critical of the environmental upgrading agenda. They have in common, however, that while trying to nudge individual firms in a slightly more sustainable direction, they leave unattended key capitalist social relations and therewith the societal–nature relations underpinning CVCs. However, if the problems of the mainstream GVC intellectual community are notable, they pale in comparison to the World Bank's techno-optimistic appraisal of GVCs' capacity to contribute to environmental safeguarding.

10.4 The World Bank's Techno-optimism

The World Bank's World Development Report (WDR) 2020—*Trading for Development in the Age of Global Value Chains* notes that GVCs 'are a mixed blessing for the environment'. However, it claims that on balance they can 'attenuate environmental concerns'. This is because they facilitate institutional learning, push the dissemination and adoption of greener technology and production methods, help establish higher standards, and 'facilitate the production of new environmentally friendly goods' (World Bank 2020, 118).

According to the report, GVCs can do so in three ways. First, 'technique effects' (i.e., new technologies) reduce the 'environmental cost per unit' (World Bank 2020, 118). Accordingly, knowledge flows among firm networks can enable the development or quicker application of more environmentally friendly techniques. In this context, secondly, '[t]he relational aspect of GVCs is also important (...) because lead firms are increasingly transferring environmentally friendly technologies to their suppliers and pushing for higher standards' (World Bank 2020, 119). Third, the report emphasizes the role of GVCs as drivers of innovation for 'less-damaging products' (World Bank 2020, 119), such as electric cars. It further claims that better state policies can remedy environmental problems. In a nutshell, innovations in technology and new products and markets combined with pro-GVC policy mean that GVCs can have a positive impact on nature.

Unfortunately, but perhaps unsurprisingly, the Bank ideologically sugarcoats its own data on the environmental destructiveness of CVCs and upholds a modernist vision of upgrading 'that evokes the stageism of classic modernization theory' (Bair et al. 2021, 1253). Its arguments are contradictory in at least six ways.

First, while it holds that technique effects can outweigh growth effects and reduce aggregate environmental degradation through more sustainable production, it factors out the impact of endless capitalist growth, and the dynamics of Jevons' Paradox. Even where there are per unit technology-driven efficiency gains in production, their potentially positive environmental impacts are negated by the total expansion of production. For example, the International Council on Clean Transportation (ICCT) shows that while many major ship classes have become less CO2 intensive, total GHG emissions from shipping increased between 2013 and 2015 due to greater numbers of Ocean traversing ships (Olmer et al. 2017, vi).

The WDR's silence on the problem of capitalist growth is reflected further in its discussion of waste. It notes that besides growing amounts of plastic waste, GVCs have 'contributed to a large share of the waste in the electronics and other GVC-intensive sectors' (World Bank 2020, 123). Its solution is to re-conceptualize E-waste as a source of 'inputs for next-generation products' in a 'circular electronics value chain', which represents a 'model of sustainability that is difficult to envisage without GVCs' (World Bank 2020, 123). Thus, the Bank presents E-waste as a means of production in new circuits of capital: capitalist growth is presented as a solution for problems that arise from capitalist growth.

The second contradiction is related to 'greener' products, in particular electric vehicles. While highlighting GHG savings in their use, the Bank omits that these goods are hazardous to the environment in new ways, mainly due to the mining of lithium and other rare earth elements used for batteries (Fornillo 2019). The latter are exported mainly by countries lower down in the imperialist chain, where ecosystems are destroyed by the extraction of these raw materials (Gosh et al. 2022). The World Bank (2020, 119) disregards this problem by asserting that negative effects of lithium mining are mainly due to weak regulations in situ rather than growth in demand by capital, e.g. in the automotive industry. But the problem cannot be reduced to an issue of local policies. In countries like Bolivia, Argentina, and Chile, lithium must be pumped from underground and then concentrated by evaporation, a process that systematically—not only under specific regulation—impacts the ecosystem 'resulting in the depletion and reduced accessibility of fresh water, and contamination of local streams' (Gosh et al. 2022, n.p.). Even if regulation were the core of the problem, policy frameworks do not emerge in a void. CVC lead firms based in the salt flats of Argentina, for instance, powerfully lobby for profit-friendly/environmentally un-friendly regulations (Fornillo and Gamba 2019, 161).

Third, the WDR 2020 assumes that technique effects are necessarily good effects and ignores how capitalist productive forces can be socially and ecologically destructive. Individual corporate strategies might establish 'greener' technologies under specific conditions. But as the destruction of nature is not necessarily an immediate threat to individual capitals, business strategies often push towards profit-making at nearly any natural cost. The newest technologies often generate irreversible damage. For example, despite life-threatening climate breakdown, 'fossil capital' (Malm 2016) has not stopped developing technologies, e.g., for hydraulic fracturing (fracking). Among other effects, the latter causes methane emissions that increasingly contribute to climate breakdown (Howarth 2019). Further, new and better technologies in mining in Chile have made the extraction of low-grade copper more valuable. Now, 'high-tech mines produce 1000x more material waste than those working with older technologies' (Arboleda 2020; cited in Werner 2022, 236).

Fourth, the World Bank ideologically portrays lead firms as, overall, benign, and it assumes arms-length market transactions between firms with no power differentials who share best-practice techniques. Profit maximization, competition, and power are systematically removed from its GVC analysis. In this way the Bank posits that:

> The knowledge flows among networks of firms can enable the development or quicker application of more environmentally friendly techniques. With their large scale, the lead firms in GVCs are able to sustain high rates of innovation (…). The relational aspect of GVCs is also important in this context because lead firms are increasingly transferring environmentally friendly technologies to their suppliers.
>
> **(World Bank 2020, 119)**

Beyond technology diffusion, it claims that lead firms also apply standards across GVCs, driven, among others, by social demands (World Bank 2020, 174). But as Ponte (2019) observes (see previous section), this notion ignores how lead firms use technologies and sustainability standards to their own benefit, often resulting not only in economic disadvantages for local workers, suppliers, and communities, but also in negative environmental effects.

Fifth, the World Bank (2020, 119) assumes that at least some environmental problems can be remedied by '[s]hifts in production toward countries with abundant natural resources [that] allow the preservation of scarce resources, helping to sustain global resources such as land and water'. It does not sustain this assumption with any evidence. Rather, it just supposes potential environmental benefits when arid countries do not have to squander water in the production of oilseeds, as they 'can import them for consumption' (World Bank 2020, 126). Here, the report remains silent about how in countries like Argentina—with plenty of arable land—deforestation and other forms of ecosystem-destruction result from the expansion of the cultivation of oilseeds used as means of production downstream in CVCs, in the biofuel and meat industries (and see below).

The sixth point refers to the WDR's ideological promotion of 'policies for preserving the environment' (World Bank 2020, 119), and specifically how they are connected to a modernist understanding of economic and political progress. The report seems to suggest that economic growth may at first lead to higher impacts on the environment. After a turning point, however, rising incomes are supposed to lead to increasing demands for environmental quality and corresponding policies, which then translate into a better environmental performance. Malm (2016, 327) has vividly criticized such assumptions as part of a bourgeois ideology known as eco-modernism: 'if only people were modern, high-tech and sophisticated enough, there wouldn't be so much pollution around'. Furthermore, the Bank once again ignores how environmental regulation is connected to global economic and power relations. On the one hand, it admits that countries might be 'reluctant to raise environmental standards because in a world of liberalized trade and investment they fear losing the interest of foreign investors' (World Bank 2020, 119). On the other hand, it fails to discuss this contradiction in relation to the above assumption that environment-friendly policies are to be achieved through GVC-development. Capitals roaming the globe for resources, production sites, and sinks, are out of sight.

Much more could be discussed here (for instance, the Bank's advocacy for pricing environmental degradation). This section has highlighted that while the World Bank recognizes some of the deleterious impacts of CVCs upon the environment, this recognition has not affected its advocacy of GVCs as a vehicle for development and climate change mitigation. To borrow an observation that Samir Amin (2016, 88) has made in a different context, the Bank 'promises everything: effectiveness (...), democracy, (...) even social justice'. WDR2020 adds to this list ecologically sustainable development. Meanwhile, 'the implementation of the policies practiced in its name produces almost the opposite' (Amin 2016, 88). Perhaps nowhere is the myopia of the environmental upgrading concept so apparent as in the feed-meat GVC.

10.5 Environmental Upgrading and Nature Destruction in and through the Feed-Meat-Chain

The feed-meat-chain exemplifies CVCs' impacts on nature at different levels—from global climate change to regional biodiversity losses, local water pollution, and the bodies of animals. One of its key components, soy, is demanded primarily as means of production (feed) by 'meat capital' (Stache 2020b) rather than directly for human nutrition (food). The ecological foundations of the feed-meat-chain are increasingly unstable, evidenced by problems of soil erosion, diminishing freshwater availability, and the decline of key non-renewable resources (Weis 2013a, 2013b). Downstream along the CVC, factory farming demonstrates in horrific detail how capitalist production abstracts from the qualities and needs of non-human nature (e.g., the capacity for suffering).

The growth of global meat production has been largely attributed to a trend of fast-rising meat consumption, especially in China. What has rarely been considered, though, is that the driving force behind the 'meatification' of diets (Weis 2013a, 2013b) (i.e., rising meat consumption, however geographically uneven) is the for-profit production of meat.

Between 1961 and 2021, global meat production increased by more than 400 per cent, from 71.3 million to 330 million tons, while the global population increased by 258 per cent in this same period. Meat production is forecast to increase further in the next decades. In 2021, 92.6 million tons of meat were produced in China alone, 48.9 million tons in the United States, 29.5 million tons in Brazil, and 44.2 million tons in the European Union (FAOSTAT, 2023)[8]. What this growth in volume does not show is the for-profit production and killing of an almost unimaginable number of sentient beings: roughly 74 billion chickens, 1.4 billion pigs, and 332 million cattle were slaughtered worldwide in 2021 (FAOSTAT, 2023).

Even if not for the ignorance of animals' sentience (and hence suffering) meat production would be irrational due to its metabolic losses. The 'cycling of grains and oilseeds through livestock to produce flesh, eggs, and milk is an inherently inefficient way to produce food' (Weis 2013b, 75). This inefficiency can also be seen in land use. A little less than half of the world's habitable land is used for agriculture. Yet, 77 per cent of the land used for agriculture is currently used for meat and dairy production,[9] while on average roughly 82 per cent of the daily supply of calories and 60 per cent of the supply of proteins stems from vegetable products.[10] Livestock—including the production of fodder, land use, land use changes, factory farming, enteric fermentation in ruminants and associated methane emissions, organic waste, and other factors—is responsible for approximately 14.5 per cent of 'human-induced'

[8] Note that these data do not show the uneven geographies of lead firms profiting from meat production, as the world's biggest meat capitals do not produce only in their countries of origin.

[9] https://ourworldindata.org/global-land-for-agriculture

[10] https://www.fao.org/faostat/en/#data/FBS

GHG emissions, thus playing a pivotal role in climate change (FAO 2013, xii).

The expansion of both soy and meat production has been mutually reinforcing in and through CVCs: 'rising crop productivity enabled livestock populations to grow', while the latter 'enabled crop production to grow to an extent that would otherwise have deflated prices' (Weis 2013b, 73). Founded upon a vast expansion of land use, between 1990 and 2021, global soy production increased from 108 to 371 million tons (FAOSTAT 2023). In South America, it covers over 61 million hectares, and in Argentina alone, nearly 17 million hectares were planted under soy in 2019 (Bernhold 2022, 179). The term 'United Soybean Republic' was coined by agribusinesses to signify their decisive role in presiding over an increasingly homogenous eco-system in the Southern Cone (Oliveira and Hecht 2016, 251ff.).

Soy value chains have generated mass profits for agro-industrial capital, and caused vast deleterious environmental and health effects (Ávila-Vázquez and Difilippo 2016; Barri 2009; Domínguez and Sabatino 2006; 2010). Argentina has turned into an 'open-air laboratory' (Gras and Hernández 2013, 27) for biotechnology and agrochemical operations. Soy production 'has converted huge tracts of some of the world's most complex ecosystems, some with as many as 600 species per [hectare], into a monoculture' with similarly depleting effects on the social life and livelihoods associated with agriculture in South America (Oliveira and Hecht 2016, 252). Disappearing biomes and an 'arc of deforestation' characterizes the region (Oliveira and Hecht 2016, 267). Westhoek et al. (2011, 17) estimated a little more than a decade ago that 'around 30% of total global terrestrial biodiversity loss may be attributed to livestock production', which is mainly due to deforestation for pasture and feed production (see Benton et al. 2021).

Soy monocropping for global feed-meat chains has also caused soil degradation, in response to which soy producers deploy chemical fertilizers, while pests are fought with pesticides that leave behind persistent toxins, damaging freshwaters and coastal ecosystems (Weis 2013b, 74). The production of huge amounts of fodder depends on highly polluting fossil energy. Pesticides are mostly based upon petrochemical inputs and like fertilizers they 'contain an under-accounted energy budget from manufacturing to transport to application' (Weis 2013b, 74f.). This is increased by the organization of the feed-meat-complex in and through CVCs and the respective long-distance material flows, for example of agricultural machinery. There is also the energy used (and the pollutions produced) when transporting soy to the factory farms all over the world.

Technical Fix Approaches and New Rifts

The problems of technical fix approaches to CVCs are highlighted by solutions that seek to enhance the efficiency of the feed-meat value chain—to reduce its environmental impact—whilst simultaneously contributing to its continued growth. These tend to use similar notions about how to fix CVC's environmental problems as the environmental upgrading agenda. The proponents of such strategies assume that the global feed-meat complex can become (more) sustainable through combinations of environmental product, process, functional and chain upgrading. Policies such as shifts to non-GM soy, better livestock farming practices, enhanced value chain 'network governance', new technologies in the life-science revolution, and shifts from beef to poultry production are posited as solutions. For example, Nepstad et al. (2006, 1596) argue that better social and environmental performance criteria can increase 'the potential for large-scale conservation' in the Amazon region, and thus mitigate the effects of soy and beef industries. Garrett et al. (2013) describe the increasing production of non-GM soy as representing an upgraded supply chain, through and laying the basis for eco-certification programmes.

Technologies such as precision farming methods or '[s]elf-driving farm equipment, powered by clean energy' (Rijsberman 2017, 4) aim to achieve greener fodder cultivation. While such technologies may decrease the environmental impact of consumption per unit, it would not contribute to slowing the growth of feed-meat-chains. In meat production, the focus is on increasing the output of meat per animal, and technologies that increase 'the efficiencies of digestion and of muscle synthesis together with the rapid growth' of animals (Scanes 2018). This may enhance per animal profitability. As Jevons noted, however, such increased profitability would encourage, rather than discourage further growth in this sector.

The OECD and FAO do not advocate the reduction of GHG emissions per unit of food to be addressed by converting the meat industry to a rational and efficient increasingly plant-based food production. Rather they promote the expansion of poultry production, as it has lower feed (and water) to flesh conversion ratios and is thus less GHG-intensive compared to cattle (OECD-FAO 2022, 52). These strategies show how upgrading in one area—fewer GHG emissions per animal—is achieved through increasing the metabolic rift in another, for example by producing chickens that are so heavy that they are unable to support their own weight. The latter increasingly observed phenomenon ignores their natural qualities and needs, and quite literally stretches their (living) existence beyond breaking point.

None of these examples of environmental upgrading advocate what would really be the most sustainable approach to the feed-meat complex—its elimination and replacement with combinations of need (rather than profit) orientated production of plant-based food for direct human consumption. Rather, they seek fixes which will justify and accelerate the complex's continued expansion. The above solutions imply the continual growth of meat capital—rather than seeking to establish food production that does not rely on metabolic losses through the cycling of feed through animals. Even if such technological developments generate a lower ratio of GHG emissions per unit of meat, the current projection by the OECD and FAO foresees a global increase in total meat production of at least 15 per cent by 2031. As a result, GHG emissions by the meat sector are projected to increase by 9 per cent in the same period (OECD-FAO 2022, 191).

The global feed-meat complex illuminates how CVCs are built upon the abstraction from the qualities and reproductive needs of non-human nature, and the vast destruction of natural environments. Mainstream GVC analysis eschews serious consideration of the specificity of capitalism and CVCs. It is not surprising, then, that those informed by the mainstream GVC approach proffer capitalist solutions predicated upon continuous economic growth, rather than based on a genuine commitment to combatting the environmentally destructive forces generated by CVCs.

10.6 Conclusions

Much of the mainstream GVC literature, particularly the WDR 2020, obscures the capitalist causes of environmental devastation. The notion of environmental upgrading promises that increased efficiency, and hence a reduced environmental impact, can be generalized across CVCs. The World Bank also suggests that lead firms can play a key role in spreading eco-friendly techniques through CVCs. However, while some individual firms may partly improve their environmental efficiency (and thus potentially become more profitable), capitalist production and growth undermine the generalizability of this process. Under capitalism, increasingly efficient use of natural resources contributes to yet greater resource use. Methodological singularism—derived from a neglect of the capitalist system of class relations—acts as blinkers on mainstream GVC analysis.

The notion of the metabolic rift illuminates how capitalist production is orientated to surplus value production through labour exploitation. In and through this process, nature is systematically appropriated and destroyed.

Grasping the devastating effects of CVCs on the environment requires comprehending societal-nature relations from the perspective of capitalist class-relations. That labour power and nature are each exploited in particular ways by capital are constants under capitalism. The way these processes occur are interrelated and exacerbated in CVCs, is historically and geographically specific and contingent, and this calls for further research.

Ultimately, capitalism's dynamic of endless accumulation, rooted in the exploitation of labour and nature, needs to be opposed and transcended. Identifying the capitalist character of value chains represents, we hope, a contribution to demystifying their purported developmental and environmental benefits. It also, hopefully, will stimulate more thought and action about what a need rather than profit-orientated economy would look like.

11
Conclusions

> We cannot solve our problems with the same thinking we used when we created them.
>
> **(attributed to Albert Einstein)**

The mainstream GVC framework obscures as much as it illuminates about contemporary global capitalism. It illuminates ways in which production and trade are managed by lead firms in globally organized hierarchies. It thus provides a useful antidote to free market ideology. However, it obscures the exploitative class relations upon which CVCs are based. It does so by failing to recognize and theorize the class-relational basis of capitalism, and the relationship between capitalism and value chains.

For these reasons we argue that an essential starting point when examining value chains is to analyse them as what they really are—Capitalist Value Chains (CVCs).

Capitalism is the most productively transformative system in human history because it is comprised of a unique dialectical relation: (A) capital pursues profit through the exploitation of labour; (B) capital exists as many individual capitalists related to each other through the market. As a result of A and B, capital accumulation is competitive, creating a historically unparalleled dynamism, and a tendency towards increasing concentration and centralization of economic power. Capitalism's dynamism is also predicated upon an historically unprecedented appropriation of nature. Labour exploitation and environmental wreckage are hard-wired into capitalism's existence. CVCs are hastening and deepening these deleterious dynamics and fostering systemic inequality and immiseration through international class relations.

The common-place idea that we require a more resilient system of CVCs to meet humanity's challenges in the twenty-first century is to fall into intellectual cul-de-sac identified by Albert Einstein in this chapter's opening quote—of attempting to solve our problems with the same ideas that created them in the first place.

Capitalist Value Chains. Benjamin Selwyn and Christin Bernhold, Oxford University Press.
 DOI: 10.1093/9780191994906.003.0011

The GVC mainstream is committed to continued economic growth through various forms of upgrading. This commitment represents a form of intellectual cognitive dissonance. On the one hand, the GVC mainstream sees the myriad inequalities and depredations associated with GVCs. On the other hand, whatever the problem, the mainstream's solution is GVC expansion and more upgrading. If insufficient growth and development are the problem, then economic upgrading is the answer. If inequality and poverty wages are the problem, then the remedy is social upgrading. If environmental destruction is the problem, then environmental upgrading is the solution. As we argue throughout this book, under capitalism, economic growth is driven forward by capital's insatiable and never-ending demand for profit rather than for human or environmental need. Capitalism in general, and CVCs in particular, are a dead-end for real human development and for the world's natural environment.

The intellectual failure of attempting to solve our problems with the same ideas that created them in the first place represents the ideological dominance—across policy, academic, and political communities—of mainstream GVC thought. Similarly, mainstream GVC proponents undertake significant efforts to convince the development community that its ideas represent and promote the most realistic forms of development. As this book shows, however, such efforts are based on partial and misleading portrayals of political economic reality, and are thus open to challenge.

This is most obvious in the ways that the GVC mainstream constructs apologetic accounts of lead firms—as coordinators, facilitators, and of potential benefactors to supplier firms eager to 'link up' with them, rather than as major concentrations of capital. It is obvious in the World Bank's attempt to retro-fit the reality of power-based economic-planning (lead firm chain governance) into the arms-length, market-based, non-power-based assumptions of comparative advantage theory. This is, as we noted in Chapter 4, the equivalent of comparing conceptual apples with empirical oranges, that is, creating a false analogy. It is facilitated by the deployment of poverty measures that portray workers who do unhealthy amounts of overtime under brutal conditions as enjoying the fruits of development through GVC integration. The ideology-as-faith basis of mainstream GVC thought is evident in its claim that environmental upgrading—entailing the continued expansion of CVCs which are specifically designed to boost capitalist growth—represents a solution to the world's environmental crisis. As if environmental crisis is not enough, some mainstream GVC scholars are playing their part in supporting the US's geopolitical objectives. The banner of GVC chain 'resilience' is being flown to sponsor the US state's efforts to contain China's rise.

Part and parcel of the GVC mainstream's ideological dominance is its construction and deployment of supportive conceptual categories. These include methodological singularism and the fallacy of composition, that is, implicitly assuming that what is achieved by one firm can be achieved by all firms; a transaction cost economics notion of chain governance where lead firms are heralded as promoters of technology-transmission and thus socio-economic progress more generally; the externalization of capitalism's destruction of non-human nature from any serious consideration of the formation and reproduction of CVCs; and above all a failure to view CVCs from the perspective of workers upon whose labour they are based, still less to consider ways in which CVCs are rooted in, and exacerbate, labour exploitation.

Such conceptual categories have helped naturalize CVCs, to such an extent that when they succumb to shocks and heightened risks, as during the Covid-19 pandemic, an entire panoply of experts, politicians, and businesspeople emerge to provide advice and guidance on how to fortify them—as if the existence of humanity depends upon their continued reproduction and expansion. The truth is the other way around. By most serious accounts, most of humanity—the world's labouring classes and those supported by/supporting them—and the planet itself, cannot afford new rounds of hyper-specialized capital accumulation. For these reasons we've attempted to develop a class-relational approach to CVCs.

At no point does the GVC mainstream consider how capitalism systemically undermines the generalizability of economic, social or environmental upgrading. In fact, the exclusion of any rigorous conception of capitalism appears to be a prerequisite for the propagation of the GVC mainstream's developmentalist illusions—that upgrading represents a 'new paradigm' of development. But, as we've shown throughout this book, the GVC mainstream's cure—more ('better') upgrading—cannot cure, and partly even worsens the disease (the problems generated by inherently uneven and environmentally destructive economic growth itself).

Our conception of capitalism includes a class-relational notion of the state. This differs from much of the GVC mainstream which conceives of the state in limited terms as 'facilitator' or institutional background of development. We understand capitalist states as arising out of and reproducing relations of exploitation in an international context. Part of this role entails attempting to boost national capitals—to raise their rates of labour exploitation and maximize surplus value capture. In the context of CVCs this entails shaping and facilitating the expansion and reproduction of exploitative international class relations. Such a comprehension informs our analysis of the role of geopolitics in CVCs.

Whilst it has been quite common lately to proclaim the 'return' of geopolitics we show how they have been ever-present in the US state's attempts to establish and protect core technologies for its firms. Our notion of the imperialist chain combines class-relations and geopolitics. ICT-based core technologies provide the technological underpinning of CVCs and of US firms' dominance of them. China's rise—its move from CVC workshop to core technology challenger to some US firms—represents an attempt to re-work its position in CVCs and in the imperialist chain. As we also show, notions of GVC resilience, whilst pitched at the universal level (as good for all GVC participants) have a strong geopolitical element, as the US state is deploying the notion as part of its attempt to contain China's rise.

Economic upgrading is the GVC mainstream's lodestar. It is portrayed by the mainstream in win–win terms—good for lead and supplier firms—generating developmental gains for workers in supplier firms and in more general terms, contributing to national economic development. We show how economic upgrading does not represent a win–win process. Rather, it occurs through dynamics of capital concentration and class differentiation: Some firms upgrade and become global suppliers (and sometimes major national players) at the expense of others. In short, economic upgrading occurs through the reshaping of social relations of production, exploitation, and surplus value capture.

This book's notion of immiserating growth regimes contributes to recent developments in labour regime theory. It shows how CVC firms and states combine to make and keep working classes poor as part of supplier firm's accumulation strategies. While exploitation is a constant under capitalism, we show how, when given the opportunity, supplier firms will deploy forms of immiserating exploitation—paying labour beneath a living wage—as a way of minimizing necessary labour and maximizing surplus value producing labour.

While many CVCs are based upon immiserating growth regimes, our discussion of social upgrading from below illuminates how workers' collective actions can, under certain circumstances, generate meaningful gains to their wages, conditions, and livelihoods. Mainstream GVC notions of social upgrading tend to deploy typologies to identify different pathways of economic integration, without delving into the social relations that underpin economic and social upgrading. By contrast, our conception of social upgrading from below is rooted in a class-relational conception of labour under capitalism, which provides a surer footing for explaining processes of immiserating growth and ways workers' can and do resist it.

The myopia of the GVC mainstream is perhaps nowhere more apparent than in its treatment of the relationship between GVCs and the natural environment. The mainstream does recognize how GVCs have a deleterious effect upon the natural environment. But, as part of its ideology as faith portrayal of the world, it then advocates continued economic growth, through environmental upgrading. This book shows, by contrast, how CVCs have exacerbated and accelerated capitalism's deep-seated appropriation and destruction of the natural environment.

What scope is there for continuing and expanding this class-relational approach across CVC and critical GVC/GPN research? We think that there are at least four potential paths of CVC research. One area that could be investigated and conceptualized further is the constitutive association between CVCs, international class relations, and the imperialist chain. How, for example, is hyperspecialization impacting upon leading state's abilities to structure the imperialist chain by enhancing the power of their own capitalist firms and classes? Relatedly, are there observable causal relations between upgrading and enhanced positions in the imperialist chain and vice versa? How have such dynamics played out historically? Put another way, what are the relationship(s) between the contested reproduction of the imperialist chain and of CVCs?

We noted that the establishment of CVCs represented, partially at least, a socio-spatial fix by sections of US capital followed by other capitalist classes to re-boot their profitability. While we've dwelled upon the first element—the socio—the second, the geographical/spatial elements of the establishment, reproduction, and developmental processes arising out of CVCs—represents a fruitful avenue for further research. How has the global division of labour been shaped and reshaped through international class relations in CVCs? What does this illuminate about the geographical dimensions of international class relations? In other words, the uneven socio-geographies of capitalist production and the distribution of (the fruits of) social labour need to be further analysed in empirical studies, and from a class relational perspective.

Thirdly, what scope is there for the development of a class relational analysis of variegated geographies of environmental destruction? The GVC mainstream has, with its notion of environmental upgrading, at least recognized some of the environmental wreckage caused by CVCs. To counter the mainstream's naïve notion that yet more growth—albeit one based upon environmental 'improvement'—is the answer to problems generated by CVCs, it is necessary to further investigate the relations and dynamics of capitalist nature destruction, and how such processes are influenced by, and underpin the formation, functioning, and uneven geographies of CVCs past, present, and future.

Fourthly, what are the politics and policies of a class-relational, pro-labour approaches to CVCs? The social upgrading perspective aims to enhance workers' wages and conditions whilst also augmenting capitalist firms' competitiveness and profitability. How does a CVC approach differ from it? Part of the CVC research agenda should be enquiring how class struggles from below that improve workers' wages, conditions, and livelihoods, can be mobilized to contest, fundamentally, capital's rule over labour, and to establish a non-capitalist, need-based economic system.

One thing that the GVC mainstream has done, through its notion of chain governance, is to illuminate just how much planning is involved in the operation and reproduction of CVCs. Moreover, the output coordinated by some lead firms involved in CVCs dwarves that of many national economies. Such planning is not subject to democratic decision-making. Far from it. If these firms were considered as national political economies, they would more likely be described as dictatorships rather than models of democratic accountability.

The alternative to accumulation-based and profit-orientated production is production for social need. But the GVC mainstream is dead set against any consideration of real alternatives to its project of endless capital accumulation. Endless profit-orientated capital accumulation is destroying the planet, increasing inequalities and subjecting ever-greater numbers of the world's population to exploitative employment. The move to restructure CVCs (e.g., by shortening or re-orienting them), if it is to be genuinely environmentally sustainable and socially equitable, must also be part of a move towards a need, rather than profit-based, political economic system.

This book's rationale has been to expose the logical failings of mainstream GVC research, the ever-more deleterious eco-social relations upon which CVCs are based, and ways in which we can think beyond this damaging system of global production. If it contributes to stimulating such conversations, then it has done its job.

Bibliography

Abu-Manneh, Bashir, 2003. 'The Illusions of Empire'. *Interventions 5* (2): pp. 159–176. doi: 10.1080/1369801031000112914.

Acosta Reveles, Irma-Lorena, 2008. 'Capitalismo Agrario y Sojización en la Pampa Argentina. Las Razones el Desalojo Laboral'. *Revista Lavboratorio. Estudios sobre Cambio Estructural y Desigualdad Social 10* (22): pp. 8–12.

Adler, Glenn, and Eddie Webster, 1995. 'Challenging Transition Theory: The Labor Movement, Radical Reform, and Transition to Democracy in South Africa'. *Politics & Society 23* (1): pp. 75–106. doi: 10.1177/0032329295023001004.

Aglietta, Michel, and Guo Bai, 2014. *China's Development: Capitalism and Empire*. 2014th ed. London, New York: Routledge Taylor & Francis Group.

Ahmed, Nazeen, and Dev Nathan, 2014. 'Improving Wages and Working Conditions in the Bangladeshi Garment Sector: The Role of Horizontal and Vertical Relations'. *Capturing The Gains Working Paper 40, University of Manchester*. https://assets.publishing.service.gov.uk/media/57a089ed40f0b64974000316/ctg-wp-2014-40.pdf.

AK Strategic Unionism, 2013. 'Jenaer Machtressourcenansatz 2.0'. In *Comeback der Gewerkschaften? Machtressourcen, innovative Praktiken, internationale Perspektiven*, edited by Stefan Schmalz and Klaus Dörre, pp. 345–375. Frankfurt and New York: Campus.

Alessandrini, Donatella, 2022. 'A Not So "New Dawn" for International Economic Law and Development: Towards a Social Reproduction Approach to GVCs'. *European Journal of International Law 33* (1): pp. 131–162. doi: 10.1093/ejil/chac005.

Alfaro, Laura, and Davin Chor, 2023. *Global Supply Chains: The Looming 'Great Reallocation'*. Working Paper 31661. doi: 10.3386/w31661. https://www.nber.org/papers/w31661.

Alford, Matthew, 2020. 'Antagonistic Governance in South African Fruit Global Production Networks: A Neo-Gramscian Perspective'. *Global Networks 20* (1): pp. 42–64. doi: 10.1111/glob.12223.

Ali, Abubakar, Amr Mahfouz, and Amr Arisha, 2017. 'Analysing Supply Chain Resilience: Integrating the Constructs in a Concept Mapping Framework via a Systematic Literature Review'. *Supply Chain Management 22* (1): pp. 16–39. doi: 10.1108/SCM-06-2016-0197.

Ali, Mona, 2016. 'Dark Matter, Black Holes and Old-Fashioned Exploitation: Transnational Corporations and the US Economy'. *Cambridge Journal of Economics 40* (4): pp. 997–1018. doi: 10.1093/cje/bev062.

Alimahomed-Wilson, Jake, and Immanuel Ness, 2018. *Choke Points: Logistics Workers Disrupting the Global Supply Chain*. London: Pluto Press.

Allegretto, Sylvia, Marc Doussard, Dave Graham-Squire, Ken Jacobs, Dan Thompson, and Jeremy Thompson, 2013. 'Fast Food, Poverty Wages: The Public Cost of Low-Wage Jobs in the Fast-Food Industry'. *UC Berkeley Labor Center, Berkley*. https://www.policymattersohio.org/wp-content/uploads/2013/10/Fast-Food-Report-FINAL.pdf.

Allen, Gregory C., 2022. 'Choking off China's Access to the Future of AI: New U.S. Export Controls on AI and Semiconductors Mark a Transformation of U.S. Technology Competition with China'. *Center for Strategic and International Studies*. https://www.csis.org/analysis/choking-chinas-access-future-ai.

Aloisi, Antonio, and Valerio de Stefano, 2022. 'Essential Jobs, Remote Work and Digital Surveillance: Addressing the COVID-19 Pandemic Panopticon'. *International Labour Review 161* (2): pp. 289–314. doi: 10.1111/ilr.12219.

Altman, Steven A., and Caroline R. Bastian, 2022. *DHL Global Connectedness Index 2022: An In-depth Report on the State of Globalization.* https://www.dhl.com/content/dam/dhl/global/delivered/documents/pdf/dhl-global-connectedness-index-2022-key-highlights-brochure.pdf.

Altvater, Elmar, 1975. 'Wertgesetz und Monopolmacht'. In *Zur Theorie des Monopols. Staat und Monopole (I). Argument-Sonderbände AS6*, edited by Wolfgang Fritz Haug, pp. 129–198. Berlin: Argument.

Amin, Samir, 2016. *Russia and the Long Transition from Capitalism to Socialism.* New York: Monthly Review Press.

AMRC, 2013. *Labor Rights in High Tech Electronics: Case Studies of Workers' Struggles in Samsung Electronics and its Asian Suppliers.* Hong Kong: Asia Monitor Resource Centre.

Amsden, Alice, 1990. 'Third World Industrialization: "Global Fordism" or a New Model?'. *New Left Review 182* (2): pp. 5–32.

Amsden, Alice, 2005. 'Promoting Industry under WTO Law'. In *Putting Development First: The Importance of Policy Space in the WTO and International Financial Institutions*, edited by Kevin P. Gallagher, pp. 216–232. London: Zed Books.

Andrews, Dan, Peter Gal, and William Witheridge, 2018. *A Genie in a Bottle? A Genie in a Bottle? Globalisation, Competition and Inflation: OECD Economics Department Working Papers No. 1462.* doi: 10.1787/deda7e54-en. https://www.oecd-ilibrary.org/content/paper/deda7e54-en.

Andrijasevic, Rutvica, and Devi Sacchetto, 2014. 'Made in the EU: Foxconn in the Czech Republic'. *The Journal of Labor & Society 17* (3): pp. 391–415. doi: 10.1163/17434580-01703006.

Ankarloo, Daniel, and Giulio Palermo, 2004. 'Anti-Williamson: A Marxian Critique of New Institutional Economics'. *Cambridge Journal of Economics 28* (3): pp. 413–429. doi: 10.1093/cje/28.3.413.

Anlló, Guillermo, Roberto Bisang, and Mercedes Campi, 2013a. 'Schumpeter de Visita en las Pampas Argentinas?' In *Claves Para Repensar El Agro Argentino*, edited by Guillermo Anlló, Roberto Bisang, and Mercedes Campi, pp. 11–30. Buenos Aires: Eudeba.

Anlló, Guillermo, Roberto Bisang, and Mercedes Campi (eds), 2013b. *Claves Para Repensar El Agro Argentino.* Buenos Aires: Eudeba.

Anlló, Guillermo, Roberto Bisang, and Mercedes Campi, 2013c. 'El modelo de Organización de la Producción Agrícola: De la Integración Vertical a la Agricultura en Red'. In *Claves Para Repensar El Agro Argentino*, edited by Guillermo Anlló, Roberto Bisang, and Mercedes Campi, pp. 152–202. Buenos Aires: Eudeba.

Anner, Mark, 2011. *Solidarity Transformed: Labor Responses to Globalization and Crisis in Latin America.* Ithaca, London: Cornell University Press.

Anner, Mark, 2012. 'Corporate Social Responsibility and Freedom of Association Rights: The Precarious Quest for Legitimacy and Control in Global Supply Chains'. *Politics & Society 40* (4): pp. 609–644. doi: 10.1177/0032329212460983.

Anner, Mark, 2013. 'Workers' Power in Global Value Chains: Fighting Sweatshop Practices at Russell, Nike and Knights Apparel'. In *Transnational Trade Unionism: Building Union Power: Building Union Power*, edited by Peter Fairbrother, Christian Lévesque, and Marc-Antonin Hennebert, pp. 23–41. 1st ed. New York: Routledge.

Anner, Mark, 2015. 'Labor Control Regimes and Worker Resistance in Global Supply Chains'. *Labor History 56* (3): pp. 292–307.

Anner, Mark, 2020. *Abandoned? The Impact of Covid-19 on Workers and Businesses at the Bottom of Global Garment Supply Chains: Research Report.* Penn State Centre for Global Workers' Rights.

Anner, Mark, 2021. 'Three Labour Governance Mechanisms for Addressing Decent Work Deficits in Global Value Chains'. *International Labour Review 160* (4): pp. 611–629. doi: 10.1111/ilr.12209.

Anner, Mark, 2022. 'Bargaining for Decent Work and Beyond: Transforming Work and Lives through Collective Bargaining Agreements in the Honduran Maquila Sector'. *The Center for Global Workers' Rights (CGWR), The Pennsylvania State University, with the Honduran Research Team and Luis Mendoza.* https://ler.la.psu.edu/wp-content/uploads/sites/4/2022/06/Honduras-maquila-report.pdf.

Appelbaum, Richard P., 2008. 'Giant Transnational Contractors in East Asia: Emergent Trends in Global Supply Chains'. *Competition & Change 12* (1): pp. 69–87. doi: 10.1179/102452908X264539.

Apple, 2014. 'Supplier Responsibility 2014 Progress Report'. www.apple.com/supplier responsibility/pdf/Apple_SR_2014_Progress_Report.pdf.

Apple, 2024. 'A Global Supply Chain: Apple Products Are Made All Over the World'. https://www.apple.com/uk/supply-chain/.

Arboleda, Martín, 2020. *Planetary Mine: Territories of Extraction Under Late Capitalism.* London: Verso.

Archetti, Eduardo, Kristi Stölen, 1975. *Explotación Familiar y Acumulación de Capital en el Campo Argentino.* Buenos Aires: Siglo Veintiuno Editores.

Armstrong, R., A. Reiter, 2024. 'Tariffs Are Hard Work'. *The Financial Times* (12 November 2024).

Armstrong Mckay, David I., Arie Staal, Jesse F. Abrams, Ricarda Winkelmann, Boris Sakschewski, Sina Loriani, Ingo Fetzer, Sarah E. Cornell, Johan Rockström, and Timothy M. Lenton, 2022. 'Exceeding 1.5°C Global Warming Could Trigger Multiple Climate Tipping Points'. *Science 377* (6611). doi: 10.1126/science.abn7950.

Arnold, Dennis, 2013a. 'Better Work or 'Ethical Fix'? Lessons from Cambodia's Apparel Industry'. *Global Labour Column 155*: pp. 1–2.

Arnold, Dennis, 2013b. 'Workers' Agency and Re-Working Power Relations in Cambodia's Garment Industry'. *Capturing The Gains, Working Paper 24, University of Manchester.* doi: 10.2139/ssrn.2237494.

Arnold, Dennis, 2017. 'Civil Society, Political Society and Politics of Disorder in Cambodia'. *Political Geography 60*: pp. 23–33. doi: 10.1016/j.polgeo.2017.03.008.

Arrighi, Giovanni, 1990. 'The Developmentalist Illusion'. In *Semiperipheral States in the World-Economy*, edited by W. G. Martin, pp. 11–42. Westport: Greenwood Press.

Arrighi, Giovanni, 1994. *The Long Twentieth Century. Money, Power and the Origins of Our Times.* London, New York: Verso.

Arrighi, Giovanni, and Jessica Drangel, 1986. 'The Stratification of the World-Economy: An Exploration of the Semiperipheral Zone'. *Review (Fernand Braudel Center) 10*: pp. 9–74.

Arriola, Christine, Sophie Guilloux-Nefussi, Seung-Hee Koh, Przemyslaw Kowalski, Elena Rusticelli, and Frank van Tongeren, 2020. 'Efficiency and Risks in Global Value Chains in the Context of COVID-19'. *OECD Economics Department Working Papers 1637*: pp. 1–43.

Asia Floor Wage, 2022. 'Calculating a Living Wage'. https://asia.floorwage.org/living-wage/calculating-a-living%20wage/#:~:text=The%20Asia%20Floor%20Wage%20is,regardless%20of%20the%20national%20currency.

Autor, David, David Dorn, Lawrence Katz, Christina Patterson, and John van Reenen, 2017. *The Fall of the Labor Share and the Rise of Superstar Firms, NBER Working Paper 2339.* Cambridge, MA: National Bureau of Economic Research.

Ávila-Vázquez, Medardo, and Flavia Silvina Difilippo, 2016. 'Agricultura Tóxica y Salud en Pueblos Fumigados de Argentina'. *Crítica y Resistencias. Revista de Conflictos Sociales Latinoamericanos 2*: pp. 23–45.

Azcuy Ameghino, Eduardo, 2000. 'Las reformas económicas neoliberales y el sector agropecuario pampeano (1991–1999)'. *Ciclos en la historia, la economía y la sociedad 10* (20): pp. 191–219.

Azpiazu, Daniel, Pablo Manzanelli, and Martin Schorr, 2011. *Concentración y Extranjerización. La Argentina en la Posconvertibilidad*. Buenos Aires: Capital Intelectual.

Baglioni, Elena, 2018. 'Labour Control and the Labour Question in Global Production Networks: Exploitation and Disciplining in Senegalese Export Horticulture'. *Journal of Economic Geography 18* (1): pp. 111–137. doi: 10.1093/jeg/lbx013.

Baglioni, Elena, 2022. 'The Making of Cheap Labour across Production and Reproduction: Control and Resistance in the Senegalese Horticultural Value Chain'. *Work, Employment and Society 36* (3): pp. 445–464. doi: 10.1177/0950017021999569.

Baglioni, Elena, and Liam Campling, 2017. 'Natural Resource Industries as Global Value Chains: Frontiers, Fetishism, Labour and the State'. *Environment and Planning A: Economy and Space 49* (11): pp. 2437–2456. doi: 10.1177/0308518X17728517.

Baglioni, Elena, Liam Campling, Neil M. Coe, and Adrian Smith (eds), 2022a. *Labour Regimes and Global Production*. Newcastle: Agenda Publishing.

Baglioni, Elena, Liam Campling, and Gerard Hanlon, 2020. 'Global Value Chains as Entrepreneurial Capture: Insights from Management Theory'. *Review of International Political Economy 27* (4): pp. 903–925. doi: 10.1080/09692290.2019.1657479.

Baglioni, Elena, Liam Campling, and Elizabeth Havice, 2017. 'The Nature of the Firm in Global Value Chains'. In *The Corporation: A Critical, Multi-disciplinary Handbook*, edited by Grietje Baars and André Spicer, pp. 314–325. Cambridge: Cambridge University Press.

Baglioni, Elena, Liam Campling, Mezzadri, Alessandra, Miyamura, Satoshi, Pattenden, Jonathan, and Benjamin Selwyn, 2022b. 'Exploitation and Labour Regimes: Production, Circulation, Social Reproduction, Ecology'. In *Labour Regimes and Global Production*, edited by Elena Baglioni, Liam Campling, Neil M. Coe, and Adrian Smith, pp. 81–100. Newcastle: Agenda Publishing.

Bair, Jennifer, 2005. 'Global Capitalism and Commodity Chains: Looking Back, Going Forward'. *Competition & Change 9* (2): pp. 153–180.

Bair, Jennifer, 2010. 'On Difference and Capital: Gender and the Globalization of Production'. *Signs: Journal of Women in Culture and Society 36* (1): pp. 203–226.

Bair, Jennifer, 2014. 'Editor's Introduction: Commodity Chains in and of the World System'. *Journal of World-Systems Research 20* (1): pp. 1–10. doi: 10.5195/jwsr.2014.574.

Bair, Jennifer, 2022. *Labour Regimes and Global Production*. 1st ed. Newcastle upon Tyne: Agenda Publishing.

Bair, Jennifer, Mathew Mahutga, Marion Werner, and Liam Campling, 2021. 'Capitalist Crisis in the "age of global value chains"'. *Environment and Planning A: Economy and Space 53* (6): pp. 1253–1272. doi: 10.1177/0308518X211006718.

Bair, Jennifer, and Marion Werner, 2011a. 'Commodity Chains and the Uneven Geographies of Global Capitalism: A Disarticulations Perspective. Guest Editorial'. *Environment and Planning A 43*: pp. 988–997.

Bair, Jennifer, and Marion Werner, 2011b. 'The Place of Disarticulations: Global Commodity Production in La Laguna, Mexico'. *Environment and Planning A 43* (5): pp. 998–1015. doi: 10.1068/a43404.

Bair, Jennifer, Marion Werner, Christian Berndt, and Marc Boeckler, 2013. 'Dis/articulating Producers, Markets, and Regions: New Directions in Critical Studies of Commodity Chains'. *Environment and Planning A 45* (11): pp. 2544–2552.

Baker, Andrew, 2006. *The Group of Seven: Finance Ministries, Central Banks and Global Financial Governance*. London, New York: Routledge.

Baldwin, Richard E., and Simon J. Evenett (eds), 2020. *COVID-19 and Trade Policy: Why Turning Inward Won't Work*. Centre for Economic Policy Research (CEPR): CEPR Press.

Baldwin, Robert E., 2008. *The Development and Testing of Heckscher-Ohlin Trade Models*. Cambridge, MA: MIT Press.

Balsa, Javier, 2007. *El Desvanecimiento del Mundo Chacarero. Transformaciones Sociales en la Agricultura Bonaerense: 1937–1988*. Bernal: Universidad de Quilmes (UNQ).

Barkai, Simcha, 2020. 'Declining Labor and Capital Shares'. *The Journal of Finance 75* (5): pp. 2421–2463. doi: 10.1111/jofi.12909.

Barker, Colin, 1978. 'A Note on the Theory of Capitalist States'. *Capital & Class 2* (1): pp. 118–126. doi: 10.1177/030981687800400108.

Barnard, Helen, Aleks Collingwood, Andrew Wenham, Eddie Smith, Ben Drake, David Leese, and Ashwin Kumar, 2018. 'UK Poverty 2018: A Comprehensive Analysis of Poverty Trends and Figures'. *Joseph Rowntree Foundation*. https://www.jrf.org.uk/uk-poverty-2018.

Barri, Fernando. 2009.'El Modelo Sojero de Desarrollo en la Argentina. Consecuencias Sociales y Ambientales en la Era de los Agronegocios'. Paper presented at XXVII Congreso de la Asociación Latinoamericana de Sociología, Buenos Aires, https://cdsa.aacademica.org/000-062/351.pdf

Barrientos, Stephanie, 2008. 'Contract Labour: The "Achilles Heel" of Corporate Codes in Commercial Value Chains'. *Development and Change 39* (6): pp. 977–990. doi: 10.1111/j.1467-7660.2008.00524.x.

Barrientos, Stephanie, Gary Gereffi, and Arianna Rossi, 2011. 'Economic and Social Upgrading in Global Production Networks: A New Paradigm for a Changing World'. *International Labour Review 150* (3–4): pp. 319–340.

Baschuk, Brace, Debby Wu, and Peter Elstrom, 2022. 'Apple's Tech Supply Chain Shows Difficulty of Dumping China'. https://www.bloomberg.com/news/articles/2022-09-30/apple-s-tech-supply-chain-shows-difficulty-of-dumping-china.

Bayari, Celal, 2018. *Economy and Market in China: The State, Wage Labour and the Construction of the 'China Price'*. Munich: University Library of Munich.

Beattie, Alan, 2021. 'Coronavirus-Induced "reshoring" Is Not Happening: Business Is Pushing Back and Goods Have Continued to Flow Despite the Pandemic'. *The Financial Times* (30 September 2020).

Benton, Tim, Carling Bieg, Helen Harwatt, Roshan Pudasaini, and Laura Wellesley, 2021. 'Food System Impacts on Biodiversity Loss: Three Levers for Food System Transformation in Support of Nature'. *The Royal Institute of International Affairs—Chatham House*. https://www.chathamhouse.org/sites/default/files/2021-02/2021-02-03-food-system-biodiversity-loss-benton-et-al_0.pdf.

Berg, Janine, Marianne Furrer, Ellie Harmon, Uma Rani, and M. Six Silbermann, 2018. *Digital Labour Platforms and the Future of Work: Towards Decent Work in the Online World*. https://discriminationlaw.org.uk/assets/documents/Berg-et-al-2018-Digital-Labour-Platforms.pdf.

Berndt, Christian, and Christin Bernhold, 2018. 'Lateinamerikanischer Neostrukturalismus: Sojaboom und wirtschaftliche Konzentration in Argentinien'. *Zeitschrift für Wirtschaftsgeographie 62* (1): pp. 30–45.

Bernhardt, Thomas, and William Milberg, 2011. 'Does Economic Upgrading Generate Social Upgrading? Insights from the Horticulture, Apparel, Mobile Phones and Tourism Sector'. *Capturing The Gains Working Paper 2011/06 University of Manchester*. https://assets.publishing.service.gov.uk/media/57a08af1ed915d622c0009cd/ctg-wp-2011-06.pdf.

Bernhold, Christin, 2021. 'Social Partners for Social Upgrading? On Corporate Strategies in Argentinian Agro-Industrial Value Chains'. *Mitteilungen der Österreichischen Geographischen Gesellschaft 163*: pp. 235–264. doi: 10.1553/moegg163s235.

Bernhold, Christin, 2022. *Global Value Chains and Uneven Development: Corporate Strategies and Class Dynamics in Argentinian Agribusiness.* 1st ed. Frankfurt am Main: Campus Verlag.

Bernhold, Christin, and Tomás Palmisano, 2022. 'Capital Concentration in and through Class Differentiation: A Case Study from Pampean Agribusiness'. *Journal of Agrarian Change 22* (2): pp. 341–361. doi: 10.1111/joac.12445.

Bernstein, Henry, 1988. 'Capitalism and Petty-Bourgeois Production: Class Relations and Divisions of Labour'. *Journal of Peasant Studies 15* (2): pp. 258–271. doi: 10.1080/03066158808438360.

Bernstein, Henry, 2008. 'The Political Economy of the Maize Filière'. *The Journal of Peasant Studies 23* (2–3): pp. 120–145. doi: 10.1080/03066159608438610.

Bernstein, Henry, 2010. *Class Dynamics of Agrarian Change. Agrarian Change and Peasant Studies.* Halifax and Winnipeg: Fernwood Publishing.

Bernstein, Henry, and Liam Campling, 2006. 'Commodity Studies and Commodity Fetishism I: Trading Down'. *Journal of Agrarian Change 6* (2): pp. 239–264.

Better Factories Cambodia, 2016. '2016 Garment Industry 33rd Compliance Synthesis Report: Cambodia'. *International Labour Organization (ILO) and International Finance Corporation.* https://researchrepository.ilo.org/esploro/outputs/report/2016-garment-industry-33rd-compliance-synthesis/995219171302676.

Bhagwati, Jagdish N., 2004. *In Defense of Globalization: With a New Afterword.* New York: Oxford University Press.

Biden, Joseph R., 2020. 'Why America Must Lead Again: Rescuing U.S. Foreign Policy after Trump'. *Foreign Affairs.* https://www.foreignaffairs.com/articles/united-states/2020-01-23/why-america-must-lead-again.

Bieler, Andreas, and Jörg Nowak, 2022. 'Labour Conflicts in the Global South: An Introduction'. In *Labour Conflicts in the Global South*, edited by Andreas Bieler and Jörg Nowak, pp. 1–12. London: Routledge.

Birke, Peter, and Felix Bluhm, 2019. 'Arbeitskräfte willkommen. Neue Migration zwischen Grenzregime und Erwerbsarbeit'. *Sozial.Geschichte Online 25*: pp. 11–43.

Bisang, Roberto, 2007. 'El Desarrollo Agropecuario en las últimas Décadas: ¿Volver a Creer?'. In *Crisis, Recuperación y Nuevos Dilemas. La Economía Argentina 2002–2007*, edited by Bernardo Kosacoff, pp. 191–266. Buenos Aires: CEPAL.

Bisang, Roberto, Guillermo Anlló, and Mercedes Campi, 2008. 'Una Revolución (No Tan) Silenciosa. Claves Para Repensar el Agro en Argentina'. *Desarollo Económico 48*: pp. 1–41.

Bisang, Roberto, and Mercedes Campi, 2013. 'El Desarrollo Agrario Argentino en las últimas Décadas: Fases en el Establecimiento de un Nuevo Paradigma Productivo'. In *Claves Para Repensar El Agro Argentino*, edited by Guillermo Anlló, Roberto Bisang, and Mercedes Campi, pp. 31–93. Buenos Aires: Eudeba.

Blakeley, Grace, 2021. 'The Big Tech Monopolies and the State'. *Socialist Register 57*: pp. 100–111.

Block, Fred, 2008. 'Swimming against the Current: The Rise of a Hidden Developmental State in the United States'. *Politics & Society 36* (2): pp. 169–206. doi: 10.1177/0032329208318731.

Bonizzi, Bruno, Annina Kaltenbrunner, and Jeff Powell, 2022. 'Financialised Capitalism and the Subordination of Emerging Capitalist Economies'. *Cambridge Journal of Economics 46* (4): pp. 651–678. doi: 10.1093/cje/beac023.

Braverman, Harry, 1974. *Labor and Capital. The Degradation of Work in the 20th Century.* New York: Monthly Review Press.

Braverman, Harry, 1998. *Labor and Monopoly Capital: The Degradation of Work in the Twentieth Century.* New York: Monthly Review Press.

Braw, Elisabeth, 2020. 'Blindsided on the Supply Side: The Coronavirus Outbreak Has Shown that Supply-Chain Disruptions Could Wreak Far Greater Havoc on the Global Economy—and National Security—than Most CEOs and Governments Realize'. *Foreign Policy*. https://foreignpolicy.com/2020/03/04/blindsided-on-the-supply-side/.

Brenner, Robert, 1977. 'The Origins of Capitalist Development: A Critique of Neo-Smithian Marxism'. *New Left Review 1* (104): pp. 25–92.

Brenner, Robert, 1982. 'The Agrarian Roots of European Capitalism'. *Past & Present 97*: pp. 16–113.

Breslin, Shaun, 2010. 'Democratizing One-Party Rule in China'. In *New Challenges to Democratization*, edited by Peter J. Burnell and Richard Youngs, pp. 136–154. London, New York: Routledge.

Brewer, Benjamin D., 2011. 'Global Commodity Chains & World Income Inequalities: The Missing Link of Inequality and the "Upgrading" Paradox'. *Journal of World-Systems Research 17* (2): pp. 308–327. doi: 10.5195/jwsr.2011.423.

Brighton Labour Process Group, 1977. 'The Capitalist Labour Process'. *Capital & Class 1*: pp. 3–26.

Brinded, Lianna, 2013. 'Bangladesh Approves 77% Pay Rise for Garment Factory Workers'. *International Business Times*. https://www.ibtimes.co.uk/bangladesh-garment-industry-rana-plaza-wage-hike-524125.

Bryan, Lowell, 2010. 'Globalization's Critical Imbalances: Future Financial Crises Could Accelerate the Rebalancing of Global Economic Activity from Developed to Emerging Markets'. *McKinsey Quarterly*. https://www.mckinsey.de/~/media/McKinsey/Featured%20Insights/Globalization/Globalizations%20critical%20imbalances/Globalizations%20critical%20imbalances.pdf.

Burawoy, Michael, 1982. *Manufacturing Consent: Changes in the Labor Process under Monopoly Capitalism*. Chicago: The University of Chicago Press.

Burawoy, Michael, 1984. 'Karl Marx and the Satanic Mills: Factory Politics under Early Capitalism in England, the United States, and Russia'. *American Journal of Sociology 90* (2): pp. 247–282. doi: 10.1086/228079.

Burawoy, Michael, 1985. *The Politics of Production: Factory Regimes under Capitalism and Socialism*. London: Verso.

Bureau of International Labor Affairs, 2024. 'List of Goods Produced by Child Labor or Forced Labor'. *U.S.Department of Labor, Bureau of International Labor Affairs*. https://www.dol.gov/agencies/ilab/reports/child-labor/list-of-goods-print?items_per_page=10&combine=rubber&field_exp_exploitation_type_target_id_1=All&tid=All&field_exp_good_target_id=All&order=name_1&sort=desc.

Burkett, Paul, 1997. 'Nature in Marx Reconsidered'. *Organization & Environment 10* (2): pp. 164–183. doi: 10.1177/0921810697102004.

Burkett, Paul, 1999. *Marx and Nature. A Red and Green Perspective*. London: Palgrave Macmillan.

Burkett, Paul, 2009. *Marxism and Ecological Economics: Toward a Red and Green Political Economy*. London: Haymarket Books.

Busch, Klaus, 1973. 'Ungleicher Tausch—Zur Diskussion über internationale Durchschnittsprofitrate, Ungleichen Tausch und Komparative Kostentheorie anhand der Thesen von Arghiri Emmanuel (1)'. *PROKLA. Zeitschrift für kritische Sozialwissenschaft 3* (8/9): pp. 47–88. doi: 10.32387/prokla.v3i8/9.1795.

Butollo, Florian, 2021. 'Digitalization and the Geographies of Production: Towards Reshoring or Global Fragmentation?'. *Competition & Change 25* (2): pp. 259–278. doi: 10.1177/1024529420918160.

Byres, T., 1997. *Capitalism from Above and Capitalism from Below: An Essay in Comparative Political Economy*. London: Palgrave Macmillan Limited.

CAFOD, 2004. 'Clean up Your Computer: Working Conditions in the Electronics Sector'. *The Catholic Agency for Overseas Development*. https://goodelectronics.org/wp-content/uploads/sites/3/2004/01/Clean-up-your-computer.pdf.

Callinicos, Alex, 2009. *Imperialism and Global Political Economy*. Cambridge, Malden: Polity.

Cambodian Center for Human Rights, 2014. '"Workers' Rights Are Human Rights": Policy Brief: The Garment Industry in Cambodia'. *Cambodian Center for Human Rights*. https://data.opendevelopmentmekong.net/dataset/96e71be5-0b9d-4601-9463-378451f83947/resource/9fe88763-91b8-4437-9d36-0c0c9dd9a00c/download/workers-rights-are-human-rights-policy-brief.pdf.

Cammack, Paul, 2006. *The Politics of Global Competitiveness*. Papers in the Politics of Global Competitiveness, No. 1: Institute for Global Studies, Manchester Metropolitan University, e-space Open Access Repository (2006).

Campi, Mercedes, 2013. 'Tecnología y Desarrollo Agrario'. In *Claves Para Repensar El Agro Argentino*, edited by Guillermo Anlló, Roberto Bisang, and Mercedes Campi, pp. 95–149. Buenos Aires: Eudeba.

Campling, Liam, 2012. 'The Tuna "Commodity Frontier": Business Strategies and Environment in the Industrial Tuna Fisheries of the Western Indian Ocean'. *Journal of Agrarian Change 12* (2–3): pp. 252–278. doi: 10.1111/j.1471-0366.2011.00354.x.

Campling, Liam, James Harrison, Ben Richardson, Adrian Smith, and Mirela Barbu, 2021. 'South Korea's Automotive Labour Regime, Hyundai Motors' Global Production Network and Trade-Based Integration with the European Union'. *British Journal of Industrial Relations 59* (1): pp. 139–166. doi: 10.1111/bjir.12506.

Campling, Liam, Satoshi Miyamura, Jonathan Pattenden, and Ben Selwyn, 2016. 'Class Dynamics of Development: A Methodological Note'. *Third World Quarterly 37* (10): pp. 1745–1767.

Campling, Liam, and Benjamin Selwyn, 2018. 'Value Chains and the World Economy: Genealogies and Reformulations'. In *Handbook of the International Political Economy of the Corporation*, edited by Andreas Nölke and Christian May, pp. 416–434. Cheltenham: Elgaronline.

Campling, Liam, Adrian Smith, and Mirela Barbu, 2022. 'Labour Regimes and Trade-Based Integration'. In *Labour Regimes and Global Production*, edited by Elena Baglioni, Liam Campling, Neil M. Coe, and Adrian Smith, pp. 247–268. Newcastle: Agenda Publishing.

Cantin, Étienne, and Marcus Taylor, 2008. 'Making the "Workshop of the World": China and the Transformation of the International Division of Labour'. In *Global Economy Contested: Power and Conflict across the International Division of Labor*, edited by Marcus Taylor, pp. 51–76. New York: Routledge.

Carswell, Grace, and Geert de Neve, 2013. 'Labouring for Global Markets: Conceptualising Labour Agency in Global Production Networks'. *Geoforum 44*: pp. 62–70. doi: 10.1016/j.geoforum.2012.06.008.

Castree, Noel, 2007. 'Labour Geography: A Work in Progress'. *International Journal of Urban and Regional Research 31* (4): pp. 853–862. doi: 10.1111/j.1468-2427.2007.00761.x.

Castree, Noel, Kevin Ward, and Neil Coe, 2003. '*Spaces of work: Global capitalism and geographies of labour*'. London: Sage.

Cattaneo, Oliver, Gary Gereffi, and Cornelia Staritz, 2010. 'Global Value Chains in a Postcrisis World: Resilience, Consolidation, and Shifting End Markets'. In *Global Value Chains in a Postcrisis World: A Development Perspective*, edited by Oliver Cattaneo, Gary Gereffi, and Cornelia Staritz, pp. 3–20. Washington DC: The World Bank.

Cattaneo, Olivier, Gary Gereffi, Sébastien Miroudot, and Daria Taglioni, 2013. *Joining, Upgrading and Being Competitive in Global Value Chains: A Strategic Framework.* World Bank Policy Research Working 6406.

Chan, Anita (ed.), 2011. *Walmart in China.* Ithaca, London: Cornell University Press.

Chan, Jenny, and Ngai Pun, 2010. 'Suicide as Protest for the New Generation of Chinese Migrant Workers: Foxconn, Global Capital, and the State'. *Asia-Pacific Journal: Japan Focus 37* (2): pp. 1–50.

Chan, Jenny, 2013. 'A Suicide Survivor: The Life of a Chinese Worker'. *New Technology, Work and Employment 28* (2): pp. 84–99. doi: 10.1111/ntwe.12007.

Chan, Jenny, Ngai Pun, and Mark Selden, 2013. 'The Politics of Global Production: Apple, Foxconn and China's New Working Class'. *New Technology, Work and Employment 28* (2): pp. 100–115.

Chan, Jenny, Mark Selden, and Ngai Pun, 2020. *Dying for an iPhone: Apple, Foxconn, and the Lives of China's Workers.* London: Haymarket Books.

Chang, Dae-oup, 2022. 'Transnational Labour Regimes and Neo-Liberal Development in Cambodia'. *Journal of Contemporary Asia 52* (1): pp. 45–70. doi: 10.1080/00472336.2020.1859122.

Chang, Ha-Joon, 2003. 'Kicking away the Ladder: Infant Industry Promotion in Historical Perspective'. *Oxford Development Studies 31* (1): pp. 21–32. doi: 10.1080/1360081032000047168.

Chase-Dunn, Christopher, and Richard Rubinson, 1977. 'Toward a Structural Perspective on the World-System'. *Politics & Society 7* (4): pp. 453–476. doi: 10.1177/003232927700700403.

Chernilo, Daniel, 2011. 'The Critique of Methodological Nationalism: Theory and History'. *Thesis Eleven 106* (1): pp. 98–117. doi: 10.1177/0725513611415789.

China Labour Watch, 2011. 'Tragedies of Globalization: The Truth behind Electronics Sweatshops'. https://chinalaborwatch.org/tragedies-of-globalization-the-truth-behind-electronics-sweatshops-2/.

China Labour Watch, 2014a. 'Another Samsung Supplier Factory Exploiting Child Labor: An Investigation of Shinyang Electronic Co Ltd'. https://chinalaborwatch.org/another-samsung-supplier-factory-exploiting-child-labor/.

China Labour Watch, 2014b. 'Two Years of Broken Promises: Investigative Report of Catcher Technology Co Ltd (Suqian), an Apple Parts Manufacturer'. https://chinalaborwatch.org/wp-content/uploads/2021/04/2014.09.02_Suqian_Catcher_FINAL_PDF_UPDATE.pdf.

China Labour Watch, 2015a. 'Analyzing Labor Conditions of Pegatron and Foxconn: Apple's Low-Cost Reality'. https://chinalaborwatch.org/analyzing-labor-conditions-of-pegatron-and-foxconn-apples-low-cost-reality/.

China Labour Watch, 2015b. 'Something's Not Right Here: Poor Working Conditions Persist at Apple Supplier Pegatron'. https://ecommons.cornell.edu/server/api/core/bitstreams/41c7722e-c1bd-4c50-b8ac-53fe05297d8f/content.

China Labour Watch, 2016a. 'Apple Making Big Profits but Chinese Workers' Wage on the Slide'. https://ecommons.cornell.edu/server/api/core/bitstreams/e1ac2936-5693-4915-8c57-915a1abf6dba/content.

China Labour Watch, 2016b. 'The Chaos in Global Supply Chain Exacerbates Terrible Working Conditions in China'. https://chinalaborwatch.org/the-chaos-in-global-supply-chain-exacerbates-terrible-working-conditions-in-china/.

Choonara, Joseph, 2009. *Unravelling Capitalism: A Guide to Marxist Political Economy.* London: Bookmarks.

Choonara, Joseph, 2018. 'The Political Economy of a Long Depression'. *International Socialism 2* (158): pp. 107–136.

Christian, Michelle M., Barbara J. Evers, and Stephanie Barrientos, 2013. 'Women in Value Chains: Making a Difference'. *Capturing The Gains, Revised Summit Briefing 6.3.* https://assets.publishing.service.gov.uk/media/57a08a22ed915d3cfd0005e6/ctg_briefing_note_6.3.pdf.

Clark, Brett, and John Bellamy Foster, 2001. 'William Stanley Jevons and the Coal Question: An Introduction to Jevons's "Of the Economy of Fuel"'. *Organization & Environment 14* (1): pp. 93–98. doi: 10.1177/1086026601141005.

Clean Clothes Campaign, 2014. 'Stitched up: Poverty Wages for Garment Workers in Eastern Europe and Turkey'. *Clean Clothes Campaign.* https://cleanclothes.org/resources/publications/stitched-up-1.

Clean Clothes Campaign, 2020a. 'Garment Workers on Poverty Pay Are Left without Billions of Their Wages during Pandemic'. https://cleanclothes.org/news/2020/garment-workers-on-poverty-pay-are-left-without-billions-of-their-wages-during-pandemic.

Clean Clothes Campaign, 2020b. 'Un(der)paid in the Pandemic. An Estimate of What the Garment Industry Owes Its Workers'. *Clean Clothes Campaign.* file:///C:/Users/user/Downloads/CCC-Report-Web-DEF.pdf.

Clean Clothes Campaign, 2021. 'Breaking Point: Wage Theft, Violence and Excessive Workloads Are Pushing Garment Workers to Breaking Point during the Pandemic'. *Clean Clothes Campaign.* https://saubere-kleidung.de/wp-content/uploads/2021/07/BreakingPoint_report__final.pdf.

Coase, Ronald H., 1937. 'The Nature of the Firm'. *Economica 4* (16): pp. 386–405. doi: 10.1007/978-1-349-24002-9_3.

Coase, Ronald H., 1960. 'The Problem of Social Cost'. *Journal of Law and Economics 3*: pp. 1–44.

Coe, Neil, 2013. 'Geographies of production III: Making space for labour'. *Progress in Human Geography 37*(2): pp. 271–284.

Coe, Neil M., Peter Dicken, and Martin Hess, 2008. 'Global Production Networks: Realizing the Potential'. *Journal of Economic Geography 8* (3): pp. 271–295.

Coe, Neil M., and Martin Hess, 2013. 'Global Production Networks, Labour and Development'. *Geoforum 44*: pp. 4–9.

Coe, Neil M., and David Jordhus-Lier, 2011. 'Constrained Agency? Re-evaluating the Geographies of Labour'. *Progress in Human Geography 35* (2): pp. 211–233.

Coe, Neil M., and David C. Jordhus-Lier, 2023. 'The Multiple Geographies of Constrained Labour Agency'. *Progress in Human Geography 47* (4): pp. 533–554. doi: 10.1177/03091325231174308.

Coe, Neil M., and Henry Wai-Chung Yeung, 2015. *Global Production Networks: Theorizing Economic Development in an Interconnected World.* Oxford: Oxford University Press.

Collier, Paul, and David Dollar, 2002. *Globalization, Growth, and Poverty: Building an Inclusive World Economy.* Washington, DC: World Bank and Oxford University Press.

Combahee River Collective, 1983. 'The Combahee River Collective Statement'. In *Home Girls: A Black Feminist Anthology*, edited by Barbara Smith, pp. 272–282. Kitchen Table: Women of Color Press.

Connell, Raewyn, and Nour Dados, 2014. 'Where in the World Does Neoliberalism Come From?: The Market Agenda in Southern Perspective'. *Theory and Society 43* (2): pp. 117–138. doi: 10.1007/s11186-014-9212-9.

Cowie, Jefferson, 1999. *Capital Moves: RCA's Seventy-Year Quest for Cheap Labor.* New York: The New Press.

Cox, Robert W., 1981. 'Social Forces, States and World Orders: Beyond International Relations Theory'. *Millennium: Journal of International Studies 10* (2): pp. 126–155. doi: 10.1177/03058298810100020501.

Crenshaw, Kimberle, 1989. 'Demarginalizing the Intersection of Race and Sex: A Black Feminist Critique of Antidiscrimination Doctrine, Feminist Theory and Antiracist Politics'. *University of Chicago Legal Forum 1989* (1).

Crossa, Mateo, 2022. 'Contorting Transformations: Uneven Impacts of the U.S.–Mexico Automotive Industrial Complex'. *Competition & Change 26* (5): pp. 533–553. doi: 10.1177/10245294211045453.

Crossa, Mateo, and Nina Ebner, 2020. 'Automotive Global Value Chains in Mexico: A Mirage of Development?'. *Third World Quarterly 41* (7): pp. 1218–1239. doi: 10.1080/01436597.2020.1761252.

Cumbers, Andrew, Gesa Helms, and Kate Swanson, 2010. 'Class, Agency and Resistance in the Old Industrial City'. *Antipode 42* (1): pp. 46–73. doi: 10.1111/j.1467-8330.2009.00731.x.

Cumbers, Andy, Corinne Nativel, and Paul Routledge, 2008. 'Labour Agency and Union Positionalities in Global Production Networks'. *Journal of Economic Geography 8* (3): pp. 369–387. doi: 10.1093/jeg/lbn008.

Cumings, Bruce, 1984. 'The Origins and Development of the Northeast Asian Political Economy: Industrial Sectors, Product Cycles, and Political Consequences'. *International Organization 38* (1): pp. 1–40.

Dao, Mai Chi, Ms.Mitali Das, Zsoka Koczan, and Weicheng Lian, 2017. *Why Is Labor Receiving a Smaller Share of Global Income? Theory and Empirical Evidence.* IMF Working Paper No. 17/169: International Monetary Fund.

Darlington, Ralph, 2023. *Labour Revolt in Britain 1910–14.* London: Pluto Press.

Das, Raju J., 2012. 'From Labor Geography to Class Geography: Reasserting the Marxist Theory of Class'. *Human Geography 5* (1): pp. 19–35. doi: 10.1177/194277861200500103.

Das, Raju J., 2017. *Marxist Class Theory for a Skeptical World.* Leiden, Boston: Brill.

Dauvergne, Peter, and Kate J. Neville, 2009. 'The Changing North–South and South–South Political Economy of Biofuels'. *Third World Quarterly 30* (6): pp. 1087–1102. doi: 10.1080/01436590903037341.

Davidson, Neil, 2018. 'Neoliberalism as a Class-Based Project'. In *The SAGE Handbook of Neoliberalism*, edited by Damien Cahill, Martijn Konings, Melinda Cooper, and David Primrose, pp. 55–68. London: SAGE.

Davidson, Helen, 2022. 'Surge in China's Military Operations Reflects 'New Normal' under Xi Jinping'. *The Guardian*, (22 December, 2022). Available at: https://www.theguardian.com/world/2022/dec/22/surge-china-military-operations-new-normal-xi-jinping

Daviron, Benoit, and Peter Gibbon, 2002. 'Global Commodity Chains and African Export Agriculture'. *Journal of Agrarian Change 2* (2): pp. 137–161.

De Loecker, Jan, and Jan Eeckhout, 2018. *Global Market Power. NBER Working Paper No. 24768.* Cambridge, MA: National Bureau of Economic Research.

De Marchi, Valentina, Eleonora Di Maria, Aarti Krishnan, and Stefano Ponte, 2019. 'Environmental Upgrading in Global Value Chains'. In *Handbook on Global Value Chains*, edited by Stefano Ponte, Gary Gereffi, and Gale Raj-Reichert, pp. 310–323. Cheltenham: Edward Elgar.

De Marchi, Valentina, Eleonora Di Maria, and Stefano Micelli, 2013. 'Environmental Strategies, Upgrading and Competitive Advantage in Global Value Chains'. *Business Strategy and the Environment 22* (1): pp. 62–72. doi: 10.1002/bse.1738.

De Marchi, Valentina, and Gary Gereffi, 2023. 'Using the Global Value Chain Framework to Analyse and Tackle Global Environmental Crises'. *Journal of Industrial and Business Economics 50* (1): pp. 149–159. doi: 10.1007/s40812-022-00253-x.

Dedrick, Jason, Kenneth L. Kraemer, and Greg Linden, 2010. 'Who Profits from Innovation in Global Value Chains? A Study of the iPod and Notebook PCs'. *Industrial and Corporate Change 19* (1): pp. 81–116.

Delgado Wise, Raúl, and Henry Veltmeyer, 2016. *Agrarian Change. Migration and Development*. Nova Scotia: Fernwood Publishing.

Deyo, Frederic C. (ed.), 1987. *The Political Economy of the New Asian Industrialism*. Ithaca, London: Cornell University Press.

Dollar, David, 2019. 'Invisible Links: Value Chains Transform Manufacturing—and Distort the Globalization Debate'. *IMF*. https://www.imf.org/en/Publications/fandd/issues/2019/06/global-value-chains-transforming-manufacturing-dollar.

Domínguez, Diego, and Pablo Sabatino, 2006. 'Con la Soja al Cuello: Crónica de un País Hambriento Productor de Divisas'. In *Los Tormentos de la Materia. Aportes Para una Ecología Política Latinoamericana*, edited by H. Alimonda, pp. 249–274. Buenos Aires: CLACSO.

Domínguez, Diego, and Pablo Sabatino, 2010. 'La Muerte que Viene en el Viento. La Problemática de la Contaminación por Efecto de la Agricultura Transgénica en Argentina y Paraguay'. In *Los Señores de la Soja: La Agricultura Transgénica en América Latina*, edited by Ana Lucia Bravo, Hugo Mereles Centurión, Diego Domínguez, Pablo Sabatino, Carla Mariela Poth, and Javier Rodríguez, pp. 31–121. Buenos Aires: CICCUS.

Doutch, Michaela, 2022. 'A Gendered Labour Geography Perspective on the Cambodian Garment Workers' General Strike of 2013/2014'. In *Labour Conflicts in the Global South*, edited by Andreas Bieler and Jorg Novak, pp. 84–97. Routledge.

Drahos, Peter, 1995. 'Global Property Rights in Information: The Story of TRIPS at the GATT'. *Prometheus 13* (1): pp. 6–19. doi: 10.1080/08109029508629187.

Drahos, Peter, 2003. *Expanding Intellectual Property's Empire: The Role of FTAs*. Regulatory Institutions Network: Research School of Social Sciences, Australian National University.

Drahos, Peter, John Braithwaite, 2017. *Information Feudalism: Who Owns the Knowledge Economy?* 1st ed. London: Routledge.

Drèze, Jean, Amartya Sen, 1989. *Hunger and Public Action*. Oxford: Clarendon Press.

Dugan, Emily, 2022a. 'What Do You Mean, Day Off?'. *The Guardian* (18 December 2022).

Dugan, Emily, 2022b. 'Workers in Thailand Who Made F&F Jeans for Tesco "Trapped in Effective Forced Labour"'. *The Guardian* (18 December 2022).

Durand, Cédric, and William Milberg, 2020. 'Intellectual Monopoly in Global Value Chains'. *Review of International Political Economy 27* (2): pp. 404–429. doi: 10.1080/09692290.2019.1660703.

ECB, 2020. 'Fostering Sustainable Growth in Europe: Keynote Speech by Christine Lagarde, President of the ECB, at the European Banking Congress'. *European Central Bank*. https://www.ecb.europa.eu/press/key/date/2020/html/ecb.sp201120~e92d92352f.en.html.

Economic Policy Institute, 2022. 'The Productivity-Pay Gap'. https://www.epi.org/productivity-pay gap/#:~:text=From%201979%20to%202020%2C%20net,(after%20adjusting%20for%20inflation).

Egels-Zandén, Niklas, and Jeroen Merk, 2014. 'Private Regulation and Trade Union Rights: Why Codes of Conduct Have Limited Impact on Trade Union Rights'. *Journal of Business Ethics 123* (3): pp. 461–473. doi: 10.1007/s10551-013-1840-x.

Eichengreen, Barry, 2024. 'Globalization and Growth in a Bipolar World'. *Journal of Policy Modeling 46* (4): pp. 714–722. doi: 10.1016/j.jpolmod.2024.03.006.

Elsby, Angus, 2020. 'Creaming off Commodity Profits: Europe's Re-export Boom and Africa's Earnings Crisis in the Coffee and Cocoa Sectors'. *Review of African Political Economy 47* (166). doi: 10.1080/03056244.2020.1842186.

Elsby, Michael W. L., Bart Hobijn, and Ayşegül Şahin, 2013. 'The Decline of the U.S. Labor Share'. *Brookings Papers on Economic Activity 2013* (2): pp. 1–63. doi: 10.1353/eca.2013.0016.

Elson, Diane, 2010. 'Gender and the Global Economic Crisis in Developing Countries: A Framework for Analysis'. *Gender & Development 18* (2): pp. 201–212. doi: 10.1080/13552074.2010.491321.

Elson, Diane, and Ruth Pearson, 1981. '"Nimble Fingers Make Cheap Workers": An Analysis of Women's Employment in Third World Export Manufacturing'. *Feminist Review 7* (1): pp. 87–107. doi: 10.1057/fr.1981.6.

Enderwick, Peter, 2011. 'A "China-Plus-One" Strategy: The Best of Both Worlds?'. *Human Systems Management 30* (1–2): pp. 85–96. doi: 10.3233/HSM-2011-0735.

Energy Institute, 2024. 'Statistical Review of World Energy. 2024, 73rd edition'. Available online at: https://www.energyinst.org/statistical-review.

Engels, Friedrich, 1883. 'Dialectics of Nature'. https://www.marxists.org/archive/marx/works/1883/don/ch09.htm.

Esping-Andersen, Gøsta, 1990. *The Three Worlds of Welfare Capitalism*. Princeton: Princeton University Press.

Fair Action, 2015. 'A Short-Term Solution: A Study of the Use of Fixed-Duration Contracts in the Cambodian Garment Industry'. https://fairaction.se/wp-content/uploads/2015/09/A-Short-Term-Solution_Fair-Action.pdf.

FAO, 2013. *Tackling Climate Change through Livestock—A Global Assessment of Emissions and Mitigation Opportunities.*

FAOSTAT, 2023. Food and Agriculture Organization of the United Nations statistics. Available at: https://www.fao.org/faostat/en/#data.

Farole, Thomas, and Deborah Winkler, 2014. *Making Foreign Direct Investment Work for Sub-Saharan Africa: Local Spillovers and Competitiveness in Global Value Chains*. Washington D.C.: The World Bank.

Feenstra, Robert C., Robert Inklaar, and Marcel P. Timmer, 2015. 'The Next Generation of the Penn World Table'. *American Economic Review 105* (10): pp. 3150–3182. doi: 10.1257/aer.20130954.

Feltri, Stefano, 2020. 'Why Coronavirus Triggered the First Global Supply-Chain Crisis'. *Promarket*. https://www.promarket.org/2020/03/05/why-coronavirus-triggered-the-first-global-supply-chain-crisis/.

Feng, Xiaojun, 2017. 'Manufacturing Conflict: The Experience of a World Factory in a Changing China'. *Modern China 43* (6): pp. 590–619. doi: 10.1177/00977004166 89037.

Ferguson, Susan, 2016. 'Intersectionality and Social-Reproduction Feminisms: Toward an Integrative Ontology'. *Historical Materialism 24* (2): pp. 38–60. doi: 10.1163/1569206X-12341471.

Fernández, Diego, 2012a. 'La Organización de la Gran Empresa Mediante Nuevos Instrumentos Financieros en la Primera Década del Siglo XXI'. In *Estudios Agrarios y Agroindustriales*, edited by Eduardo Azcuy Ameghino, pp. 93–135. Buenos Aires: Ediciones Imago Mundi.

Fernández, Diego, 2012b. 'Vinculaciones entre los Procesos de Cambio Tecnológico y Concentración Económica en la Agricultura Pampeana en la Década del ´90'. *Documentos del CIEA 8*: pp. 99–114.

Fernández, Diego, 2013. 'Tendencias y Evidencias Sobre el Avance del Proceso de Concentración Económica en las Región Pampeana Tras 2002'. *Documentos del CIEA 9*: pp. 77–99.

Fernandez-Stark, Karina, Penny Bamber, and Gary Gereffi, 2011. 'The Fruit and Vegetable Global Value Chain: Economic Upgrading and Workforce Development'. In *Skills for Upgrading: Workforce Development and Global Value Chains in Developing Countries*, edited by Gary Gereffi, Karina Fernandez-Stark, and Penny Psilos, pp. 13–74. Durham: Duke Center on Globalization, Governance & Competitiveness, RTI International.

Fernandez-Stark, Karina, Penny Bamber, and Gary Gereffi, 2012. *Inclusion of Small- and Medium-sized Producers in High-value Agro-food Value Chains*. Durham: Duke Center on Globalization, Governance & Competitiveness.

Fornillo, Bruni (ed.), 2019. *Litio en Sudamérica. Geopolítica, energía y territorios*. Buenos Aires: CLACSO; Editorial El Colectivo; IEALC.

Fornillo, Bruno, and Martina Gamba, 2019. 'Política, ciencia y energía en el "Triángulo del litio"'. In *Litio en Sudamérica. Geopolítica, energía y territorios*, edited by Bruni Fornillo, pp. 133–172. Buenos Aires: CLACSO; Editorial El Colectivo; IEALC.

Fortune, 2024. 'Fortune Global 500'. https://fortune.com/ranking/global500/

Foster, John Bellamy, 1999. 'Marx's Theory of Metabolic Rift: Classical Foundations for Environmental Sociology'. *American Journal of Sociology 105* (2): pp. 366–405. doi: 10.1086/210315.

Foster, John Bellamy, 2021. 'The New Cold War on China'. *Monthly Review*. https://monthlyreview.org/2021/07/01/the-new-cold-war-on-china/.

Foster, John Bellamy, and Ian Angus, 2016. 'In Defense of Ecological Marxism: John Bellamy Foster Responds to a Critic'. *Climate and Capitalism*. https://climateandcapitalism.com/2016/06/06/in-defense-of-ecological-marxism-john-bellamy-foster-responds-to-a-critic/.

Foster, John Bellamy, and Brett Clark, 2018. 'The Expropriation of Nature'. *Monthly Review*. https://monthlyreview.org/2018/03/01/the-expropriation-of-nature/.

Foster, John Bellamy, Brett Clark, and Richard York, 2010. *The Ecological Rift. Capitalism's War on the Earth*. New York: Monthly Review Press.

Foster, John Bellamy, and Robert W. McChesney, 2012. 'The Global Stagnation and China'. *Monthly Review 63* (9): pp. 3–21.

Foster, John Bellamy, Robert W. McChesney, and R. Jamil Jonna, 2011. 'Monopoly and Competition in Twenty-First Century Capitalism'. *Monthly Review 62* (11): p. 1. doi: 10.14452/mr-062-11-2011-04_1.

Foster, John Bellamy, and Intan Suwandi, 2020. 'COVID-19 and Catastrophe Capitalism: Commodity Chains and Ecological-Epidemiological-Economic Crises'. In *Routledge Handbook of Marxism and Post-Marxism*, edited by Alex Callinicos, Stahis Kouvelakis, and Lucia Pradella, pp. 545–559. New York: Routledge.

Fox-Hodess, Katy, 2019. 'Worker Power, Trade Union Strategy, and International Connections: Dockworker Unionism in Colombia and Chile'. *Latin American Politics and Society 61* (03): pp. 29–54. doi: 10.1017/lap.2019.4.

Fox-Hodess, Katy, 2022. 'Global Solidarity on the Docks'. *New Labor Forum 31* (1): pp. 50–58. doi: 10.1177/10957960211061727.

Francis, A. David, 1960. 'I. John Methuen and the Anglo-Portuguese Treaties of 1703'. *The Historical Journal 3* (2): pp. 103–124. doi: 10.1017/S0018246X00022858.

Freeman, Richard, 2006. *The Great Doubling: The Challenge of the New Global Labor Market: Draft*. Harvard University.

Fridell, Gavin, and Chris Walker, 2019. 'Social Upgrading as Market Fantasy: The Limits of Global Value Chain Integration'. *Human Geography 12* (2): pp. 1–17. doi: 10.1177/194277861901200201.

Friedman, Eli, 2014a. 'Alienated Politics: Labour Insurgency and the Paternalistic State in China'. *Development and Change 45* (5): pp. 1001–1018. doi: 10.1111/dech.12114.

Friedman, Eli, 2014b. *Insurgency Trap: Labor Politics in Postsocialist China*. Ithaca, London: ILR Press, an imprint of Cornell University Press.

Friedman, Milton, 1985. 'The Meaning of Freedim'. *The US Army War College Quarterly: Parameters 15* (1): pp. 2–7. doi: 10.55540/0031-1723.1379.

Fröbel, Folker, Jürgen Heinrichs, and Otto Kreye, 1978. '"The New International Division of Labour"'. *Social Science Information 17* (1): pp. 123–142. doi: 10.1177/053901847801700107.

Fuchs, Christian, 2016. 'Digital Labor and Imperialism'. *Monthly Review 67* (8): pp. 14–24.

Fukuyama, Francis, 2021. 'In Praise of Industrial Policy'. *American Purpose*. Updated 16 October. https://www.persuasion.community/p/in-praise-of-industrial-policy.

Gallagher, John, and Ronald Robinson, 1953. 'The Imperialism of Free Trade'. *The Economic History Review 6* (1): pp. 1–15. doi: 10.2307/2591017.

Gallagher, Kevin P. (ed.), 2005. *Putting Development First: The Importance of Policy Space in the WTO and International Financial Institutions*. London: Zed Books.

Garrett, Rachel D., Ximena Rueda, and Eric Lambin, 2013. 'Globalization's Unexpected Impact on Soybean Production in South America: Linkages between Preferences for Non-genetically Modified Crops, Eco-certifications, and Land Use'. *Environmental Research Letters* (8): p. 44055.

Garton, Eric, and Michael Mankins, 2020. 'The Pandemic Is Widening a Corporate Productivity Gap'. *Harvard Business Review*. https://hbr.org/2020/12/the-pandemic-is-widening-a-corporate-productivity-gap.

Gereffi, Gary, 1978. 'Drug Firms and Dependency in Mexico: The Case of the Steroid Hormone Industry'. *International Organization 32* (1): pp. 237–286.

Gereffi, Gary, 1994a. 'Capitalism, Development and Global Commodity Chains'. In *Capitalism and Development*, edited by Leslie Sklair, pp. 211–231. London, New York: Routledge.

Gereffi, Gary, 1994b. 'The Organization of Buyer-Driven Global Commodity Chains: How U.S. Retailers Shape Overseas Production Networks'. In *Commodity Chains and Global Capitalism*, edited by Gary Gereffi and Miguel Korzeniewicz, pp. 95–122. Westport: Praeger.

Gereffi, Gary, 1995. 'Global Production Systems and Third World Development'. In *Global Change, Regional Response: The New International Context of Development*, edited by Barbara Stallings, pp. 100–142. Cambridge: Cambridge University Press.

Gereffi, Gary, 1996. 'Global Commodity Chains: New Forms of Coordination and Control among Nations and Firms in International Industries'. *Competition & Change 1* (4): pp. 427–439.

Gereffi, Gary, 2001. 'Shifting Governance Structures in Global Commodity Chains, with Special Reference to the Internet'. *American Behavioral Scientist 44* (10): pp. 1617–1637.

Gereffi, Gary, 2018. *Global Value Chains and Development: Redefining the Contours of 21st Century Capitalism*. Cambridge: Cambridge University Press.

Gereffi, Gary, and Karina Fernandez-Stark, 2016. *Global Value Chain Analysis: A Primer*. Durham: Duke Center on Globalization, Governance & Competitiveness.

Gereffi, Gary, John Humphery, Raphael Kaplinsky, and Timothy J. Sturgeon, 2001. 'Introduction: Globalisation, Value Chains and Development'. In *The Value of Value Chains: Spreading the Gains from Globalisation*, edited by Gary Gereffi, and Raphael Kaplinsky, pp. 1–8. Sussex: Institute of Development Studies (IDS).

Gereffi, Gary, John Humphrey, and Timothy J. Sturgeon, 2005. 'The Governance of Global Value Chains'. *Review of International Political Economy 12* (1): pp. 78–104. doi: 10.1080/09692290500049805.

Gereffi, Gary, and Raphael Kaplinsky (eds), 2001. *The Value of Value Chains: Spreading the Gains from Globalisation. IDS Bulletin*. Sussex: Institute of Development Studies (IDS).

Gereffi, Gary, and Miguel Korzeniewicz (eds), 1994. *Commodity Chains and Global Capitalism*. Westport: Praeger.

Gereffi, Gary, Miguel Korzeniewicz, and Roberto Korzeniewicz, 1994. 'Introduction: Global Commodity Chains'. In *Commodity Chains and Global Capitalism*, edited by Gary Gereffi and Miguel Korzeniewicz, pp. 1–14. Westport: Praeger.

Gereffi, Gary, and Joonkoo Lee, 2016. 'Economic and Social Upgrading in Global Value Chains and Industrial Clusters: Why Governance Matters'. *Journal of Business Ethics 133* (1): pp. 25–38. doi: 10.1007/s10551-014-2373-7.

Gereffi, Gary, Pavida Pananond, and Torben Pedersen, 2022. 'Resilience Decoded: The Role of Firms, Global Value Chains, and the State in COVID-19 Medical Supplies'. *California Management Review 64* (2): pp. 46–70. doi: 10.1177/00081256211069420.

Germann, Julian, 2023. 'Wrestling with Unevenness: Sino-American Rivalry, State Strategy and the Reformation of German Capitalism'. *Global Political Economy 2* (1): pp. 77–97. doi: 10.1332/WDGH8153.

Gerschenkron, Alexander, 1962. *Economic Backwardness in Historical Perspective: A Book of Essays*. Charlestown, Massachusetts: Belknap Press of Harvard University Press.

Gerstenberger, Heide, 2022. *Market and Violence: The Functioning of Capitalism in History*. Leiden, Boston: Brill.

Gibbon, Peter, Jennifer Bair, and Stefano Ponte, 2008. 'Governing Global Value Chains: An Introduction'. *Economy and Society 37* (3): pp. 315–338.

Giles, Chris, 2020. 'Global Economy to Suffer Worst Blow since the 1930s, Warns IMF'. *The Financial Times* (14 April 2020).

Gill, Stephen, 1998. 'New Constitutionalism, Democratisation and Global Political Economy'. *Pacifica Review: Peace, Security & Global Change 10* (1): pp. 23–38. doi: 10.1080/14781159808412845.

Giménez, Martha E., 2019. *Marx, Women, and Capitalist Social Reproduction: Marxist Feminist Essays*. Leiden: Brill.

Giménez, Martha E., 2021. 'Kapitalistische soziale Reproduktion: Eine Alternative zur Intersektionalität?: Historisch-materialistische Beobachtungen'. *Zeitschrift Marxistische Erneuerung* (126): pp. 72–81.

Glassman, Jim, 2011. 'The Geo-political Economy of Global Production Networks'. *Geography Compass 5* (4): pp. 154–164. doi: 10.1111/j.1749-8198.2011.00416.x.

Godfrey, Shane, 2013. *A Study of Changes and Continuities in the Organization and Regulation of Work with an Empirical Examination of the South African and Lesotho Clothing/Retail Value Chain*. Thesis presented for the Degree of Doctor of Philosophy in the Department of Sociology, Faculty of Humanities, University of Cape Town.

Goger, Annelies, Stephanie Barrientos, Gary Gereffi, and Shane Godfrey, 2014. *Capturing the Gains in Africa: Making the Most of Global Value Chain Participation*. Duke University, Center on Globalization, Governance and Competitiveness at the Social Science Research Institute.

Goldberg, Pinelopi Koujianou, and Nina Pavcnik, 2007. 'Distributional Effects of Globalization in Developing Countries'. *Journal of Economic Literature 45* (1): pp. 39–82. doi: 10.1257/jel.45.1.39.

GoodElectronics, 2010. 'Is EICC Protecting Apple and Foxconn on Recent Worker Suicides?' https://goodelectronics.org/is-eicc-protecting-apple-and-foxconn-on-recent-worker-suicides/.

GoodElectronics, 2018. 'Low Workers' Wages Undercut and Limit Living Expenses in Guangdong Province, China'. https://goodelectronics.org/workers-wage-living-expenses-report-covering-four-tier-cities-guangdong-province-china/.

Gopinath, Gita, 2020. 'The Great Lockdown: Worst Economic Downturn since the Great Depression'. *IMF Blog*. https://www.imf.org/en/Blogs/Articles/2020/04/14/blog-weo-the-great-lockdown-worst-economic-downturn-since-the-great-depression.

Gosh, Jayati, Shouvik Chakraborty, and Debamanyu Das, 2022. 'Climate Imperialism in the Twenty-First Century'. *Monthly Review*. https://monthlyreview.org/2022/07/01/climate-imperialism-in-the-twenty-first-century/.

Goswami, Namrata, 2023. 'China Prioritizes 3 Strategic Technologies in Its Great Power Competition: Space, AI, and Quantum Computing and Communication Are China's Top Technology Priorities. How Advanced Are Its Capabilities in Each?' *The Diplomat*. https://

thediplomat.com/2023/04/china-prioritizes-3-strategic-technologies-in-its-great-power-competition/.
Gowan, Peter, 1999. *The Global Gamble: Washington's Faustian Bid for World Dominance.* London: Verso.
Gras, Carla, and Valeria Hernández, 2013. *El Agro como Negocio. Producción, Sociedad y Territorios en la Globalización.* Buenos Aires: Editorial Biblos.
Gray, Kevin, 2015. *Labor and Development in East Asia: Social Forces and Passive Revolution.* London: Routledge.
Graz, Jean-Christophe, Jimena Sobrino Piazza, and André Walter, 2022. 'Labour Standards in Global Production Networks: Assessing Transnational Private Regulation and Workers' Capacity to Act'. *Development and Change 53* (4): pp. 912–937. doi: 10.1111/dech.12712.
Greenhouse, Steven, 2015. 'How Walmart Persuades Its Workers Not to Unionize'. https://www.theatlantic.com/business/archive/2015/06/how-walmart-convinces-its-employees-not-to-unionize/395051/.
Grossman, Gene M., and Esteban Rossi-Hansberg, 2008. 'Trading Tasks: A Simple Theory of Offshoring'. *American Economic Review 98* (5): pp. 1978–1997. doi: 10.1257/aer.98.5.1978.
Gruber, Lloyd, 2001. 'Power Politics and the Free Trade Bandwagon'. *Comparative Political Studies 34* (7): pp. 703–741. doi: 10.1177/0010414001034007001.
Guschanski, Alexander, and Özlem Onaran, 2021. *Greenwich Papers in Political Economy: The Effect of Global Value Chain Participation on the Labour Share—Industry Level Evidence from Emerging Economies.* GPERC82. https://www.postkeynesian.net/downloads/events/guschanski_and_onaran_2021.pdf.
Hadjimichalis, Costis, 1984. 'The Geographical Transfer of Value: Notes on the Spatiality of Capitalism'. *Environment and Planning D 2*: pp. 329–345.
Hadjimichalis, Costis, 1987. *Uneven Development and Regionalism: State, Territory and Class in Southern Europe.* London: Croom Helm.
Hammer, Nikolaus, Réka Plugor, Peter Nolan, and Ian Clark, 2015. 'New Industry on a Skewed Playing Field: Supply Chain Relations and Working Conditions in UK Garment Manufacturing. Focus Area—Leicester and the East Midlands'. *University of Leicester.* https://figshare.le.ac.uk/articles/report/New_industry_on_a_skewed_playing_field_supply_chain_relations_and_working_conditions_in_UK_garment_manufacturing_Focus_area_-_Leicester_and_the_East_Midlands/10145732/1?file=18284381.
Hammer, Nikolaus, Lone Riisgaard, 2015. 'Labour and Segmentation in Value Chains'. In *Putting Labour in Its Place: Labour Process Analysis and Global Value Chains,* edited by Kirsty Newsome, Philip Taylor, Jennifer Bair, and Al Rainnie. London: Palgrave.
Harman, Chris, 1984. *Explaining the Crisis: A Marxist Re-Appraisal.* London: Bookmarks.
Harman, Chris, 2001. 'Beyond the Boom'. *International Socialism 90* (Spring): pp. 41–70.
Hart-Landsberg, Martin, 2013. *Capitalist Globalization: Consequences, Resistance, and Alternatives.* 1st ed. New York: NYU Press.
Harvey, David, 2005a. *Brief History of Neoliberalism.* Oxford University Press.
Harvey, David, 2005b. *Spaces of Neoliberalization. Towards a Theory of Uneven Geographical Development.* Stuttgart: Franz-Steiner Verlag.
Harvey, David, 2010. *The Enigma of Capital.* paper prepared for the American Sociological Association Meetings in Atlanta, August 16th, 2010. Available at: https://davidharvey.org/2010/08/the-enigma-of-capital-and-the-crisis-this-time/
Harvey, David, 2017. *Marx, Capital and the Madness of Economic Reason.* Oxford University Press.
Harvey, Fiona, and Damian Garrington, 2022. 'World is on "Highway to Climate Hell", UN Chief Warns at Cop27 Summit'. *The Guardian 2022* (11.07.2022).

Hayek, Friedrich A. von, 1980. *Individualism and Economic Order*. Chicago: University of Chicago Press.

Haynes, Mike, 2021. 'Working from Home—an Employer Win?' https://leftiehistorian.wordpress.com/2021/05/05/working-from-home-an-employer-win-3-min-read/.

Henderson, Jeffrey, Peter Dicken, Martin Hess, Neil Coe, and Henry Wai-Chung Yeung, 2002. 'Global Production Networks and the Analysis of Economic Development'. *Review of International Political Economy 9* (3): pp. 436–464.

Henwood, Doug, 1995. 'Clinton's Trade Policy'. In *Free Trade and Economic Restructuring in Latin America: A NACLA Reader*, edited by Fred Rosen and Deidre McFadyen, pp. 27–38. New York: Monthly Review Press.

Herod, Andrew, 1997. 'From a Geography of Labor to a Labor Geography: Labor's Spatial Fix and the Geography of Capitalism'. *Antipode 29* (1): pp. 1–31. doi: 10.1111/1467-8330.00033.

Herod, Andrew, 2001. *Labor Geographies: Workers and the Landscapes of Capitalism*. New York: Guilford Press.

Herod, Andrew, Graham Pickren, Al Rainnie, and Susan McGrath Champ, 2014. 'Global Destruction Networks, Labour and Waste'. *Journal of Economic Geography 14* (2): pp. 421–441. doi: 10.1093/jeg/lbt015.

Hesketh, Chris, 2017. *Spaces of Capital/Spaces of Resistance: Mexico and the Global Political Economy*. University of Georgia Press.

Hess, Martin, and Henry Wai-Chung Yeung, 2006. 'Whither Global Production Networks in Economic Geography? Past, Present, and Future'. *Environment and Planning A 38* (7): pp. 1193–1204. doi: 10.1068/a38463.

Hickel, Jason, 2019. 'Is It Possible to Achieve a Good Life for All within Planetary Boundaries?' *Third World Quarterly 40* (1): pp. 18–35. doi: 10.1080/01436597.2018.1535895.

Hickel, Jason, and Giorgos Kallis, 2020. 'Is Green Growth Possible?'. *New Political Economy 25* (4): pp. 469–486. doi: 10.1080/13563467.2019.1598964.

Hodal, Kate, and Peter Bengtsen, 2017. 'Chinese Factory Supplying Major Laptop Brands Accused of Student Labour Abuses'. *The Guardian* (6 October 2017).

Hodgson, Geoffrey M., 2001. *How Economics Forgot History: The Problem of Historical Specificity in Social Science*. 1st ed. London: Routledge.

Hopewell, Kristen, 2020. *Clash of Powers: US–China Rivalry in Global Trade Governance*. Cambridge University Press.

Hopkins, Terence, and Immanuel Wallerstein, 1977. 'Patterns of Development of the Modern World-System'. *Review (Fernand Braudel Center) 1* (2): pp. 111–145.

Hopkins, Terence, and Immanuel Wallerstein, 1982. 'Structural Transformations of the World-Economy'. In *World-Systems Analysis. Theory and Methodology*, edited by Terence Hopkins and Immanuel Wallerstein, pp. 121–142. London: Sage Publications.

Hopkins, Terence, and Immanuel Wallerstein, 1986. 'Commodity Chains in the World Economy Prior to 1800'. *Review (Fernand Braudel Center) 10* (1): pp. 157–170.

Horner, Rory, 2017. 'Beyond Facilitator? State Roles in Global Value Chains and Global Production Networks'. *Geography Compass 11* (2): e12307. doi: 10.1111/gec3.12307.

Howarth, Robert W., 2019. 'Ideas and Perspectives: Is Shale Gas a Major Driver of Recent Increase in Global Atmospheric Methane?' *Biogeosciences 16* (15): pp. 3033–3046. doi: 10.5194/bg-16-3033-2019.

Howson, Kelle, Fabian Ferrari, Funda Ustek-Spilda, Nancy Salem, Hannah Johnston, Srujana Katta, Richard Heeks, and Mark Graham, 2022. 'Driving the Digital Value Network: Economic Geographies of Global Platform Capitalism'. *Global Networks 22* (4): pp. 631–648. doi: 10.1111/glob.12358.

Hsiao, Jingyue, 2023. 'Wistron Exits iPhone Business in India Reportedly Due to Low Profit and Work Culture'. *Digittimes Asia* (23 May 2023).

Hughes, Alex, James A. Brown, Mei Trueba, Alexander Trautrims, Ben Bostock, Emily Day, Rosey Hurst, and Mahmood F. Bhutta, 2023. 'Global Value Chains for Medical Gloves during the COVID-19 Pandemic: Confronting Forced Labour through Public Procurement and Crisis'. *Global Networks 23* (1): pp. 132–149. doi: 10.1111/glob.12360.

Hughes, Neil C., 1998. 'Smashing the Iron Rice Bowl'. *Foreign Affairs 77* (4): p. 67. doi: 10.2307/20048966.

Human Rights Now, 2018. 'Cambodia: HRN Calls for Improvements in Working Conditions and Prevention Measures among Global Sportswear Brands, such as ASICS, Puma and Nike Following Mass Faintings by Female Workers at Factories'. *Human Rights Now*. http://hrn.or.jp/eng/news/2018/03/06/cambodia-mass-faintings/.

Humphrey, John, 2006. 'Policy Implications of Trends in Agribusiness Value Chains'. *The European Journal of Development Research 18* (4): pp. 572–592.

Humphrey, John, and Hubert Schmitz, 2000. *Governance and Upgrading: Linking Industrial Cluster and Global Value Chain Research*. IDS Working Paper 120.

Hung, Ho-fung, 2015. *The China Boom: Why China Will Not Rule the World*. New York: Columbia University Press.

ILO, 2018. 'How Has Garment Workers' Pay Changed in Recent Years in Cambodia?: Cambodian Garment and Footwear Sector Bulletin 7'. *International Labour Organization*. https://www.ilo.org/publications/how-has-garment-workers-pay-changed-recent-years-cambodia.

ILO, 2021. 'Can Digital Labour Platforms Create Fair Competition and Decent Jobs?'. *International Labour Organization*. https://webapps.ilo.org/digitalguides/en-gb/story/world-employment-social-outlook-2021#introduction.

IMF, 1999. 'United States: Selected Issues. IMF Staff Country Report no.99/101: IMF Staff Country Report no.99/101'. *IMF*. https://www.imf.org/external/pubs/ft/scr/1999/cr99101.pdf.

IMF, 2007. *World Economic Outlook, April 2007: Spillovers and Cycles in the Global Economy*.

Jabsky, Marina, and Charlene Obernauer, 2019. 'Time Off Task. Pressure, Pain, and Productivity at Amazon: Amazon Workers Report'. *New York Committee for Occupational Safety and Health*. https://nycosh.org/resource/amazon-workers-report/.

Jefferies, William, 2021. 'China's Accession to the WTO and the Collapse that Never Was'. *Review of Radical Political Economics 53* (2): pp. 300–319. doi: 10.1177/0486613420948968.

Jenkins, Rhys, 2018. 'Globalisation, Trade Liberalisation and Industrial Pollution in Latin America. Industry and Environment in Latin'. In *Industry and Environment in Latin America*, edited by Rhys Jenkins, pp. 13–42. London, New York: Routledge.

Jepson, Wendy, 2005. 'Spaces of Labor Activism, Mexican-American Women and the Farm Worker Movement in South Texas Since 1966'. *Antipode 37* (4): pp. 679–702. doi: 10.1111/j.0066-4812.2005.00521.x.

Jessop, Bob, 2001. 'Institutional Re(turns) and the Strategic Relational Approach'. *Environment and Planning A 33* (7): pp. 1213–1235. doi: 10.1068/a32183.

Jevons, William Stanley, 1866. *The Coal Question: An Inquiry Concerning the Progress of the Nation and the Probable Exhaustion of Our Coal-mines*. London: Macmillan.

Jha, Praveen, and Amit Chakraborty, 2016. 'Global Production Networks and Labour Process'. In *Labour in Global Value Chains in Asia*, edited by Dev Nathan, Meenu Tewari, and Sandip Sarkar, pp. 398–420. Cambridge, UK, New York, NY: Cambridge University Press.

Johnson, Carter, and Anlexandre Tanzi, 2023. 'Dollar Usage in Global Payments in July Rises to Record, Swift Says'. *Bloomberg, 24 August*. https://www.bloomberg.com/news/articles/2023-08-24/dollar-usage-in-global-payments-in-july-rises-to-record-swift-says?leadSource=uverify%20wall.

Jordhus-Lier, David C., and Neil M. Coe, 2024. 'The Roles and Intersections of Constrained Labour Agency'. *Antipode 56* (3): pp. 941–962. doi: 10.1111/anti.13003.

Joyce, Simon, 2020. 'Rediscovering the Cash Nexus, Again: Subsumption and the Labour–Capital Relation in Platform Work'. *Capital & Class 44* (4): pp. 541–552. doi: 10.1177/0309816820906356.

Kagermann, Henning, Wolfgang Wahlster, and Johannes Helbig, 2013. *Recommendations for Implementing the Strategic Initiative INDUSTRIE 4.0: Securing the Future of German Manufacturing Industry: Final Report of the Industrie 4.0 Working Group.* https://www.din.de/resource/blob/76902/e8cac883f42bf28536e7e8165993f1fd/recommendations-for-implementing-industry-4-0-data.pdf.

Kaplinsky, Raphael, 1998. *Globalisation, Industrialisation and Sustainable Growth: The Pursuit of the NTH Rent.* University of Sussex: Institute of Development Studies.

Kaplinsky, Raphael, 2000. 'Globalisation and Unequalisation: What Can Be Learned from Value Chain Analysis?'. *The Journal of Development Studies 37* (2): pp. 117–146.

Kaplinsky, Raphael, 2005. *Globalization, Poverty and Inequality: Between a Rock and a Hard Place.* Cambridge: Wiley.

Kaplinsky, Raphael, and Mike Morris, 2001. *A Handbook for Value Chain Research.* IDRC.

Kapsos, Steven, and Evangelia Bourmpoula, 2013. *Employment and Economic Class in the Developing World.* Geneva: ILO.

Karabarbounis, Loukas, and Brent Neiman, 2014. 'The Global Decline of the Labor Share'. *The Quarterly Journal of Economics 129* (1): pp. 61–103. doi: 10.1093/qje/qjt032.

Kashyap, Aruna, 2015. '"Work Faster or Get Out": Labor Rights Abuses in Cambodia's Garment Industry'. *Human Rights Watch.* https://www.hrw.org/report/2015/03/12/work-faster-or-get-out/labor-rights-abuses-cambodias-garment-industry.

Katz, Cindi, 2004. *Growing Up Global: Economic Restructuring and Children's Everyday Lives.* Minneapolis, Minn.: Univ. of Minnesota Press.

Kay, Cristóbal, 2002. 'Why East Asia Overtook Latin America: Agrarian Reform, Industrialisation and Development'. *Third World Quarterly 23* (6): pp. 1073–1102. doi: 10.1080/0143659022000036649.

Kerswell, Timothy, 2013. 'Productivity and Wages: What Grows for Workers without Power and Institutions'. *Social Change 43* (4): pp. 507–531. doi: 10.1177/0049085713502591.

Kizu, Takaaki, Stefan Kühn, and Christian Viegelahn, 2016. *Linking Jobs in Global Supply Chains to Demand: ILO Research Paper No. 16.* https://www.ilo.org/publications/linking-jobs-global-supply-chains-demand.

Klingler-Vidra, Robyn, and Steven Hai, 2024. 'China's Chip Industry Is Gaining Momentum—It Could Alter the Global Economic and Security Landscape'. *The Conversation.* Updated 15 October. https://theconversation.com/chinas-chip-industry-is-gaining-momentum-it-could-alter-the-global-economic-and-security-landscape-222958.

Knights, David, and Hugh Willmott (eds), 2016. *Labour Process Theory.* New York: Springer.

Knorringa, Peter, and Lee Pegler, 2006. 'Globalisation, Firm Upgrading and Impacts on Labour'. *Tijdschrift voor Exonomische en Sociale Geografie 97* (5): pp. 470–479.

Knox, Robert, and Ashok Kumar, 2023. 'Reexamining Race and Capitalism in the Marxist Tradition—Editorial Introduction'. *Historical Materialism 31* (2): pp. 25–48. doi: 10.1163/1569206x-bja10012.

Knutsen, Hege M., Sylvi B. Endersen, Ann C. Bergene, and David C. Jordhus-Lier, 2015. 'Labor, Geography of'. *International encyclopedia of the social & behavioral sciences 2* (13): pp. 163–168.

Krishnan, Aarti, Valentina De Marchi, and Stefano Ponte, 2022a. 'Environmental Upgrading and Downgrading in Global Value Chains: A Framework for Analysis'. *Economic Geography 99* (1): pp. 25–50. doi: 10.1080/00130095.2022.2100340.

Krishnan, Lrk, and Divya Krishnan, 2022b. 'Employment Practices at Apple; Social and Legal Issues Disrupting India's Industrial Relations Landscape'. *Journal of the International Academy for Case Studies 28* (4): pp. 1–10.

Kühn, Stefan, 2019. 'Global Employment and Social Trends'. *World Employment and Social Outlook 2019* (1): pp. 5–24. doi: 10.1002/wow3.150.

Kumar, Ashok, 2020. *Monopsony Capitalism: Power and Production in the Twilight of the Sweatshop Age*. Cambridge: Cambridge University Press (CUP).

Labour Behind the Label, 2020. 'Boohoo & COVID-19: The People behind the Profits'. *Labour Behind the Label*. https://labourbehindthelabel.net/wp-content/uploads/2020/06/LBL-Boohoo-WEB.pdf.

Lapegna, Pablo, 2017. 'The Political Economy of the Agro-export Boom under the Kirchners: Hegemony and Passive Revolution in Argentina'. *Journal of Agrarian Change 17*: pp. 313–329.

Le, Lam, 2021. 'Workers in Vietnam Lived inside Factories to Keep Samsung's Products on Shelves during the Pandemic'. *Rest of The World*. https://restofworld.org/2021/samsung-worker-factories-pandemic/.

LeBaron, Genevieve, Penelope Kyritsis, Perla Polanco Leal, and Michael Marshall, 2021. *The Unequal Impacts of Covid-19 on Global Garment Supply Chains: Evidence from Ethiopia, Honduras, India, and Myanmar*. Sheffield: University of Sheffield.

Lee, Joonkoo, and Gary Gereffi, 2013. 'The Co-Evolution of Concentration in Mobile Phone Global Value Chains and Its Impact on Social Upgrading in Developing Countries'. *Capturing The Gains Working paper 25 University of Manchester*. https://www.researchgate.net/publication/256053886_The_Co-Evolution_of_Concentration_in_Mobile_Phone_Global_Value_Chains_and_Its_Impact_on_Social_Upgrading_in_Developing_Coun tries.

Lee, Joonkoo, and Gary Gereffi, 2015. 'Global Value Chains, Rising Power Firms and Economic and Social Upgrading'. *Critical Perspectives on International Business 11* (3/4): pp. 219–339.

Lee, Joonkoo, Gary Gereffi, and Dev Nathan, 2013. 'Mobile Phones: Who Benefits in Shifting Global Value Chains?' *Capturing the Gains, Revised Summit Briefing 6.1, University of Manchaster*. https://dukespace.lib.duke.edu/server/api/core/bitstreams/f159a5ce-f71b-47c3-92e9-e66a55be9c43/content.

Leguizamón, Amalia, 2014. 'Modifying Argentina: GM Soy and Socio-environmental Change'. *Geoforum 53*: pp. 149–160.

Leyden, Dara, 2024. 'The Struggle for Upgrading: Electronics Global Value Chains and Labour Regimes in Thailand', PhD thesis, Queen Mary University of London, 2024.

Li, Minqi, 2015. *China and the Twenty-first-Century Crisis*. Chicago: University of Chicago Press.

Li, Minqi, 2021. 'China: Imperialism or Semi-Periphery?'. *Monthly Review*. https://monthlyreview.org/2021/07/01/china-imperialism-or-semi-periphery/.

Li, Minqi, 2023. 'From "996" to "Lying Flat": China's Regime of Accumulation'. *Socialist Register 59*: pp. 190–209.

Lier, David Christoffer, 2007. 'Places of Work, Scales of Organising: A Review of Labour Geography'. *Geography Compass 1* (4): pp. 814–833. doi: 10.1111/j.1749-8198.2007.00047.x.

Lin, Justin, and Ha-Joon Chang, 2009. 'Should Industrial Policy in Developing Countries Conform to Comparative Advantage or Defy it? A Debate between Justin Lin and Ha-Joon Chang'. *Development Policy Review 27* (5): pp. 483–502. doi: 10.1111/j.1467-7679.2009.00456.x.

Liu, Qianer, 2023. 'How Huawei Surprised the US with a Cutting-edge Chip Made in China'. *The Financial Times* (30 November 2023).

Locke, Richard M., 2013. *The Promise and Limits of Private Power: Promoting Labor Standards in a Global Economy*. Cambridge Studies in Comparative Politics. Cambridge, UK: Cambridge University Press.

López, Tatiana, 2023. *Labour Control and Union Agency in Global Production Networks: A Case Study of the Bangalore Export-garment Cluster*. Cham: Springer Nature.

Lucas, Louise, 2018. 'The Chinese Communist Party Entangles Big Tech'. *The Financial Times* (19 July 2018).

Lund-Thomsen, Peter, 2013. 'Labor Agency in the Football Manufacturing Industry of Sialkot, Pakistan'. *Geoforum 44*: pp. 71–81. doi: 10.1016/j.geoforum.2012.04.007.

Lüthje, Boy, and Florian Butollo, 2017. 'Why the Foxconn Model Does Not Die: Production Networks and Labour Relations in the IT Industry in South China'. *Globalizations 14* (2): pp. 216–231. doi: 10.1080/14747731.2016.1203132.

Lüthje, Boy, Stefanie Hürtgen, Peter Pawlicki, and Martina Sproll, 2013. *From Silicon Valley to Shenzhen: Global Production and Work in the IT Industry*. Lanham, MD: Rowman & Littlefield.

Lütten, John, 2021. 'Zum Gebrauchswert des Klassenbegriffs'. In *Auf den Schultern von Karl Marx*, edited by Thomas Sablowski, Judith Dellheim, Alex Demirović, Katharina Pühl, and Ingar Solty, pp. 207–226. 1st ed. Münster: Westfälisches Dampfboot.

Lütten, John, Christin Bernhold, and Felix Eckert, 2021. 'Zur Kritik des Intersektionalismus'. *Z. Zeitschrift für marxistische Erneuerung* (126): pp. 18–30.

MacKinnon, Danny, 2012. 'Beyond Strategic Coupling: Reassessing the Firm–Region Nexus in Global Production Networks'. *Journal of Economic Geography 12* (1): pp. 227–245. doi: 10.1093/jeg/lbr009.

Magdoff, Harry, 1978. *Imperialism: From the Colonial Age to the Present*. New York, London: Monthly Review Press.

Magdoff, Harry, 1992. 'Globalization—To What End?'. *Socialist Register 28*: pp. 44–75.

Malm, Andreas, 2012. 'China as Chimney of the World'. *Organization & Environment 25* (2): pp. 146–177. doi: 10.1177/1086026612449338.

Malm, Andreas, 2016. *Fossil Capital: The Rise of Steam Power and the Roots of Global Warming*. London, New York: Verso.

Mankiw, N. Gregory, and Mark Taylor, 2008. *Macroeconomics: European Edition*. London: W. H. Freeman & Co Ltd.

Martin, Nathan D., David Brady, 2007. 'Workers of the Less Developed World Unite? A Multilevel Analysis of Unionization in Less Developed Countries'. *American Sociological Review 72* (4): pp. 562–584. doi: 10.1177/000312240707200404.

Martinelli, Aris, 2022. 'Collectivism, Individualism and Solidarity in Global Value Chain Restructuring in the Global North: Workers' Resistance in the Swiss Machinery Industry'. *Economic and Industrial Democracy 43* (3): pp. 1391–1419. doi: 10.1177/0143831X211009958.

Martinez, Nain, and Diana Terrazas-Santamaria, 2024. 'Beyond Nearshoring: The Political Economy of Mexico's Emerging Electric Vehicle Industry'. *Energy Policy 195*: p. 114385. doi: 10.1016/j.enpol.2024.114385.

Marx, Karl, 1844a. 'Economic and Philosophic Manuscripts of 1844'. In *Collected Works (MECW): Volume 3*, edited by Karl Marx and Friedrich Engels, pp. 229–346. New York: International Publishers.

Marx, Karl, 1844b. 'On the Jewish Question'. https://www.marxists.org/archive/marx/works/1844/jewish-question/.

Marx, Karl, 1847. 'The Poverty of Philosophy'. https://www.marxists.org/archive/marx/works/1847/poverty-philosophy/ch02c.htm.

Marx, Karl, 1977. *Capital. A Critique of Political Economy*. Volume 1. New York: Vintage.

Marx, Karl, 1875. 'Critique of the Gotha Programme'. In *Collected Works (MECW): Volume 24*, edited by Karl Marx and Friedrich Engels, pp. 75–99. New York: International Publishers.

Marx, Karl, 1989. 'Theories of Surplus Value'. In *Collected Works (MECW)*, edited by Karl Marx and Friedrich Engels, pp. 6–578. New York: International Publishers.

Marx, Karl, 1990. *Capital. A Critique of Political Economy. Volume I*. London: Penguin.

Marx, Karl, 1991. *Capital. A Critique of Political Economy. Volume III*. London: Penguin.

Marx, Karl, 1993. *Grundrisse. Foundations of the Critique of Political Economy*. London, New York: Penguin.

Marx, Karl, and Friedrich Engels, 1848. 'Manifesto of the Communist Party'. In *Collected Works (MECW): Volume 6*, edited by Karl Marx and Friedrich Engels, pp. 483–519. New York: International Publishers.

Mavroidis, Petros C., and André Sapir, 2021. *China and the WTO: Why Multilateralism Still Matters*. Princeton University Press.

Mayer, Frederick W., and Nicola Phillips, 2017. 'Outsourcing Governance: States and the Politics of a "Global Value Chain World"'. *New Political Economy 22* (2): pp. 134–152. doi: 10.1080/13563467.2016.1273341.

Mayer, Frederick W., Nicola Phillips, and Anne C. Posthuma, 2017. 'The Political Economy of Governance in a "Global Value Chain World"'. *New Political Economy 22* (2): pp. 129–133. doi: 10.1080/13563467.2016.1273343.

Mazzucato, Mariana, 2018. *The Entrepreneurial State: Debunking Public vs. Private Sector Myths*. London: Penguin.

McDougall, Walter A., 1982. 'Technocracy and Statecraft in the Space Age—Toward the History of a Saltation'. *The American Historical Review 87* (4): p. 1010. doi: 10.2307/1857903.

McDowell, Linda, 2008. 'Thinking through Work: Complex Inequalities, Constructions of Difference and Trans-national Migrants'. *Progress in Human Geography 32* (4): pp. 491–507. doi: 10.1177/0309132507088116.

McGee, Patrick, and Andrew Edgecliffe-Johnson, 2020. 'Companies' Supply Chains Vulnerable to Coronavirus Shocks: Shortages of Components Likely to Be Far Worse than Expected, Warn Experts'. *Financial Times* (9 March 2020).

McGrath, Siobhan, 2018. 'Dis/articulations and the Interrogation of Development in GPN Research'. *Progress in Human Geography 42* (4): pp. 509–528. doi: 10.1177/0309132517700981.

McKinsey, 2020a. 'Resetting Supply Chains for the Next Normal'. https://www.mckinsey.com/capabilities/operations/our-insights/resetting-supply-chains-for-the-next-normal.

McKinsey, 2020b. *Risk, Resilience, and Rebalancing in Global Value Chains*. http://dln.jaipuria.ac.in:8080/jspui/bitstream/123456789/14300/1/Risk-resilience-and-rebalancing-in-global-value-chains-full-report.pdf.

McMillan, Margaret, and !ñigo Verduzco-Gallo, 2011. 'New Evidence on Trade and Employment: An Overview'. In *Trade and Employment: From Myths to Facts*, edited by Marion Jansen, Ral Peters, and José Manuel Salazar-Xirinachs, pp. 23–60. Geneva: International Labour Office.

McMullen, Anna, 2013. 'Shop 'til They Drop: Fainting and Malnutrition in Garment Workers in Cambodia'. *Labour Behind the Label, Community Legal Education Centre*. https://www.google.com/url?sa=t&source=web&rct=j&opi=89978449&url=https://cleanclothes.org/resources/national-cccs/shop-til-they-drop&ved=2ahUKEwi9oN7-kp-JAxXnhv0HHWbFG3QQFnoECBIQAQ&usg=AOvVaw2tbLgxgHzTcw76r5LV934X.

McNally, Christopher A., 2012. 'Sino-Capitalism: China's Reemergence and the International Political Economy'. *World Politics 64* (4): pp. 741–776. doi: 10.1017/s0043887112000202.

McNally, David, 2017. 'Intersections and Dialectics: Critical Reconstructions'. In *Social Reproduction Theory: Remapping Class, Recentering Oppression*, edited by Tithi Bhattacharya, pp. 94–111. London: Pluto Press.

Mearsheimer, John J., 2021. 'The Inevitable Rivalry: America, China, and the Tragedy of Great-Power Politics'. *Forreign Affairs 100*: pp. 48–58.

Meschi, Elena, and Marco Vivarelli, 2009. 'Trade and Income Inequality in Developing Countries'. *World Development 37* (2): pp. 287–302. doi: 10.1016/j.worlddev.2008.06.002.

Mezzadri, Alessandra, 2016. 'Class, Gender and the Sweatshop: On the Nexus between Labour Commodification and Exploitation'. *Third World Quarterly 37* (10): pp. 1877–1900.

Milberg, William, 2008. 'Shifting Sources and Uses of Profits: Sustaining US Financialization with Global Value Chains'. *Economy and Society 37* (3): pp. 420–451. doi: 10.1080/03085140802172706.

Milberg, William, and Deborah Winkler, 2011. 'Trade Crisis and Recovery: Restructuring of Global Value Chains'. *Capturing the Gains Briefing Note 1*. https://assets.publishing.service.gov.uk/media/57a08ac9ed915d3cfd00093c/ctg_briefing_note_1.pdf.

Milberg, William, and Deborah Winkler, 2013. *Outsourcing Economics: Global Value Chains in Capitalist Development*. Cambridge, New York: Cambridge University Press.

Milios, John, and Dimitris P. Sotiropoulos, 2009. *Rethinking Imperialism: A Study of Capitalist Rule*. Basingstoke: Palgrave Macmillan.

Miller, Chris, 2022. *Chip War: The Fight for the World's Most Critical Technology*. New York: Simon and Schuster.

Miller, Doug, 2013. *Towards Sustainable Labour Costing in UK Fashion Retail*. Capturing The Gains, Working Paper 14, University of Manchester. doi: 10.2139/ssrn.2212100.

Miroudot, Sébastien, 2020. 'Resilience versus Robustness in Global Value Chains: Some Policy Implications'. In *COVID-19 and Trade Policy: Why Turning Inward Won't Work*, edited by Richard E. Baldwin and Simon J. Evenett, pp. 117–130. Centre for Economic Policy Research (CEPR): CEPR Press.

Mirrlees, Tanner, 2024. 'The US and China's Digital Tech War: A New Rivalry within and beyond the US Empire?'. *Socialist Register 60*: pp. 105–140.

Moatsos, Michail, 2021. 'Global Extreme Poverty: Present and Past since 1820'. In *How Was Life? Vol. II: New Perspectives on Well-being and Global Inequality since 1820*, pp. 186–212. Paris: OECD Publishing, https://doi.org/10.1787/3d96efc5-en.

Moore, Jason, 2015. *Capitalism in the Web of Life. Ecology and the Accumulation of Capital*. London, New York: Verso Books.

Moore, Jason W., 2011. 'Transcending the Metabolic Rift: A Theory of Crises in the Capitalist World-ecology'. *Journal of Peasant Studies 38* (1): pp. 1–46. doi: 10.1080/03066150.2010.538579.

Morgan, Kevin, 2018. 'Strategic Coupling: East Asian Industrial Transformation in the New Global Economy'. *Regional Studies 52* (3): pp. 458–459.

Mosley, Layna, 2008. 'Workers' Rights in Open Economies: Global Production and Domestic Institutions in the Developing World'. *Comparative Political Studies 41* (4–5): pp. 674–714. doi: 10.1177/0010414007313119.

Muradian, Roldan., O'Connor, Martin., and Martinez-Alier, Joan, 2002. "Embodied Pollution in Trade: Estimating the 'Environmental Load Displacement' of Industrialised Countries." *Ecological Economics 41*, pp. 51–67.

Muzlera, José, 2021. *Diccionario del agro iberoamericano*. [CABA], [Buenos Aires, Argentina]: [publisher not identified]; TeseoPress Design (www.teseopress.com).

Nathan, Dev, 2013. 'Industrial Relations in a Global Production Network: What Can Be Done'. *Economic and Political Weekly 48* (30): pp. 29–33.

National Defence University, 2000. *Joint Vision 2020: America's Military-Preparing for Tomorrow.* National Defense University Washington DC Institute for National Strategic Studies.

Naughton, Barry, 2007. *The Chinese Economy: Transitions and Growth.* Cambridge, Mass.: MIT Press.

Naylor, Lindsay, 2017. 'Reframing Autonomy in Political Geography: A Feminist Geopolitics of Autonomous Resistance'. *Political Geography 58*: pp. 24–35. doi: 10.1016/j.polgeo.2017.01.001.

Neiman, Guillermo, 2010. 'Los Estudios sobre el Trabajo Agrario en la última Década: Una Revisión para el Caso Argentino'. *Mundo Agrario 10* (20): pp. 1–19.

Nepstad, Daniel C., Claudia M. Stickler, and Oriana T. Almeida, 2006. 'Globalization of the Amazon Soy and Beef Industries: Opportunities for Conservation'. *Conservation Biology 20* (6): pp. 1595–1603. doi: 10.1111/j.1523-1739.2006.00510.x.

Ness, Immanuel, 2016. *Southern Insurgency: The Coming of the Global Working Class.* London: Pluto Press.

Newsome, Kirsty, 2010. 'Work and Employment in Distribution and Exchange'. *Industrial Relations Journal 41* (3): pp. 190–205. doi: 10.1111/j.1468-2338.2010.00563.x.

Newsome, Kirsty, 2015. 'Value in Motion: Labour and Logistics in the Contemporary Political Economy'. In *Putting Labour in Its Place: Labour Process Analysis and Global Value Chains*, edited by Kirsty Newsome, pp. 29–44. Basingstoke, Hampshire: Palgrave Macmillan.

Newsome, Kirsty, Philip Taylor, Jennifer Bair, and Al Rainnie (eds), 2015. *Putting Labour in Its Place: Labour Process Analysis and Global Value Chains.* London: Palgrave.

Nikulin, Dagmara, Joanna Wolszczak-Derlacz, and Aleksandra Parteka, 2022. 'Working Conditions in Global Value Chains: Evidence for European Employees'. *Work, Employment and Society 36* (4): pp. 701–721. doi: 10.1177/0950017020986107.

Nolan, Peter, 2001. *China and the Global Economy: National Champions, Industrial Policy and the Big Business Revolution.* New York: Springer.

Norfield, Tony, 2011. 'T-shirt Economics: Labour in the Imperialist World Economy'. *Global Labour University.* http://column.global-labour-university.org/2012/08/t-shirt-economics-labour-in-imperialist.html.

Nowak, Jörg, 2022. 'Do Choke Points Provide Workers in Logistics with Power? A Critique of the Power Resources Approach in Light of the 2018 Truckers' Strike in Brazil'. *Review of International Political Economy 29* (5): pp. 1675–1697. doi: 10.1080/09692290.2021.1931940.

O'Connor, Sarah, 2021. 'Why I Was Wrong to Be Optimistic about Robots: Humans Are Being Crunched into a Robot System Working at a Robot Pace'. *The Financial Times* (9 February 2021).

O'Mara, Margaret, 2019. *The Code: Silicon Valley and the Remaking of America.* London: Penguin.

OECD, 2005. *OECD Economic Surveys 2005/13: China.*

OECD, 2014. *Global Value Chains: Challenges, Opportunities, and Implications for Policy.* Report prepared for submission to the G20 Trade Ministers Meeting. https://g20.utoronto.ca/2014/Global%20Value%20Chains%20Challenges%20Opportunities%20and%20Implications%20for%20Policy.pdf.

OECD, 2021. *Building More Resilient and Sustainable Global Value Chains through Responsible Business Conduct.* https://mneguidelines.oecd.org/rbc-and-trade.htm.

OECD-FAO, 2022. 'Agricultural Outlook 2022–2031'. https://read.oecd-ilibrary.org/agriculture-and-food/oecd-fao-agricultural-outlook-2022-2031_f1b0b29c-en#page1.

Office for National Statistics, 2021. 'Homeworking Hours, Rewards and Opportunities in the UK: 2011 to 2020'. https://www.ons.gov.uk/employmentandlabourmarket/peopleinwork/

labourproductivity/articles/homeworkinghoursrewardsandopportunitiesintheuk2011to2020/2021-04-19.

Oliveira, Gustavo, and Susanna Hecht, 2016. 'Sacred Groves, Sacrifice Zones and Soy Production: Globalization, Intensification and Neo-nature in South America'. *Journal of Peasant Studies 43* (2): pp. 251–285. doi: 10.1080/03066150.2016.1146705.

Olmer, Naya, Bryan Comer, Biswajoy Roy, Xiaoli Mao, and Dan Rutherford, 2017. *Greenhouse Gas Emissions from Global Shipping, 2013–2015*. ICCT, International Council on Clean Transportation.

Ong, Aihwa, 1987. *Spirits of Resistance and Capitalist Discipline: Factory Women in Malaysia*. Albany, NY: State University of New York Press.

Ong, Aihwa, 1991. 'The Gender and Labor Politics of Postmodernity'. *Annual Review of Anthropology 20* (1): pp. 279–309. doi: 10.1146/annurev.anthro.20.1.279.

Oxfam, 2017. *An Economy for the 99%: It's Time to Build a Human Economy that Benefits Everyone, Not Just the Privileged Few*. https://www-cdn.oxfam.org/s3fs-public/file_attachments/bp-economy-for-99-percent-160117-en.pdf.

Oxfam, 2019. 'Poverty Pay and Abuse of Workers on Farms and Plantations Linked to UK Supermarkets'. https://www.oxfam.org.uk/mc/dwxejj/.

Padmanabhan, Neethi, 2012. 'Globalisation Lived Locally: A Labour Geography Perspective on Control, Conflict and Response among Workers in Kerala'. *Antipode 44* (3): pp. 971–992. doi: 10.1111/j.1467-8330.2011.00918.x.

Pagano, Ugo, 2014. 'The Crisis of Intellectual Monopoly Capitalism'. *Cambridge Journal of Economics 38* (6): pp. 1409–1429. doi: 10.1093/cje/beu025.

Palma, José Gabriel, 2005. 'The Seven Main "Stylized Facts" of the Mexican Economy since Trade Liberalization and NAFTA'. *Industrial and Corporate Change 14* (6): pp. 941–991. doi: 10.1093/icc/dth076.

Palmer, Doug, 2023. 'What Cold War? U.S. Trade with China Hits New High: Two-way Trade between the United States and China Set a New Record in 2022'. *Politico* (02/07/2023).

Panitch, Leo, and Sam Gindin, 2005. 'Superintending Global Capital'. *New Left Review 35* (101).

Panitch, Leo, and Sam Gindin, 2015. 'Rethinking Production, Finance and Hegemonic Decline in IPE'. In *Handbook of the International Political Economy of Production*, edited by Kees van der Pijl, pp. 23–42. Cheltenham: Edward Elgar Publishing.

Panitch, Leo, and Sam Gindin, 2019. 'Trumping the Empire'. In *Socialist Register 2019, Volume 55: A World Turned Upside Down*, edited by Leo Panitch and Gregory Albo, pp. 1–25. New York: Monthly Review Press.

Panitch, Leo, and Colin Leys, 2001. 'Preface'. In *Socialist Register 2001, Volume 37: Working Classes. Global Realities*, edited by Leo Panitch, and Colin Leys, vii–x1. https://socialistregister.com/index.php/srv/issue/view/438.

Panwar, Rajat, Jonatan Pinkse, and Valentina De Marchi, 2022. 'The Future of Global Supply Chains in a Post-COVID-19 World'. *California Management Review 64* (2): pp. 5–23. doi: 10.1177/00081256211073355.

Parnreiter, Christof, 2007. *Historische Geographien, Verräumlichte Geschichte. Mexico City und das Mexikanische Städtenetz von der Industrialisierung bis zur Globalisierung*. Stuttgart: Franz Steiner Verlag.

Parnreiter, Christof, and Christin Bernhold, 2020. 'Global Commodity Chains'. In *International Encyclopedia of Human Geography*, edited by Audrey Kobayashi, pp. 169–176. Amsterdam, Netherlands, Cambridge, MA: Elsevier.

Parnreiter, Christof, Laszlo Steinwärder, and Klara Kolhoff, 2024. 'Uneven Development through Profit Repatriation: How Capitalism's Class and Geographical Antagonisms Intertwine'. *Antipode, online first*: pp. 1–25. doi: 10.1111/anti.13089.

Parteka, Aleksandra, and Joanna Wolszczak-Derlacz, 2020. 'Wage Response to Global Production Links: Evidence for Workers from 28 European Countries (2005–2014)'. *Review of World Economics 156* (4): pp. 769–801. doi: 10.1007/s10290-020-00380-4.

Patel, Raj, and Jason W. Moore, 2017. *A History of the World in Seven Cheap Things: A Guide to Capitalism, Nature, and the Future of the Planet: A Guide to Capitalism, Nature, and the Future of the Planet.* Oakland, CA: University of California Press.

Pattenden, Jonathan, 2018. 'The Politics of Classes of Labour: Fragmentation, Reproduction Zones and Collective Action in Karnataka, India'. *Journal of Peasant Studies 45* (5): pp. 1039–1059. doi: 10.1080/03066150.2018.1495625.

Peck, Jamie, 2018. 'Pluralizing Labour Geography'. In *The New Oxford Handbook of Economic Geography*, edited by Gordon L. Clark, Maryann P. Feldman, Meric S. Gertler, and Dariusz Wójcik, pp. 465–484. Oxford: Oxford University Press (OUP).

Peet, Richard, 1983. 'Relations of Production and the Relocation of United States Manufacturing Industry since 1960'. *Economic Geography* (59): pp. 112–143.

Pega, Frank, Bálint Náfrádi, Natalie C. Momen, Yuka Ujita, Kai N. Streicher, Annette M. Prüss-Üstün, Alexis Descatha, Tim Driscoll, Frida M. Fischer, Lode Godderis, Hannah M. Kiiver, Jian Li, Linda L. Magnusson Hanson, Reiner Rugulies, Kathrine Sørensen, and Tracey J. Woodruff, 2021. 'Global, Regional, and National Burdens of Ischemic Heart Disease and Stroke Attributable to Exposure to Long Working Hours for 194 Countries, 2000–2016: A Systematic Analysis from the WHO/ILO Joint Estimates of the Work-related Burden of Disease and Injury'. *Environment international 154*: p. 106595. doi: 10.1016/j.envint.2021.106595.

Pen, Ratana, and Phalla Chea, 2015. 'Large-Scale Land Grabbing in Cambodia: Failure of International and National Policies to Secure the Indigenous Peoples' Rights to Access Land and Resources'. *Heinrich Böll Stiftung.* https://kh.boell.org/en/2015/03/25/large-scale-land-grabbing-cambodia-failure-international-and-national-policies-secure.

Peretti, Miguel, 1999. 'Competitividad de la empresa agropecuaria argentina en la década de los '90''. *Revista Argentina de Economía Agraria 2* (1): pp. 27–41.

Persson, Linn, Bethanie M. Carney Almroth, Christopher D. Collins, Sarah Cornell, Cynthia A. de Wit, Miriam L. Diamond, Peter Fantke, Martin Hassellöv, Matthew MacLeod, Morten W. Ryberg, Peter Søgaard Jørgensen, Patricia Villarrubia-Gómez, Zhanyun Wang, and Michael Zwicky Hauschild, 2022. 'Outside the Safe Operating Space of the Planetary Boundary for Novel Entities'. *Environmental Science & Technology 56* (3): pp. 1510–1521. doi: 10.1021/acs.est.1c04158.

Phillips, Nicola, 2011. 'Informality, Global Production Networks and the Dynamics of "Adverse Incorporation"'. *Global Networks 11* (3): pp. 380–397. doi: 10.1111/j.1471-0374.2011.00331.x.

Phillips, Wendy, Jens K. Roehrich, Dharm Kapletia, and Elizabeth Alexander, 2022. 'Global Value Chain Reconfiguration and COVID-19: Investigating the Case for More Resilient Redistributed Models of Production'. *California Management Review 64* (2): pp. 71–96. doi: 10.1177/00081256211068545.

Pickles, John, and Adrian Smith, 2016. *Articulations of Capital: Global Production Networks and Regional Transformations.* Chichester, West Sussex, UK, Malden, MA: Wiley Blackwell.

Pike, Andy, 2007. 'Contesting Closures: The Limits and Prospects of Social Agency'. In *Reclaiming the Economy: Alternatives to Market Fundementalism*, edited by Andrew Chambers, and Geoffrey Whittman, pp. 64–78. Biggar: Scottish Left Review Press.

Pleyers, Geoffrey, 2024. 'For a Global Sociology of Social Movements: Beyond Methodological Globalism and Extractivism'. *Globalizations 21* (1): pp. 183–195. doi: 10.1080/14747731.2023.2173866.

Pogge, Thomas, and Sanjay G. Reddy, 2006. 'Unknown: Extent, Distribution and Trend of Global Income Poverty'. *Economic and Political Weekly 41* (22): pp. 2241–2247.
Polanyi, Karl, 2001. *The Great Transformation: The Political and Economic Origins of Our Times*. Boston: MA: Beacon Press.
Ponte, Stefano, 2019. *Business, Power, and Sustainability in a World of Global Value Chains*. London: Zed Books.
Ponte, Stefano, 2020. 'Green Capital Accumulation: Business and Sustainability Management in a World of Global Value Chains'. *New Political Economy 25* (1): pp. 72–84. doi: 10.1080/13563467.2019.1581152.
Ponte, Stefano, and Joachim Ewert, 2009. 'Which Way Is "Up" in Upgrading? Trajectories of Change in the Value Chain for South African Wine'. *World Development 37* (10): pp. 1637–1650.
Porter, Michael E., 1990. 'The Competitive Advantage of Nations'. *Harvard Business Review* (March–April): pp. 73–91.
Poulantzas, Nicos, 1969. 'The Problem of the Capitalist State'. *New Left Review 0* (58): p. 67.
Pradella, Lucia, 2015. *Globalisation and the Critique of Political Economy: New Insights from Marx's Writings*. Abingdon, New York: Routledge.
Prentice, Rebecca. 2021. Labour rights from labour wrongs? Transnational compensation and the spatial politics of labour rights after Bangladesh's Rana Plaza garment factory collapse. *Antipode, 53*(6): pp. 1767–1786.
Pringle, Tim, 2011. *Trade Unions in China: The Challenge of Labour Unrest*. Abingdon: Routledge.
Projekt Klassenanalyse, 1974. *Materialien zur Klassenstruktur der BRD: Erster Teil: Theoretische Grundlagen und Kritiken*. Berlin: VSA-Verlag.
Pun, Ngai, and Jenny Chan, 2012. 'Global Capital, the State, and Chinese Workers'. *Modern China 38* (4): pp. 383–410. doi: 10.1177/0097700412447164.
Pun, Ngai, and Anita Koo, 2015. 'A "World-Class" (Labor) Camp/us: Foxconn and China's New Generation of Labor Migrants'. *positions: asia critique 23* (3): pp. 411–435. doi: 10.1215/10679847-3125811.
Pun, Ngai, and Chris Smith, 2007. 'Putting Transnational Labour Process in Its Place: The Dormitory Labour Regime in Post-socialist China'. *Work, Employment and Society 21* (1): pp. 27–45. doi: 10.1177/0950017007073611.
Qiang, Christine Zhenwei, Yan Liu, and Victor Steenbergen, 2021. 'Global Value Chains in the Time of COVID-19 (Coronavirus)'. In *An Investment Perspective on Global Value Chains*, edited by Christine Zhen-Wei Qiang, Yan Liu, and Victor Steenbergen, pp. 188–218. Washington, DC: International Bank for Reconstruction and Development/World Bank Group.
Quentin, David, and Liam Campling, 2018. 'Global Inequality Chains: Integrating Mechanisms of Value Distribution into Analyses of Global Production'. *Global Networks 18* (1): pp. 33–56. doi: 10.1111/glob.12172.
Rackwitz, Hans, 2022. 'Der ökologische Gesellschaftskonflikt als Klassenfrage: Konvergenzen, Divergenzen und Wechselwirkungen von Klassen- und Naturverhältnissen'. In *Die Wiederkehr der Klassen: Theorien, Analysen, Kontroversen*, edited by Jakob Graf, Kim Lucht, and John Lütten, pp. 91–122. Frankfurt/New York: Campus Verlag.
Raikes, Philip, Michael Friis Jensen, and Stefano Ponte, 2000. 'Global Commodity Chain Analysis and the French Filière Approach: Comparison and Critique'. *Economy and Society 29* (3): pp. 390–417.
Raj-Reichert, Gale, 2016. 'Promoting Decent Work in Global Supply Chains: The Electronics Industry'. In *Sectoral Studies on Decent Work in Global Supply Chains: Comparative Analysis of Opportunities and Challenges for Social and Economic Upgrading*, edited by the International Labour Office, pp. 125–164. Geneva.

Ravallion, Martin, 2010. 'The Developing World's Bulging (but Vulnerable) Middle Class'. *World Development 38* (4): pp. 445–454.

Raworth, Kate, 2004. 'Trading away Our Rights: Women Working in Global Supply Chains'. *Oxfam*. http://www.worldshake.org/wsfairtrade/leermeer/Downloads/Oxfam%20Rapporten/2004_trading%20away%20our%20rights.pdf.

Raworth, Kate, and Thalia Kidder, 2009. 'Mimicking "Lean" in Global Value Chains: It's the Workers Who Get Leaned on'. In *Frontiers of Commodity Chain Research*., edited by Jennifer Bair, pp. 165–189. Stanford: Stanford University Press.

Reardon, Thomas, and Rose Hopkins, 2006. 'The Supermarket Revolution in Developing Countries: Policies to Address Emerging Tensions among Supermarkets, Suppliers and Traditional Retailers'. *The European Journal of Development Research 18* (4): pp. 522–545. doi: 10.1080/09578810601070613.

Reed, Adolph, 2014. 'Adolph Reed, Jr. Responds'. *New Labor Forum 23* (1): pp. 65–67. doi: 10.1177/1095796013513240.

Reed, John, and Kathrin Hille, 2023. 'Apple and Foxconn Win Labour Reforms to Advance Indian Production Plans: Lobbying in Karnataka Leads to Landmark Legislation that Anticipates iPhone Production in Southern State'. *The Financial Times* (10 March 2023).

Ren, Hao, Zhongjin Li, and Eli Friedman (eds), 2016. *China on Strike: Narratives of Workers' Resistance*. Chicago: Haymarket Books.

Reuveny, Rafael, and William R. Thompson, 2001. 'Leading Sectors, Lead Economies, and Economic Growth'. *Review of International Political Economy 8* (4): pp. 689–719. doi: 10.1080/09692290110077629.

Rijsberman, Frank, 2017. 'The Key Role of the Meat Industry in Transformation to a Low-Carbon, Climate Resilient, Sustainable Economy'. *Meat Science 132*: pp. 2–5. doi: 10.1016/j.meatsci.2017.04.013.

Rikap, Cecilia, 2021. *Capitalism, Power and Innovation: Intellectual Monopoly Capitalism Uncovered*. London: Routledge.

Roach, Stephen, 1996. 'Lessons in Restructuring'. *Financial Times* (22 October 1996).

Roberts, Anthea, 2023. 'From Risk to Resilience: How Economies Can Thrive in a World of Threats'. *Foreign Affairs 102* (6): pp. 123–133.

Roberts, Anthony, and Thai Binh Tran, 2022. 'The Globalization of Production, National Labour Regulations and Income Inequality in the Global North and South, 1980–2013'. *Global Networks 23* (4): pp. 687–714. doi: 10.1111/glob.12392.

Roberts, John Michael, 2022. *Digital, Class, Work: Before and During COVID-19*. Edinburgh: Edinburgh University Press.

Robinson, Joan, 1973. 'The Need for a Reconsideration of the Theory of International Trade'. In *Collected Economic Papers*, edited by Joan Robinson, pp. 14–24. Oxford: Basil Backwell.

Robinson, Joan, 1977. 'What Are the Questions?'. *Journal of Economic Literature 15* (4): pp. 1318–1339.

Robinson, Pamela K., and Helen Rainbird, 2013. 'International Supply Chains and the Labour Process'. *Competition & Change 17* (1): pp. 91–107. doi: 10.1179/1024529412Z.00000000027.

Robinson, Wiliam I., Salvador Rangel, and Hilbourne A. Watson, 2022. 'The Cult of Cedric Robinson's Black Marxism: A Proletarian Critique'. *The Philosophical Salon*. https://thephilosophicalsalon.com/the-cult-of-cedric-robinsons-black-marxism-a-proletarian-critique/.

Roediger, David R., and Elizabeth D. Esch, 2012. *The Production of Difference: Race and the Management of Labor in U.S. History*. Oxford: Oxford University Press.

Roediger, David R., and Philip S. Foner, 1989. *Our Own Time: A History of American Labor and the Working Day*. Westport, CT: Greenwood Press.

Rogaly, Ben, 2009. 'Spaces of Work and Everyday Life: Labour Geographies and the Agency of Unorganised Temporary Migrant Workers'. *Geography Compass 3* (6): pp. 1975–1987. doi: 10.1111/j.1749-8198.2009.00290.x.

Rolf, Steven, 2021. *China's Uneven and Combined Development.* Springer International Publishing.

Rolf, Steven, 2023. 'The Revenge of Multiplicity: Chinese Capitalism under Systemic Competition'. *Global Political Economy 2* (1): pp. 121–138. doi: 10.1332/LXGV9552.

Rosenberg, Justin, 1994. *The Empire of Civil Society: A Critique of the Realist Theory of International Relations.* London: Verso.

Rosenberg, Justin, and Christopher Boyle, 2019. 'Understanding 2016: China, Brexit and Trump in the History of Uneven and Combined Development'. *Journal of Historical Sociology 32* (1): e32–e58. doi: 10.1111/johs.12217.

Rossi, Arianna, 2013. 'Does Economic Upgrading Lead to Social Upgrading in Global Production Networks? Evidence from Morocco'. *World Development 46*: pp. 223–233. doi: 10.1016/j.worlddev.2013.02.002.

Rossi, Arianna, 2019. 'Social Upgrading'. In *Handbook on Global Value Chains,* edited by Stefano Ponte, Gary Gereffi, and Gale Raj-Reichert, pp. 272–284. Cheltenham: Edward Elgar.

Rostow, Walt W., 1990. *The Stages of Economic Growth: A Non-communist Manifesto.* 3rd ed. Cambridge: Cambridge University Press.

Russell, Shana A., 2018. 'Intersectionality: A Young Scholar Responds'. *Science & Society 82* (2): pp. 287–291. doi: 10.1521/siso.2018.82.2.287.

Rutherford, Tod, 2010. 'De/Re-Centring Work and Class?: A Review and Critique of Labour Geography'. *Geography Compass 4* (7): pp. 768–777. doi: 10.1111/j.1749-8198.2010.00328.x.

Ruwanpura, Kanchana N., 2016. 'Garments without Guilt? Uneven Labour Geographies and Ethical Trading—Sri Lankan Labour Perspectives'. *Journal of Economic Geography 16* (2): pp. 423–446. doi: 10.1093/jeg/lbu059.

Ruwanpura, Kanchana N., 2022. *Garments without Guilt?: Global Labour Justice and Ethical Codes in Sri Lankan Apparels.* Cambridge University Press.

Ruwanpura, Kanchana N., and Alex Hughes, 2016. 'Empowered Spaces? Management Articulations of Gendered Spaces in Apparel Factories in Karachi, Pakistan'. *Gender, Place & Culture 23* (9): pp. 1270–1285. doi: 10.1080/0966369X.2015.1136815.

Sachs, Jeffrey, 2005. *The End of Poverty: Economic Possibilities for Our Time.* London, New York: Penguin.

SACOM, 2008. 'The Dark Side of Cyberspace: Inside the Sweatshops of China's Computer Hardware Production'. *Students and Scholars against Corporate Misbehaviour.* https://electronicswatch.org/the-dark-side-of-cyberspace_3378.pdf.

SACOM, 2010. 'Workers as Machines: Military Management in Foxconn'. *Students and Scholars against Corporate Misbehaviour.* https://www.somo.nl/wp-content/uploads/2010/08/military-management-in-Foxconn.pdf.

Saintano, Michael, 2024. 'US Dock Workers Agree on Deal with Port Operators to End Strike'. *The Guardian* (4 October 2024).

Salmivaara, Anna, 2018. 'New Governance of Labour Rights: The Perspective of Cambodian Garment Workers' Struggles'. *Globalizations 15* (3): pp. 329–346. doi: 10.1080/14747731.2017.1394069.

Salyga, Jakubas, 2020. 'Why Migrant Farm Workers Are Living Four to a Caravan in a Time of Social Distancing'. *Jacobin* (5 February 2020).

Sánchez Enrique, and Daniela Verónica, 2016. 'Trabajo Rural Temporario y Fragmentación Normativa en Argentina'. *Revista Pilquen. Sección Ciencias Sociales 19* (2): pp. 25–37.

Savage, Luke, 2023. 'The Capitalist Road to Serfdom'. https://jacobin.com/2023/02/capitalist-road-to-serfdom-surveillance-wage-labor.

Scanes, Colin G., 2018. 'Animal Agriculture: Livestock, Poultry, and Fish Aquaculture'. In *Animals and Human Society*, edited by Colin G. Scanes and Samia Toukhsati, pp. 133–179. Amsterdam: Academic Press.

Scheiber, Noam, 2015. 'Growth in the "Gig Economy" Fuels Work Force Anxieties'. *The New York Times* (12 July 2016).

Schling, Hannah, 2022. '"Just-In-Time" Migrant Workers in Czechia: Racialization and Dormitory Labour Regimes'. In *Labour Regimes and Global Production*, edited by Elena Baglioni, Liam Campling, Neil M. Coe, and Adrian Smith, pp. 301–316. Newcastle: Agenda Publishing.

Schmalz, Stefan, Carmen Ludwig, and Edward Webster, 2018. 'The Power Resources Approach: Developments and Challenges'. *Global Labour Journal 9* (2). doi: 10.15173/glj.v9i2.3569.

Schorr, Martín (ed.), 2013. *Argentina en la Posconvertibilidad: ¿Desarrollo o Crecimiento Industrial? Estudios de Economia Politica.* Buenos Aires: Editorial Miño y Dávila.

Schumpeter, Joseph A., 1987. *Capitalism, Socialism and Democracy.* London: Allen and Unwin.

Schwartz, Herman M., 2018. *States versus Markets: Understanding the Global Economy.* 4th ed. London, New York, Oxford, New Delhi, Sydney: Bloomsbury Publishing.

Sell, Susan, 2003. *Private Power, Public Law: The Globalization of Intellectual Property Rights.* Cambridge: Cambridge University Press.

Selwyn, Ben, 2013a. 'The Global Retail Revolution, Fruiticulture and Economic Development in North-east Brazil'. *Review of International Political Economy 20* (1): pp. 153–179. doi: 10.1080/09692290.2011.633850.

Selwyn, Ben, 2019. 'Poverty Chains and Global Capitalism'. *Competition & Change 23* (1), pp. 71–97. https://doi.org/10.1177/1024529418809067.

Selwyn, Benjamin, 2007. 'Labour Process and Workers' Bargaining Power in Export Grape Production, North East Brazil'. *Journal of Agrarian Change 7* (4): pp. 526–553. doi: 10.1111/j.1471-0366.2007.00155.x.

Selwyn, Benjamin, 2008. 'Bringing Social Relations back in: (Re) conceptualising the "Bullwhip Effect" in Global Commodity Chains'. *International Journal of Management Concepts and Philosophy 3* (2): pp. 156–175. doi: 10.1504/IJMCP.2008.021272.

Selwyn, Benjamin, 2011. 'Trotsky, Gerschenkron and the Political Economy of Late Capitalist Development'. *Economy and Society 40* (3): pp. 421–450. doi: 10.1080/03085147.2011.574425.

Selwyn, Benjamin, 2012a. 'Beyond Firm-centrism: Re-integrating Labour and Capitalism into Global Commodity Chain Analysis'. *Journal of Economic Geography* (12): pp. 205–226.

Selwyn, Benjamin, 2012b. *Workers, State and Development in Brazil. Powers of Labour, Chains of Value.* Manchester: Manchester University Press.

Selwyn, Benjamin, 2013b. 'Social Upgrading and Labour in Global Production Networks: A Critque and an Alternative Conception'. *Competition and Change 17* (1): pp. 75–90.

Selwyn, Benjamin, 2015. 'Commodity Chains, Creative Destruction and Global Inequality: A Class Analysis'. *Journal of Economic Geography 15* (2): pp. 253–274. doi: 10.1093/jeg/lbu014.

Selwyn, Benjamin, 2017. *The Struggle for Development.* Cambridge: Polity Press.

Selwyn, Benjamin, Liam Campling, Alessandra Mezzadri, Elena Baglioni, Satoshi Miyamura, and Jonathan Pattenden, 2023. 'Exploitation and Global Value Chains'. In *Handbook of Research on the Global Political Economy of Work*, edited by Maurizio Atzeni, Dario

Azzellini, Alessandra Mezzadri, Phoebe V. Moore, and Ursula Apitzsch, pp. 126–136. Cheltenham, UK, Northampton, MA: Edward Elgar Publishing.

Selwyn, Ben, and Leyden, Dara, 2021. 'World Development under Monopoly Capitalism'. *Monthly Review 73* (6). Available at: https://monthlyreview.org/2021/11/01/world-development-under-monopoly-capitalism/

Selwyn, Benjamin, and Dara Leyden, 2022. 'Oligopoly-driven Development: The World Bank's Trading for Development in the Age of Global Value Chains in Perspective'. *Competition & Change 26* (2): pp. 174–196. doi: 10.1177/1024529421995351.

Selwyn, Benjamin, Bettina Musiolek, and Artemisa Ijarja, 2020. 'Making a Global Poverty Chain: Export Footwear Production and Gendered Labor Exploitation in Eastern and Central Europe'. *Review of International Political Economy 27* (2): pp. 377–403. doi: 10.1080/09692290.2019.1640124.

Sevastopulo, Demitri, Aime Williams, and Gregory Meyer, 2020. 'Donald Trump Orders Meat-Processing Plants to Stay Open: Fears of Food Shortages as Coronavirus Forces Facilities to Shut and US Cases Top 1m'. *The Financial Times 2020* (29 April 2020).

Shadlen, Kenneth C., 2005a. 'Exchanging Development for Market Access? Deep Integration and Industrial Policy under Multilateral and Regional-Bilateral Trade Agreements'. *Review of International Political Economy 12* (5): pp. 750–775. doi: 10.1080/09692290500339685.

Shadlen, Kenneth C., 2005b. *Policy Space for Development in the WTO and Beyond: The Case of Intellectual Property Rights*. Global Development and Environment Institute Working Paper 05-06.

Shaffer, Paul, Ravi Kanbur, and Richard Sandbrook (eds), 2019. *Immiserizing Growth: When Growth Fails the Poor*. Oxford: Oxford University Press.

Shaikh, Anwar, 2016. *Capitalism: Competition, Conflict, Crises*. New York: Oxford University Press.

Sharma, Ruchir, 2022. 'China's Economy will not Overtake the US until 2060, if Ever'. *Financial Times* (24 October 2022).

Shenkar, Oded, 2005. *The Chinese Century: The Rising Chinese Economy and Its Impact on the Global Economy, the Balance of Power, and Your Job*. Upper Saddle River, N.J.: Wharton School Pub.

Shepardson, David, and Karen Pierog, 2021. 'Foxconn Mostly Abandons $10 Billion Wisconsin Project Touted by Trump'. *Reuters*. https://www.reuters.com/business/foxconn-sharply-scales-back-wisconsin-investment-2021-04-20/.

Shepherd, Ben, and Susan Stone, 2012. *Global Production Networks and Employment: A Developing Country Perspective*. OECD Trade Policy Paper 154, 14.

Shih, Willy C., 2020. 'Global Supply Chains in a Post-pandemic World'. *Harvard Business Review*. https://hbr.org/2020/09/global-supply-chains-in-a-post-pandemic-world.

Shivakumar, Sujai, and Charles Wessner, 2022. 'Semiconductors and National Defense: What Are the Stakes?'. *Center for Strategic and International Studies*. https://www.csis.org/analysis/semiconductors-and-national-defense-what-are-stakes.

Siegmann, Karin, Jeroen Merk, and Peter Knorringa, 2014. 'Voluntary Initiatives in Global Value Chains: Towards Labour-Led Social Upgrading?'. *The Institute of Social Sciences, Working Paper no. 586*. https://repub.eur.nl/pub/76957/Metis_202349.pdf.

Silver, Beverly J., 2003. *Forces of Labor: Workers' Movements and Globalization since 1870*. New York: Cambridge University Press.

Silvey, Rachel, 2003. 'Gender Geographies of Activism: Motherhood, Migration, and Labour Protest in West Java, Indonesia'. *Asian Journal of Social Science 31* (2): pp. 340–363. doi: 10.1163/156853103322318261.

Sitrin, Marina A., 2012. *Everyday Revolutions: Horizontalism and Autonomy in Argentina*. London: Zed Books.

Smil, Vaclav, 2017. *Energy Transitions: Global and National Perspectives, second edition.* Santa Barbara, CA: Praeger.

Smith, Adam, 1976. *An Inquiry into the Nature and Causes of The Wealth of Nations: Volume One.* London: Printed for W Strahan and T Cadell.

Smith, Adrian, 2015. 'The State, Institutional Frameworks and the Dynamics of Capital in Global Production Networks'. *Progress in Human Geography 39* (3): pp. 290–315. doi: 10.1177/0309132513518292.

Smith, Adrian, Mirela Barbu, Liam Campling, James Harrison, and Ben Richardson, 2018. 'Labor Regimes, Global Production Networks, and European Union Trade Policy: Labor Standards and Export Production in the Moldovan Clothing Industry'. *Economic Geography 94* (5): pp. 550–574. doi: 10.1080/00130095.2018.1434410.

Smith, Chris, 2006. 'The Double Indeterminacy of Labour Power: Labour Effort and Labour Mobility'. *Work, Employment and Society 20* (2): pp. 389–402.

Smith, Chris, and Jenny Chan, 2015. 'Working for Two Bosses: Student Interns as Constrained Labour in China'. *Human Relations 68* (2): pp. 305–326. doi: 10.1177/0018726714557013.

So, A. Y., and Yin-wa Chu, 2012. 'The Transition from Neoliberalism to State Neoliberalism in China at the Turn of the Twenty-first Century'. In *Developmental Politics in Transition: The Neoliberal Era and Beyond*, edited by Kyung-Sup Chang, Ben Fine, and Linda Weiss, pp. 166–187. Basingstoke: Palgrave Macmillan.

SOMO, 2012. 'Workers' Rights in the Global Electronics Sector: Report of the May 2012 makeITfair and GoodElectronics Round Table'. *Centre for Research on Multinational Corporations.* https://goodelectronics.org/wp-content/uploads/sites/3/2012/11/Workers%E2%80%99-rights-in-the-global-electronics-sector.pdf.

Sosa Varrotti, and Andrea Patricia, 2019. 'Las megaempresas del agronegocio: un estudio del modelo agrario a partir de las prácticas empresariales'. *Estudios Socioterritoriales. Revista de Geografía* (26): e026. doi: 10.37838/unicen/est.26-026.

Srnicek, Nick, 2017. *Platform Capitalism.* Cambridge: Polity Press.

Stache, Christian, 2017. *Kapitalismus und Naturzerstörung. Zur kritischen Theorie des gesellschaftlichen Naturverhältnisses.* Opladen, Berlin, Toronto: Budrich UniPress.

Stache, Christian, 2020a. 'Conceptualising Animal Exploitation in Capitalism: Getting Terminology Straight'. *Capital & Class 44* (3): pp. 401–421. doi: 10.1177/0309816819884697.

Stache, Christian, 2020b. 'It's Not Humans, It's Animal Capital!'. In *Capitalist Commodification of Animals*, edited by Brett Clark and Tamar Diana Wilson, pp. 9–31. Bingley: Emerald Publishing Limited.

Stache, Christian, and Christin Bernhold, 2021. 'The Bourgeois Meat Hegemony'. *Österreichische Zeitschrift für Soziologie 46* (2): pp. 167–186. doi: 10.1007/s11614-021-00454-z.

Stamm, Andreas, 2008. 'Agribusiness and Poverty Reduction: What Can Be Learned from the Value Chain Approach?'. In *Agri-Food Commodity Chains and Globalising Networks*, edited by Christina Stringer and Richard Le Heron, pp. 23–34. Burlington: Ashgate.

Standing, Guy, 2017. *The Corruption of Capitalism: Why Rentiers Thrive and Work Does Not Pay.* Biteback Publishing.

Staritz, Cornelia, and Mike Morris, 2013. 'Local Embeddedness and Economic and Social Upgrading in Madagascar's Export Apparel Industry'. *Capturing The Gains Working Paper 21, University of Manchester.*

Starrs, Sean Kenji, 2014. 'The Chimera of Global Convergence'. *New Left Review 87* (1): pp. 81–96.

Starrs, Sean Kenji, 2019. 'Can China Unmake the American Making of Global Capitalism'. In *Socialist Register 2019, Volume 55: A World Turned Upside Down*, edited by Leo Panitch, and Gregory Albo, pp. 173–200. New York: Monthly Review Press.

Ste. Croix, Geoffrey Ernest Maurice de, 1981. *The Class Struggle in the Ancient Greek World from the Archaic Age to the Arab Conquests*. Ithaca: Cornell University Press.

Steffen, Will, Katherine Richardson, Johan Rockström, Sarah E. Cornell, Ingo Fetzer, Elena M. Bennett, Reinette Biggs, Stephen R. Carpenter, Wim de Vries, Cynthia A. de Wit, Carl Folke, Dieter Gerten, Jens Heinke, Georgina M. Mace, Linn M. Persson, Veerabhadran Ramanathan, Belinda Reyers, and Sverker Sörlin, 2015. 'Sustainability. Planetary Boundaries: Guiding Human Development on a Changing Planet'. *Science 347* (6223): p. 1259855. doi: 10.1126/science.1259855.

Stein, Ben, 2006. 'In Class Warfare, Guess Which Class Is Winning'. *New York Times* (11.26.2006).

Stenmanns, Julian, and Stefan Ouma, 2021. 'Logistik der imperialen Lebensweise: Zur Weltökologie maritimer Güterketren'. In *Globale Warenketten und ungleiche Entwicklung: Arbeit, Kapital, Konsum, Natur*, edited by Karin Fischer, Christian Reiner, and Cornelia Staritz, 266–282. 1st ed. Wien: Mandelbaum.

Stevano, Sara, 2023. 'The Workplace at the Bottom of Global Supply Chains as a Site of Reproduction of Colonial Relations: Reflections on the Cashew-Processing Industry in Mozambique'. *Gender, Work & Organization 30* (2): pp. 496–509. doi: 10.1111/gwao.12757.

Stevenson, Tom, 2023. 'America's Undying Empire: Why the Decline of US Power Has Been Greatly Exaggerated'. *The Guardian* (30 November 2023).

Stiglitz, Joseph E., 2005. 'More Instruments and Broader Goals: Moving toward the Post-Washington Consensus'. In *Wider Perspectives on Global Development*, edited by Anthony Shorrocks, pp. 16–48. London: Palgrave Macmillan.

Stiglitz, Joseph E., 2007. *Making Globalization Work*. New York: W.W. Norton.

Stone, Maddie, 2021. 'The Shipping Industry Faces a Climate Crisis Reckoning—Will It Decarbonize?'. *The Guardian* (12 November 2021).

Strange, Roger, and James Newton, 2006. 'Stephen Hymer and the Externalization of Production'. *International Business Review 15* (2): pp. 180–193. doi: 10.1016/j.ibusrev.2005.07.007.

Strauss, Kendra, 2020. 'Labour Geography II: Being, Knowledge and Agency'. *Progress in Human Geography 44* (1): pp. 150–159. doi: 10.1177/0309132518803420.

Sturgeon, Timothy J., 2001. 'How Do We Define Value Chains and Production Networks?'. In *The Value of Value Chains: Spreading the Gains from Globalisation. IDS Bulletin*, edited by Gary Gereffi, and Raphael Kaplinsky, pp. 9–18. Sussex: Institute of Development Studies (IDS).

Sturgeon, Timothy J., 2009. 'From Commodity Chains to Value Chains'. In *Frontiers of Commodity Chain Reserach*, edited by J. Bair, pp. 110–135. Stanford: Stanford University Press.

Sullivan, Anthony, 2022. 'Britain's 'Dark Factories': Specters of Racial Capitalism Today'. *Fashion Theory 26* (4): pp. 493–508. doi: 10.1080/1362704X.2022.2046861.

Sullivan, Dylan, Michail Moatsos, and Jason Hickel, 2024. 'Capitalist Reforms and Extreme Poverty in China: Unprecedented Progress or Income Deflation?'. *New Political Economy 29* (1): pp. 1–21. doi: 10.1080/13563467.2023.2217087.

Sullivan, Jake, 2023. 'Remarks by National Security Advisor Jake Sullivan on Renewing American Economic Leadership at the Brookings Institution'. *The White House*. https://www.whitehouse.gov/briefing-room/speeches-remarks/2023/04/27/remarks-by-national-security-advisor-jake-sullivan-on-renewing-american-economic-leadership-at-the-brookings-institution/.

Sumner, Andrew, 2007. 'Meaning versus Measurement: Why Do 'Economic' Indicators of Poverty Still Predominate?' *Development in Practice 17* (1): pp. 4–13. doi: 10.1080/09614520601092485.

Sumner, Andrew, Christopher Hoy, and Eduardo Ortiz-Juarez, 2020. *Estimates of the Impact of COVID-19 on Global Poverty.* WIDER Working Paper 2020/43. doi: 10.35188/UNU-WIDER/2020/800-9. https://www.econstor.eu/handle/10419/229267.

Suwandi, Intan, 2019. *Value Chains: The New Economic Imperialism.* New York: Monthly Review Press.

Taglioni, Daria, and Deborah Winkler, 2016. *Making Global Value Chains Work for Development.* Washington DC: The World Bank.

Tamaoka, Masayuki, 1994. 'The Regressivity of a Value Added Tax: Tax Credit Method and Subtraction Method—A Japanese Case'. *Fiscal Studies 15* (2): pp. 57–73. doi: 10.1111/j.1475-5890.1994.tb00197.x.

Taylor, Marcus, 2007. 'Rethinking the Global Production of Uneven Development'. *Globalizations 4* (4): pp. 529–542.

Taylor, Marcus, and Sébastien Rioux, 2017. *Global Labour Studies.* Medford, MA: Polity.

Taylor, Philip, Kirsty Newsome, Jennifer Bair, and Al Rainnie, 2015. 'Labour and the Changing Landscapes of the Call Centre'. In *Putting Labour in Its Place: Labour Process Analysis and Global Value Chains*, edited by Kirsty Newsome, Philip Taylor, Jennifer Bair, and Al Rainnie, pp. 266–286. London: Palgrave.

Teipen, Christina, and Fabian Mehl, 2021. 'Global Value Chains and Industrial Relations in the Global South: Social Upgrading Paths in Different Industries'. *Journal of Labor and Society 24* (1): pp. 214–236. doi: 10.1163/24714607-20212008.

Teixeira, Tiago, 2024. 'Variegated Forms of Corporate Capture: The State, MNCs, and the Dark Side of Strategic Coupling'. *Global Networks 24* (1). doi: 10.1111/glob.12433.

Teubal, Miguel, 2006. 'Expansión del Modelo Sojero en la Argentina. De la Producción de Alimentos a los Commodities'. *Realidad Económica 220*: pp. 71–96.

Teubal, Miguel, and Tomas Palmisano, 2010. 'El Conflicto Agrario: Características y Proyecciones'. In *Del Paro Agrario a las Elecciones de 2009. Tramas, Reflexiones y Debates*, edited by Norma Giarracca and Miguel Teubal, pp. 193–252. Buenos Aires: Antropofagia.

The Growth Lab at Harvard University, 2024. 'The Atlas of Economic Complexity'. https://atlas.cid.harvard.edu/explore/stack?country=231&year=2021&queryLevel=location&startYear=1995&productClass=HS&tradeDirection=import&product=undefined&target=Partner&partner=location-43.

The People's Vaccine, 2022. 'Frequently Asked Questions'. https://peoplesmedicines.org/faq/.

The White House, 2021a. *Building Resilient Supply Chains, Revitalizing American Manufacturing, And Fostering Broad-Based Growth: 100-Day Reviews under Executive Order 14017.* https://www.whitehouse.gov/wp-content/uploads/2021/06/100-day-supply-chain-review-report.pdf.

The White House, 2021b. 'Executive Order on America's Supply Chains'. https://www.whitehouse.gov/briefing-room/presidential-actions/2021/02/24/executive-order-on-americas-supply-chains/.

Thompson, Edward P., 1968. *The Making of the English Working Class.* Pelican.

Trotsky, Leon, 2009. *History of the Russian Revolution.* New York: Haymarket Books.

Trotsky, Leon, 2020. *In Defence of Marxism.* London: Wellred Books.

Tsing, Anna, 2009. 'Supply Chains and the Human Condition'. *Rethinking Marxism 21* (2): pp. 148–176.

TWI, 2021. 'What Is a Smart Factory? (A Complete Guide)'. https://www.twi-global.com/technical-knowledge/faqs/what-is-a-smart-factory.

UN, 2014. *World Urbanization Prospects: The 2014 Revision.*

UNCTAD, 2013. *World Investment Report 2013: Global Value Chains-Investment and Trade for Development.*

UNCTAD, 2017. *Trade and Development Report 2017: Beyond Austerity: Towards a Global New Deal.*

UNCTAD, 2018. *Trade and Development Report 2018: Power, Platforms and the Free Trade Delusion.*

UNCTAD, 2019. *Trade and Development Report 2019: Financing a Global Green New Deal.* https://policycommons.net/artifacts/15227/trade-and-development-report-2019/40109/.

UNCTAD, 2023. *World Seaborne Trade.Handbook of Statistics 2023.* https://hbs.unctad.org/world-seaborne-trade/.

UNHR, 2018. 'Press Release: United Nations Experts Raise Concerns of Human Rights Violations against Women Workers at Samsung Vietnam'. https://ipen.org/documents/press-release-united-nations-experts-raise-concerns-human-rights-violations-against-women.

UNIDO, 2006. *Yearbook of Industrial Statistics.* New Yor: United Nations.

UNIDO, 2015. *Global Value Chains and Development: UNIDO's Support towards Inclusive and Sustainable Industrial Development.*

United Nations. General Assembly, 1949. *Universal Declaration of Human Rights (Vol. 3381). Department of State*, United States of America.

United States Space and Command, 1998. *Long Range Plan: Executive Summary.* US Space Command.

Valentine, Gill, 2007. 'Theorizing and Researching Intersectionality: A Challenge for Feminist Geography'. *The Professional Geographer 59* (1): pp. 10–21. doi: 10.1111/j.1467-9272.2007.00587.x.

van der Pijl, Kees, 2012. 'Is the East Still Red? The Contender State and Class Struggles in China'. *Globalizations 9* (4): pp. 503–516. doi: 10.1080/14747731.2012.699921.

Varman, Rahul, 2012. 'The Neoclassical Apology for Monopoly Capital'. *Monthly Review 64* (6): pp. 29–47. doi: 10.14452/MR-064-06-2012-10_2.

Villulla, Juan Manuel, 2015. *Las Cosechas Son Ajenas. Historia de los Trabajadores Rurales Detras del Agronegocio.* Buenos Aires: Editorial Cienflores.

Vine, David, 2021. 'Lists of U.S. Military Bases Abroad, 1776–2021'. *American University Digital Research Archive.* https://www.basenation.us/uploads/5/7/1/7/57170837/vine_david_lists_of_us_military_bases_abroad_1776-2021_final_2021_07_04.xlsx.

Vivoda, Vlado, 2023. 'Friend-shoring and Critical Minerals: Exploring the Role of the Minerals Security Partnership'. *Energy Research & Social Science 100*: p. 103085. doi: 10.1016/j.erss.2023.103085.

Vogel, Lise, 2018. 'Beyond Intersectionality'. *Science & Society 82* (2): pp. 275–287. doi: 10.1521/siso.2018.82.2.275.

Wade, Robert H., 2002. 'America's Empire Rules an Unbalanced World'. https://www.nytimes.com/2002/01/03/opinion/IHT-americas-empire-rules-an-unbalanced-world.html.

Wade, Robert H., 2003. 'What Strategies Are Viable for Developing Countries Today? The World Trade Organization and the Shrinking of "Development Space"'. *Review of International Political Economy 10* (4): pp. 621–644. doi: 10.1080/09692290310001601902.

Wade, Robert H., 2004. 'On the Causes of Increasing World Poverty and Inequality, or Why the Matthew Effect Prevails'. *New Political Economy 9* (2): pp. 163–188. doi: 10.1080/1356346042000218050.

Wade, Robert H., 2014. 'The Paradox of US Industrial Policy: The Developmental State in Disguise'. In *Transforming Economies: Making Industrial Policy Work for Growth, Jobs and Development*, edited by José M. Salazar-Xirinachs, Irmgard Nübler, and Richard Kozul-Wright, pp. 379–400. Geneva: International Labour Office.

Wade, Robert H., 2023. 'The New Great Game: Big-Power Politics behind the Come-back of Industrial Strategy and Managed Trade'. *Global Policy 31*: pp. 1–11.
Walker, Richard, and Daniel Buck, 2007. 'The Chinese Road: New Left Review'. *46*: p. 39.
Wall, Tom, 2021. "Fire and Rehire' Tactics Rife at Firms that Are in Profit and Claiming Covid Cash: Observer Analysis of Those Companies Condemned by Unions Also Shows that Some Raised Executive Pay'. *The Guardian 2021* (18 April 2021).
Wallerstein, Immanuel, 1974a. 'Dependence in an Interdependent World: The Limited Possibilities of Transformation within the Capitalist World Economy'. *African Studies Review 17* (1): pp. 1–26.
Wallerstein, Immanuel, 1974b. *The Modern World System. Capitalist Agriculture and the Origins of the European World-Economy in the Sixteenth Century*. New York, London: Academic Press.
Wallerstein, Immanuel, 1988a. 'Development: Lodestar or illusion?'. *Economic and Political Weekly 23* (39).
Wallerstein, Immanuel, 1988b. 'The Bourgeois(ie) as Concept and Reality'. *New Left Review 167*: pp. 91–106.
Wallerstein, Immanuel, 2003. *The Decline of American Power: The U.S. in a Chaotic World*. New York: New Press.
Wallerstein, Immanuel, 2009. 'Crisis of the Capitalist System: Where Do We Go from Here?' https://mronline.org/wp-content/uploads/2020/09/Wallerstein20November 20200920Wolpe20Lecture-1.pdf.
Wallerstein, Immanuel, 2011a. *The Modern World-System I: Capitalist Agriculture and the Origins of the European World-Economy in the Sixteenth Century*. 1st ed. Berkeley, CA: University of California Press.
Wallerstein, Immanuel Maurice, 2011b. *The Modern World-System IV: Centrist Liberalism Triumphant, 1789–1914*. Berkeley, Calif., London: University of California Press.
Wang, Fei-Ling, 2010. 'Conflict, Resistance and the Transformation of the Hukou System'. In *Chinese Society: Change, Conflict and Resistance*, edited by Elizabeth J. Perry, and Mark Selden. 3rd ed., pp. 98–118. Florence: Taylor and Francis.
Watson, Matthew, 2017. 'Historicising Ricardo's Comparative Advantage Theory, Challenging the Normative Foundations of Liberal International Political Economy'. *New Political Economy 22* (3): pp. 257–272. doi: 10.1080/13563467.2016.1216535.
Watts, Jonathan, 2006. 'Chinese Court Freezes Assets of Journalists in iPod Exposé'. *The Guardian* (30 August 2006).
Weber, Max, 2019. *Economy and Society: A New Translation*. Cambridge: Harvard University Press.
Webster, Edward, 2015. 'Labour after Globalisation: Old and New Sources of Power'. *Institute of Social and Economic Research (ISER), Working Paper, no. 2015/1*.
Weis, Tony, 2013a. *The Ecological Hoofprint: The Global Burden of Industrial Livestock*. London: Zed Books.
Weis, Tony, 2013b. 'The Meat of the Global Food Crisis'. *Journal of Peasant Studies 40* (1): pp. 65–85. doi: 10.1080/03066150.2012.752357.
Weiss, Linda, 2005. 'Global Governance, National Strategies: How Industrialized States Make Room to Move under the WTO'. *Review of International Political Economy 12* (5): pp. 723–749. doi: 10.1080/09692290500339768.
Weiss, Linda, 2021. 'Re-emergence of Great Power Conflict and US Economic Statecraft'. *World Trade Review 20* (2): pp. 152–168. doi: 10.1017/s1474745620000567.
Wen, Yun, 2020. *The Huawei Model: The Rise of China's Technology Giant*. Chicago: University of Illinois Press.

Werner, Marion, 2012. 'Beyond Upgrading: Gendered Labor and the Restructuring of Firms in the Dominican Republic'. *Economic Geography 88* (4): pp. 403–422. doi: 10.1111/j.1944-8287.2012.01163.x.

Werner, Marion, 2016. *Global Displacements. The Making of Uneven Development in the Caribbean.* New Jersey: Wiley-Blackwell.

Werner, Marion, 2019. 'Geographies of Production I: Global Production and Uneven Development'. *Progress in Human Geography 43* (5): pp. 948–958. doi: 10.1177/0309132518760095.

Werner, Marion, 2022. 'Geographies of Production III: Global Production in/through Nature'. *Progress in Human Geography 46* (1): pp. 234–244. doi: 10.1177/03091325211022810.

Werner, Marion, Jennifer Bair, and Victor Ramiro Fernández, 2014. 'Linking Up to Development? Global Value Chains and the Making of a Post-Washington Consensus'. *Development and Change 45* (6): pp. 1219–1247. doi: 10.1111/dech.12132.

Westhoek, Henk, Trudy Rood, Maurits van den Berg, Jan Janse, Durk Nijdam, Reudink, Melchert, and Elke Stehfest, 2011. *The Protein Puzzle: The Consumption and Production of Meat, Dairy and Fish in the European Union.* PBL Netherlands Environmental Assessment Agency 500166001. https://www.pbl.nl/sites/default/files/downloads/Protein_Puzzle_web_1.pdf.

Wickramasingha, Shyamain, and Neil M. Coe, 2022. 'Conceptualizing Labor Regimes in Global Production Networks: Uneven Outcomes across the Bangladeshi and Sri Lankan Apparel Industries'. *Economic Geography 98* (1): pp. 68–90.

Williamson, Oliver E., 1973. 'Markets and Hierarchies: Some Elementary Considerations'. *The American Economic Review 63* (2): pp. 316–325.

Williamson, Oliver E., 1979. 'Transaction-Cost Economics: The Governance of Contractual Relations'. *The Journal of Law and Economics 22* (2): pp. 233–261.

Wolford, Wendy, 2010. *This Land Is Ours Now: Social Mobilization and the Meanings of Land in Brazil.* Durham: Duke University Press.

Wood, Ellen Meiksins, 1998. *The Retreat from Class: A New 'True' Socialism.* London, New York: Verso.

Wood, Ellen Meiksins, 2016. 'Global Capital, National States'. In *Historical Materialism and Globalisation: Essays on Continuity and Change: E-book*, edited by Mark Rupert, and Hazel Smith, pp. 17–39. London: Routledge.

Workers Rights Consortium, 2013. 'Global Wage Trends for Apparel Workers, 2001–2011'. *Center for American Progress, Just Jobs, Workers Rights Consortium.* https://www.americanprogress.org/wp-content/uploads/sites/2/2013/07/RealWageStudy-3.pdf.

World Bank, 2019. *World Development Report 2019: The Changing Nature of Work.* Washington, D.C.: World Bank Publications.

World Bank, 2020. *World Development Report 2020: Trading for Development in the Age of Global Value Chains.* Washington, D.C.: World Bank Publications.

World Bank, 2024. "World Development Indicators". World Bank. Washington. https://databank.worldbank.org/

Wright, Erik Olin, 2000. 'Working-Class Power, Capitalist-Class Interests, and Class Compromise'. *American Journal of Sociology 105* (4): pp. 957–1002. doi: 10.1086/210397.

Wright, Erik Olin, 2015. 'Why Class Matters: An Interview with Erik Olin Wright'. https://jacobin.com/2015/12/socialism-marxism-democracy-inequality-erik-olin-wright.

Xing, Yuqing, Elisabetta Gentile, and David Dollar (eds), 2021. *Global Value Chain Development Report 2021: Beyond Production.*

Xiwei, Zhong, Yang Xiangdong, 2007. 'Science and Technology Policy Reform and Its Impact on China's National Innovation System'. *Technology in Society 29* (3): pp. 317–325. doi: 10.1016/j.techsoc.2007.04.008.

Ye, Jingzhong, 2015. 'Land Transfer and the Pursuit of Agricultural Modernization in China'. *Journal of Agrarian Change 15* (3): pp. 314–337. doi: 10.1111/joac.12117.

Yeung, Henry Wai-chung, 2023. 'Troubling Economic Geography: New Directions in the Post-pandemic World'. *Transactions of the Institute of British Geographers 48* (4): pp. 672–680. doi: 10.1111/tran.12633.

Yeung, Henry Wai-Chung, 2009. 'Transnational Corporations, Global Production Networks, and Urban and Regional Development: A Geographer's Perspective on Multinational Enterprises and the Global Economy'. *Growth and Change 40* (2): pp. 197–226. doi: 10.1111/j.1468-2257.2009.00473.x.

Yeung, Henry Wai-Chung, 2015. 'Regional Development in the Global Economy: A Dynamic Perspective of Strategic Coupling in Global Production Networks'. *Regional Science Policy & Practice 7* (1): pp. 1–23.

Yeung, Henry Wai-Chung, and Neil Coe, 2015. 'Toward a Dynamic Theory of Global Production Networks'. *Economic Geography 91* (1): pp. 29–58.

York, Richard, 2010. 'The Paradox at the Heart of Modernity: The Carbon Efficiency of the Global Economy'. *International Journal of Sociology 40* (2): pp. 6–22. doi: 10.2753/IJS0020-7659400201.

Zaman, Sawlat., and Jean Jenkins, 2024. 'Creating a local managerial regime in global context: The case of the Bangladesh ready-made garment sector'. *Industrial Relations Journal 55*(6): pp. 425–445.

Zampoukos, Kristina, 2021. 'Thinking through Intersectionality at Work: A Feminist-and-Labour Geographer's Approach'. In *Working Life and Gender Inequality: Intersectional perspectives and the*, edited by Angelika Sjöstedt, Katarina Giritli Nygren, and Marianna Fotaki, pp. 272–290. London, New York: Routledge.

Zhou, Qian, 2023. 'What Are the Tax Incentives in China to Encourage Technology Innovation?: China Briefing'. https://www.china-briefing.com/news/tax-incentives-china-to-encourage-technology-innovation-updated/.

Index

For the benefit of digital users, indexed terms that span two pages (e.g., 52–53) may, on occasion, appear on only one of those pages.

Tables and figures are indicated by an italic *t*, *f*.

The manufacturer's authorised representative in the EU for product safety is Oxford University Press España S.A. of el Parque Empresarial San Fernando de Henares, Avenida de Castilla, 2 – 28830 Madrid (www.oup.es/en or product.safety@oup.com). OUP España S.A. also acts as importer into Spain of products made by the manufacturer.

www.ingramcontent.com/pod-product-compliance
Ingram Content Group UK Ltd.
Pitfield, Milton Keynes, MK11 3LW, UK
UKHW020842150926
475595UK00010B/190/J
* 9 7 8 0 1 9 8 8 8 7 8 3 6 *